The Logical Design of Operating Systems
Second Edition

Lubomir Bic

Department of Information and Computer Science

University of California, Irvine

Alan C. Shaw

Department of Computer Science

University of Washington

Prentice Hall, Englewood Cliffs, New Jersey 07632

Library of Congress Cataloging-in-Publication Data

BIC, LUBOMIR
    The logical design of operating systems.

    Rev. ed. of: The logical design of operating
systems / Alan C. Shaw. 1974.
    Bibliography.
    Includes index.
    1. Operating systems (Computers)   2. Multiprogramming
(Electronic computers)   I. Shaw, Alan C.
II. Shaw, Alan C.   Logical design of
operating systems.   III. Title.
QA76.76.063B53 1987   005.4'3   87-12421
ISBN   0-13-540139-9

Editorial/production supervision and
    interior design: **Ellen B. Greenberg**
Cover design: **Lundgren Graphics, LTD.**
Cover Cartoon: **Don Martinetti**
Manufacturing buyer: **Barbara Kelly Kittle**

Printed in the United States of America
10 9 8 7 6 5 4 3 2 1

ISBN   0-13-540139-9   025

PRENTICE-HALL INTERNATIONAL (UK) LIMITED, LONDON
PRENTICE-HALL OF AUSTRALIA PTY. LIMITED, SYDNEY
PRENTICE-HALL CANADA INC., TORONTO
PRENTICE-HALL HISPANOAMERICANA, S.A., MEXICO
PRENTICE-HALL OF INDIA PRIVATE LIMITED, NEW DELHI
PRENTICE-HALL OF JAPAN, INC., TOKYO
SIMON & SCHUSTER ASIA PTE. LTD., SINGAPORE
EDITORA PRENTICE-HALL DO BRASIL, LTDA., RIO DE JANEIRO

To Zuzana
  Lubomir Bic

To Heather, David, and Elizabeth
  Alan Shaw

Contents

Preface

This is the second edition of A. C. Shaw, THE LOGICAL DESIGN OF OPERATING SYSTEMS, Prentice-Hall, Inc. 1974. The book has been completely rewritten to include the many changes in the field since the early 1970's while still retaining the basic conceptual material presented in the first edition. Thus, for example, the discussion on concurrent programming has been expanded substantially. There is a new chapter on protection and security, and examples from significant contemporary systems such as Unix® (Unix is a trademark of Bell Laboratories) are used throughout.

We have tried to present the principles and techniques required for engineering and understanding operating systems, rather than describe case studies on how specific systems are implemented on different computers. However, many examples from real systems are given to illustrate the application of particular concepts. The term "logical design" was retained in the title to stress our continued concern with the logical organization of operating systems, the interactions of their components, and with the methods of reasoning about these systems.

The book is intended for both students and professionals in computer science and engineering, having a basic knowledge of machine organization, assembly language, programming languages, and data structures. The prerequisite background can be obtained in an introductory one-term course in each of the above subjects. While THE LOGICAL DESIGN OF OPERATING SYSTEMS, SECOND EDITION was being written, we used it as the primary text for a one-term undergraduate course at the University of

California at Irvine and at the University of Washington. It is suitable for a one- or two-term course at the advanced undergraduate level.

Operating systems have two main functions: they provide services to users to simplify their tasks, and they manage systems resources to assure efficient operation. Each of the seven chapters treats either or both of these functions. Chapter 1 provides an overview of the organization of systems hardware and software, including a rationale for operating systems and an historical perspective. In Chapter 2, we develop the process model and concurrent programming techniques as a means for describing and building systems, and as a framework for solving problems of synchronization, communication, and resource control. Chapter 3 then investigates process and resource management from the point of view of the operating system, discussing implementation data structures and primitive operations at the kernel level of a system. The manipulation of processes and resources can sometimes lead to situations where processes are blocked indefinitely—an undesirable state called deadlock. Methods for deadlock detection, prevention, and recovery are treated in Chapter 4. Chapter 5 is concerned with techniques for the management and sharing of main storage, both real and virtual. In Chapter 6, we study file systems, including methods for handling secondary storage and input/output operations. The last chapter, Chapter 7, addresses the problems of protection and security, and offers some practical solutions as well as some theoretical models.

The book contains many constructive exercises which the reader is strongly encouraged to solve. In learning new ideas about computer software systems, it is particularly important that the ideas be translated to practical realizations and tested experimentally. For this reason, we also recommend that the exercises be implemented, where appropriate.

Lubomir Bic

Alan Shaw

NOTATION

The notation used in this book is based on the programming language Pascal. While Pascal would not normally be used to write an operating system, we have chosen it for two reasons. First, Pascal is a modern block structured language and hence, permits algorithms to be expressed in a highly organized and readable fashion. The second and perhaps more important reason is that Pascal is widely used in both educational institutions and in industry. Hence, it will permit a large number of readers to study the basic principles of operating systems without having to acquire a new language.

To further improve the readability of algorithms in this book, we have taken some liberties with Pascal by introducing several convenient new constructs, and by relaxing the syntax to create a pseudo programming language when appropriate. Below we summarize the most significant changes/extensions:

1. It is frequently necessary to write an "infinite" loop. In Pascal, the constructs

    while *true* **do** *S*

    or

    repeat *S* **until** *false*

    would be used, where *S* represents the loop body. We introduce the following more intuitive construct for the same purpose:

    loop *S* **end**

    which repeats the statement *S* indefinitely. This construct is used in a number of modern programming languages such as Modula-2.

2. The body of a **while** loop may be empty, that is:

    while *B* **do**;

    where *B* is an arbitrary Boolean expression. This represents a "wait" loop in that it does not execute any statements. Instead, it only keeps testing the expression *B* on each iteration. When *B* is made true (by some other process), the loop terminates and execution continues with the next statement.

3. The operators "$+_n$" and "$-_n$" denote addition and subtraction modulo a constant *n*. They are defined on integers in the range from 0 to $n - 1$. The meaning of "$z := x +_n y$" is as follows:

    if $x + y < n$ **then** $z := x + y$ **else** $z := x + y - n$

    Similarly, the meaning of "$z := x -_n y$" is:

    if $x - y \geq 0$ **then** $z := x - y$ **else** $z := x - y + n$

Intuitively, the two operations "wrap around" the range of integers 0 through $n - 1$. For example, the program segment

```
x := 0;
loop write(x); x := x +₄ 1 end
```

would output the sequence 0, 1, 2, 3, 0, 1, 2, 3, 0, 1, 2, 3, ... indefinitely.

4. To apply an operation to all elements of a set, we use the construct:

for all p in L do S

This represents a more abstract form of a loop in that it does not specify the order in which the elements are processed. It also ignores the details of how the set is implemented. That is, L could be a linked list, an array, a tree, etc. The loop body S is executed for each element p in L regardless of L's structure.

A related statement is:

for all p in L such that B do S

This also executes S for each element p in L but only if p satisfies the Boolean expression B.

5. The symbols "$\land$", "$\lor$", and "$\neg$" are used to denote logical AND, logical OR, and negation, respectively.

6. The construct **cobegin** ... **coend** is used to denote concurrent execution of programs. The exact semantics are defined in the text (Section 2.2.2).

1

The Organization
of Computer Systems

The term *logical design* is used in this book to denote a general method of *reasoning* about operating systems that allows their systematic design and the study of their organization and behavior. Our emphasis is on general principles as opposed to ad hoc "tricks"; thus, programming techniques are not discussed in great detail, nor do we present a case study of a particular commercial system, even though many examples from the latter are given to illustrate particular points.

We begin this book by examining the large gap between the requirements and expectations placed on computer systems by the user community and the rather limited capabilities of existing hardware. This gap must be bridged by the software constituting the operating system and a variety of other utility and support programs. We then outline the tasks to be performed by operating systems, their organization and structure, and the different points of view from which operating systems may be studied. The remainder of this chapter offers a brief survey of the historical development of existing operating systems to provide the necessary perspective for studying modern concepts and approaches.

1.1 BRIDGING THE HARDWARE/USER GAP

The vast majority of existing computer systems are based on the principles of a stored-program computer formulated by the mathematician John von Neumann in the late 1940s.

The basic components and their interconnections constituting such a computer are shown in Figure 1-1 in the form of a high-level block diagram. At the heart of this system are a *linear memory* of cells, referred to as *main* (or primary) *memory*, and a *processor.* The memory is used to hold a *program*, a sequence of machine instructions, that is to be executed by the processor. To make this basic computational scheme of any practical value, two other major components must be included. The first is a *communication* subsystem to permit data to be exchanged between the user and the machine. The other is a *secondary storage* subsystem to hold programs and data currently not loaded in main memory. This is needed because the system's main memory is usually volatile (i.e., it loses its contents when power is turned off) and also quite limited in size. We will refer to the secondary storage and the communication subsystems jointly as the *input/output (IO) subsystem*; individual devices then will be called *IO devices*. (*Note:* In the literature, the term IO devices is used sometimes to refer to only communication devices and other times to both communication and secondary storage devices. The former is typically the case when device types and their properties are studied, while the latter occurs when the programming of IO routines is discussed. We will use the term throughout the book as defined previously.)

The processor, frequently called the *central processing unit* (CPU), continuously repeats a basic cycle of *fetching* instructions from memory and *executing* them. The order in which instructions are fetched and executed is governed by a special register called the *instruction* (or program) *counter*, which holds the memory address of the instruction to be executed next. The basic algorithm executed by the CPU may be described as follows:

```
loop
    Fetch next instruction;
    Increment instruction counter;
    Execute the instruction
end {loop}
```

Unfortunately, there is still a long way to go from this abstract computational scheme of a stored-program von Neumann computer to a truly practical machine. The main problems stem from the limited capabilities of the hardware components. In particular, the machine instructions executed by a CPU perform only very simple tasks. Among these are arithmetic and logical operations on binary numbers, comparisons of two bit strings, altering the sequence of instruction execution by setting the instruction

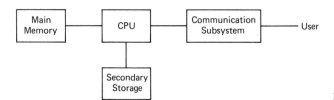

Figure 1-1   Components of a computer.

counter, or reading and writing an element of information from or to one of its subsystems. The user, on the other hand, needs to think in terms of the problems to be solved (i.e., in terms of high-level data structures and the corresponding operations to manipulate these). Furthermore, the user would like to have simple, uniform interfaces to the different subsystems and to be able to treat entire programs or program segments as well as various collections of data as single entities, which could be created, destroyed, copied, and transferred between different locations using only a small set of high-level commands.

The gap between the capabilities of existing hardware and the needs and expectations of a user must be eliminated or at least partially reduced by software. There is a number of different software subsystems provided for this purpose in any modern computing facility. The most common are language processors (assemblers, compilers, or interpreters), linkers and loaders, text editors, various utility and service programs, and, of course, the operating system. All these software components serve as a *bridge* between the bare machine hardware and the user. In this book, we concentrate primarily on tasks performed by operating systems. We will examine the discrepancies between hardware capabilities and user needs in more detail and discuss the operating system's role in alleviating the problem.

1.2 LIMITATIONS OF HARDWARE RESOURCES

1.2.1 Processors, Memories, and IO Devices

Most computers today are hardware realizations of the basic von Neumann model of computation depicted in Figure 1-1. They consist of a processor, a linear directly accessible main memory, one or more secondary storage devices, and a set of communication devices. For each of these hardware subsystems, however, there exists a wide spectrum of possible choices, depending on the intended application domain and the cost of the system. In the case of a personal computer, the processor and memory chips could occupy the area of a few printed circuit boards; a single floppy disk drive and a CRT terminal with a keyboard could suffice for permanent storage and communication with the user. The hardware for a supercomputer, on the other hand, typically occupies entire rooms. Correspondingly, the tasks performed by the operating system and other system programs vary from a few rudimentary functions, for example, to hide the details of input/output programming in a personal microcomputer, to sophisticated routines to guarantee acceptable performance and to ensure efficient utilization of resources in a general-purpose multiuser system. A major objective of operating systems is to eliminate any unnecessary idle times of the different hardware components. To better understand performance and resource utilization issues, let us first examine the essential characteristics of the various hardware components constituting a modern computer installation.

CPU.   This is usually the fastest component of a typical computer. Its speed is measured in CPU cycles, which are typically in the 0.01- to 0.1-microsecond (μs) range.

The actual number of instructions executed per unit of time, however, is highly dependent on the rate at which instructions and operands may be transferred from and to main memory.

Main Memory.   The speed of main memory is measured in memory cycles, ranging from 0.1 to 1 μs, where one memory cycle is the time to perform one read or write operation. When compared with the CPU cycle, main memory is an order of magnitude slower than CPU. Since the discrepancy occurs at the very low level of instruction execution, it cannot be solved by any software mechanisms; rather, additional hardware is necessary. The most common solution is to provide fast *registers* and various types of *caches*, which are small, high-speed memories used to hold the most current instructions and data operated on by the CPU.

Secondary Storage.   A wide variety of devices are capable of holding large amounts of information over virtually unlimited periods of time. The most common of these are magnetic disks (both hard and floppy disks) and magnetic tapes. Some properties of concern to the system designer and user are the following:

1. *Capacity.* This is the maximum amount of data that can be stored on the device.
2. *Record size.* A physical record is the smallest set of contiguous information that may be addressed on a device. The device may allow *fixed* or *variable-length* records.
3. *Access method.* Direct access of any record on a device may be possible, or the device may be restricted to *sequential* access only. In direct access, a hardware record address directs the read/write mechanism directly to the record. With sequential access only, a specific record is reached by explicitly skipping forward or backward over intervening records; the normal mode of operation is to access the records sequentially in the same linear sequence in which they are stored.
4. *Removability.* Magnetic tapes, floppy disks, and some types of hard disks are *removable,* permitting *off-line* storage of files on these devices. This feature substantially increases the amount of possible storage provided for a user by allowing only those devices containing active files to be mounted. Removable devices may also be used to transfer information between different machines, thus serving as "communication" devices.
5. *Data transfer rate.* This is the rate of speed, usually expressed in bits, bytes, or words per second, at which data can be transferred between main memory and the device.
6. *Latency.* After a read or write command is accepted by a device controller, it normally takes an additional time increment, the *latency* time, before the start of the accessed record is under the read or write heads and the data transfer can begin. This is either the start-up time for magnetic tape to accelerate to its rated speed from a dead stop or the rotational delay of disks.
7. *Seek time.* Disk devices with moving read/write heads must precede each read or

write operation by a *seek*, which physically moves the head over the track containing the desired record.

In addition to these seven characteristics, the cost of a device is a major factor. As one would expect, cost increases with the speed and convenience of accessing data.

Table 1-1 lists typical characteristics of the three main classes of secondary storage devices in terms of the preceding properties. The main liabilities of magnetic tape for file storage are the sequential accessing requirement and the inability in practice to make selective changes to records that would increase their length or to insert new records without rewriting the entire tape. On the other hand, tapes are inexpensive, small, and removable—features that make them useful for archival storage and for storing sequential files. Disks are currently the most widely used secondary storage devices, primarily because of their combination of large capacity, direct access capability, and low price, relative to tapes and electronic random-access memory (RAM).

Communication Devices.   Similar to secondary storage devices, the range of existing devices intended primarily for communication between the machine and the user (or some other machine) is very wide. We can distinguish different types of input and output devices. In the past, *card readers* and *paper tape readers* were typical representatives of input devices, while output was performed using the corresponding card and paper tape *punchers*. Due to the rapid advancement of interactive computing in recent years, these devices have almost completely disappeared from the market. Their most common replacements are various types of CR terminals (for cathode-ray terminal) consisting of a screen for output and a keyboard for input. There are many different types of terminals. The simplest are character-oriented displays for text output. For simple graphics applications, vector-oriented terminals, capable of producing drawings composed of straight-line segments of different length and orientation, may be used. The

TABLE 1-1   TYPICAL CHARACTERISTICS OF SECONDARY STORAGE DEVICES

	Magnetic Tape	Hard Disk	Floppy Disk
Capacity	$\sim 10^8$ B/reel	$\sim 10^7 - 10^9$ B/unit	$\sim 10^5$ B/unit
Record size	V	F or V	F or V
Access method	S	D	D
Removability	R	R or NR	R
Data transfer rate	~ 15 kB–1 MB/s	~ 150 kB–1.5 MB/s	~ 3–5 kB/s
Latency	~ 5 ms	~ 8 ms	~ 80 ms
Seek time	NA	~ 30 ms	~ 400 ms

B: bytes; kB: kilobytes; MB: megabytes
F: fixed length; V: variable length
S: sequential; D: direct
R: removable; NR: nonremovable

most sophisticated terminals are raster (bit map) displays, which can generate arbitrary pictures, including text, as patterns of black and white or colored dots, called pixels.

The category of output-only devices consists of various types of printers and graphic plotters, both of which produce output in the form of human-readable (hard) copies. Similar to terminals, there is a wide variety of printers, ranging from simple dot-matrix or line-oriented printers used for text output, to sophisticated photostatic or laser printers capable of generating arbitrary images on paper, transparencies, or other media. For line-oriented output, especially for large technical drawings, pen-oriented (single or multicolor) plotters are typically employed.

For transferring large amounts of data between different machines, magnetic tapes or removable disks are frequently used. Thus a tape or disk may be considered both a storage device and a source/destination of input/output data, depending on one's point of view. The properties characterizing the different communication devices of most interest to the system designer and user are the following:

1. *Record size.* As was the case with secondary storage devices, the record size determines the unit of data transferred with each operation. The most common unit used with simple CR terminals and slower output devices is one character; with fast printers and terminals, complete lines or even pages of text or blocks of vector or bit-mapped output may be transmitted with each operation.

2. *Data transfer rate.* This measures the maximum speed at which data may be transmitted to or from the device. The rate at which output data is transmitted between the processor and a character-oriented CR terminal ranges typically between 10 and 1000 bytes per second. Considerably higher rates may be required for graphics terminals. For example, a bit-map terminal used for real-time animation requires that the entire frame of $n \times m$ pixels be replaced several times per second to make the movement of objects on the screen appear smooth. This requires data transfer rates in the megabytes per second range, depending on the values of n and m.

In the case of printers and plotters, speed is determined largely by the technology used. Devices based on mechanical impact are usually capable of producing 100 to 3000 lines per minute; this translates to a data transfer rate of approximately 200 to 6000 bytes per second. Devices that do not require any movement of mechanical parts to produce an image, for example those based on static electricity, achieve data transfer rates that are generally one order of magnitude higher than those of electromechanical devices.

We have already discussed the speed of tapes and removable disks, which may be used for input and output. The only other device to consider is the keyboard, for which the actual rate of data input depends on the speed of the human user; a rate of 5 keystrokes per second (achieved only over very short periods of time) is considered the limit for this type of device.

When devices are connected to a system remotely, the rate at which data may be transmitted along such connections must also be considered. Public telephone lines typically support transfer rates up to 500 bytes per second. With dedicated long-distance transmission lines, rates of up to 5000 bytes per second may be achieved. Special-purpose short-distance communication media, such as Ethernet, achieve a transfer rate in the megabyte range. When modems are used to connect terminals to the communication lines, the transmission rate is usually determined by the sophistication of the modem used; typically, modems support transmission rates of 40 to 1000 bytes per second.

1.2.2 The Processor/Device Interface

Programmed IO.   Let us consider the possible ways of attaching the various IO devices described in Section 1.2.1 to a computer system. In the simplest case, each device is equipped with a separate *device controller* connected directly to the CPU via sets of lines called *buses*. A typical configuration is shown in Figure 1-2. In the minimal case, an *address* bus and a *data* bus are provided. The address bus is used by the CPU to select a particular memory location or an IO device; the data bus carries data between the CPU and the selected target. The controllers are needed to transform commands issued by the CPU into the appropriate electrical impulses expected by the actual devices and, conversely, transform the device status information into a representation that can be understood by the CPU. Each controller also contains a *hardware buffer* capable of holding one record (e.g., a character or a print line) to be transferred to or from the device. The CPU is responsible for carrying out all data transfers between the main memory (or some internal registers) and the device buffer. In the case of output, it copies the record into the buffer and informs the device that data are available. When the device completes the output operation, it indicates so by raising a *flag*, which is tested (implicitly or explicitly) by the CPU. When the test is successful, the CPU may copy the next record into the device buffer and initiate the device to perform the corresponding operation. This protocol, informally called *handshaking*, is repeated until all data are output. To perform input, an analogous protocol is followed. The CPU commands the device to place an input record into the hardware buffer. When this is completed, the device

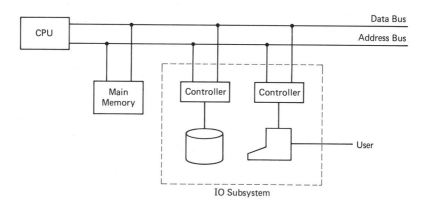

Figure 1-2 A simple hardware configuration.

indicates so by raising a flag. At this point, the CPU may remove the record from the buffer and issue the next command to the device.

The preceding input/output scheme, where the CPU is responsible for actually moving all data between main memory and the devices, is referred to as *programmed IO*. It is the simplest and least expensive approach in terms of the required hardware, but it is also the least efficient in terms of resource utilization. To illustrate this, let us compare the speed of the CPU's instruction execution with the IO rate of the different devices as discussed in Section 1.2.1; differences of possibly many orders of magnitude exist. For example, to issue the sequence of commands for moving the read/write arm of a disk requires only a few CPU cycles (i.e., a few microseconds), but the actual seek time of a disk is on the order of 30 to 400 milliseconds (ms). If the CPU were to remain idle until the disk completed the operation, a significant amount of CPU time would be wasted. Similar ratios may be detected with most hard-copy output devices. For example, to print a line on an average line printer may require 50 μs of CPU time, whereas the actual printing time could be as much as 50 ms, a difference of three orders of magnitude. If the CPU were to wait for the completion of each data transfer, its utilization would be grossly inefficient. Furthermore, only one device could be active at any time. One way to alleviate this problem is to overlap the operation of the CPU with that of individual devices so that the CPU is able to initiate a data transfer operation and to continue execution without waiting for the device to complete. In this way, many devices, as well as the CPU itself, may operate concurrently.

A major issue to be resolved when CPU and IO overlap is how to test a device for completion of an operation. This condition is indicated by a hardware flag, which must be tested by the CPU. There are three commonly used schemes to perform this test. In the first, the test is performed implicitly as part of each IO instruction. The main limitation of this approach is that the CPU is blocked for the entire duration of the IO operation (i.e., until the data transfer is completed). The second scheme utilizes a special machine instruction, test-device-flag, that returns the value *true* or *false*, depending on the current value of the flag. This permits the CPU to test the device periodically and, if it is still busy, perform some other useful work. The main problem with this approach, known as *polling*, is to determine how frequently the device flag should be tested (polled); if it is done too frequently, a significant portion of the computation is wasted on executing the test-device-flag instruction just to find out that the device is still busy. If, on the other hand, it is inserted into the instruction stream too sparsely, the device may be left idle for extensive periods of time.

The third and most efficient way of testing the device flag is to employ the concept of *interrupts*. In this approach, rather than forcing the CPU to explicitly test the device flag using a special instruction, a hardware mechanism is provided that tests the flag as part of every machine instruction executed by the CPU. If the flag is set, the hardware automatically interrupts the current sequence of instruction execution and transfers control to a predefined location in memory. Starting at this location must be a routine, called the *interrupt handler*, whose task is to decide on the actions to be taken in the given situation. In general, more than one device may have caused the IO interrupt. The interrupt handler must determine which device needs attention, analyze its status, restart it with the next operation when appropriate, and return control to the interrupted program.

In more sophisticated systems, hardware to distinguish several types of interrupts is often provided. Depending on the interrupt type, control is transferred to one of n possible locations in memory. These are ordered according to fixed priorities. If the CPU is executing the interrupt-handler routine associated with a given priority, the hardware automatically inhibits all interrupts at the same or lower priority levels. Such an arrangement, called a *multiple-priority* interrupt system, helps to improve resource utilization since different events may be handled according to their relative importance.

The following is a simplified description of a hardware instruction cycle, including the testing for interrupts.

```
loop
    w := M[ic];    {Fetch next instruction}
    ic := ic + 1;  {Increment instruction counter}
    Execute(w);
    if Interrupt then
    begin
        Store(ic);
        case interrupt__cause of
            C₁ : ic := int₁;
            C₂ : ic := int₂;
            ⋮
            Cₙ : ic := intₙ
        end {case}
    end
end {loop}
```

This algorithm performs the instruction fetch and execution as in the simple instruction cycle described in Section 1.1; we use M to denote main memory and ic as the instruction counter. The algorithm then tests for an interrupt condition and, when satisfied, it saves the state of the machine (minimally, the content of the instruction counter) immediately preceding the interrupt. At this point, the normal execution flow is diverted to one of the routines starting at location int_j, depending on the interrupt cause C_j. The selected routine is inserted into the normal stream of processing in much the same way as a normal subroutine, except that the call is issued implicitly by the hardware. This is illustrated in Figure 1-3; an interrupt condition of type C_j has been raised during the execution of instruction i, which causes the sequence of instructions $k, k + 1, \ldots$ to be executed. The instruction *Return__from__Interrupt* causes the normal sequence of execution to be resumed at the instruction $i + 1$.

Figure 1-4 illustrates graphically the main distinction between the three possible device completion techniques. Horizontal lines represent times when the CPU and the device are busy; vertical arrows indicate the points of interaction between the two. The

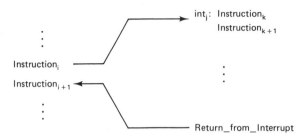

Figure 1-3 Execution of an interrupt routine.

heavy portion of the horizontal CPU line corresponds to the IO routine, that is, the code that copies a record of data from or to the device buffer and initiates the device's operation. In the first approach (Figure 1-4a), each IO instruction waits for the completion of the data transfer. There is no overlap between the CPU and the device. In the case of polling (Figure 1-4b), the CPU must periodically issue the test-device-flag instruction, shown by dashed arcs in the figure. When the device is busy, the CPU continues its normal computation; when it is idle, the restart routine is executed. Note that a device remains idle from the time it completes an operation until the next test instruction is performed. In the third approach, dashed arrows represent interrupts issued by the device

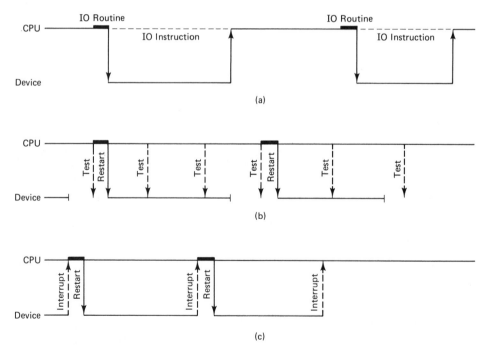

Figure 1-4 CPU/Device interaction: (a) IO instruction waits (b) CPU polls device (c) Device interrupts CPU.

upon completing a data transfer. This automatically invokes the device restart routine (interrupt routine), and hence device idle time is reduced to a minimum.

Direct Memory Access.   When using programmed IO (regardless of the device completion technique employed), the CPU carries the burden of physically moving all data between main memory and the device buffers. This is acceptable with slow, character-oriented devices, such as manually operated keyboards or line printers, since the CPU is capable of executing thousands of instructions before the device completes the transfer of a single character. In the case of fast devices, however, the overhead resulting from initiating and monitoring each individual transfer of data between the device and main memory is too high to permit an efficient utilization of the CPU. To alleviate this problem, additional hardware may be provided in each device controller to permit data to be transferred directly between the device and main memory. Using this concept, called *direct memory access* (DMA), the CPU only commands the device to perform the transfer of a block of characters while the actual operation is carried out directly by the DMA controller. The CPU may use polling or, more commonly, interrupts to determine when the DMA controller has completed the current transfer and is ready for the next operation.

Even when DMA controllers are employed with faster devices, there is still a significant amount of work to be done by the CPU for each data transfer. In particular, it must analyze the status of each interrupting device to detect possible errors and attempt to correct these, and it must perform various kinds of device-specific code conversions and formatting functions. All these tasks may be usefully delegated to a specialized processor, referred to as a *channel*. This may be viewed as a more sophisticated form of a DMA controller, responsible for managing several devices at the same time and supervising the data transfers between each of these devices and main memory. Figure 1-5 shows the block diagram of a typical general-purpose computing facility consisting of a CPU, main memory, and a variety of different IO devices connected to the system via several channels. (Usually, a channel does not interface directly to a device; rather, it is connected through a simple device controller. These controllers are omitted from the figure for clarity.)

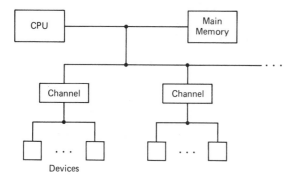

Figure 1-5 A general-purpose computing facility.

1.3 FUNCTIONS OF OPERATING SYSTEMS

1.3.1 A Minimal Operating System

There are many possible hardware organizations that implement the basic von Neumann model of computation; fortunately, most of these are extensions and variations of a few standard configurations. Figure 1-2 shows the simplest form of such a machine, which maps very closely onto the abstract machine of Figure 1-1. In particular, the CPU and the memory perform the functions of a sequential stored-program computer, as outlined previously. The secondary storage and the communication subsystems are represented by a disk unit and a user terminal, respectively.

This simple hardware configuration is typical of some of the older computer systems and, more importantly, most present-day microcomputers. Conceptually, its operation is very simple in that it follows exactly the basic von Neumann model of computation: The memory contains a sequence of machine-level instructions that the CPU fetches and executes using the program counter. The main difficulties stem from the need to attach a variety of different IO devices, since each device type expects different sequences of commands to initiate and supervise its operation. For example, to output a character to a manually operated terminal may require a relatively simple control sequence, consisting of selecting the appropriate device through the address bus and placing the desired character on the data bus. To output one or more characters to a moving-head disk, on the other hand, involves several hundreds or even thousands of machine instructions; this is due to the extremely complex interfaces of electromechanical devices, which need to first perform a seek operation to position the read/write head over the appropriate track and then await the rotational delay until the desired location passes under the read/write head before any transfer of data can begin.

The spectrum of possible error conditions and other status information returned by such devices is correspondingly complex. The problem is aggravated further by the fact that no widely accepted standards for the operation of IO devices exist; different sequences of instructions are usually required not only for each major device class (e.g., a user terminal), but also for each individual device type within that class. To liberate the programmer from the burden of coping with such hardware-dependent issues, operating systems provide specialized *IO routines* for the various types of devices; from the user's point of view, these may be used in much the same way as if higher-level IO instructions actually existed. In this way, the operating system bridges the gap between the programmer's needs and the limited capabilities of the underlying hardware.

Another major problem to be solved with any computer system concerns the *initial loading* of programs into main memory after the power is turned on, since electronic storage circuits contain no meaningful information at that time. To accomplish this, mechanisms are provided to transfer initially some minimal amount of information and, subsequently, entire user programs residing on secondary storage devices into main memory. In terms of hardware, the required support is quite minimal. It consists of circuitry that reads one data record into some fixed set of contiguous main memory locations and then transfers control (i.e., sets the instruction counter of the machine) to a fixed address in that set, usually the first. The circuitry can be activated by an external Load button pressed by the operator to start the system. In small systems (e.g., personal computers) no explicit load button may be provided; instead, turning on the power activates the initial loading circuitry.

To illustrate the resulting effect, let the main memory of a computer be designated $M[0]$, $M[1]$, $M[2]$, . . . , where each location $M[i]$ may contain 1 byte (or word) of information. Suppose that pressing the Load button causes one record of 80 bytes of information to be read from a predetermined area on a disk unit into the memory area $M[0]$ . . . $M[79]$; this is then followed by the setting of the instruction counter to zero. Algorithmically, this may be described as follows:

Press__Load: **for** $i := 0$ **to** 79 **do** *Read*$(M[i])$; {*end of loop*}
                  Transfer__to$(M[0])$;

When this hardware algorithm terminates, the CPU begins to fetch and execute instructions starting at memory location $M[0]$. To read a complete program, the first 80-byte record, the one read by Press__Load, must contain machine instructions for reading the next record or set of records into subsequent memory locations. Let each address, instruction, and datum in our primitive machine occupy 1 byte. Assume that the program to be read is stored on a secondary storage device where each record has the following format:

Byte	Contents
0	Loading address, LA, for first byte of program/data part of record
1	Number of bytes, n, to be loaded; $n \leq 78$
2 to 79	Program/data part; the absolute code

The last record contains $n = 0$, and the loading address byte is interpreted as the first instruction (the entry point) of the program; Figure 1-6 shows the required records in order. Finally, let storage locations $M[r]$, . . . , $M[r + 79]$ be a reserved read-in area, where r is arbitrarily assigned as the starting location of the read-in area. Then a one-record absolute loader, read into memory as the first record when the Load button is pressed, performs the following actions:

```
loop
    for i := 0 to 79 do Read(M[r + i]);
    LA := M[r];
    n := M[r + 1];
    if n = 0 then Transfer__to(LA);
    for i := 0 to n − 1 do
        M[LA + i] := M[r + 2 + i]
end {loop}
```

LA1	n1	Program/Data
LA2	n2	Program/Data
⋮	⋮	⋮
Entry Address	0	

Figure 1-6 Program for initial loading.

The loading process is a vivid example of bootstrapping—pulling oneself up by one's own bootstraps.

The initial program loading and the IO support consisting of predefined routines as described are two major areas in which the operating system contributes to reducing the hardware/user gap. A third major component provided by virtually all general-purpose operating systems is a *file system*, which helps the user to manage different programs and data collections on secondary storage. The file system may be viewed as another level of abstraction: by building on the IO routines provided by the operating system for easier control of the various devices, a higher-level interface is created, which permits entire programs and data collections to be manipulated as single objects (i.e., files). Typically, commands to create, destroy, copy, append, or transfer files are provided. Again we observe the bridging effect of the operating system, which extends the existing machine hardware to meet the more abstract point of view expected by the user.

1.3.2 Principles of Multiprogramming

With the introduction of interrupts, DMA controllers, and channels, we have provided hardware mechanisms that permit the CPU to keep many devices operating simultaneously and, at the same time, perform some other computation. A single program, however, is rarely able to exploit this potential. Rather, a typical program alternates between phases of input, computation, and output and limits itself to using just a few of the existing devices. Consider, for example, a simple program that reads a file, performs some computation on the data, and outputs the results. Even with the most sophisticated interrupt and DMA facilities, the overlap between CPU and devices is limited to that of Figure 1-7. The CPU is drastically underutilized during the input or output phase; we say the system is *IO-bound*. Conversely, all devices are idle during the compute phase; in this case, the system is said to be *compute-bound*. Furthermore, even when processors (CPU, channels) are kept busy most of the time, the utilization of other computer resources is often poor; for example, if the program is small, much of main memory is unused. If more than one program were simultaneously active, not only would the amount of idle resources decrease, but also system throughput and turnaround time for individual programs would improve. This was the original reasoning that led to the development of *multiprogrammed* systems.

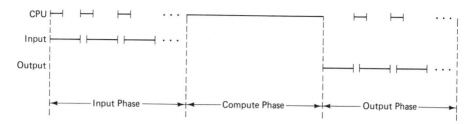

Figure 1-7 Typical CPU/IO overlap in a single program.

The basic idea behind the multiprogramming concept is to maintain more than one independent program in main memory. A particularly good choice would be to overlap an IO-bound program A (e.g., updating a large data file) and a compute-bound program B (e.g., solving a set of partial differential equations). While A is waiting for IO, B can compute; on IO completion, control is switched back to A. Figure 1-8 illustrates the execution of two such programs in both a single-programmed and multiprogrammed environment. The time saved by multiprogramming is evident in this example. Note that multiprogramming involves the sharing of *time* on processors and the sharing of *space*

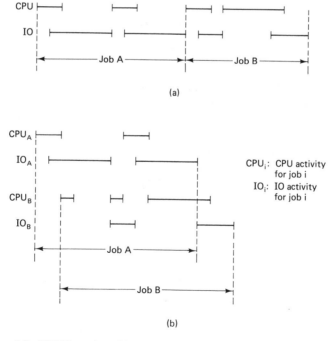

Figure 1-8 CPU/IO overlap with singleprogramming and multiprogramming: (a) One job at a time (b) Multiprogramming A and B.

in main memory, as well as the potential sharing of other resources. An additional space-saving benefit accrues from the ability to share code resident in main memory. If several programs require the same language translator or request the same system service, a single copy of these routines may be shared asynchronously. The economic and technical success of hardware and software resource sharing through multiprogramming is beneficial to users in one other, perhaps the most important, way; it makes it feasible to provide a wide variety of services.

Currently, most medium- and large-scale systems are multiprogrammed. However, the advantages of this mode of operation are not gained without a price. First, a number of hardware components must be added to make multiprogramming feasible. The operating system then must be extended from a simple collection of IO and file-management routines to a complex resource manager capable of accommodating the wide spectrum of needs and expectations of individual users. As with the simple operating system described in Section 1.2.1, a multiprogramming operating system serves as a bridge between the existing hardware and the user. In particular, it hides the details of storage and IO devices from the user by providing high-level operations for input and output, and it provides a file system for managing programs and data files on secondary storage. In addition, an operating system for multiprogramming must carry out a number of other important tasks. Most significantly, it must attempt to *hide the fact that resources are shared among different users.* That is, except for the slower speed at which services are performed, each user should have the illusion of having the system entirely to himself, unless some exchange of information is explicitly desired. The following points summarize the basic tasks an operating system must perform to permit multiprogramming:

1. *Bridge the gap between the machine and the user level.* The operating system must hide many aspects of the actual hardware by providing higher levels of instructions. This applies especially to low-level hardware IO instructions that the users do not wish to use for reasons of convenience or that may be restricted to only certain classes of programs for reasons of security and data integrity. A number of other primitives may also be provided by the operating system to the users, for example, to facilitate the handling of files on secondary storage. All such primitives may be viewed as abstractions that hide the details of the underlying machine language implementation necessary to control the existing hardware.

2. *Manage the available resources needed by different users.* The operating system is responsible for allocating hardware and software resources. It must periodically reevaluate the system's status and possibly change the assignment of available resources (i.e., CPU, memory, devices, and files) to processes in order to maximize their utilization. The problem is one of matching the efficient use of these resources against constraints imposed by the users, such as response time.

3. *Enforce protection policies.* Since the system is shared by many different users, we must ensure the integrity of the operating system and user programs from accidental or malicious damage. Most parts must also be protected against snooping

by user programs or even the system itself. This is not only a question of preventing the destruction of information but is also a problem of assuring privacy and ownership. Private user files or parts of the operating system may require guarantees against unauthorized reading or execution. In addition, an owner of a file (data or program) should be able to permit any reading, writing, or execution to specified classes or groups of users.

4. *Provide facilities for synchronization and communication.* In a multiprogramming system, different processes may be executing concurrently. In many situations, two or more processes may compete for a common resource (e.g., a file) that they need to read and modify. To preserve the integrity of the file's content, it may be necessary to impose an order in which the file may be accessed. Similarly, processes may wish to cooperate by exchanging information at various stages of their execution. Thus a multiprogramming operating system must provide synchronization and communciation primitives to permit the implementation of such schemes.

To accomplish these four major tasks, a multiprogramming operating system should be equipped with some form of the following hardware and software mechanisms:

1. *DMA hardware.* We have already discussed the need to liberate the CPU from the burden of performing low-level IO operations; this may be accomplished by providing direct memory access controllers or IO channels. With multiprogramming, this requirement is even more pronounced since there are always many programs awaiting execution, thus generating sufficient demand for both CPU time and IO. The available computing resources may be utilized by switching the CPU among those programs currently not requiring any IO services, while DMA controllers or channels are kept busy supervising data transfers between devices and main memory for IO-bound processes.

2. *(Priority) interrupt mechanism.* In a multiprogrammed computer system, there exists a variety of possible events to which the operating system must respond. Among these are the completion of IO operations reported by channels, hardware malfunctions, errors generated during computation (e.g., overflow or division by zero), and external signals generated by the operator. To have an efficient way of coping with such events, the interrupt mechanisms discussed earlier are extended to handle not only the completion of IO but all the other events as well. Different priority levels for interrupts are necessary because of the relative importance of programs waiting for an interrupt signal to awaken them and because the existence of timing constraints between an event and its processing. For example, a machine error must normally be treated immediately, an interrupt indicating that input is available from a data-acquisition device may require service within a very short period of time or data could be lost, and an IO completion interrupt from a magnetic tape could be handled at some indefinite time in the future, depending on the priority of the particular program using the tape. A built-in set of hardware priorities for broad classes of interrupts and the ability to inhibit and enable interrupts by programs permit the system dynamically to establish precedence relationships among interrupt-causing events. When an interrupt occurs, the hardware must quickly save the current state of the system, determine the cause of the interrupt, and change the CPU state to initiate an appropriate interrupt-handling routine.

3. *Timer.* A program-controllable timer should be included in the hardware to control the sharing of time among several processes. The timer is set to a particular value, which it decrements periodically by a small constant. When it reaches zero, it produces an interrupt that permits the operating system to gain control of the CPU. This facility is necessary to prevent an ongoing computation from monopolizing the CPU for extensive periods of time and thus causing other resources to be underutilized.

4. *Storage and instruction protection.* To efficiently prevent erratic or malicious processes from destroying or invading the privacy of other processes, including system processes, it is important to have hardware facilities for protecting areas of main memory and for restricting the set of machine instructions available to a particular process. For example, it is not generally desirable for a user program directly to inhibit interrupts.

5. *Dynamic address relocation.* When a program waits for some lengthy event, such as the completion of an IO operation, it is sometimes desirable to remove it temporarily from main memory to permit other programs to utilize the otherwise wasted space. To increase flexibility in *swapping* programs in and out of main memory, it should be possible to load a given program into different locations each time it is removed. Furthermore, a program should be permitted to only partially reside in main memory. Hardware that permits such dynamic relocation without lengthy transformations of the program is necessary to improve the efficiency of the system.

1.3.3 Operating Systems as Virtual Machines

In the previous two sections we concentrated on showing the tasks executed by an operating system primarily from the *performance* point of view. We argued that, by using interrupt mechanisms and devices with direct memory access, it is possible to free the CPU from most of IO processing, while permitting different IO devices to operate concurrently. The objective of multiprogramming is then to generate sufficient workload so that much of the available CPU and device time can be exploited. A second major benefit of multiprogramming is the ability to simultaneously share the machine's resources so that, for example, more than one user may interact with the system at the same time. To make this approach practical, however, it is necessary to guarantee some acceptable response time to each user at his or her terminal. This implies that even programs that display an ideal behavior in terms of a balanced resource utilization must not be permitted to run for extensive periods of time if other programs are waiting. Rather, all active processes must receive some fair share of the available computational resources, especially CPU time. One common system policy is to serve all active processes in turn by assigning to each a small quantum (possibly variable in length) of the available CPU time. This *time-sharing* concept uses the basic principles of multiprogramming to create the illusion of a separate *virtual machine* for each user. Conceptually, each of these virtual machines is an exact image of the actual machine except for its speed, which is divided by the number of currently active users.

The basic mechanism used to create such a virtual machine is the use of *abstraction*, introduced implicitly in Section 1.1 when discussing the problem of bridging the hardware/user gap. For example, IO instructions are implemented as procedures or macros provided by the system. From the user's point of view, however, they are primitive operations that the higher-level virtual machine is capable of executing as its "machine" language. Similarly, operations to manipulate files are viewed as primitives executable by another virtual machine, which, in turn, may utilize the virtual IO operations to perform its function. Another example of a virtual machine is the command language through which the users control the system's operation. Each command (e.g., to load and start a program or to retrieve some information about the system status) may involve many lower-level operations on part of the system; from the user's point of view, however, the operating system appears as a virtual machine with the set of commands as its "machine" language.

Abstraction may be applied repeatedly to create multiple levels of virtual machines. At each level, certain physical constraints of existing hardware components are eliminated. A prime example of one such constraint is the limited size of main memory. If a given program exceeds the available memory space, it must somehow be partitioned into smaller segments, which are loaded into memory when needed. If no abstraction is used (i.e., the physical memory is visible at the user level), the programmer is responsible for determining which parts of the program are to reside in memory at any given time. Modern operating systems have liberated the programmer from this burden by implementing the concept of *virtual memory*; at the programming level the illusion of a contiguous and, for most practical purposes, unbounded storage space is created. This is accomplished by making the operating system responsible for transferring those program segments relevant to the current computation between main memory and secondary storage. Thus the operating system extends the actually existing physical memory into a virtual memory presented to the programmer.

The preceding examples illustrate the fundamental concept of abstraction, which governs much of modern operating system technology. We will return to this concept in Section 1.5, which discusses different ways to organize and structure operating systems.

1.4 TYPES OF OPERATING SYSTEMS

A very large number of operating systems exists today and new systems are continuously being developed. To permit any comparisons to be made, we categorize operating systems along the following three dimensions: (1) the size of the underlying hardware configuration, (2) the level of resource sharing, and (3) the types of interaction permitted.

1.4.1 Size of the Underlying Hardware Configuration

Operating System for Microcomputers.   Typically, the CPU of a microcomputer consists of one chip, the microprocessor, which is connected to the remaining hardware components by a set of shared buses. In the past, the addressing capabilities of microcomputers have been usually limited to 8 or 16 bits (i.e., the storage consisted of 2^8 or 2^{16} bytes or words), which severely restricted the range of programs that could be executed on such systems. This limitation is disappearing as new 32-bit microprocessors are being developed. The main emphasis of microcomputers, however, is still on low cost, which implies that peripheral devices are limited to one or two disk drives (hard or floppy disks), a CR terminal with a keyboard, and possibly a printer. Conforming with the objective of low cost, the operating systems for microcomputers are quite simple. Their functions are restricted to initializing the system when it is turned on, providing IO routines to permit user programs to transfer data between main memory and IO devices, and providing a file system to manipulate program and data files. Oftentimes, microcomputers (or even larger systems) are used as intelligent peripheral devices or personal *workstations*. In that case, communication facilities must also be provided by the operating system to permit the workstation to exchange information with the host computer. Workstations are also usually equipped with graphic facilities, which imply special high-resolution terminals and special devices to interact with the image, such as a light pen or a "mouse." Examples of such sophisticated workstations are Apollo's Series 3000 Personal Workstation, which is based on the Motorola MC68020 microprocessor, Digital Equipment Corporation's VAXstation 100 (based on the MicroVAX), and Sun Microsystems' Sun-Workstation.

Operating Systems for Minicomputers.   Early minicomputers had characteristics very similar to those of present-day microcomputers, except that the CPU was not manufactured as one chip. In recent years, minicomputers have been significantly upgraded in terms of both hardware and software. In particular, the instruction set has been extended to perform floating-point operations and to handle words of 32 or even 64 bits in length, the addressing capability has been further extended through hardware-supported mapping schemes, and special high-speed memories and other hardware facilities have been added to increase performance. As a result, operating systems for minicomputers must place greater emphasis on efficient resource utilization than those for microcomputers; in general, they perform most of the functions of a general-purpose time-sharing or multiprogramming system.

Operating Systems for Mainframe Computers.   The term mainframe was coined in the late 1970s to designate large general-purpose computing facilities. Such systems are intended to support many interactive as well as batch processes at the same time and offer a wide spectrum of services and facilities to each user. Consequently, they must be equipped with a powerful CPU (or even multiple CPUs) with addressing capabilities of 32 or more bits, large main memories, and a multitude of secondary storage and communication devices. Due to the rapid development of minicomputers in recent years, the difference between mini- and mainframe computers is, however, beginning to disappear. Thus, from the operating system's point of view, there are no significant conceptual differences between the two types of systems; it is only the extent and complexity of the underlying hardware configuration that is reflected in the size of the corresponding operating system.

1.4.2 Level of Resource Sharing

Any program executing on a computer system makes use of some of the available hardware and software resources. Depending on whether these resources may be used only by one program at a time or whether they can be shared, we can distinguish two fundamental types of operating systems:

Single-programmed Operating Systems.   In the simplest form, the system may permit only one program to be active at any given time; once it is loaded into main memory it remains there until its completion. Typical examples of such systems are operating systems for microcomputers. In some larger systems, a technique called *swapping* is sometimes employed to better utilize available resources. Such operating systems maintain one active program in main memory and several programs on secondary storage. When the currently executing program needs to wait (e.g., for the completion of an IO operation), it is swapped out of main memory and another program is loaded instead. Operating systems that support swapping may actually be viewed as border-line cases between single- and multiprogrammed operating systems.

Multiprogrammed Operating Systems.   To improve the utilization of a system's resources, multiprogramming is most commonly used. As discussed in Section 1.3.2, the operating system maintains more than one program in main memory simultaneously to permit effective sharing of CPU time, storage space, and other resources among the active programs. The resource sharing actually extends into the operating system itself in that programs comprising the operating system are also multiprogrammed in most large systems. Multiprogramming is most commonly used in systems shared by several users. It may, however, be useful in single-user systems as well. This is the case when the user is permitted to have several active processes running concurrently or when the operating system itself maintains several active processes at the same time.

1.4.3 Type of Interaction Permitted

The third dimension along which operating systems may be categorized is the type of interface available to the user. The main determining factor is the system's response time (i.e., the speed at which services are delivered to the user). These operating systems may be divided into the following three classes.

Operating Systems for Batch Processing.   In this type of environment, user jobs are submitted in sequential batches on input devices and there is no interaction between users and their jobs during processing. The user is completely isolated from the job and, as a result, equates system response time with the job *turnaround time*, defined as the actual time it takes to complete a job, counting from the point it has been submitted to the system. This time is generally satisfactory if it can be measured in small numbers of minutes or hours. Consequently, the operating system can follow a relatively flexible scheduling policy. Batch processing may be done in both single- and multiprogrammed environments.

Interactive Operating Systems.   Systems in this class permit users to interact with their computations in the form of a dialog. They may be designed as single-user systems, possibly allowing several processes to run simultaneously on behalf of the user, or they may provide computational services to many users concurrently. In the latter, the effect of simultaneous access is achieved by sharing processor time and other resources among all users in a manner that guarantees response to each command within a few seconds. This is accomplished by extending the principles of multiprogramming into the concept of time sharing, as discussed in Section 1.3.3; that is, the CPU is allocated to each user process for a small time quantum to create the illusion of a separate computer for each user.

Real-time Operating Systems.   Many applications are designed to service external processes having strict timing constraints on response. Usually, interrupt signals are used to command the attention of the system; if they are not handled promptly (within microseconds, milliseconds, or seconds, depending on the type of process), information may be lost or the external process may be seriously degraded or misrepresented. These systems are often designed for a particular application, for example telecommunications, air traffic control, robotics, weapons control, or the control of manufacturing processes in an industrial plant. In some of these applications, failure to meet timing constraints can have disastrous effects.

In many cases, operating systems provide for any or all of batch processing, time sharing, or real-time control. For example, both real-time and time-sharing systems usually permit batch jobs to be submitted, which are processed in the "background" (i.e., whenever there is no higher-priority activity to perform).

1.5 STRUCTURE OF OPERATING SYSTEMS

An operating system may be viewed as the manager of a variety of hardware and software resources. The primary hardware resources are processors, memories, and IO devices, while software resources constitute programs and data files. The operating system forms a layer of software that creates the illusion of a machine quite different from the actual underlying hardware. Most of the details of the hardware are hidden from ordinary users by the operating system, which instead provides a diverse repertoire of commands and facilities to satisfy the needs of different users. Since operating systems are usually large and complex collections of software routines, the designers must place great emphasis on their internal organization and structure. In this section we examine the various possible internal organizations of operating systems.

1.5.1 A Monolithic Structure

The most primitive form of operating system, developed mostly during the early days of computing, is a *monolithic* entity, consisting of a set of programs that execute on the bare hardware. In such an operating system, modules serving different functions, such as processor management, memory management, or device management, may generally be distinguished. Their execution, however, usually results in a single 'process', in that control is being passed from one module to another by procedure calls and branches. User programs may be viewed as subroutines invoked by the operating system whenever it is not performing any system functions. When a user program is invoked, it continues executing until one of several possible conditions occurs:

1. The program terminates, resulting in an action similar to a procedure return.
2. A time-out signal is generated, signaling that the program has exceeded some assigned maximum amount of CPU time.
3. The program requests some service action to be taken by the operating system (e.g., an IO operation); this may be accomplished through a regular call to a system procedure or through a special instruction, a supervisor call (SVC), that forces execution into a privileged mode.
4. An interrupt occurs (in systems that provide an interrupt facility), indicating that a device or some other event requires the attention of the operating system.

In all four cases, control is returned to the operating system, which analyzes the cause of the return and, after performing the necessary management functions, invokes another user process. The basic concept of a monolithic operating system is shown in Figure 1-9, where p_1 though p_n represent user programs and HW represents the bare machine hardware.

Due to the multitude of different functions that need to be performed in a modern computing facility and the inherent nondeterminism resulting from the concurrent activities of different users and different hardware components, operating systems are becoming larger and more complex. As a result, their internal structuring has played an important role not only during the development phase but throughout their entire lifetime. A good structure is essential to allow subsequent modifications (maintenance) and possible enhancements to be carried out easily and usually has a significant impact on the system's performance. To cope with these requirements, the monolithic organization of early operating systems must be rejected in favor of a more refined internal structure.

1.5.2 The Kernel Approach

The philosophy underlying this approach is to concentrate on the design of an operating system *kernel* or nucleus, which embodies only the most vital low-level functions per-

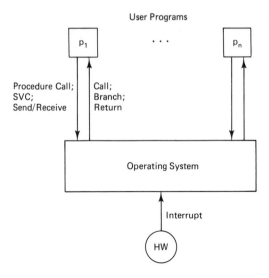

User Programs

Figure 1-9   A monolithic operating system.

formed by an operating system. It is a level of software that, not unlike a monolithic operating system, hides the underlying hardware. However, it provides only a *minimal* set of operations from which the rest of the operating system may be constructed.

Most present-day systems are organized as collections of concurrent processes. We will define the concept of a process in Section 2.1; for the purposes of the present discussion, a process can be viewed as an active entity—a program or a collection of programs that, when assigned a CPU, is capable of executing. In the simplest form, each user and each important system task (e.g., memory management or the servicing of a device) can be viewed as a separate process, running concurrently with other processes. To implement this point of view is one of the most important tasks of the kernel. The kernel hides the physical CPU by performing the functions associated with CPU management and allocation. It is responsible for dividing the available CPU time among all active processes according to some fair system policy. All details of the allocation are hidden inside the kernel and hence all active processes appear to run simultaneously, albeit at different speeds. Hence the kernel provides a fundamental abstraction; it creates a *virtual CPU* for every active process. To permit processes to interact, some synchronization and/or communication primitives must also be provided by the kernel. Figure 1-10 shows this operating system structure, where u_i and s_j represent user and system processes, respectively. The dotted lines among processes indicate that synchronization or communication signals may be exchanged among processes. The actual flow of such information, however, passes through the kernel (i.e., by kernel-defined primitives).

One of the first systems based on the kernel approach was Brinch-Hansen's multiprogramming system for the RC 4000 computer (Brinch Hansen, 1970). The kernel of this system provides four primitives for process control: *create*, *start*, *stop*, and *remove*. The first of these permits any process to create new processes as its progenies (children). To these it can then apply the remaining three operations to control their behavior. Hence

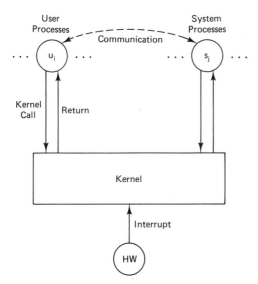

Figure 1-10 A process-oriented operating system.

processes are ordered in a natural hierarchy according to their creation. They may communicate with one another by sending messages. The main data structures provided by the kernel are a pool of buffers to hold messages in transit and a message queue for each process. The following four primitives can then be used by processes to exchange messages (a semicolon is used to separate input parameters from output parameters):

1. *send_message(receiver, message; buffer).* The kernel places the contents of *message* into a free buffer and enters it in the queue of the process named *receiver*. If this process is waiting for the arrival of a message, it is activated. The sender process continues after the output variable *buffer* is set to identify the particular buffer used by the kernel for this message transmission.

2. *wait_message(; sender, message, buffer).* The process executing this primitive is blocked until at least one message is present in its message queue. When the process is allowed to continue, the three output variables contain the name of the sender, a copy of the message, and identification of the buffer in which the message was received, respectively. (The latter may be used by a subsequent *send_answer* primitive.)

3. *send_answer(result, answer, buffer).* This primitive copies *result* and *answer* into *buffer*, where *result* specifies the answer type (possible answer types are regular answer and dummy answer, as explained later); *buffer* identifies the buffer in which a message was originally received by *wait_message*. The buffer containing the answer is then entered in the queue of the original sender; if the sender is waiting for this answer, it is activated.

4. *wait_answer(result, answer; buffer).* The process executing this primitive is de-

layed until an answer arrives; the variable *result* again specifies the answer type (regular or dummy), and *buffer* identifies the particular buffer used for the transmission.

The normal message protocol requires the use of all four primitives. The sender emits a *send_message* followed at some point by a *wait_answer*, while the receiver issues a *wait_message* and, subsequently, a *send_answer*. A dummy answer is inserted by the kernel when the addressed receiver process does not exist; the answer type is given in the parameter *result* used by the last two primitives.

The send and receive primitives are also used for performing input and output operations. This is possible by viewing collections of input and output data as external processes with which internal processes can communicate. This uniform point of view permits the use of the same four kernel primitives for both interprocess communication and programming of input and output routines.

1.5.3 A Process Hierarchy

The kernel approach as shown in Figure 1-10 permits a much cleaner way of structuring an operating system than the monolithic approach. However, it divides modules or processes into only two sets, those constituting the kernel and those built on top of it. Hence, deciding which functions should be part of the kernel is very critical. If the kernel is relatively large, it itself becomes subject to some internal structuring, since its correct and efficient functioning is vital to the rest of the system. If it is small, most of the operating system is implemented outside. Viewing it as a homogeneous collection of concurrent processes is not sufficient in this case. Instead, additional structure must be imposed above the kernel level to capture the way processes interact and possibly depend on each other's services. To avoid the critical decision on what functions should be part of the kernel, the operating system may instead be structured as a multilevel hierarchy. This is achieved by imposing additional levels of abstraction on different processes. The lowest level is typically responsible for the task of virtualizing the CPU for all processes found at higher levels, as was the case in the pure kernel approach described previously. The next higher level then usually deals with the problem of memory management. It attempts to hide the actual physical memory by providing a *virtual memory* in much the same way as the lowest level accomplishes the virtualization of the CPU. This memory abstraction may be implemented in two forms: (1) a single virtual memory may be shared by all processes above this level, or (2) a separate virtual memory space can be provided for each process. With the latter approach, processes are entirely independent since each runs in its own memory space and has its own CPU; any interactions take place exclusively through the kernel-supplied synchronization and communication primitives.

At higher levels, the principles of abstraction may be applied again to impose further structure on the remaining processes above the CPU and memory virtualization levels. For example, a level of virtual IO devices may be created by hiding the details of the actual physical units. Similarly, logical files are a convenient high-level abstraction of collections of data accessed by processes.

One of the first and most influential approaches to such a systematic approach was taken by Dijkstra in the THE operating system (Dijkstra, 1968a), which we will use to illustrate the structuring of an operating system as different layers of abstraction imposed on processes. In THE, processes are arranged in a hierarchy where each level defines a successively more abstract virtual machine. As one moves up the hierarchy, more resource management tasks are performed. Thus, processes at one level can assume the availability of resources handled by processes at lower levels; in other words, certain classes of resources may be ignored at each level. For example, if dynamic allocation of main storage is performed at level i, then processes at level j, where $j > i$, can essentially ignore storage problems in the most general case.

The THE system has the process hierarchy shown in Figure 1-11. Level 0 performs the virtualization of the CPU and, in the case of THE, provides two primitives (the P

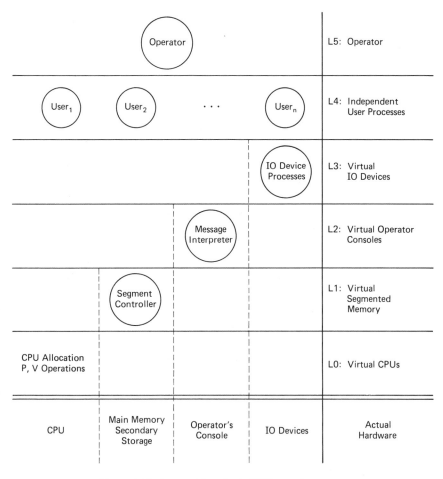

Figure 1-11 Process hierarchy in THE operating system.

and *V* operations, which will be discussed Section 2.4.1) as the lowest-level synchronization mechanisms. Processes above level 0 need not be concerned with the number of physical processors available. Level 1 contains the segment controller process, whose task it is to hide the details of main and secondary storage (core memory and a magnetic drum in the case of THE). Thus processes above this level deal only with segments of information, independently of their location in the two types of storage. Level 2 of the hierarchy abstracts the concept of the operator console. Even though there is only one physical console in the system, all processes above level 2 have the illusion of having their own console. The message interpreter at level 2 takes care of all the message traffic between these processes and the operator at the actual physical console. Processes at the next higher level, 3, perform all tasks associated with buffering of input streams and unbuffering of output streams. This essentially accomplishes the virtualization of the physical IO devices, such as the printer or paper tape reader. These processes have been placed above the level of the message interpreter since they must be able to communicate with the system's operator. Level 4 contains all user processes; each has at its disposal a complete virtual machine, consisting of a separate set of IO devices, an operator console, segmented storage, and a CPU. Save for the communication primitives, processes at this level are completely isolated and thus protected from one another. Finally, the operator process may be viewed as residing at the highest level, 5, which permits it to control all other processes at lower levels.

1.5.4 A Functional Hierarchy

The basic concept of organizing an operating system into a hierarchy of abstractions is appealing because it is then possible to develop and understand the system by a successive refinement process, starting with the lowest level and proceeding by building on the primitives provided by the levels below. The abstraction levels, however, do not necessarily correspond to the various processes in a system. In fact, it is quite difficult to arrange processes into a clearly defined hierarchy since there may be mutual dependencies among processes that prevent one being placed above the other in a strict hierarchy.

Consider the two tasks of process management and memory management. If each is handled by one process, several interdependencies may occur. For example, to create a new process, the process management subsystem may call on the services of the memory management to create the necessary space for the new process. Similarly, when processes are activated or deactivated, some memory management functions may also be performed. On the other hand, the memory manager may need to call on some process scheduling facilities to satisfy allocation requests when memory is full. This mutual dependency of processes prevents their clear separation into distinct hierarchy levels. A second problem that results when processes are associated with levels of a hierarchy is a significant overhead in communication between processes at different levels.

To solve this obvious disparity between processes and hierarchy levels, Habermann, Flon, and Cooprider (1976) suggested that an operating system should not be organized into levels of processes but levels of *functions* performed by the various processes. In such an organization, each level consists of a set of functions whose names are statically known. The levels $L_0, L_1, \ldots, L_n$ are ordered such that functions defined at level L_i are also known to L_{i+1} and, at the discretion of L_{i+1}, also to levels L_{i+2}, and so on. L_0 corresponds to the hardware instructions of the target machine. Each level, in fact, is regarded as providing a new computer—a virtual machine—to the next higher level.

Since processes generally perform more than one function, any given process may span several levels of the hierarchy. This permits the necessary interleaving of processes resulting from mutual dependencies. Consider again the two tasks of process and memory management. The former embodies the various functions of process creation, destruction, activation, and suspension. The latter deals with the creation and destruction of segments and with their management in primary and secondary storage. When viewed as embodiments of functions, it is possible to interleave processes such that interdependencies among the various functions follow a strict hierarchical ordering, as illustrated in Figure 1-12. The functions of process creation and destruction need the functions of segment creation and destruction and are thus placed above the latter. For similar reasons, process scheduling is placed above the segment management function. Finally, segment creation and destruction are above process scheduling and thus may call on this function when satisfying a memory request.

An example of an existing system that explicitly uses such a comblike process hierarchy is the Pilot operating system (Redell et al., 1980). It interleaves the functions of the file system, responsible for the management of files on secondary storage, and the virtual memory subsystem, which extends the addressing capability of the system beyond the size of the available physical memory. The lower-level functions of both subsystems were included in the Pilot kernel.

1.5.5 Object-oriented Structure

Instead of viewing the operating system as a collection of concurrent processes, some systems have taken a more general approach by viewing the system as a collection of

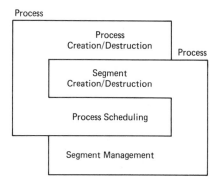

Process

| Process Creation/Destruction |
| Segment Creation/Destruction |
| Process Scheduling |
| Segment Management |

Process

Figure 1-12 Interleaving of functions.

objects. A process is only one type of object; other possible object types may include procedures, storage pages, communication ports, hardware devices, synchronization primitives, and a variety of other concepts. Possible interactions among objects are determined by *capabilities*, which may be viewed as pointers to objects, each also containing a set of rights that define the operations applicable to that object. A kernel is provided whose task is to enforce this abstract point of view. In particular, the kernel is responsible for maintaining the existing object type definitions and for controlling the access privileges to each object. This is usually accomplished by permitting only the kernel to directly access and manipulate capabilities. When a process wishes to perform some operation on some other object, it must issue a kernel call, naming the capability for the object to be manipulated and the operation to be performed. The kernel validates the request and, if legal, permits the operation to be carried out.

The resulting structure of an object-oriented operating system is a network of objects interconnected by capabilities, as illustrated in Figure 1-13. The principles of abstraction are also applied here, but not to create successively refined layers of virtual machines as described earlier. Rather, each object itself embodies an abstraction of some concept; it hides the internal implementation of that concept and provides a set of operations applicable to the object. Consider, for example, a process scheduler, an agent responsible for selecting processes and placing these into a queue, where they await execution by the CPU. In an object-oriented system, the scheduler may deal with two types of objects, processes and ports (queues). Its main task is to select processes from a scheduling port and place these according to some scheduling policy into a dispatching port. The scheduler does so by using the operations *receive* and *send*, defined on objects of type port, which accomplish the dequeuing and enqueuing of the named process at the appropriate ports. The scheduler does not need to know anything about the internal representation and functioning of either object type; its working environment consists of process and port objects, which it manipulates by the corresponding send and receive operations.

One of the most sophisticated object-oriented systems is Intel's iAPX 432. It uses processor and process objects to implement scheduling and dispatching, as outlined previously. Its interprocess communication facility permits any object to be passed among

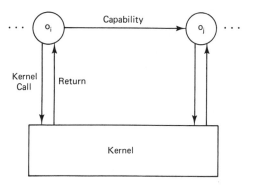

Figure 1-13 An object-oriented operating system.

different processes. It provides storage objects, which may be used to obtain space for programs and data in virtual memory. Finally, it permits programs and data to be maintained by the file system on secondary storage in the form of objects. (We will explain some of these concepts in more detail in relevant sections of this book.)

1.6 HISTORICAL PERSPECTIVE

This section briefly describes the historical evolution of computer hardware and software systems to provide the necessary context for studying present-day computer systems.

1.6.1 Early Systems

From about 1949, when the first stored-program digital computer actually started executing instructions, until 1956, the basic organization and mode of operation of computers remained relatively constant (with some farsighted but mostly unsuccessful exceptions). Their classical von Neumann architecture was predicated on strictly sequential instruction execution including input/output operations. When loading and running programs, users worked at the console directly on line to the machine, setting registers, stepping through instructions, examining storage locations, and generally interacting with their computation at the lowest machine level. Programs were written in absolute machine language (decimal or octal notation) and were processed by an absolute loader.

In these early years, programming aids were either nonexistent or minimal—simple assemblers and interpreters at the most sophisticated installations, with little use of library routines. As the importance of symbolic programming was recognized and assembly systems came into more widespread use, a standard operating procedure evolved: A loader reads in an assembler; the assembler assembles into absolute code symbolic decks of user source programs and library routines; the assembled code is written on magnetic tape or paper cards, and a loader is again used to read these into main memory; the absolute program is then executed. Each step required manual assistance from an operator and consumed a great deal of time, especially in comparison with the computer time to process the cards at that step.

The first generation of operating systems was motivated by the preceding inefficiencies, as well as by other considerations. These additional factors included the expense of on-line operation, the availability of other languages (the FORTRAN system being most prominent), the development of library programs and services especially related to input/output operations, and the awkwardness of translating into absolute code, which required that *all* program sections and subroutines needed for a given run be translated together initially and everytime a change was made in any program. The first batch systems automated the standard load/translate/load/execute sequence with a central control program to retrieve and load required system programs (an assembler, compiler, loader, or library subroutine) and to handle job-to-job transitions. Language translators were rewritten to produce relocatable rather than absolute code. Linking loaders were developed to allow source and relocatable object language decks to be mixed together; library programs could then also be stored in relocatable object form.

Services from a human operator were required for running the physical batch input and output equipment, for setup of nonstandard jobs, and for taking corrective action on system failure. The originator of a job was banished, at least in principle, from the machine and gradually was convinced that the "best" way of treating a computer complex was as a large input/output box. In these operating systems, protection was a most difficult and frustrating problem; it was relatively easy for the system to be destroyed by itself or by a user or for one user to read past his program into the next program. Resource allocation, for main storage and IO devices primarily, was the task of language processors and user programs rather than the operating system.

1.6.2 Second-generation Hardware and Software

The generations of computer hardware have been defined in terms of their component technology: vacuum tubes in the first generation, transistors in the second, integrated circuits in the third, and large to very large scale integration in the fourth. From the perspective of operating systems, these distinctions are less important than those that can be made in hardware and software architecture; the time periods are roughly the same.

From about 1959 to 1963, several significant hardware developments came into widespread use and stimulated advances in operating systems. Perhaps the most important hardware innovation was the IO channel, a primitive computer with its own instruction set, registers, and control, that controls the communication and data transmission between the main computer and IO devices. On receiving an IO request from a CPU, the channel executes and controls the operation, asynchronously and in parallel with continued CPU execution; overlapping of IO and CPU operations is then possible. Main storage is shared by the CPU and channel and contains programs and data for both. Initially, the CPU could interrogate the status of the channel, but it soon became clear that one could operate more efficiently if the channel could also interrupt CPU processing to deliver a message, most frequently the completion of an IO operation.

Complicated input/output programming systems were written to take advantage of the potential efficiencies of this new architecture. These included software buffering facilities to permit automatic reading ahead of programs and queuing output for delayed writing of output and interrupt-handling routines to respond to IO interrupts and return control to interrupted programs.

Interrupts were expanded to signal exceptional internal conditions, such as an arithmetic overflow, and instructions were added for the selective enabling and disabling of the interrupt mechanisms. Internal clocks that could be programmed to interrupt the CPU after a specified time interval became available; these allowed a supervisory routine to control the amount of CPU time allocated for each user, permitting the automatic detection of some erroneous or excessively long programs.

It was natural for users, on the one hand, to delegate interrupt-handling and IO services to a central system, and for installation managers, on the other hand, to begin to insist that users employ these services. Sophisticated programmers would still often write their own packages. System protection remained a serious and unsolved problem; system crashes were caused by both experienced and beginning programmers in an almost too easy fashion.

During this period, libraries were expanded considerably to include utility routines, such as sorts or card-to-tape converters, and more language processors; direct-access files (usually disks) began to replace magnetic tape for storing the system and libraries. With the added and more complex tasks of the operating system—the "machine" viewed by a typical user becoming further removed from the actual hardware—it was necessary to specify in a more systematic way the characteristics and requirements of a job; job-control languages were added for this purpose.

We can summarize this generation as a settling-in period for sequential batch processing, with many exploratory efforts to use data channels, interrupts, and auxiliary storage efficiently. However, one-job-at-a-time processing still resulted in low channel activity for heavy compute jobs and low CPU activity for heavy IO jobs, even if maximum overlap of CPU and channel operations was obtained.

1.6.3 Systems of the Third Generation

From about 1962 to 1969, multiprogramming, permitting more than one active program in memory at the same time, came into almost universal use in large operating systems. Time sharing, which allows simultaneous access to the system by several interactive users, was also developed as an alternative to batch processing. Large fast-access disk units provided on-line storage for systems and user library programs, as well as for user jobs waiting to be processed. Hardware for storage and instruction protection was incorporated on many computers, main memory systems with relocation hardware that permitted the implementation of large virtual memories appeared on some large machines, and multiprocessor configurations became more common.

The problems of resource allocation and protection became more critical and difficult in a multiprogramming environment, where many processes were simultaneously requesting both shared and exclusive use of resources of the system, often had to transmit signals to one another, and were potentially malicious or erratic. It was during this period that the subject of operating systems emerged as a central part of software engineering and computer science. For the first time, systematic techniques for designing, analyzing, and simulating operating systems became available to at least a limited extent.

1.6.4 The Fourth Generation and Beyond

During the 1970s and early 1980s, technology continued to develop at a rapid pace. Large-scale integration (LSI) and very large scale integration (VLSI) have made it possible to manufacture large quantities of powerful hardware components at very low cost. Whereas general-purpose multiprogrammed and time-shared computer installations were typical representatives of systems of the third generation, the availability of inexpensive hardware has caused three new major trends in modern systems: the development of *personal* computers, *parallel* systems, and computer *networks*. The first of these trends is a direct result of declining hardware cost; it is now possible to manufacture microcomputers for personal computing that are as powerful as many of the earlier mini- or even mainframe computers but at a fraction of their cost. Due to their relatively simple hardware and single-user mode of operation, no major innovations in operating system technology have been necessary; rather, most of the principles governing operating systems for earlier large computers may be applied in the case of microcomputers.

Many application areas exceed the capabilities of any single-processor system. When the technological limits of building high-speed logic circuits are reached, the only way to increase performance is to use multiple processing units operating in parallel. The development of such systems has been the subject of intensive research in recent years and has produced three fundamental approaches to organizing multiple processing units into one system: *pipelining*, *array processing*, and *general multiprocessing*.

A pipelining computer achieves parallelism by overlapping different stages of instruction execution. This is possible by providing separate hardware units for each stage operating in parallel. Pipelining usually leads to significant improvements in performance. An array processor uses multiple processing units to achieve spatial parallelism. There is a single sequential stream of instructions; however, each is broadcast to many processing elements during the same cycle. Thus the same instruction operates on many different operands at the same time. Such architectures are referred to as SIMD (single-instruction/multiple-data) architectures.

The primary objective of pipelined and array processors is increased performance through parallel processing. Consequently, the operating systems for such computers must be designed to efficiently exploit the available hardware parallelism. This applies particularly to the scheduling of tasks, servicing of interrupts, and the organization of memory and IO buffers necessary to supply data to processors at the required speed.

The third direction in parallel computer architecture attempts to construct systems consisting of independent processing elements, each executing its own sequence of instructions with a separate set of data elements. Such systems are called *multiprocessors* and their principle of operation is termed MIMD (multiple-instruction/multiple-data). If all processors share the same main memory, the architecture is frequently referred to as a *tightly coupled network*. Compared to pipelined and array computers, multiprocessors are the most general in their ability to support different types of applications. A number of systems have already been built for both general-purpose computing and specific applications. However, only systems with a relatively small number of processors (rarely exceeding a few dozen) have been successful commercially.

The main limitation to massively parallel systems is their programmability; it is, in general, very difficult to divide computation among large numbers of processors and to synchronize their progress. If this is to be performed at the operating system level, the overhead is too great to efficiently exploit hundreds or even thousands of processors. To solve this problem, new computational models that abandon the basic concept of the stored-program von Neumann computer and that can exploit inherent parallelism more directly have been proposed. The most noteworthy are data-driven, demand-driven, and logic-based models (Treleaven, Brownbridge, and Hopkins, 1982; van Emden and Kowalski, 1976). Presently, only a few experimental machines have actually been built and much research remains to be done before commercial production can begin.

The third major trend in modern systems is the development of *loosely coupled* computer networks, where each node is an autonomous computer connected to other nodes by communication links. Networks may be local (local area networks, or LANs), connecting just a few computer systems in the same room or building, or they may be geographically distributed, where nodes located in different cities or even on different continents are connected by telephone or satellite links. Since nodes typically vary in size and type, different operating systems may be used in each node. Each, however, must be extended to match the increased hardware complexity resulting from the physical interconnections and to provide additional services, such as a general mailing system or remote log-in and file-transfer facilities. In more sophisticated networks, an even distribution of the current workload may also be attempted. In this case, each node must be able to delegate computation to other nodes that may currently be less busy or be better equipped for the given task. Each node must also provide the necessary protection, error handling, and accounting mechanisms.

1.7 SUMMARY

In this chapter we have discussed the features of existing hardware and contrasted these with the needs and desires of the users. The following major discrepancies responsible for the large hardware/user gap have been identified: different speeds of hardware components (i.e., CPU, main memory, and IO devices); different types of interfaces for various components; the absence of user-oriented high-level primitives at the hardware level; and limitations in memory size. We have also introduced some of the characteristics, functions, and organization principles of operating systems from several points of view. In summary, operating systems have two main roles: (1) they provide services for users to simplify their tasks, and (2) they manage systems resources to assure efficient operation. Having gained this initial insight into the general problem domain, we are now ready to study the various functions of operating systems in more detail.

2

Concurrent Programming Methods

2.1 THE CONCEPT OF A PROCESS

When developing a complex system, structuring is of utmost importance. The system must be decomposed into modules that perform well-defined functions and interact with one another through well-defined interfaces. In operating systems, an additional challenge is the high degree of nondeterminism: many functions or services are invoked in response to certain events, which may occur at unpredictable times and with a varying degree of frequency. We can order these events informally according to their typical frequency of occurrence. At the highest level are requests from communication and storage devices needing attention from the CPU. The next level constitutes requests for resources such as physical devices, blocks of memory, or software components. Finally, commands entered by interactive users or the operator through terminals and possible hardware or software errors constitute yet another level. All these events typically arrive at unpredictable times and may require that different modules or subsystems of the operating system be invoked.

To cope with the highly nondeterministic nature of this environment in some elegant way, the concept of a *sequential process* is introduced. Informally, a sequential process (sometimes called *task*) is the activity resulting from the execution of a program with its data by a sequential processor (CPU). Conceptually, each process has its own processor and program stored in physical memory. In reality, two different processes

36

might be sharing the same program or the same processor. The operating system is then viewed as a collection of processes, all running concurrently. They operate almost independently of one another, *cooperate* by sending messages and synchronization signals to each other, and *compete* for resources. Each process is dedicated to a specific function, and its interactions with other processes are limited to only a few well-defined interfaces.

Most existing computers are equipped with only one CPU, which must be shared among all processes in order to advance the state of their respective computations. To permit a system to be viewed as a collection of concurrent processes, the details of CPU sharing must be invisible at the process level. This is accomplished by the lowest level of the operating system, usually referred to as the *kernel*, whose task is to "virtualize" the CPU, that is, to create the illusion of a separate CPU for each running process. The kernel may also provide a separate storage, a virtual memory, for each process. Under these assumptions, each process may be viewed in isolation; it interacts with other processes only through a limited number of primitives also provided by the kernel.

In systems equipped with only one processor, the achieved concurrency among processes (both user and system processes) is only *logical* since only one process may be executing at any given time. Thus the main benefit of introducing the concept of a process is the improved overall structure of the system. By examining the logic of processes and ignoring the number of physical processors and the details of physical memory allocation, it is possible to develop hardware-independent solutions to a number of systems and application problems. The solutions ensure that systems of processes cooperate correctly, regardless of whether or not they share physical resources. The process concept has several other implications in operating systems. It has permitted the isolation and specification of many primitive operating systems tasks, has simplified the study of the organization and dynamics of an operating system, and has led to the development of useful design methodologies.

In the case of multiprocessors equipped with more than one processing element dedicated to general computation or in systems equipped with IO channels, *physical* concurrency is possible. The process notion is invaluable here for dealing with the additional problems of distributing computation to the available processors; typically, each process is viewed as an independent entity that may be scheduled for execution on a processor.

2.2 CONSTRUCTS FOR PROCESS CREATION

Traditionally, only the operating system itself was permitted (and able) to create new processes. This view has changed in modern computer systems, which permit users to create their own subsystems consisting of many concurrent processes. Depending on the sophistication of the system, process creation may be done either *statically* or *dynamically*. In the first case, each process p may contain the declaration of a fixed set of subprocesses, all of which will be activated when process p begins execution. More flexibility is attained when processes may be spawned (and terminated) dynamically during execution.

2.2.1 Process Flow Graphs

Programming constructs for creating and terminating processes should be able to express a variety of precedence relations among processes. Figure 2-1 illustrates the kinds of precedence constraints that are possible among processes, if we assume that a system has a common start and finish point. The execution of a process p_i is represented by a directed edge of a graph. Each edge in the figure denotes an execution-time trace of a set of processes, and the graph connectivity describes the start and finish precedence

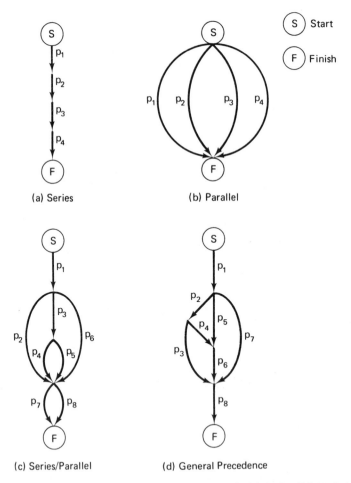

Figure 2-1 Precedence relations among processes: (a) Serial (b) Parallel (c) Serial/Parallel (d) General Precedence.

constraints on the processes. For convenience, these graphs will be called *process flow graphs*. (Abstractly, a process flow graph is a directed acyclic graph; any such graph may be interpreted as a process flow graph.)

All components in the serial/parallel example are properly nested. Let $S(a, b)$ denote the serial connection of process a followed by process b and let $P(a, b)$ denote the parallel connection of processes a and b. Then a process flow graph is *properly nested* if it can be described by the functions S and P, and only function composition.[†]

Example

The first three graphs in Figure 2-1 can be described as

$$S(p_1, S(p_2, S(p_3, p_4)))$$

$$P(p_1, P(p_2, P(p_3, p_4)))$$

and

$$S\left(p_1, S\left(P\left(p_2, P\left(S(p_3, P(p_4, p_5)), p_6\right)\right), P(p_7, p_8)\right)\right)$$

respectively.

The general precedence graph (d) in the figure is *not* properly nested. We prove this by first observing that any description by function composition must include at the most interior level an expression either of the form $S(p_i, p_j)$ or $P(p_i, p_j)$ for p_i, p_j in $\{p_k | k = 1, \ldots, 8\}$. $P(p_i, p_j)$ cannot appear, since Figure 2-1d does not contain any subgraph of this form. All serially connected p_i and p_j have at least one other process p_k that starts or finishes at the node, say n_{ij}, between p_i and p_j; however, if $S(p_i, p_j)$ appears in the expression, the connection of p_k to p_i or p_j through node n_{ij} could not be described. Therefore, $S(p_i, p_j)$ cannot be used either, and a properly nested description is not possible.

The following three examples of parallelism give rise to properly nested process flow graphs:

1. *Evaluation of arithmetic expressions.* If side effects or numerical accuracy do not dictate a fixed sequential evaluation, the subexpressions of arithmetic expressions can be evaluated in parallel; the amount of parallelism that can occur is limited by the depth of the expression tree. Figure 2-2 shows an example of an arithmetic expression and the corresponding expression tree. (Edges are labeled by the code executed by the corresponding process.) Many problems in which the primary data structure is a tree can be logically described in terms of parallel computations.

2. *Sorting.* During the ith pass in a standard two-way merge sort, pairs of sorted lists of length 2^{i-1} are merged into lists of length 2^i; each merge can be performed in parallel within a pass (see Figure 2-3 on page 41).

[†]This property is very similar to the "proper nesting" of block structure in programming languages and of parentheses within expressions.

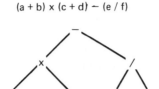

$$(a + b) \times (c + d) - (e / f)$$

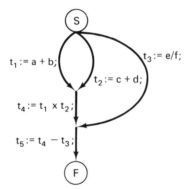

Expression Tree

Process Flow Graph   **Figure 2-2**   Process flow graph.

3. *Matrix multiplication.* On performing the matrix multiplication $A = B \times C$, all elements of A can, potentially, be computed simultaneously.

2.2.2 cobegin/coend

These primitives, originally called **parbegin** and **parend** (Dijkstra, 1968), specify explicitly a sequence of program segments that may be executed concurrently. They have the form

$$\textbf{cobegin } C_1 \mid C_2 \mid \dots \mid C_n \textbf{ coend}$$

where each C_i is an autonomous segment of code. It results in the creation of a separate process for each C_i, executing independently of all other processes within the **cobegin/coend** construct.

The **cobegin/coend** primitives are a simple extension of the S and P functions defined in Section 2.2.1 for the purposes of describing properly nested process flow graphs. The following reasoning shows the correspondence. If we view each code seg-

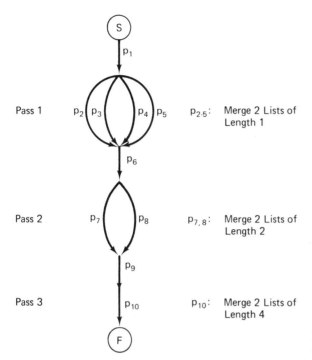

Pass 1 p_2 p_3 p_4 p_5 $p_{2\text{-}5}$:   Merge 2 Lists of Length 1

Pass 2 p_7 p_8 $p_{7,8}$:   Merge 2 Lists of Length 2

Pass 3 p_{10} p_{10}:   Merge 2 Lists of Length 4

Figure 2-3   Merge-sort of a list of eight elements.

ment C_i as a separate process, then the preceding **cobegin/coend** construct corresponds to the following set of nested functions:

$$P\left(C_1, P\left(C_2, \ldots P(\ldots, C_n) \ldots\right)\right)$$

Each code segment C_i can be decomposed into a sequence of processes $p_{i_1}, p_{i_2}, \ldots,$ p_{i_m}, where each p_{i_j} corresponds to some program segment in C_i. Thus each C_i in the preceding expression may be expressed using the function S as follows:

$$S\left(p_{i_1}, S\left(p_{i_2}, \ldots S(\ldots, p_{i_m}) \ldots\right)\right)$$

In an analogous way, any expression composed of the functions P and S may be transformed into an equivalent expression using the **cobegin/coend** constructs. This implies that the two notations are equivalent in their expressive power and both are limited to only properly nested flow graphs. General process flow graphs, such as that of Figure 2-1d, may sometimes be transformed into properly nested graphs by forcing one or more of the processes to wait. For example, by delaying the start of process p_6 (in Figure 2-1d) until the completion of the two processes p_3 and p_7, the graph becomes properly nested and thus may be expressed using the **cobegin/coend** constructs. Unfortunately, such transformations are not possible if the involved processes need to be active at the same time. For example, if p_3 and p_7 need to communicate with p_6, p_6 cannot be delayed.

Example

The following code performs the parallel evaluation of the arithmetic expression of Figure 2-2:

```
cobegin
    cobegin t1 := a + b | t2 := c + d coend;
    t4 := t1 * t2;
    |
    t3 := e/f;
coend;
t5 := t4 - t3;
```

2.2.3 The fork, join, and quit Primitives

The primitives **fork**, **join**, and **quit** (Conway, 1963; Dennis and Van Horn, 1966) provide a more general means for describing parallel activity in a program than the **cobegin/coend** constructs.

Execution by a process p of the instruction "**fork** x" causes a new process q to start executing at the instruction labeled x; p and q then execute simultaneously. If a process p executes the instruction "**quit**," p terminates. The instruction "**join** t, y" has the following effect:

```
- - - - - -
t := t - 1;
if t = 0 then go to y;
- - - - - -
```

The area enclosed by the dotted lines is considered an *indivisible* operation.

A program segment for evaluating the expression of Figure 2-2 is

```
        n := 2;
        fork p3;
        m := 2;
        fork p2;
        t1 := a + b; join m, p4; quit;
p2 :    t2 := c + d; join m, p4; quit;
p4 :    t4 := t1 × t2; join n, p5; quit;
p3 :    t3 := e/f; join n, p5; quit;
p5 :    t5 := t4 - t3;
```

This is certainly less transparent than the program of Section 2.2.2. However, iterations can be described more clearly, as illustrated by the following example from image processing.

We are given an array $A[0..n + 1, 0..n + 1]$ consisting of 0's and 1's representing a digitized picture. It is desired to *smooth* the picture by replacing each interior point $A[i, j]$ by 1 if the majority of $A[i, j]$'s immediate eight neighbors are 1, and by 0 otherwise. This process is called *local averaging* and is logically a parallel computation. We assume that the smoothed picture is stored in a new array, B.

```
type picture = array[0 .. n + 1, 0 .. n + 1] of integer;
procedure Local_average(A: picture, n: integer, var B: picture);
var t, i, j: integer; i, j: private;
begin
    t := n ↑ 2;
    for i := 1 to n do
    for j := 1 to n do
        fork e;
    quit;
e : if A[i − 1, j − 1] + A[i − 1, j] + A[i − 1, j + 1]
        + A[i, j − 1] + A[i, j] + A[i, j + 1] + A[i + 1, j − 1]
        + A[i + 1, j] + A[i + 1, j + 1] ≥ 5
    then B[i, j] := 1 else B[i, j] := 0;
    join t, r;
    quit;
r : end {Local_average}
```

To create private copies of variables within parallel processes, variables may be declared as "private" to a process by the declaration

$$x_1, x_2, \ldots, x_n : \textbf{private}$$

The variables x_i then only exist for the process "executing" the private declarations; in addition, any new process created by the latter (using a **fork**) will receive its own copy of the private variables of the parent process.

The statements **fork**, **join**, and **quit** suffice to describe any process flow graph. The following is a program for the graph of Figure 2-1d, where S_i denotes the program statements for process p_i:

```
      t6 := 2; t8 := 3;
      S1; fork p2; fork p5; fork p7; quit;
p2 :  S2; fork p3; fork p4; quit;
p5 :  S5; join t6, p6; quit;
p7 :  S7; join t8, p8; quit;
p3 :  S3; join t8, p8; quit;
p4 :  S4; join t6, p6; quit;
p6 :  S6; join t8, p8; quit;
p8 :  S8; quit;
```

The main disadvantage of these primitives is that they may be used indiscriminately anywhere within a program. When invoked inside of loops or other control statements, the program structure may become rather obscure. Nevertheless, various forms and derivatives of the **fork**, **join**, and **quit** primitives are implemented in many modern operating systems.

Example

1. The UNIX operating system employs a variant of the **fork** primitive that simply replicates the process executing the **fork**. It has the form

$$procid = \textbf{fork} \; (\;)$$

Execution of this statement causes the current process, called *parent*, to be replicated. The only distinction between the parent and the newly created process, called *child*, is the variable *procid*; in the parent it has the process number of the child as its value, whereas in the child its value is zero. This permits each of the two processes to determine its identity and to proceed accordingly. Typically, the next statement following **fork** is of the form

> **if** *procid* = 0
> **then** do child processing
> **else** do parent processing

One of the processes, say the child, may "overlay" itself by performing the instruction **exec** as part of the "do child processing" clause. This instruction specifies a new program as one of its parameters, which then continues execution as the child process.

2. In the previous example, the **fork** statement was part of the *command* language of UNIX. Frequently, such primitives are incorporated directly in a programming language. One example of such a language is Mesa (Lampson and Redell, 1980), which permits *any* procedure $q(. . .)$ to be invoked as a separate process. The two statements used to spawn and coordinate concurrent processes have the following form:

> $p \leftarrow$ **fork** $q(. . .)$;
> $var\_list \leftarrow$ **join** p;

The **fork** statement creates a new process that begins executing the procedure q concurrently with the parent process. In Mesa, each process is treated as an *object* and thus it may be assigned to a variable. In the preceding statement, the variable p represents the child process. Note that, unlike the *procid* variable in UNIX, the variable p contains not just a process identifier but the process object itself. This permits processes to be treated as any other variable; for example, a process may be passed to another procedure as a parameter.

To synchronize the termination of a child process with the parent's computation, the **join** primitive is used. It forces the parent process to wait for the termination of the child process p. Each procedure in Mesa must explicitly specify a list of values to be returned as the result of the procedure's computation. When a child process terminates, the results of the corresponding procedure may be transmitted to the parent process by assigning them to variables listed as part of the **join** statement. In the preceding example, the results returned from the procedure q executed by the child process p are assigned to the variables listed in var_list upon p's termination. At that point, the parent process would continue its execution with the next instruction following the **join**.

2.2.4 Explicit Process Declarations

Some languages have combined the virtues of both **fork/join/quit** and **cobegin/coend** by providing mechanisms that explicitly designate segments of code to be separate processes but permit their invocation to be controlled during execution. The following discussion presents a simplified version of the mechanisms provided by the language ADA (U.S. Department of Defense, 1981). (The syntax is slightly modified to conform to the notation used throughout this section.)

Processes, called tasks in ADA, are declared as follows:

```
process p
    declarations
begin
    . . .
end
```

The key word **process** designates the segment of code between **begin** and **end** as a separate unit of execution named p. Preceding the **begin/end** block is a list of declarations, containing local variables, functions, procedures, and possibly other process definitions. As soon as the process p is activated, all processes defined within the declaration portion of that process are activated as well. This mechanism represents a *static* creation of processes.

To provide more flexibility, processes may be declared *dynamically* by replacing the key word **process** by the phrase **process type**. This can be interpreted as defining a process *template*, instances of which may be created dynamically during execution by using a special command **new**. The following program skeleton illustrates the distinction between static and dynamic process creation:

```
process p
    process p₁
        declarations for p₁
    begin
        . . .
    end
    process type p₂
        declarations for p₂
    begin
        . . .
    end
    other declarations for p
begin
    . . .
    q := new p₂
    . . .
end
```

The process p_1 is declared statically within the declaration part of p and hence will be activated as soon as the process p begins execution. The process p_2, on the other hand, is declared as a template (a process type), and thus an instance of p_2 will be created only as a result of the explicit call **new** p_2, performed during the execution of the body of process p. The new instance of p_2 will be named q.

The preceding mechanisms permit any number of processes to be declared and spawned at arbitrary times and in arbitrary order during execution. However, they do not permit processes to interact with one another in any way. For example, a process cannot delay itself to await the termination of some other process. When compared with the **fork/join/quit** primitives, the term **new** acts as a **fork** and the **end** statement is similar to a **quit**; however, there is no construct corresponding to the primitive **join**. This implies that additional mechanisms must be provided if more controlled interactions, such as those depicted in Figure 2-1c and d, are to be enforced.

2.3 PROCESS INTERACTIONS

2.3.1 The Critical Section Problem

When several processes may asynchronously change the contents of a common data area, it is necessary to protect the data from simultaneous access and change by two or more processes. The updated area may not, in general, contain the intended changes if this protection is not provided. The common data shared by several processes most often describes a *resource*; updating the data corresponds to allocating or freeing elements of the resource. In general, the resource could be some hardware elements, such as IO devices or storage, or it could be software, such as files.

Consider two processes p_1 and p_2, both asynchronously incrementing a common variable x representing the number of units of a resource:

```
cobegin
p₁ :   . . .
           x := x + 1;
       . . .
       |
p₂ :   . . .
           x := x + 1;
       . . .
coend
```

Each of the two high-level instructions $x := x + 1$ is normally translated into several machine-level instructions. Let us assume that these instructions are (1) load the value of x into some internal register, (2) increment that register, and (3) store the new value into the variable x. Let C_1 and C_2 be central processors with internal registers R_1 and R_2, respectively, and sharing main storage. If p_1 were executing on C_1 and p_2 on C_2, then either of the two execution sequences shown next could occur over time. (In the diagram, when two statements are shown on the same line, they are assumed to execute simultaneously on their respective processors; i.e., the time line in each sequence runs from top to bottom.)

Sequence 1:

p_1 :	$R1 := x;$	p_2 :	...
	$R1 := R1 + 1;$		...
	$x := R1;$		...
	...		$R2 := x;$
	...		$R2 := R2 + 1;$
	...		$x := R2;$

Sequence 2:

p_1 :	$R1 := x;$	p_2 :	...
	$R1 := R1 + 1;$		$R2 := x;$
	$x := R1;$		$R2 := R2 + 1;$
	...		$x := R2;$

Let x contain the value v at the time execution begins. At the time of completion, x would contain $v + 2$, the correct value, if the execution followed sequence 1, but would contain $v + 1$ if it followed sequence 2. Both values of v could also be realized if p_1 and p_2 were time sharing a single processor with control switching between the processes by means of interrupts. If p_1 and p_2 were invoked as part of an airline reservation system and x represented the number of available seats on a particular flight, customers and management would be very unhappy if x contained $v + 1$ instead of $v + 2$. Similarly, if x contained the number of blocks of memory allocated to different processes, the possibility of sequence 2 would be intolerable. Clearly, *each* increment of x should count. The solution is to allow only one process at a time into the *critical section* (CS) "$x := x + 1;$". In general, the critical section could consist of any number of statements.

The problem and its environment can now be stated more precisely. We are given several sequential processes, which can communicate with each other through a common data store. The programs executed as part of the processes each contain a critical section in which access to the common data is made; these processes are considered to be cyclic. The problem is to implement the processes so that, at any moment, only *one* of them is in its critical section; once a process, say p, enters its CS, no other process may do the same until p has left its CS. The following assumptions are made about the system:

1. Writing into and reading from the common data store are each indivisible operations; simultaneous reference (loads or stores) to the same location by more than one processor will result in sequential references in an unknown order.
2. Critical sections may not have priorities associated with them.

3. The relative speeds of the processes are unknown.

4. A program may halt outside of its CS.

The system of cyclic processes for the CS problem is assumed to have the following program forms:

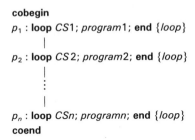

where *CSi* is the CS for process i, the statement on each line is the code for process p_i, and $n \geq 2$.

Software Solution (Dijkstra, 1968). The problem will be initially restricted to two processes as illustrated in Figure 2-4. Our primary aim is to prevent p_1 and p_2 from being in their respective CSs together (*mutual exclusion*). At the same time, three possible types of *blocking* must be avoided:

1. A process operating well outside its CS (i.e., not attempting to enter its CS) cannot be preventing another process from entering its CS.

2. It must not be possible for one of the processes to repeatedly enter its CS while the other process never gets its chance (it "starves").

3. Two processes about to enter their CSs cannot, by entering infinite waiting loops

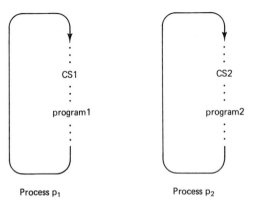

Figure 2-4 Two processes with critical sections.

or by an ''after you''–''after you'' type of intercommunication, postpone indefinitely the decision on which one actually enters.

We will now try to develop solutions to the problem and illustrate some of the pitfalls that exist. The problem is easily solved if we insist that p_1 and p_2 enter their CSs alternately; one common variable (*turn*) can keep track of whose turn it is:

```
var turn: integer
turn := 2;
cobegin
p1 :    loop
             while turn = 2 do ; {wait loop}
             CS1; turn := 2; program1
        end {loop}
        |
p2 :    loop
             while turn = 1 do ; {wait loop}
             CS2; turn := 1; program2
        end {loop}
coend
```

Unfortunately, if p_1 were run on a much faster processor than p_2, or if *program1* were much longer than *program2*, or if p_1 halted in *program1*, this solution would hardly be satisfactory. One process well outside its CS can prevent the other from entering its CS, thus violating the previous requirement 1.

To avoid this possible blocking, two common variables, $c1$ and $c2$, may be used as flags to indicate whether a process is inside or outside of its CS. A process p_i wishing to enter its CS indicates its intent by setting the flag ci to *false*. It then waits for the other flag to become *true* and enters the CS. Upon termination of the CS, it resets its flag to *true*, thus permitting the other process to continue.

```
var c1, c2: boolean
c1 := c2 := true;
cobegin
p1 :    loop
             c1 := false;
             while ¬c2 do ; {wait loop}
             CS1; c1 := true; program1
        end {loop}
        |
p2 : . . . (analogous to p1)
coend
```

Mutual execution is avoided with this solution, but mutual blocking of the third type listed previously is now possible. Both $c1$ and $c2$ may be set to *false* at the same time and the processes would loop forever in their **while** statements. The obvious way to rectify this is to reset c_1 and c_2 to *true* after testing whether they are *false*:

```
var c1, c2: boolean
c1 := c2 := true;
cobegin
p₁ :   loop
            c1 := false;
            if ¬c2 then c1 := true;
                else begin
                        CS1; c1 := true; program1
                    end
        end {loop}
        |
p₂ : . . .
coend
```

Unfortunately, this solution may lead to both the second and third type of blocking. When the execution timing is such that one process, say p_2, always tests the c_1 flag just after it was set to *false* by p_1 and, as a result, sets c_2 to *true* before it is tested by p_1, p_1 will always succeed in entering its CS, while p_2 is forced to wait.

The third type of blocking occurs when both processes begin execution at the same time and proceed at exactly the same speed. They keep setting and testing their mutual flags indefinitely, without ever entering their CSs. Note, however, that such indefinite postponement is much less likely to occur here than with the previous solution, since both processes must maintain the same speed indefinitely; if one becomes slower or faster, the mutual blocking is resolved. With the previous solution, both processes remained in their respective **while** loops forever, regardless of speed.

The three attempts at solving the CS problem illustrate some of the subtleties underlying process synchronization. The first complete solution to the critical section problem was proposed by the mathematician T. Dekker. While his solution prevents both mutual execution and mutual blocking, it is quite complex to understand and to verify (see Exercise 2-8). Peterson (1981) proposed a much simpler and elegant algorithm, which we now present as the final complete software solution to the critical section problem.

```
var c1, c2: boolean; turn: integer
c1 := c2 := true;
cobegin
p₁ :   loop
            c1 := false;
            turn := 1;
            while ¬c2 ∧ turn = 1 do ; {wait loop}
            CS1; c1 := true; program1
        end {loop}
        |
```

```
p₂:   loop
          c2 := false;
          turn := 2;
          while ¬c1 ∧ turn = 2 do ; {wait loop}
          CS2; c2 := true; program2
      end {loop}
   coend
```

Consider first the problem of mutual blocking. If it were possible, at least one of the processes, say p_1, would have to somehow circle through its **while** loop forever. This is not possible for the following reason. While p_1 is in its loop, the second process p_2 may be doing one of three general things: (1) not trying to enter its CS, (2) waiting in its own **while** loop, or (3) repeatedly executing its own complete loop. In the first case, p_1 detects that $c2$ is *true* and proceeds into its CS. The second case is impossible because *turn* is either 1 or 2, which permits one of the processes to proceed. Similarly, the third case is impossible since p_2 will set *turn* to 2 and, consequently, not pass through its **while** statement test. It will not be able to proceed until p_1 has executed its CS.

Mutual execution is also prevented by the preceding solution. To show that this is the case, assume that p_1 has just passed its test and is about to enter its CS. At this time, $c1$ must be *false*. Let us examine if there is any way for p_2 to enter $CS2$, thus violating the mutual execution requirement. There are two cases to consider:

1. p_1 has passed its test because $c2$ was *true*. This implies that p_2 is currently not trying to enter its CS; that is, p_2 is outside the segment of code delimited by the instructions $c2 := false$ and $c2 := true$. If it now tries to enter it must first set *turn* to 2. Since $c1$ is *false*, it will fail its test and will have to wait until p_1 has left its critical section.

2. p_1 has passed its test because *turn* was equal to 2. This implies that, regardless of where p_2 is at this time, it will find $c1 = false$ and $turn = 2$ when it reaches its test and will not be permitted to proceed.

2.3.2 Cooperating Processes

The critical section problem is a situation in which processes *compete* for a resource, which may not be accessed by more than one such process at any given time. Note that each process could exist without the other; their interaction is needed only to resolve simultaneous access to the resource. A different situation arises when two or more processes *cooperate* in solving a common goal. In this case, each of them is aware of, and usually depends on, the existence of the other. Similar to concurrent processes of the critical section type, cooperating processes have a need to exchange information with one another. In the simplest case, only synchronization signals are necessary.

Processes engaged in what is typically characterized as a *producer/consumer* situation fall into this category. Figure 2-5 describes this situation for one consumer and one producer process that communicate by a shared buffer storage. The producer's task

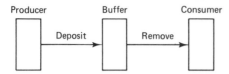

Figure 2-5 A producer and a consumer communicating through a buffer.

is to generate (produce) new blocks of data, which it deposits in the buffer. These are removed (consumed) from the buffer storage by the consumer process. This is an abstraction of the situation where, for example, a main process produces an output record and then transfers it to the next available buffer while, asynchronously, an output process removes a record from buffer storage and then prints it. (Alternatively, the producer may be interpreted as an input process, while the consumer is a main process using the input data.) Since both processes run concurrently at possibly varying speeds, it must be guaranteed that the producer does not overwrite any data in the buffer storage before the consumer can remove it. Similarly, the consumer must be able to wait for the producer when the latter falls behind and does not fill the buffer storage on time. Hence the two processes must be able to exchange information about the current state of the storage, in this case the number of data blocks present.

In many situations it is desirable that processes exchange more information with one another than just synchronization signals. For example, the system could provide some service routine, implemented as a separate process. Other processes could make use of that service by sending to it the necessary input data in the form of messages. Upon performing the desired computations with the received data, the service could return the results to the calling process in the form of a reply message. Such processes are usually referred to as *communicating* processes. They demonstrate the need for a general interprocess communication facility to allow processes to establish logical channels with one another through which arbitrary messages could be exchanged.

2.4 SEMAPHORE PRIMITIVES

2.4.1 The *P* and *V* Operations

There are two unappealing features of the software solutions to the critical section problem:

1. The solutions are mystifying and unclear; a simple conceptual requirement, mutual exclusion in CSs, results in complex and awkward additions to programs.
2. During the time when one process is in its CS, another process may be continually looping, accessing and testing common variables. To do this, the waiting process must ''steal'' memory cycles from the active process; if the processes are sharing a single processor, then the waiting process is consuming valuable CPU time without really accomplishing anything. The result is a general slowing down of the system by processes that are not doing any useful work.

Dijkstra (1965) introduced two new primitive operations that considerably simplified the communication and synchronization of processes and, depending on their implementation, may also solve the second problem just pointed out. In their abstract form, these primitives, designated P and V, operate on nonnegative integer variables called *semaphores*. Let s be such a semaphore variable. The operations are defined as follows:

1. $V(s)$: Increment s by 1 in a single *indivisible* action; the fetch, increment, and store cannot be interrupted, and s cannot be accessed by another process during the operation.

2. $P(s)$: Decrement s by 1, if possible. If $s = 0$, then it is not possible to decrement s and still remain in the domain of nonnegative integers; the process invoking the P operation then *waits* until it is possible. The successful testing and decrementing of s are also an indivisible operation. (We defer until Section 2.4.4 any discussion of how the waiting is accomplished when $s = 0$.)

If several processes simultaneously call for P or V operations on the same semaphore, these operations occur sequentially in an arbitrary order; similarly, if more than one process is waiting on a P operation and the affected semaphore becomes positive (due to the execution of a V), the particular waiting process that is selected to complete the operation is arbitrary and unknown.

It is the semaphore variables that are used to synchronize processes. The P primitive includes a potential wait of the calling process, whereas the V primitive may possibly activate some waiting process. The indivisibility of P and V assures the integrity of the values of the semaphores.

2.4.2 Mutual Exclusion Using Semaphore Operations

Semaphore operations allow a simple and straightforward solution to the critical section problem. Let *mutex* be a semaphore variable used to protect the CSs. A program solution for n processes operating in parallel is

```
var mutex: semaphore
mutex := 1;
cobegin
p₁ :   loop ... end {loop}
          |
          ⋮

pᵢ :   loop
              P(mutex); CSi; V(mutex); programi
          end {loop}
          |
          ⋮

pₙ :   loop ... end {loop}
coend;
```

The value of *mutex* is 0 when any process is in its CS; otherwise, *mutex* = 1. The semaphore has the function of a simple lock. Mutual exclusion is guaranteed, since only one process can decrement *mutex* to zero with the *P* operation; all other processes attempting to enter their CSs while *mutex* is zero are forced to wait by *P*(*mutex*). Mutual blocking is not possible, because simultaneous attempts to enter CSs when *mutex* = 1 must, by our definition, translate into *sequential P* operations. When a semaphore can take only the values 0 or 1, it will be called a *binary* semaphore.

2.4.3 Semaphores in Producer/Consumer Situations

Each process in a computer system can be characterized by the number and type of resources it *consumes* (uses) and *produces* (releases). These could be "hard" resources, such as main storage, tape drives, or processors, or "soft" resources, such as full buffers, critical sections, messages, or files. Semaphores can be used to maintain resource counts and to synchronize processes, as well as to lock out critical sections. For example, a process can block itself by a *P* operation on a semaphore *s* and can be awakened by another process executing *V* on *s*:

```
var s: semaphore
s := 0;
cobegin
p₁ :   begin
           ⋮
               P(s);      {Wait for signal from p₂}
           ⋮
       end
       |
p₂ :   begin
           ⋮
               V(s);      {Send wakeup signal to p₁}
           ⋮
       end
coend
```

p_1 can also be viewed as consuming the resource designated *s* through the instruction $P(s)$, while p_2 produces units of *s* through $V(s)$. In this section, we illustrate the use of semaphores in typical resource producer/consumer applications.

Example: The Bounded Buffer Problem (Dijkstra, 1968)

Consider again the producer/consumer situation described in Section 2.3.2. A producer process produces information and then adds it to buffer storage; in parallel with this, a consumer process removes information from buffer storage and then processes it. Let buffer storage consist of *n* equal-sized buffers, each buffer capable of holding one record. We will use two semaphores as resource counters:

e = number of empty buffers (i.e., buffers that are currently available to the producer)

f = number of full buffers (i.e., buffers filled by the producer but not yet used by the consumer)

Assume that adding to or taking from a buffer constitutes critical sections; let b be a binary semaphore used for mutual exclusion. The processes may then be described as

```
var e, f, b: semaphore
e := n; f := 0; b := 1
cobegin
producer :    loop
                  produce next record;
                  P(e); P(b); add to buffer; V(b); V(f)
              end {loop}
                  |
consumer :    loop
                  P(f); P(b); take from buffer; V(b); V(e)
                  process record
              end {loop}
coend
```

Incrementing and decrementing e and f must be indivisible, or their values could be in error; hence, P and V operations are used. One could alternately define e and f as ordinary variables and treat their changes as critical sections. Some additional logic, however, must be included to take care of the possible waits when the variables are decremented. If the buffers were implemented as an array, mutual exclusion, enforced by the semaphore b, might not be necessary in the preceding, since the producer and the consumer always refer to different elements; however, if linked lists of buffers are employed or the program is generalized to m producers and n consumers (m, $n \geq 1$), mutual exclusion is necessary.

2.4.4 Implementing Semaphore Operations

Most currently available computers do not provide direct hardware instructions corresponding to the P and V semaphore operations. However, it is not difficult to program the logical equivalents of these operations on a computer that can both *test* and *set* a storage location in *one* (*indivisible*) operation. Let our version of such an instruction be designated $TS(X)$, where the storage location X can contain either a 0 (*false*) or a 1 (*true*); we will treat X as a Boolean variable. Then $TS(X)$ performs the following actions:

```
- - - - - -
R := X;
X := false ;
- - - - - -
```

where R is a program-addressable register of the machine executing the TS. (Assume that R can hold either of the values *true* or *false*.) Thus, $TS(X)$ always sets X to *false* and stores the previous value of X in the register R where it can later be accessed.

To simplify the algorithms in the following sections, we will ignore the register R and treat $TS(X)$ as an *indivisible* Boolean function that returns the value previously assigned to R:

```
function TS(X: Boolean): Boolean;
begin
    TS := X;
    X := false
end {TS}
```

In other words, the $TS(X)$ function always sets the value of X to *false* and indicates, by setting the value of TS to *true* or *false*, whether a change has been made to the value of X: TS is set to *true* if the value of X has changed from *true* to *false*, and it is set to *false* if no change has taken place.

2.4.4.1 Implementation with a Busy Wait

Let us first consider a restricted version of the semaphore operations, which operate on *binary* semaphores, that is, semaphores that may only have the value 0 (*false*) or 1 (*true*). We denote such restricted operations as Pb and Vb. Pb has the same definition as P, but Vb is slightly different; the effect of $Vb(sb)$ is $sb := 1$. (Note that Vb has no effect if the semaphore is already 1.)

The Pb and Vb operations on a binary semaphore sb may be implemented as follows:

$Pb(sb)$ is equivalent to: **while** $\neg TS(sb)$ **do** ; {*wait loop*}

$Vb(sb)$ is equivalent to: $sb := true$

When the semaphore sb has the value *false*, a process attempting to execute Pb will wait by repeatedly executing the **while** loop. This form of waiting is referred to as *busy waiting*, since the process consumes memory cycles and processor time while executing the loop.

The P and V operations on a *general* semaphore s may be implemented using the preceding operations Pb and Vb and two binary semaphores, $mutex_s$ and $delay_s$. For each operation $P(s)$ we use

```
Inhibit interrupts;
Pb(mutexs);
s := s - 1;
if s < 0 then begin Vb(mutexs); Pb(delays) end;
Vb(mutexs);
Enable interrupts;
```

Each $V(s)$ is replaced by

```
Inhibit interrupts;
Pb(mutexₛ);
s := s + 1;
if s ≤ 0 then Vb(delayₛ) else Vb(mutexₛ)
Enable interrupts;
```

Initially, s is set to the desired semaphore value and is decremented with each P operation and incremented with each V operation. Since s may become negative, it is viewed as serving a dual purpose: as long as it is greater than or equal to zero, it corresponds to the actual semaphore value; whenever it becomes negative, it represents the number of processes suspended on that semaphore. The suspension is accomplished using the binary semaphore $delay_s$, which is initialized to *false*.

A process executing a P or V is protected from processor preemption by inhibiting interrupts for the duration of these operations. Under reasonable assumptions, lengthy busy waits will not occur. Note that without inhibiting interrupts a situation referred to as *deadlock* can occur. To illustrate this possibility, assume that a process executing in the middle of a P or V operation is preempted, and the processor is assigned to some other higher-priority process. If the latter now attempted to execute a P or V operation on the same semaphore, it would find $mutex_s = false$ and, as a result, remain in the corresponding **while** loop of the Pb operation forever.

On a single-processor system, inhibiting interrupts is normally sufficient to prevent processes, other than the one executing the P or V operation, from simultaneously accessing the semaphore. On a multiprocessor, however, inhibiting interrupts on one processor does not prevent processes running on another processor from accessing the semaphore. This is achieved by the Pb operation on the binary semaphore $mutex_s$, initialized to *true*; it guarantees that at most one P or one V operation is acting on any given semaphore.

Busy waits for CSs may not be inefficient if they are "short" waits. Frequently, CSs may be executed relatively quickly. (They should be planned to have this property if at all possible.) It may then be possible to *inhibit interrupts* during the entire CS execution. In an environment involving more general CSs and synchronizations, where, for example, a process may be blocked waiting for an IO operation to be completed, or a hardware resource to become available, or a message from another process that can arrive at any arbitrary time, lengthy busy waits may be unsatisfactory. They can degenerate a multiprogrammed system into a uniprogrammed system, as well as increase to intolerable levels the response time for real-time events.

2.4.4.2 Avoiding the Busy Wait

A busy wait is avoided by providing for possible suspension (*blocking*) of processes on P operations and possible activation of processes on V operations. We develop one possible implementation of this general strategy in this section.

A process p that cannot proceed on a $P(s)$ will be blocked by saving p's state vector (i.e., the information necessary to restart the process; see Section 3.2.3) and inserting p on a *blocked list* L_s associated with the semaphore s. The operation then selects another ready process q from a global *ready list RL* and transfers control to it. Thus q continues executing on the processor instead of the process p. Such a process reassignment is usually called a *context switch*. If L_s is not empty, a $V(s)$ will select some process, say q, to be activated. If there is a free processor, q will be started immediately; otherwise, it is moved to the ready list *RL*. Interrupts are inhibited during the execution of P and V operations to prevent a possible deadlock as with the busy-wait solution of Section 2.4.4.1.

The P and V operations are then defined:

```
P(s) :
        Inhibit interrupts;
        Pb(mutex_s);
        s := s − 1;
        if s < 0 then
        begin      {context switch}
            Block process invoking P;
            q := Remove__from__RL;
            Vb(mutex_s);
            Transfer control to q with interrupts enabled
        end else
        begin
            Vb(mutex_s);
            Enable interrupts
        end
```

It is assumed that *Remove__from__RL* always returns a process name from *RL*;[†] at this point, we are not concerned with the particular process selected from *RL*. Note that $P(s)$ must be considered an indivisible machine operation. Thus if a process p is blocked on invoking $P(s)$, the instruction counter of its saved state vector will point to the next instruction following $P(s)$.

```
V(s):
        Inhibit interrupts;
        Pb(mutex_s);
        s := s + 1;
        if s ≤ 0 then
```

[†]It is convenient to always maintain one *idle* or *dummy* process on *RL* for each processor; in this way, *RL* will never be empty when a real working process becomes blocked. An idle process is selected by *Remove__from__RL only* when *RL* contains no working processes.

```
begin
    q := Remove__from__Lₛ;
    if there are free processors
    then Start executing q on a free procesor
    else Add q to RL
end;
Vb(mutexₛ);
Enable interrupts;
```

As with the busy wait implementation of Section 2.4.4.1, we allow the semaphore to have negative values. If a semaphore s is negative, its absolute value $|s|$ gives the number of blocked processes on L_s. Since interrupts are inhibited and a busy wait exists in the **while** loop, it is important that the preceding code be short and efficient for the same reasons discussed earlier. Note that it is still possible to have long, even infinite, busy waits in a multiprocessor system. Suppose that a single cyclic process were constantly executing P and V on one processor and that each of the remaining processors were looping on a Pb operation. Timing conditions could be such that the first process always entered the CS and left the others looping forever. This situation can be prevented by expanding the CS entry mechanism so that it grants entry on a round-robin basis.

Possibilities for the contents and organization of process data structures, the various lists, and process schedulers will be discussed in Chapter 3. We have also omitted several error checks that must be included in a real implementation; for example, what happens in $V(s)$ if $s \leq 0$ on entry and L_s is empty?

2.5 HIGHER-LEVEL SYNCHRONIZATION METHODS

The objection raised against the **fork**, **join**, and **quit** primitives used to spawn and synchronize processes, namely, their poor ability to support elegant structuring of programs, applies also to the P and V operations presented in Section 2.4.4.2. This problem stems from the fact that P and V operations are very low level primitives and, as such, are too general. For example, they do not permit a segment of code to be designated explicitly as a critical section. Rather, the effect of a critical section must be enforced by correctly using the P and V operations (i.e., by enclosing the desired segment between a pair of P and V operations and presetting the corresponding semaphore to 1. Violating any of these rules destroys the desired effect. Furthermore, semaphore operations embody two distinct concepts: (1) the blocking and waking up of processes, and (2) counting. Often, these tasks are related, in that the blocking or waking up of processes is performed when the counter reaches a certain value. Conceptually, however, they are independent and thus should be kept apart.

Since P and V operations may be used anywhere in a program, the task of understanding and verifying the desired behavior of programs becomes very difficult. For example, the following programming errors are usually extremely difficult to find: the omission of a V operation from a program or its mere bypassing when execution follows some unexpected path; this could result in a situation where processes are blocked forever, a situation commonly referred to as *deadlock*. Equally dangerous is an unintentional execution of a V operation, permitting more than one process to enter a critical section.

The following sections present several constructs that have been used or proposed as alternatives to the low-level P and V operations on semaphores.

2.5.1 Conditional Critical Regions

2.5.1.1 Definition and Use

To overcome the deficiencies of semaphores, a structuring method called *conditional critical region* (CCR) was defined by Hoare (1972) and Brinch-Hansen (1973). The basic idea is to explicitly designate a portion of code (region) to be a critical section and to specify the variables to be protected by that section, as well as the conditions under which it may be entered.

Each CCR is associated with a collection of variables to be protected by that region. Such a collection is referred to as a *resource* and must be declared as follows:

$$\textbf{resource } r :: v_1, v_2, \ldots, v_n$$

All variables v_1 through v_n, constituting the resource r, may be accessed only within a CCR that has the following syntax:

$$\textbf{region } r \textbf{ when } B \textbf{ do } S$$

The variable B is a Boolean expression that guards access to the critical section; only when B is true will the segment of code, S, be entered. Furthermore, the implementation of CCR must guarantee mutual exclusion: at any given time, only one process is permitted to enter the code segment associated with the resource r.

Example

> The following code illustrates the use of CCRs to implement the bounded buffer problem introduced in Section 2.4.3. In addition to the synchronization primitives, the code shows also the details of the buffer manipulation. The buffer is defined as an array of n elements (characters). The variables *nextin* and *nextout* are used as indexes into the buffer array; *nextin* points to the element to be filled next by the producer, and *nextout* points to the element to be emptied next by the consumer. Each pointer is incremented modulo n (denoted as $+_n$) after the appropriate operation. This implements the circular nature of the buffer. The number of valid elements not yet consumed is maintained in the variable *full__cnt*. This is consulted before each produce or consume operation to prevent the two indexes *nextin* and *nextout* from overtaking each other.

```
type buf_storage = array[0 .. n − 1] of char;
resource b :: Buf: buf_storage; nextin, nextout: integer;
. . .
process producer
loop
    produce data;
    region b when full_cnt < n do
        Buf[nextin] := data;
        nextin := nextin +ₙ 1;
        full_cnt := full_cnt + 1
    end {region}
end {loop}

process consumer
loop
    region b when full_cnt > 0 do
        data := Buf[nextout];
        nextout := nextout +ₙ 1;
        full_cnt := full_cnt − 1
    end {region}
    consume data
end {loop}
```

2.5.1.2 Implementation

Despite their advantages over simple P and V operations, CCRs are not very common in existing operating systems. The main reason is the difficulty in implementing them efficiently. Since conditions in CCRs may refer to local variables, each process must evaluate its own conditions. Consider the following semaphore-based implementation suggested by Brinch Hansen (1973), where each construct

region r when B do S

translates into the code

```
P(mutex);
del_cnt := del_cnt + 1;
while ¬B do
begin
    V(mutex);
    P(delay);
    P(mutex)
end;
del_cnt := del_cnt − 1;
S;
for i := 1 to del_cnt do
    V(delay);
V(mutex)
```

where *mutex*, *delay*, and *del__cnt* are defined as follows:

> **var** *mutex*, *delay*: **semaphore**; *del__cnt*: **integer**;
> *mutex* := 1; *delay* := 0; *del__cnt* := 0

Figure 2-6 illustrates the three main stages a process may pass through when attempting to enter a CCR. First, the process performs a *P* operation on the semaphore *mutex*, which guarantees that only one process may test the condition *B* at any given time; all other processes trying to enter the same region wait in a queue, Q_{mutex}, associated with the semaphore *mutex*. When the condition *B* is satisfied, the process completes the region by executing the statement *S*; otherwise, it releases the semaphore *mutex* and enters another queue, Q_{delay}, by executing the operation $P(delay)$. All processes waiting for some condition on the resource *r* enter the same queue Q_{delay}. The variable *del__cnt* records the number of processes in that queue.

Whenever some process passes its test and successfully completes the statement *S*, it is possible that one or more of the conditions expected by processes in the queue Q_{delay} are satisfied. Thus, after completing the statement *S*, all processes in that queue are transferred to the first queue Q_{mutex} to enable them to test their condition *B* again. This is accomplished by executing a $V(delay)$ operation for each process on Q_{delay}.

Note that it is possible for a process to be transferred in vain between Q_{delay} and Q_{mutex} several times before its condition *B* holds. But this can only occur as frequently as processes successfully execute the CCR. This controlled amount of "busy waiting" is the price we pay for the conceptual simplicity achieved by using arbitrary Boolean expressions as synchronizing conditions.

2.5.2 Monitors

2.5.2.1 Definition and Use

Conditional critical regions, while an improvement over simple *P* and *V* operations, still have the undesirable property of being scattered throughout programs. The desire to concentrate all accesses to the shared object, i.e., the critical resource to be accessed on a one-at-a-time basis, led to the development of the monitor concept (Hoare, 1974; Brinch Hansen, 1973b). The idea of a monitor is based on the principles of *abstract data types*,

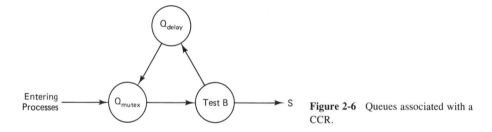

Figure 2-6   Queues associated with a CCR.

which suggest that for any distinct data type there should be a well-defined set of operations through which any instance of that data type must be manipulated. Following this idea, a monitor is defined as a collection of data (representing the resource to be controlled by the monitor) and a set of procedures to manipulate that resource.

The implementation of the monitor construct must guarantee the following:

1. Access to the resource is possible only via one of the monitor procedures.
2. Procedures are mutually exclusive; that is, at any given time only one process may be executing inside the monitor. During that time, other processes calling a monitor procedure are delayed until the process leaves the monitor.

The monitor, as just defined, is sufficient to implement a critical section by preventing simultaneous access to a resource. However, it does not provide any means for processes to communicate with one another. In particular, a mechanism is needed that would permit a process to leave the monitor and to suspend itself while waiting for some condition to be satisfied. When the condition becomes true, the suspended process must be reactivated and permitted to resume execution inside the monitor.

To solve this problem, monitors provide a special type of variable called *condition*, and two operations, **wait** and **signal**, which operate on conditions and can only be used inside monitor procedures. The operation **wait** on condition c, denoted as

$$c.\textbf{wait}$$

causes the executing process to be suspended (blocked) and placed on a queue associated with the condition c. Performing the **signal** operation on c, denoted as

$$c.\textbf{signal}$$

causes one (if any) of the processes waiting for the condition c to be eligible for reentering the monitor. Here we assume that the process that has waited the longest time will be chosen.

It should be emphasized that conditions are not variables in the classical sense; that is, there is no value associated with a condition. Rather, each condition variable may be viewed as a *name* chosen by the programmer to refer to a specific event or state of computation. To illustrate this concept, assume that a process may proceed only when some variable, say X, has a value greater than zero. We can define a condition variable, say $X\_is\_positive$, and use it to exchange information about the truth value of the expression $X > 0$ among different processes. Whenever a process finds this value to be *false*, it performs the operation $X\_is\_positive.\textbf{wait}$, which suspends that process on a queue associated with the condition variable $X\_is\_positive$. When some other process changes the content of X to a positive value, it may inform the suspended process of this event by performing the operation $X\_is\_positive.\textbf{signal}$. Note that the condition variable *X__is__positive* does not actually contain the value *true* or *false* of the expression *X* > 0.

There is one important issue to be resolved with the **signal** operation. Since it is used to indicate that a condition *c*, on which some other process *q* may be suspended, is now satisfied, there may be two processes eligible to run inside the monitor after a **signal** is issued: (1) the process executing *c*.**signal** and (2) the process *q* selected for reactivation (if there was a waiting process). By the monitor definition, only one process may be active inside a monitor at any one time, and thus one of the two processes must wait. In the original proposal, Hoare defined the semantics of the **signal** operation such that the process executing *c*.**signal** is suspended. This process is assigned the highest priority and thus reenters the monitor as soon as the previously reactivated process exits the monitor (or blocks itself by executing a **wait** operation). We will investigate other alternatives to implementing condition signaling in Section 2.5.2.3.

Example

To illustrate the use of a monitor, consider a solution to the bounded buffer problem:

```
buffer: monitor;
type buf__storage=array[0 .. n − 1] of char;
var
    Buf: buf__storage;
    nextin, nextout, full__cnt: integer;
    notempty, notfull: condition;
procedure deposit(data: char);
begin
    if full__cnt = n then notfull.wait
    Buf[nextin] := data;
    nextin := nextin +n 1;
    full__cnt := full__cnt + 1;
    notempty.signal
end;

procedure remove(data: char);
begin
    if full__cnt = 0 then notempty.wait
    data := Buf[nextout];
    nextout := nextout +n 1;
    full__cnt := full__cnt − 1;
    notfull.signal
end;

begin
    full__cnt := nextin := nextout := 0   {initialization}
end {buffer}
```

The two monitor procedures may be invoked by any process through the calls *buffer.deposit(stuff)* and *buffer.remove(stuff)*, respectively, where *stuff* is a variable of type **char**.

2.5.2.2 Implementation

To implement the monitor facility, we must guarantee the following:

1. Execution of procedures must be mutually exclusive.
2. A **wait** must block the current process on the corresponding condition.
3. When a process exits or is blocked on a condition and there are processes waiting to enter or reenter the monitor, one must be selected. If there is a process suspended as the result of executing a **signal** operation, then it is selected; otherwise, one of the processes from the initial queue of entering processes is selected (processes blocked on conditions remain suspended).
4. A **signal** must determine if any process is waiting on the corresponding condition. If this is the case, the current process is suspended and one of these waiting processes is reactivated (say, using a first-in/first-out discipline); otherwise, the current process continues.

We will show how monitors can be implemented using semaphores to satisfy the preceding requirements. The following semaphores and variables are employed:

mutex	is a semaphore initialized to 1; it is used to guard mutual access to procedures inside the monitor.
urgent	is a semaphore preset to 0; it is used to suspend a process when executing a **signal** operation.
condsem$_i$	represents a collection of semaphores, one for each condition c_i; these are used to suspend a process executing a **wait** operation; all *condsem$_i$* are initialized to 0.
urgentcnt	is a counter preset to 0; it contains the number of processes suspended as the result of a **signal** operation.
condcnt$_i$	is a counter associated with the condition c_i; it contains the number of processes suspended on that condition.

The body of each procedure inside the monitor is then surrounded by entry and exit code as follows:

```
P(mutex);
procedure body;
if urgentcnt > 0 then V(urgent) else V(mutex)
```

Each $c.$**wait** within the procedure body is coded as

```
condcnt := condcnt + 1;
if urgentcnt > 0 then V(urgent) else V(mutex);
P(condsem);  {process waits here}
condcnt := condcnt - 1
```

Each $c.$**signal** within the procedure body is implemented as

```
urgentcnt := urgentcnt + 1;
if condcnt > 0 then begin V(condsem); P(urgent) end;
urgentcnt := urgentcnt - 1
```

In this implementation, access to the monitor is regarded as a privilege that is explicitly passed from one process to another. Only when no one wishes to keep this privilege is *mutex* finally released. Various simplifications of this implementation are possible in special cases, for example, when a procedure contains no **wait** or **signal** operation, or under certain restrictions, for example, when **signal** may be used only as the last instruction in any procedure (see Exercise 2-19).

2.5.2.3 Other Monitor Variants

Wait *and* Notify *Primitives*.   The **signal** operation as defined previously causes the current process to be suspended. A simple variant of **signal** is the **notify** primitive, defined for the programming language Mesa (Lampson and Redell, 1980). **Notify** does not suspend the current process; it only indicates to a waiting process, without actually activating it, that the corresponding condition has been satisfied. The waiting process is resumed only when the current process exits the monitor.

In this scheme, however, a process suspended because a particular condition B was found *false* cannot be guaranteed that the condition will be *true* when the process resumes execution. To understand why such a guarantee cannot be given, consider two processes, $p1$ and $p2$, both of which are currently blocked as a result of executing the statements

if not $B1$ then $c1$.wait

and

if not $B2$ then $c2$.wait

respectively. Assume that the process currently executing inside the monitor causes both conditions to become *true* and indicates this fact by executing the statements $c1.$**notify** and $c2.$**notify**. When it exits the monitor, one of the waiting processes, say $p1$, is permitted to reenter the monitor. During its execution (*after* the $c2.$**notify** was issued), $p1$

may modify the contents of any variable inside the monitor, thus possibly making the condition *B2 false* again. Consequently, when *p2* is permitted to reenter, it cannot assume *B2* to be *true*. Rather, it must reevaluate *B2* to determine its current value and, if *false*, suspend itself again.

In general, **wait** statements should therefore be enclosed in a loop of the form

while not *B* **do** *c*.**wait**

instead of writing

if not *B* **then** *c*.**wait**

as would be done in monitors using **signal**.

2.5.2.4 Priority Waits

For the implementation of monitors as described in Section 2.5.2.2, it was assumed that when more than one process is waiting on the same condition, a **signal** will cause the longest waiting process to be resumed. In the design of an operating system, there are many cases where such simple scheduling on the basis of first-come/first-served is not adequate. To give a closer control over scheduling strategy, Hoare (1974) introduced a *conditional* (or scheduled) **wait**, which includes a priority for the waiting process. This has the form

c.**wait**(*p*)

where *c* is the condition variable on which the process is to be suspended, and *p* is an integer specifying a priority.

When the condition *c* is signaled and there is more than one process waiting, the one that specified the lowest value of *p* is resumed. The following example of an alarm clock illustrates the use of priority waits.

Example

```
alarmclock: monitor;
var
    now: integer;
    wakeup: condition;

procedure wakeme(n: integer);
var alarmsetting: integer;
begin
    alarmsetting := now + n;
    while now < alarmsetting do wakeup.wait(alarmsetting);
    wakeup.signal   {In case more than one process is to
                        wake up at the same time}
end;
```

```
procedure tick;
begin
        now := now + 1;
        wakeup.signal
end;


begin
    now := 0   {initialization}
end {alarmclock}
```

The monitor *alarmclock* enables a process to delay itself for a stated number *n* of time units, or ticks, by calling the procedure *wakeme*. This procedure presets the wakeup time to *now* + *n* and suspends the calling process by performing a **wait** operation. The priority associated with the suspended process is the value of the alarm setting.

The procedure *tick* is assumed to be invoked automatically by hardware (e.g., through an interrupt) at regular intervals. It increments the value of the current time, *now*, and wakes up the process with the lowest alarm setting time. This process compares the time *now* with its *alarmsetting*; if *now* is less than *alarmsetting*, it goes back to ''sleep'' by executing the **wait** operation. Otherwise, it performs a **signal** operation to wake up another process that might have its alarm preset to the same time and leaves the monitor.

2.5.3 Path Expressions

2.5.3.1 Definition and Use

Following the principles of abstract data types, monitors have the property of keeping a given resource and all operations that may be performed on that resource in one centralized place, the monitor body. By definition, all procedures are guaranteed to be mutually exclusive. Additional synchronization, however, must be programmed explicitly by using the **wait** and **signal** mechanisms. These mechanisms, which tend to be scattered throughout the bodies of various monitor procedures, impair the readability of the monitor code and hence are detrimental to the usefulness of the construct. Path expressions, first introduced by Campbell and Habermann (1974), represent an effort to remedy this problem by providing a direct scheme for expressing constraints on the order in which operations in concurrent programs may be executed. There are many variations of path-expression formalisms. In this book we restrict ourselves to the *open path expressions*, which have been incorporated into the programming language Pascal by Campbell and Kolstad (1980).

Path expressions are used within modules called *objects* that are similar to monitors in that a resource and the corresponding legal operations are defined in one central place. Unlike monitors, procedures within objects are not automatically mutually exclusive, and no **signal** or **wait** operations are provided. Instead, all constraints are declared in the beginning of the object using a path expression. This specifies the synchronization constraints for all procedures (or functions) within the object, invoked by possibly different processes. A path expression has the form

path *restriction__expression* **end**

where *restriction__expression* is defined recursively as follows:

1. A procedure name P is a *restriction__expression*; by itself, a single procedure name implies no restriction.
2. If $P1$ and $P2$ are *restriction__expressions*, then each of the following is also a *restriction__expression*:
   (a) $P1$, $P2$ denotes *concurrent execution*. No restriction is imposed on the order in which $P1$ and $P2$ are invoked or on the number of concurrent invocations (i.e., any number of each can execute concurrently).
   (b) $P1$; $P2$ denotes *sequential execution*. One invocation of $P1$ must complete before each invocation of $P2$. The execution of $P2$ in no way inhibits the initiation of $P1$; thus many different invocations of $P1$ and $P2$ may be active concurrently, as long as the number of $P2$'s that have begun execution is less than the number of $P1$'s that have completed.
   (c) n:$(P1)$ denotes *resource restriction*. It allows at most n separate invocations of $P1$ to coexist simultaneously.
   (d) $[P1]$ denotes *resource derestriction*. It allows an arbitrary number of invocations of $P1$ to coexist simultaneously.

By combining these operators, using parentheses to indicate precedence among the different operations, powerful constraints may be expressed in a very elegant way. The following examples are provided to illustrate the expressive power of path expressions.

Example

1. **path** 1:$(P1)$ **end**
   Procedure $P1$ must be executed sequentially; only one invocation may be active at a time.
2. **path** 1:$(P1)$, $P2$ **end**
   Multiple invocations of $P1$ result in sequential execution, while no restriction is placed on $P2$ (i.e., any number of invocations of $P2$ are permitted).
3. **path** 1:$(P1)$, 1:$(P2)$ **end**
   A maximum of one $P1$ and $P2$ can execute concurrently.
4. **path** 6:$(5$:$(P1)$, 4:$(P2))$ **end**
   As many as five invocations of $P1$ and four invocations of $P2$ can proceed concurrently as long as the limit of six total invocations is not exceeded.
5. **path** 5:$(P1$; $P2)$ **end**
   Each invocation of $P2$ must be preceded by an execution completion of $P1$; at most five

invocations of *P*1 followed by *P*2 may proceed concurrently (i.e., *P*1 can get ahead of *P*2 by at most five invocations).

6. **path** 1:([*P*1], [*P*2]) **end**
   Both procedures *P*1 and *P*2 operate in mutual exclusion; either is authorized to proceed (with multiple invocations) as long as requests for its invocation exist; when all requests have been satisfied, either procedure may start again.

7. The bounded buffer problem is solved using path expressions as follows:

```
buffer: object;
path n:(1:(deposit); 1:(remove)) end;
type buf_storage = array[0 .. n − 1] of char;
var Buf: buf_storage; nextin, nextout: integer;

procedure deposit(data: char);
begin
    Buf[nextin] := data;
    nextin := nextin +ₙ 1
end

procedure remove(data: char);
begin
    data := Buf[nextout];
    nextout := nextout +ₙ 1
end
```

The semicolon in the path expression indicates that each *remove* must be preceded by a *deposit*. The number *n* specifies that at most *n* *deposits* can be made before *remove* must be called. The number 1 preceding a procedure prevents multiple simultaneous invocation of that procedure.

When compared to the solution using a monitor, two improvements may be observed. First, the structure of the preceding solution is easier to understand since all constraints are concentrated in one place, the path expression. In this simple example the improvement may seem negligible. With more intricate problems, however, the improvement in structure could be significant. The second improvement is an increased potential for parallelism. Although the operations *remove* and *deposit* are mutually exclusive when a monitor is used, the solution using path expressions permits these to be executed concurrently. This does not cause any problems because different elements of the buffer are accessed by the two procedures.

The major limitation to path expressions is their poor ability to deal with conditional operations. Frequently, it is desirable to make a decision whether to execute a particular operation based on information available only at run time. To cope with such situations, path expressions would have to be extended by incorporating additional control constructs.

2.5.3.2 Implementation

The implementation of path expressions can be expressed using P and V operations (Campbell and Habermann, 1974). For each of the four constructs denoting concurrent execution, sequential execution, resource restriction, and resource derestriction, there is a well-defined sequence of P and V operations that may be generated by a compiler. These sequences are included in the procedure named in the path expression. In general, each procedure is preceded by a sequence called *prolog* and is terminated with a sequence called *epilog*. Let us examine the necessary rules for transforming each of the four possible constructs into the appropriate prologs and epilogs of the named procedures.

Since each construct may be embedded inside a more complex path expression, it is typically surrounded by sequences of generated synchronization operations. We will refer to the sequence on its left as L and the sequence on its right as R. Each transformation rule operates on a string of the form $L\ C\ R$, where C is the construct currently being translated, L is a sequence of P or PP operations (defined later) or it may be empty, and R is a sequence of V or VV operations (defined later) or it is empty.

Initially, a given path expression

path restriction_expression end

is transformed into the following form:

⟨ restriction_expression ⟩

This then is transformed recursively according to the following rules in an outside-in manner, that is, starting with the outermost constructs and proceeding inward until individual procedure names are reached. Angle brackets are used to show the scope of the prologs and epilogs derived so far.

1. Concurrent execution: $\langle L\ P1,\ P2\ R \rangle$ is replaced by $\langle L\ P1\ R \rangle \langle L\ P2\ R \rangle$.

2. Sequential execution: $\langle L\ P1;\ P2\ R \rangle$ is replaced by $\langle L\ P1\ V(s1) \rangle \langle P(s1)\ P2\ R \rangle$, where $s1$ is a new semaphore initialized to 0.

3. Resource restriction: $\langle L\ n{:}(P1)\ R \rangle$ is replaced by $\langle P(s2)\ L\ P1\ R\ V(s2) \rangle$, where $s2$ is a new semaphore initialized to n.

4. Resource derestriction: $\langle L\ [P1]\ R \rangle$ is replaced by $\langle PP(c,\ s,\ L)\ P1\ VV(c,\ s,\ R) \rangle$, where c is an integer initialized to 0, s is a semaphore initialized to 1, and the operations PP and VV are defined as follows:

$$
\begin{array}{ll}
PP(c,\ s,\ L){:}\ P(s); & \qquad VV(c,\ s,\ R){:}\ P(s); \\
\qquad c := c + 1; & \qquad\qquad c := c - 1; \\
\qquad \textbf{if } c = 1 \textbf{ then } L; & \qquad\qquad \textbf{if } c = 0 \textbf{ then } R; \\
\qquad V(s) & \qquad\qquad V(s)
\end{array}
$$

Example

The path expression used with the bounded buffer example,

path n:(1:(*deposit*); 1:(*remove*)) **end**

is transformed through the following sequence of rules:

1. Create new semaphore $s0 := n$; apply resource restriction rule:

⟨$P(s0)$ 1:(*deposit*); 1:(*remove*) $V(s0)$⟩

2. Create new semaphore $s1 := 0$; apply sequential execution rule:

⟨$P(s0)$ 1:(*deposit*) $V(s1)$⟩ ⟨$P(s1)$ 1:(*remove*) $V(s0)$⟩

3. Create new semaphore $s2 := 1$; apply resource restriction rule:

⟨$P(s2)$ $P(s0)$ *deposit* $V(s1)$ $V(s2)$⟩ ⟨$P(s1)$ 1:(*remove*) $V(s0)$⟩

4. Create new semaphore $s3 := 1$; apply resource restriction rule:

⟨$P(s2)$ $P(s0)$ *deposit* $V(s1)$ $V(s2)$⟩ ⟨$P(s3)$ $P(s1)$ *remove* $V(s0)$ $V(s3)$⟩

The preceding derivation thus produces the following prologs and epilogs for the buffer procedures:

1. The prolog of procedure *deposit* is $P(s2)$ $P(s0)$.
2. The epilog of procedure *deposit* is $V(s1)$ $V(s2)$.
3. The prolog of procedure *remove* is $P(s3)$ $P(s1)$.
4. The epilog of procedure *remove* is $V(s0)$ $V(s3)$.

2.6 MESSAGE-BASED SYNCHRONIZATION SCHEMES

All the synchronization mechanisms presented so far were based on the assumption that processes share some portion of memory. In the case of simple P and V operations, this is limited to sharing semaphores. With CCRs, sharing of condition variables, counters, and semaphores is necessary. Finally, with monitors or path expressions, entire blocks of code must be shared among processes.

It is not always desirable or even possible that processes share some portion of memory. For example, for reasons of security, processes often need to run in isolation, each in its own logical space, with all interactions under strict control of each participating process. Using any of the shared constructs (e.g. a monitor), this cannot be guaranteed since global data from each process sharing the monitor is accessible by any of the procedures inside the monitor's body. Hence the monitor could cause arbitrary flow of information among processes.

A second reason for abandoning the idea of shared constructs is the increasing importance of distributed systems. In such environments, each processor may have its own local memory, and hence no sharing of data is possible among processes running on different processors. For these two reasons, mechanisms for interprocess communication and synchronization other than those based on shared memory must be provided.

2.6.1 send and receive Primitives

As the names suggest, **send** and **receive** primitives are used to exchange messages between processes. Unlike other synchronization primitives, such as P and V, there is not a universally accepted definition of **send** and **receive**; depending on a particular system, many different interpretations may be found. A generic form of these two primitives could be described as

$$\textbf{send}(p, \textit{msg})$$
$$\textbf{receive}(q, \textit{msg})$$

send causes the message $\textit{msg}$, which could be an arbitrary data object, to be sent to the process named p. The primitive **receive** is used to obtain a message. It names the process, q, from which a message is expected. When the message arrives, it is deposited in the variable $\textit{msg}$. Some implementations permit the parameters p or q to be omitted, indicating that, in the case of **send**, a message is to be *broadcast* to all processes, whereas, in the case of **receive**, messages are to be accepted from any process.

To understand the variety of **send** and **receive** primitives, we must try to answer the following fundamental questions:

1. When a message is emitted, does the sending process have to wait until the message has been accepted by the receiver, or can it continue processing?
2. What should happen when a **receive** is issued and there is no message waiting?
3. Does the sender have to specify exactly one receiver to which it wishes to transmit a message, or can messages be accepted by any of a group of receivers?
4. Does the receiver have to specify exactly one sender from which it wishes to accept a message, or can it accept messages arriving from different senders?

Depending on the answers to these questions, we can distinguish several classes of interprocess communication schemes. The first two questions are concerned with the issues of *synchronous* versus *asynchronous* communication, while questions 3 and 4 address the problems of *explicit* versus *implicit naming* of processes. Let us consider these schemes and their possible combinations in turn.

There are two possible answers to question 1: If the sending process is blocked until the message is accepted, the **send** primitive is called *blocking* or *synchronous*. If, on the other hand, the process may proceed while the message is being transferred to the destination process, the **send** is said to be *nonblocking* or *asynchronous*.

Analogous to the blocking and nonblocking **send**, question 2 distinguishes two types of **receive** operations: in the first case, when issuing a **receive** and there is no message waiting, the process is blocked; such a **receive** is called blocking. Another alternative is to permit the receiving process to continue when no messages are waiting, thus virtually ignoring the **receive** operation; this type of **receive** is called nonblocking.

Questions 3 and 4 address the problem of naming. In the case of **send**, a process may wish to transmit a message nonselectively to any of a number of processes that may wish to receive it. This operation is usually referred to as *broadcasting* or **send** with *implicit naming*. Similarly, a process may need to receive a message from a number of possible senders, depending on the order of their arrival. Such operation will be called a **receive** with *implicit naming*.

The semantics of the various types of **send** and **receive** primitives may be summarized as follows (Shatz, 1984):

send	Blocking	Nonblocking
Explicit naming	Send message m to receiver r Wait until message is accepted	Send message m to receiver r
Implicit naming	Broadcast message m Wait until message is accepted	Broadcast message m

receive	Blocking	Nonblocking
Explicit naming	Wait for message from sender s	If there is a message from sender s, then receive it; else proceed
Implicit naming	Wait for message from any sender	If there is a message from any sender, then receive it; else proceed

Various combinations of these primitives may be provided to implement a variety of different facilities for process interactions. In the simplest case, where both operations are blocking (with explicit or implicit naming), the communication scheme is called *synchronous*; both processes must reach well-defined points (the respective **send** and **receive** operations) before they can proceed. When one or both primitives are nonblocking, the communication is called *asynchronous*; it permits the process executing a nonblocking operation to proceed without waiting for the other process.

Blocking **send/receive** primitives provide powerful mechanisms for solving a variety of process coordination problems. In the case of **send**, the blocking version with implicit naming is of little practical use because of the complexities of synchronizing the **send** with *all* possible receivers. Hence, broadcasting is usually done in the nonblocking form. The blocking versions of **receive**, on the other hand, are both very useful. In particular, in the absence of a **receive** with implicit naming, solutions to many important problems would be very difficult to construct, as illustrated by the following example.

Example

The following algorithm is a solution to the bounded buffer problem, with one producer, one consumer, and a buffer of length 1. *Only* blocking **send/receive** with explicit naming are used.

```
producer:                        consumer:
   loop                             loop
      produce__data                    receive(producer, data)
      send(consumer, data)             consume__data
   end {loop}                       end {loop}
```

Although this solution is very simple, it would be quite difficult to extend it for a buffer greater than 1, using only **send/receive** primitives with explicit naming. When a combination of both explicit and implicit naming is available, the following solution can be given (both primitives are still blocking):

```
process producer;
   loop
      produce__data;
      send(buffer__manager, data);
   end {loop};

process consumer;
   loop
      send(buffer__manager, request);
      receive(buffer__manager, data);
      consume__data;
   end {loop};

process buffer__manager;
   loop
      if full__cnt = 0 then
      begin
         receive(producer, data);
         Buf [nextin] := data;
         nextin := nextin +_n 1;
         full__cnt := full__cnt + 1
      end else
      if full__cnt = n then
```

```
begin
    data := Buf [nextout];
    receive(consumer, request);
    send(consumer, data);
    nextout := nextout +ₙ 1;
    full_cnt := full_cnt − 1;
end else
begin
    receive(*, temp);   {* means any sender}
    if * = producer then
    begin
        Buf [nextin] := temp;   {temp contains data}
        nextin := nextin +ₙ 1;
        full_cnt := full_cnt + 1
    end else   {* = consumer; temp contains request}
    begin
        data := Buf [nextout];
        send(consumer, data);
        nextout := nextout +ₙ 1;
        full_cnt := full_cnt − 1;
    end
end
end {loop}
```

The *producer* process is simple; it continuously produces data, which it sends to the *buffer_manager* process using a blocking **send**; the destination process is named explicitly. The *consumer* process is more complicated in that it must first send a request for data to the *buffer_manager* process before issuing the *receive* command. To understand why this is necessary, let us examine the *buffer_manager* process itself. If $full\_cnt = 0$, the buffer is empty and thus the only operation the *buffer_manager* can possibly perform is to await the arrival of data from the *producer*. Similarly, if $full\_cnt = n$, indicating that the buffer is completely full, the next interaction must be between the *buffer_manager* and the *consumer*. If neither condition holds, the *buffer_manager* should be able to interact with either of the two processes. Unfortunately, the *buffer_manager* does not know which of the two processes, if any, is ready to engage in an exchange of data. Consequently, it would not know whether to issue a **send**(*consumer*, *data*) or a **receive**(*producer*, *data*) operation. To solve this problem, a **receive** statement with implicit naming, denoted as **receive**(*, *temp*), is used, where * stands for ''any'' sending process. Since both the producer and the consumer use **send** as their first message operation, the *buffer_manager* is able to nondeterministically respond to a request from either the *producer* or the *consumer*.

An example of a highly influential system that employs only synchronous communication with explicit naming yet permits a process to nondeterministically receive data from more than one sender is CSP, *Communicating Sequential Processes*, proposed by Hoare (1978). A program in CSP defines a collection of sequential processes operating in parallel; a construct similar to **cobegin/coend** is used to define and start processes. Interprocess communication is accomplished by two simple *input* and *output* commands, analogs to the blocking **receive** and **send** operations introduced in this section. Exchange of data occurs when one process explicitly names another as destination for output *and* the second process names the first as source for input. When both conditions are satisfied, the value to be output is copied from the first process to the second. There is no automatic buffering between processes; in general, an input or output command is delayed until the other process is ready with the corresponding output or input.

To make the use of the communication primitives more effective, the concept of *guarded commands*, first introduced by Dijkstra (1975), is implemented in CSP. A statement preceded by a guard, which can be an arbitrary Boolean condition, is executed only if the guard evaluates to *true*. When an input command is preceded by a guard, it is selected for execution only when the process named in the command is ready to execute the corresponding output command. If several guarded input commands are enabled at the same time, only one is selected; the others have no effect. The selection is made arbitrarily. This feature of CSP virtually implements a form of a *selective input* command (similar to the selective accept statement of ADA, discussed in Section 2.6.2), which permits processes to communicate in a nondeterministic fashion, depending on the availability of input data at run time.

In CSP, as well as in the preceding solution to the bounded buffer problem, all **send/receive** operations were assumed to be *blocking*. While a solution to the same problem using only the *nonblocking* versions of the **send/receive** primitives is possible, their main purpose is aimed at a different type of problem. First, the definition of these primitives implies that the system must provide some kind of a buffering facility in order to hold all outstanding messages until they are requested by the receiving process. However, this is itself a requirement for a solution to the bounded buffer problem. Hence devising a solution for the bounded buffer problem using the nonblocking **send/receive** primitives is not meaningful since the implementation of these primitives requires such buffers to already exist.

Furthermore, problems such as the bounded buffer example are typical examples in synchronization, implying that some kind of blocking is expected to occur. Since, by definition, there is no waiting with the nonblocking **send/receive**, these operations lose the flavor of synchronization primitives and take on the form of a more general "mailing" facility. Both types of problems, synchronization as well as the asynchronous exchange of messages, are important in a general-purpose computing facility; thus many operating systems provide several different versions of **send** and **receive** to satisfy the needs of different applications.

Ports and Mailboxes.   In the absence of **receive** primitives with *implicit* naming (or the form of guarded input commands used in CSP), a process is limited to only one potential source of messages at any given time. If the **receive** is nonblocking, it can be embedded into a loop to simulate the effect of implicit naming as a form of "busy waiting." This solution is, however, quite inefficient. A common approach to avoiding the limitations of explicit naming that does not suffer from the performance problem of busy waiting is to use *indirect* communication. The basic idea is to make the queues holding messages between senders and receivers visible to the processes. That is, a **send** primitive does not use the name of a process as its destination; rather, it addresses the queue to which the message is to be appended. Similarly, the receiving process names the queue from which a message is to be accepted.

A queue that may be named by more than one sender and more than one receiver process is called a *mailbox*. This scheme is illustrated in Figure 2-7a. It provides the most general communication facility since any of the *n* senders may emit messages, which may be intercepted by any of the *m* receivers. Unfortunately, in a distributed environment the implementation of the **receive** operation can be quite costly since **receives** referring to the same mailbox may reside on different computers. Therefore, a limited form of a mailbox, usually called a *port*, is frequently implemented. In this case the port is associated with only one receiver. Hence all messages, coming from possibly different processes but addressed to the same port, are sent to one central place, associated with the receiver, as shown in Figure 2-7b.

2.6.2 Remote Procedure Calls

The use of synchronization primitives based on shared variables may not be always desirable or, in the case of distributed systems, may not even be possible. The problem with using the **send/receive** primitives, on the other hand, is their low level of interaction. The programmer is forced to abandon the structuring concepts of procedures and other high-level modules and interject **send/receive** primitives in much the same way as *P* and *V* operations on semaphores. *Remote procedure calls* (RPCs) have been introduced as a high-level concept for process communication to overcome both of these problems.

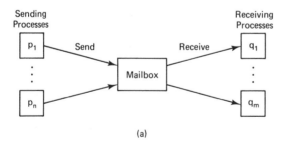

(a)

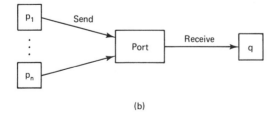

(b)

Figure 2-7 Indirect process communication: (a) through a mailbox (b) through a port.

As far as the programmer is concerned, a RPC has the same effect as a regular procedure call: it transfers control to another procedure while suspending the caller. A return statement executed by the called procedure then transfers control back to the caller, where execution continues with the instruction following the call. In this respect, the called procedure may be viewed as a service invoked by the caller. The main distinction between regular procedures and remote procedures (RPs) is that the latter reside in separate address spaces and hence no global variables may be shared. To exchange information, the calling procedure must pass all values to the called procedure as input parameters. Similarly, results are returned to the caller as output parameters.

From the caller's point of view, a RP appears and behaves exactly as any other procedure. Ideally, the caller should not even have to be aware of the fact that the called procedure is remote. At the implementation level, however, RPs are quite different from regular procedures. The problem is that a RP will be executing in a separate address space, possibly on a different computer, and hence cannot become part of the calling process. Rather, a separate process must be created to execute the RP. This process may be created dynamically or statically.

In the first case, a new process is created (and destroyed) for each invocation of the procedure. The overhead resulting from this dynamic approach may be eliminated if a permanent process, say *RP__guard*, exists, which repeatedly invokes the embedded procedure for each call. In this case, coordination of the processes must be enforced, which may be accomplished using the low-level **send/receive** primitives. Each RPC is implemented as a pair of synchronous **send** and **receive** statements, where **send** transmits the input parameters and **receive** awaits the arrival of the corresponding results. The RP itself must begin with a **receive** statement and terminate with a **send**. This implementation is illustrated by the following code skeleton:

```
Implementation of RPC:              Process containing RP:


    . . .                           process RP__guard;
    send(RP__guard, parameters);    loop
    receive(RP__guard, results);        receive(caller, parameters);
    . . .                               body of RP;
                                        send(caller, results)
                                    end {loop}
```

Let us now consider how the concept of RPCs can be incorporated into a high-level language. The calling process does not have to be aware of any distinctions between regular and remote procedures, and hence the same call statement can be used for both, leaving it up to the compiler to generate the appropriate statements. The RP itself, however, is different in that it must be embedded in a process, as described previously. Hence, some notation must be provided to designate a procedure as remote. We will consider the approach taken in ADA (U.S. Department of Defense, 1981), which provides a powerful mechanism called *rendezvous*. In its simplest form, an **accept** statement is used to designate a segment of code to serve as a remote procedure. This statement, which may be placed anywhere within a program, has the following form:

$$\textbf{accept } E(p_1, \ldots, p_n) \textbf{ do } S \textbf{ end}$$

where E is the procedure name, p_i are its parameters, and S represents the procedure body.

Its counterpart in the calling program is a standard procedure call of the form $E(q_1, \ldots, q_n)$, where q_i are the actual parameters to be passed to the **accept** statement. To explain the semantics of the **accept** statement, assume that p is the process issuing the call and q is the process executing the corresponding **accept** statement.

1. If the process p issues the call before process q has reached the corresponding **accept** statement, p becomes blocked. When q executes the **accept** statement, it proceeds by executing the procedure body, S. After completion of this rendezvous, both processes continue their execution concurrently. This is illustrated in Figure 2-8a.

2. If process q reaches the **accept** statement before the procedure call has been issued by p, q becomes blocked. As soon as a call is made, the rendezvous takes place and the process q resumes execution. While q executes the procedure body S, process p is suspended. As in the first case, both processes continue concurrently upon termination of S. Figure 2-8b illustrates this case.

In its exposed form, the **accept** statement suffers the same problem as a blocking **receive** with explicit naming: it does not permit the process executing this statement to wait selectively for the arrival of one of several possible requests. This would make sharing of such a RP limited to a predetermined order of arrivals. To eliminate this deficiency, ADA provides a **select** statement that permits several **accept** statements to be active at the same time. Furthermore, a Boolean statement may be associated with each **accept** statement that prevents its execution if its value is *false* at the time the **select**

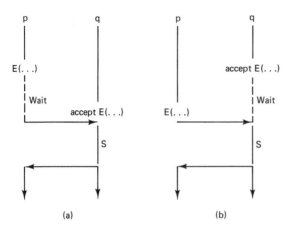

Figure 2-8 Execution of a rendezvous: (a) Calling process is delayed (b) Called process is delayed.

statement is executed. The **accept** statements are embedded in a **select** statement as follows:

```
select
    [when B₁:]
        accept E₁(. . .) do S₁ end
    or
    [when B₂:]
        accept E₂(. . .) do S₂ end
    or
    . . .
    [when Bₙ:]
        accept Eₙ(. . .) do Sₙ end
    [else] R
end {select}
```

The construct has the following semantics: The **when** clause associated with each **accept** statement is optional, as indicated by the square brackets. When omitted, its value is assumed to be *true*. Execution of the **select** statement causes one of the embedded **accept** statements to be executed. To be selected, the corresponding **when** clause must yield the value *true*, and there must be at least one pending procedure call to that **accept** statement performed by some other process. If there are more than one such eligible **accept** statements, the system is assumed to choose among these according to some fair internal policy. If, on the other hand, none of the **accept** statements is eligible, the **else** clause, comprising the statement *R*, is executed.

The **else** clause is optional. If it is omitted, the **select** statement behaves as follows: If none of the **when** clauses evaluates to *true*, an *error* is generated. Otherwise, the process is suspended until a call to one of the **accept** statements, for which the **when** clause evaluates to *true*, is performed. At this time the body S_i of that **accept** statement is executed and both processes continue concurrently.

Example

This example shows the solution to the bounded buffer problem using a selective **accept** statement (Shatz, 1984):

```
process buffer;
select
    when full__cnt < n:
        accept deposit(data: char) do
            Buf [nextin] := data;
            nextin := nextin +ₙ 1;
            full__cnt := full__cnt + 1
        end
```

```
              or
              when full__cnt > 0:
                  accept remove(data : char) do
                      data := Buf [nextout];
                      nextout := nextout +_n 1;
                      full__cnt := full__cnt − 1
                  end
              end {select}
```

The two operations on the buffer may be invoked by other processes issuing the procedure calls *buffer.deposit(stuff)* and *buffer.remove(stuff)*, respectively.

In conclusion, RPs could be considered as closing the gap between procedure-oriented synchronization schemes and those based on message passing. From the programmer's point of view, RPs are high-level constructs that fit well the philosophy of block-structured programming languages. Their implementation, on the other hand, is in terms of simple message-passing primitives, which makes them suitable to distributed environments (Andrews and Schneider, 1983).

2.7 CLASSIC SYNCHRONIZATION PROBLEMS

In Section 2.6 we used the critical section problem and the bounded buffer problem to study the various approaches to process synchronization. In this section we present three additional well-known problems that have been used extensively in the literature. These problems are not only important in their own right in concurrent programming; they also serve to demonstrate the capabilities of different synchronization schemes. We will contrast two different solutions for each of the problems to further illustrate the concepts discussed in preceding sections.

2.7.1 The Readers/Writers Problem

The readers/writers problem, first formulated and solved by Courtois, Heymans, and Parnas (1971), arises when two types of processes, referred to as readers and writers, need to share a common resource, such as a file. Writers are permitted to modify the resource and thus must have exclusive access. Readers, on the other hand, may share the resource concurrently with an unlimited number of other readers. In addition, some fairness policy must be enforced to prevent indefinite exclusion of readers or writers or both.

Depending on the latter requirement, there are several different variants of the basic readers/writers problem. In the original paper, two solutions using P and V operations were given. The first adopts the policy that readers have priority over writers. That is, no reader should be kept waiting unless a writer has already obtained permission to use the resource. Note that this policy will result in an indefinite postponement (starvation) of writers if there is a continuous stream of read requests.

The second policy gives priority to writers. When a writer arrives, only those readers already granted permission to read are allowed to complete their operation. All new readers arriving after the writer are postponed until the writer's completion. This policy may result in an indefinite postponement of read requests when there is an uninterrupted stream of writers arriving at the resource.

2.7.1.1 Solution Using CCRs

The following is a modified version of the solution to the readers/writers problem assuming the policy where writers have priority over readers (Brinch Hansen, 1973).

```
resource v :: read_cnt, write_cnt: integer;
resource w;
read_cnt := write_cnt := 0;
procedure reader;
begin
    region v when write_cnt = 0 do read_cnt := read_cnt + 1;
    read;
    region v do read_cnt := read_cnt − 1
end;

procedure writer;
begin
    region v do write_cnt := write_cnt + 1;
    region v when read_cnt = 0 do ; { proceed only when read_cnt = 0}
    region w do write;
    region v do write_cnt := write_cnt − 1
end
```

The resource v consists of two integer variables, *read_cnt* and *write_cnt*, which define the number of readers currently using the resource and the number of writers currently waiting for or using the resource. Mutual exclusion of readers and writers is achieved by letting readers wait until the number of writers is zero, and vice versa. Mutual exclusion of individual writers is ensured by the critical region associated with the resource w.

The priority rule is enforced by increasing the number of writers as soon as one of them wishes to use the resource. This will delay any subsequent read requests until all pending writer requests are satisfied.

2.7.1.2 Solution Using a Monitor

With the two priority policies for readers and writers as formulated by Courtois, Heymans, and Parnas (1971), one of the process types has absolute priority over the other. Consequently, it is possible for one of these to monopolize the resource while processes of the other type are delayed indefinitely. To prevent this from occurring, Hoare (1974) proposed a solution that obeys the following priority policy: A new reader should not be permitted to start if there is a writer waiting; and all readers waiting at the end of a write operation should have priority over the next writer. This solution is given in the form of a monitor as follows:

```
readers/writers monitor;
var read_cnt: integer;
    busy: Boolean;
    OK_to_read, OK_to_write: condition;

procedure start_read;
begin
    if busy ∨ ¬empty(OK_to_write) then OK_to_read.wait;
    read_cnt := read_cnt + 1;
    OK_to_read.signal;
end;

procedure end_read;
begin
    read_cnt := read_cnt − 1;
    if read_cnt = 0 then OK_to_write.signal;
end;

procedure start_write;
begin
    if read_cnt ≠ 0 ∨ busy then OK_to_write.wait;
    busy := true;
end;

procedure end_write;
begin
    busy := false;
    if ¬empty(OK_to_read) then OK_to_read.signal
    else OK_to_write.signal
end;

begin
    read_cnt := 0;
    busy := false
end
```

The monitor's procedures are called by reader and writer processes as follows:

start_read	is called by reader who wishes to read.
end_read	is called by reader who has finished reading.
start_write	is called by writer who wishes to write.
end_write	is called by writer who has finished writing.

The variables *read__cnt* and *busy* have a similar function as in the previous solution using CCRs. The condition variables *OK__to__read* and *OK__to__write* are used by readers and writers to suspend themselves until the appropriate condition is signaled.

The constructs $\neg$*empty(OK__to__read)* and $\neg$empty(*OK__to__write*) are Boolean functions used to test whether the queues associated with the conditions *OK__to__read* and *OK__to__write* are empty. These functions were also proposed by Hoare (1974) as extensions to the basic monitor definition. They permit convenient solutions to problems such as the readers/writers problem.

2.7.2 The Dining Philosophers Problem

To illustrate the subtleties of deadlock and indefinite postponement in process synchronization, Dijkstra (1968) formulated and proposed a solution to a problem that became known as the dining philosophers problem. Five philosophers, p_i, sit around a table in the middle of which is a bowl of spaghetti. There is a plate in front of each philosopher and there are five forks on the table, one between each two plates, as illustrated in Figure 2-9. At unspecified times, each of the philosophers may wish to eat. To do that, he must first pick up the two forks next to his plate; only then is he allowed to start eating. When he is finished (after a finite time), he places the forks back on the table. Philosophers are considered to be processes and forks are resources. The problem is to design the philosopher processes so that none of them starve because of the unavailability of forks.

There are two main concerns when developing a solution to this problem. First, a deadlock situation, in which each philosopher acquires one of the forks and waits indefinitely for the other to be released, must be prevented. Second, it should not be possible for two or more philosophers to conspire in such a way that one of the remaining philosophers could be prevented indefinitely from acquiring his two forks.

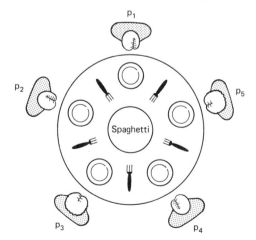

Figure 2-9 Five dining philosophers.

2.7.2.1 Solution Using a Monitor

```
dining__philosophers: monitor;
type
    f = array[0 . . 4] of integer;
    f__available = array[0 . . 4] of condition;
var
    forks: f;
    forks__available: f__available;

procedure start__eating(i);
begin
    if forks(i) ≠ 2 then forks__available(i).wait;
    forks(i −₅ 1) := forks(i −₅ 1) − 1;
    forks(i +₅ 1) := forks(i +₅ 1) − 1;
end;

procedure stop__eating(i);
begin
    forks(i −₅ 1) := forks(i −₅ 1) + 1;
    forks(i +₅ 1) := forks(i +₅ 1) + 1;
    if forks(i −₅ 1) = 2 then forks__available(i −₅ 1).signal;
    if forks(i +₅ 1) = 2 then forks__available(i +₅ 1).signal;
end;

begin
    for i := 0 to 4 do forks(i) := 2;
end {dining__philosophers}
```

The solution uses an array of five counters, $forks(i)$, to keep track of how forks are being used. Each $forks(i)$ is associated with one philosopher, i, and is initially preset to 2. It indicates how many forks the philosopher i has at his disposal at each given moment.

When philosopher i is ready to eat, he calls the procedure $start\_eating(i)$. If $forks(i)$ is less than 2, indicating that one or both of his neighbors are currently eating, the philosopher i is forced to wait; otherwise, the procedure decrements the number of forks available to the two neighboring philosophers, $i -_5 1$ and $i +_5 1$, and permits philosopher i to proceed.

Upon termination, philosopher i calls the procedure $stop\_eating(i)$, which increments the fork counts of the two neighboring philosophers. If either of these two counts is equal to 2, the procedure signals to the corresponding philosopher that he now may attempt to acquire his forks.

This solution prevents deadlock in a simple way: each philosopher is forced to pick up the two forks at the same time (i.e., within the same critical section). The problem with indefinite postponement is, however, still possible. Two philosophers may conspire to prevent a third one from ever getting his turn, thus starving him to death.

To illustrate this situation, assume that philosophers 1 and 3 are currently eating and philosopher 2 calls his *start__eating*(2) procedure. If in the future *start__eating*(3) is always called before *stop__eating*(1) and *start__eating*(1) is always called before *stop__eating*(3), philosopher 2 will be blocked forever.

2.7.2.2 Solution Using Path Expressions (Campbell and Kolstad, 1980)

```
dining__philosophers: object;
path 4:(start__eating; stop__eating) end;
type f = array[0 . . 4] of
    object
        path 1:(pickup; putdown) end;
        procedure pickup begin end;
        procedure putdown begin end;
    end;
var fork: f;

procedure start__eating(i);
begin
    fork[i].pickup;
    fork[i +₅ 1].pickup;
end;

procedure stop__eating(i);
begin
    fork[i].putdown;
    fork[i +₅ 1].putdown;
end
end {dining__philosophers}
```

Whenever a philosopher i wishes to eat, he calls the procedure *dining__philosophers.start__eating(i)*, which, in turn, calls the two procedures *fork[i].pickup* and *fork[i +₅ 1].pickup*. Upon termination, the philosopher calls the procedure *dining__philosophers.stop__eating(i)*, which invokes the procedures *fork[i].putdown* and *fork[i +₅ 1].putdown*. The *pickup* and *putdown* procedures have no bodies; they are used only to control access to the forks.

The path expression within each of the five fork objects prescribes how the fork may be used: it must first be picked up and then put down; and only one philosopher at a time may pick it up. The path expression within the outer object permits at most four philosophers at a time to compete for access to the forks. This simple constraint prevents deadlock from occurring.

The indefinite postponement problem is also solved by the preceding solution. If a philosopher calls the procedure *start__eating* while the other four philosophers are all inside their *start__eating/end__eating* procedures or are actually eating, he is forced to wait. A permission to continue will, however, be granted as soon as any of the currently busy philosophers terminates by executing the procedure *stop__eating*. The latter have no way of preempting or otherwise delaying the one currently waiting.

2.7.3 Disk Head Scheduler

On a moving head disk, the time to move the read/write head increases monotonically with the distance traveled. If several programs wish to move the head, the average waiting time can be reduced by selecting first the request that moves the head the shortest distance. Unfortunately, this policy could delay a request indefinitely by servicing a stream of requests that accesses data within close proximity of each other.

An alternative policy that avoids this kind of starvation but still handles requests efficiently is one that minimizes the changes in direction of movement of the head. At any time, the head is moved in only one direction, and it services the program requesting access to the nearest disk track in that direction. If there is no such request, the direction is reversed, and the head makes the next sweep across the disk surface, servicing all requests in that direction. This scheme has also been termed the ''elevator'' algorithm, since it simulates the behavior of a lift in a multistory building (Hoare, 1974).

2.7.3.1 Solution Using a Monitor

```
disk__head__scheduler: monitor;
var
    type direction = (up, down);
    headpos: integer; dir: direction; busy: Boolean;
    upsweep, downsweep: condition;

procedure request(dest);
begin
    if busy then
        if headpos < dest ∨ (headpos = dest ∧ dir = up)
        then upsweep.wait(dest)
        else downsweep.wait(n − dest);
    busy := true;
    headpos := dest;
end;

procedure release;
begin
    busy := false;
    if dir = up then
        if ¬ empty(upsweep) then upsweep.signal else
        begin
            dir := down;
            downsweep.signal
        end else
        if ¬ empty(downsweep) then downsweep.signal else
```

```
              begin
                 dir := up;
                 upsweep.signal
              end
      end;


      begin
         headpos := 0; dir := up; busy := false
      end {disk__head__scheduler}
```

This solution is for a disk consisting of n cylinders, numbered from 0 to $n - 1$. The head may move *up*, toward the outermost cylinder $n - 1$, or *down*, toward the innermost cylinder 0.

There are two entries to the disk head scheduler. Procedure *request(dest)* is called by a process just before issuing the instruction to move the head to the cylinder *dest*. The procedure *release* is called when the process has made all the transfers it needs on the current cylinder.

The variable *headpos* records the current position of the head, the Boolean variable *busy* records whether the disk is currently being accessed, and the variable *dir* keeps track of the current direction in which the head is moving.

When a request is issued and the disk is busy, the caller is placed on one of two waiting queues associated with the conditions *upsweep* and *downsweep*. The decision on which queue a process is to be placed depends on the current head position, the destination, and the direction of the current sweep: if the head is moving up toward the destination, then the *upsweep* queue is used; otherwise, the process must wait for the direction to change and thus is placed on the *downsweep* queue.

Within each queue, processes are ordered by priority: on the *upsweep* queue the priority is given by the distance between the destination and the innermost cylinder (i.e., *dest*); on the *downsweep* queue it is the distance of the destination from the outermost cylinder (i.e., $n - dest$).

The *release* procedure signals one of the waiting processes (if any) to proceed. If the head is moving up and the *upsweep* queue is not empty, the process with the smallest priority on that queue is enabled. Similarly, on a downsweep, the smallest priority process from the *downsweep* queue is enabled. The direction of the sweep is reversed whenever the corresponding queue is empty.

2.7.3.2 Solution Using RPCs

```
      select
          accept save__request(dest) do
              if headpos < dest ∨ (headpos = dest ∧ dir = up)
              then enter(upsweep__queue)
              else enter(downsweep__queue)
          end
```

```
    or
        when ¬busy ∧ (dir = up ∧ ¬empty(upsweep_queue) ∨
                        dir = down ∧ ¬empty(downsweep_queue)):
        accept process_request do
            busy := true
            if dir = up then headpos := first(upsweep_queue)
            else headpos := first(downsweep_queue)
        end
    or
        accept release do
            busy := false;
            if dir = up ∧ empty(upsweep_queue) then dir := down;
            if dir = down ∧ empty(downsweep_queue) then dir := up
        end
    end {select}
```

The selective **accept** construct of ADA does not permit a process to suspend itself while waiting on some condition to be satisfied and then later to reenter the same **select** statement. We have therefore divided the requests for accessing the disk into two procedures, which must be called in sequence. The first of these procedures, *save_request(dest)* enters the process into one of two queues, *upsweep_queue* or *downsweep_queue*, according to the current direction of the sweep, the current head position, and the destination. The second procedure, *process_request*, which must be called after each call to *save_request*, is invoked only when the disk is not busy and, in addition, only when the queue associated with the current sweep direction is not empty. The procedure body then sets *busy* to *true* and the head position to the first element on the appropriate queue. The task of the *release* procedure is to free the disk and to reverse the sweep direction if the corresponding queue is empty.

EXERCISES

2.1. Rewrite the following program using **cobegin/coend** statements. Make sure that it exploits maximum parallelism but *always* produces the same result as the sequential execution.

$$W := X1 * X2;$$

$$V := X3 * X4;$$

$$Y := V * X5;$$

$$Z := V * X6;$$

$$Y := W * Y;$$

$$Z := W * Z;$$

$$ANS := Y + Z;$$

2.2. Write a procedure using **cobegin/coend** to compute the dot product $\Sigma_{i=1}^{n} a_i b_i$ of two vectors in parallel.

2.3. The following expression describes the serial/parallel precedence relationship among six processes, p_1 through p_6:

$$P\Big(S\big(P\big(p_3, S\big(p_1, P\big(p_6, p_5\big)\big)\big), p_2\big), p_4\Big)$$

Transform this expression into a program using:
(a) fork, join, quit primitives
(b) cobegin/coend

2.4. Write a two-way merge-sort procedure using **fork, join, quit**, and **private**. You may assume that you are to sort a globally defined array $A[1..n]$ of integers and that you have a procedure *merge* that will merge two sorted subranges of A in place.

2.5. Why must most of the **join** operation be indivisible?

2.6. Write a program for parallel matrix multiplication using the primitives **fork, join, quit**, and **private**.

2.7. Two processes, p and q, in ADA interact as follows:

- p starts q.
- While p computes: "$x1 := some\_computation$,"
  q computes "$y1 := some\_computation$."
- A rendezvous takes place during which p computes "$y2 := y1 + x1$."
- While p computes "$x2 := some\_computation$,"
  q computes "$y3 := y2 + some\_computation$."
- A second rendezvous takes place during which p computes "$y4 := y3 + x2$."

Write the ADA code for the two processes p and q.

2.8. The following solution to the critical section problem was given by T. Dekker. (The original solution contained labels and goto statements, which we have replaced with loop constructs.)

```
var c1, c2: boolean; turn: integer;
c1 := c2 := true;
turn := 1;
cobegin
p₁ : loop
        c1 := false;
        while ¬c2 do
          if turn = 2 then
          begin
            c1 := true;
            while turn = 2 do ; {wait loop}
            c1 := false;
          end
        CS1; turn := 2;
        c1 := true; program1
     end {loop}
```

$$p_2 : \ldots$$

Show how this solution prevents mutual execution. Is mutual blocking of any of the forms described in Section 2.3.1 possible?

2.9. Use semaphores to describe the synchronization of the eight processes in the general precedence graph of Figure 2-1d.

2.10. Simulate the traffic at an intersection of two one-way streets using semaphore operations. In particular, the following rules should be satisfied:

- Only one car can be crossing at any given time.

- When a car reaches the intersection and there are no cars approaching from the other street, it should be allowed to cross.

- When cars are arriving from both directions, they should take turns to prevent indefinite postponement of either direction.

2.11. What is the effect of interchanging (a) $P(b)$ and $P(e)$ or (b) $V(b)$ and $V(f)$ in the producer process in the bounded buffer example of Section 2.4.3?

2.12. Consider the possible parallel activities in the compiler depicted in Figure 2-10. Each of the four processes p_1 through p_4 is cyclic and communicates with one or more other processes through the common data areas *AL*, *ILC*, and *OM*. Process p_1 adds atom pointers to *AL* that are consumed by p_2. p_2 produces intermediate language code for *ILC* that is consumed by p_3. p_1, p_2, and p_3 produce output messages in *OM* that are consumed by p_4. Let the common data areas be arrays defined as

$$AL[0 \ldots al - 1], \ ILC[0 \ldots ilc - 1], \ OM[0 \ldots om - 1], \qquad \text{where } al, ilc, om \geq 1$$

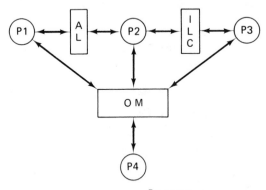

Data:		Processes:	
AL:	Atom List	P1:	Scan
ILC:	Intermediate Language	P2:	Syntax and Semantics
	Code	P3:	Code Generation
OM:	Output Messages	P4:	Output

Figure 2-10 Parallel processes in a compiler.

They are organized as cyclic buffers. Assume that each data area request or release involves only one element of an array. Write the relevant code for each process for adding and removing elements of common storage and for assuring their correct synchronization using semaphore operations. All four processes are to execute concurrently.

2.13. A simple batch operating system may be described as a set of three processes interacting as follows (Andrews and Schneider, 1983):

```
program OPSYS;
var input_buffer: array[0 .. N − 1] of card_image;
    output_buffer: array[0 .. N − 1] of line_image;

process reader;
var card: card_image;
begin
    loop
        read card from cardreader;
        deposit card in input_buffer
    end {loop}
end;

process executer;
var card: card_image; line: line_image;
begin
    loop
        fetch card from input_buffer;
        process card and generate line;
        deposit line in output_buffer
    end {loop}
end;

process printer;
var line: line_image;
begin
    loop
        fetch line from output_buffer;
        print line on lineprinter
    end {loop}
end
end
```

Modify and augment this batch operating system using semaphore operations to properly buffer the *card_image* data that flows from the *reader* to the *executer* and the *line_image* data that flows from the *executer* to the *lineprinter*.

2.14. Are the implementations of the general semaphore operations using binary semaphore operations presented in Section 2.4.4.1 still correct if $Vb(mutex_s)$ is moved to precede the s test in either the P or the V operation?

2.15. Consider the instruction *TSB(X, L)* that performs a test, set, and branch as one indivisible operation as follows:

if *X* **then go to** *L* **else** *X* := *true*;

Implement the *P* and *V* operations on binary semaphores using *TSB*.

2.16. Consider the following synchronization primitives (Reed and Kanodia, 1979):

- *ADVANCE(A)*: increments the variable *A* by 1.
- *AWAIT(A, C)*: blocks the process executing this instruction until $A \geq C$.

Using these primitives, develop a solution to the bounded buffer problem with (a) buffer size 1, and (b) buffer size n $(n > 1)$.

2.17. We have seen that monitors can be implemented with semaphore operations. To show that monitors and semaphores have equal expressive power, we have to show that semaphores can be implemented with monitors. Assuming that monitors can be implemented with something other than semaphores, write a monitor that implements the general *P* and *V* operations.

2.18. Let a *bounded semaphore s* be a general semaphore that cannot exceed a given value *smax* > 0. The corresponding *P* and *V* operations are then defined as

$P(s)$:   wait until $s > 0$; then decrement *s* by 1

$V(s)$:   wait until $s < smax$; then increment *s* by 1

Write a monitor to implement bounded semaphores.

2.19. Under each of the following assumptions the code implementing a monitor (Section 2.5.2.2) may be simplified. Show the new code for each case:
(a) The monitor contains no **wait** or **signal** operations.
(b) The last instruction of the monitor body is **signal**. (Other **signal** operations may occur earlier in the body.)
(c) The use of **signal** is restricted such that it may occur *only* as the last instruction of any monitor.

2.20. Recall the semantics of monitors in Mesa (Section 2.5.2.3) where a signaller (''notifier'') retains the monitor rather than immediately relinquishing control to a waiting process.
(a) Show how a general semaphore, initialized to zero, can be implemented using a Mesa monitor.
(b) Show how Mesa monitors can be implemented using semaphores.

2.21. Consider two monitors *m1* and *m2* and assume that a procedure *p1* in *m1* calls a procedure *p2* in *m2*. When *p2* blocks itself by executing a **wait** operation, the monitor *m2* is, by definition, released and may be entered by other processes. It is, however, not clear what should happen to *m1* in such a *nested monitor call*: should it remain locked or should it be released together with *m2*? Discuss possible consequences of the two choices. In particular, consider what happens when the original process is permitted to reenter *m2* while *m1* is released.

2.22. (a) Repeat Exercise 2.18 (implementation of bounded semaphores) using path expressions.

(b) Translate the path expressions of part (a) to a P and V implementation using the rules of Section 2.5.3.2.

2.23. Using path expressions, define an object that implements a bounded stack. The object should provide three operations:

- *push*: inserts an element on top of the stack.
- *pop*: deletes the top element from the stack.
- *top*: returns the top element of the stack (when the stack is empty, a special null element is returned).

Your solution should permit a maximum amount of parallel access.

2.24. Modify and augment the simple batch operating system of Exercise 2.13 using each of the following synchronization mechanisms:
(a) Conditional critical regions
(b) Monitors
(c) Path expressions
(d) Send/receive primitives
(e) Remote procedure calls (ADA)

2.25. There are two processes, c_1 and c_2, that at unpredictable times call another process p. The task of p is to count how many times it has been called by each c_i process. Once in a while, a fourth process q calls p to get the accumulated counts for the c_i processes. When the counts are reported to q, p resets both counters to 0. Write the process p using the selective **accept** statement of ADA.

2.26. Modify the solution to the readers/writers problem given in Section 2.7.1.1 such that readers have priority over writers.

2.27. The following solution to the readers/writers problem was proposed by Courtois, Heymans, and Parnas (1971):

```
var read_cnt, write_cnt: integer;
    mutex, r, w: semaphore;

procedure reader;
begin
    P(mutex);
    read_cnt := read_cnt + 1;
    if read_cnt = 1 then P(w);
    V(mutex);
    read;
    P(mutex);
    read_cnt := read_cnt - 1;
    if read_cnt = 0 then V(w);
    V(mutex)
end;


procedure writer;
```

```
begin
    P(w);
    write;
    V(w)
end
```

Show that this solution satisfies the basic requirements of the readers/writers problem. Is starvation of readers or writers possible?

2.28. The following is a variation of the readers/writers problem applicable in database environments. Assume that a data record is either free or is locked in one of three possible modes: I (for intention), S (for shared), or X (for exclusive). More than one lock can be applied to a given record as long as the locks are compatible with one another. The following table specifies how locks can be acquired:

		Current Lock Mode		
		I	S	X
Lock request:	I	Grant	Deny	Deny
	S	Deny	Grant	Deny
	X	Deny	Deny	Deny

where "grant" means the record acquires the new lock and the process continues, and "deny" means the process is blocked until the lock request can be satisfied. Thus, a record can have either (1) no locks, (2) one or more I locks, (3) one or more S locks, or (4) one X lock. Assume that any number of processes may be attempting to access a given record concurrently, using the following sequence of operations: *lock record in desired mode; use record; unlock record.* Locking and unlocking are done with the following procedures:

LI: lock in I mode	RI: remove one of the I locks
LS: lock in S mode	RS: remove one of the S locks
LX: lock in X mode	RX: remove the X lock

(a) Using semaphores for synchronization, write the code for these six procedures so that the locking restrictions are satisfied.

(b) Does your solution potentially lead to starvation of some process? If so, show how starvation can occur; if not, prove it.

2.29. Repeat Exercise 2.28 using a monitor to encapsulate the six procedures.

2.30. (a) Repeat Exercise 2.28 using path expressions.

   (b) Translate the path expressions of part (a) to a P and V implementation using the rules of Section 2.5.3.2.

2.31. Consider the following solution to the readers/writers problem:

```
procedure reader;
begin
    region v do rc := rc + 1;
    read;   {this is outside of the region body}
    region v do rc := rc - 1
end
```

```
procedure writer;
begin
    region v when rc = 0 do write
end
```

(Initially, $rc = 0$.) Does this solution satisfy the general requirements of the readers/writers problem? Is starvation of readers or writers possible?

2.32. Assume that each of the five philosophers, i, in the dining philosophers problem executes the following segment of code:

```
P(mutex);
    P(fork[i]);
    P(fork[i +₅ 1]);
V(mutex);
    eat;
V(fork[i]);
V(fork[i +₅ 1])
```

Does this code satisfy all requirements of the dining philosophers problem?

2.33. Using conditional critical regions, solve the readers/writers problem according to the priority policy of Section 2.7.1.2.

2.34. The 'elevator' algorithm for disk head scheduling in Section 2.7.3 favors requests at the center cylinders of the disk at the expense of requests at the two extremities. A fair scheduling method is a *circular scan* algorithm that services requests in order from the first through the last cylinder and then moves *directly* back to the first cylinder for the next pass. Give a monitor solution to the disk head scheduling problem that uses the circular scan policy.

3

Process and Resource Control

In Chapter 2, we introduced the concept of a process and described a number of primitives for the creation and destruction of processes and for enforcing controlled interaction. These primitives were described primarily from the user's point of view. We considered processes and resources as single entities, without defining their individual components and internal structure. This chapter presents a framework for representing processes and resources at the level of the operating system. We also assumed that processes could be created, destroyed, blocked, reactivated, or otherwise manipulated, without specifying how such operations are actually implemented. This chapter examines possible realizations of these operations as low-level kernel procedures. Finally, a major portion of Chapter 2 was devoted to the synchronization of and cooperation among processes. These require that processes can be blocked while waiting for a condition to be satisfied. In this chapter, we illustrate the concepts of blocking and unblocking of processes by introducing two low-level operations for requesting and releasing resources. These may be viewed as more general forms of the P and V operations on semaphores. This will permit us to study some of the subtleties of process scheduling and dispatching, which constitute an important part of the operating system but were invisible at the high level of process coordination studied in Chapter 2.

3.1 THE OPERATING SYSTEM KERNEL

The operating system *kernel* or *nucleus* is a basic set of *primitive operations* and *processes* from which the remainder of the system may be constructed. The distinction between a process and a primitive operation in this context deserves some explanation. When a primitive operation is invoked by a process, it takes the form of a subroutine call (or a macro expansion) and is part of the calling process, and often a critical section within this process. On the other hand, a process requesting a service from another process sends a request message to that process and, frequently, blocks itself until the service has been rendered; that is, the two processes are thought of as almost independent activities running concurrently. The service process, say a member of the kernel, can be written to remain in blocked status until it receives a request, or it could be continuously polling the system for work. In the first case, one could also treat the process as an operation, the distinction being one of conceptual convenience. A practical consideration here is that a process call is more complicated and consumes more time and space.

One often thinks of kernel operations as processes, regardless of the implementation method, because a process requesting a systems service does not normally have the capability (resources) to perform that service for itself; if it wishes to do so, some other process must grant the requesting process the required resources. One example is a supervisor-call instruction, which causes a hardware action that changes the state of the machine to make additional resources available (e.g., the ability to execute channel initiation instructions).

The set of kernel operations can be divided into four classes according to their purpose:

1. Primitives for process creation, destruction, and basic interprocess communication.

2. Primitives for allocating and releasing units of various resources such as main memory, secondary storage, IO devices, or files.

3. Input and output primitives; essentially, these are read, write, and control operations for initiating and supervising the transfer of data between main memory and the various IO devices.

4. Operations to handle interrupts triggered by various system events; among these are the termination of a process, completion of an IO operation, request of some service to be performed by the operating system, an error caused by a program, or hardware malfunctioning.

In this chapter we are concerned primarily with the first two types of kernel operations (i.e., those for process and resource management). Discussion of IO operations and the corresponding interrupt-handling routines will be postponed until Chapter 6.

The highest level of user processes in an operating system is usually established in response to a request (e.g. a "login" command) expressed in the system's control or command language. We will assume that a highest-level supervisory or "envelope" process p_j is created for each user j. In many systems, this is actually the case; where it is not, it is still convenient conceptually to assume the existence of such a process, even though its function may be performed centrally by some systems process. The process p_j has the responsibility for initiating, monitoring, and controlling the progress of j's work through the system and for maintaining a global accounting and resource data structure for the user. The latter may include static information such as user identification, maximum time and IO requirements (for batch processing), priority, type (e.g., interactive or batch), and other resource needs; it may also include dynamic information related to resource use and other processes created as progenies.

In general, p_j creates a number of such progeny processes, each corresponding to some requested unit of work. These processes may in turn create additional ones, either in sequence or in parallel. Thus, as computation progresses, a corresponding tree hierarchy of processes grows and shrinks. The processes are not totally independent, but

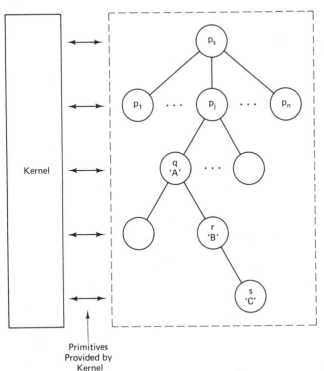

Primitives
Provided by
Kernel

Figure 3-1 A process creation hierarchy.

interact with each other and parts of the operating system such as resource managers, schedulers, and file system components, using communication primitives provided by the kernel.

These ideas are illustrated in Figure 3-1, where an operating system process p_s has created user process $p_1, \ldots, p_n$, and the process p_j, in turn, has created the processes q, r, s. All processes utilize the primitives provided by the underlying kernel. (The significance of the labels A, B, and C will be explained shortly.)

3.2 DATA STRUCTURES FOR PROCESSES AND RESOURCES

Every process and resource is normally represented by a data structure containing its basic state, identification, and accounting information. These data structures are referred to as systems *control blocks* or *descriptors*. Collectively, they represent the state of the operating system and, as such, are accessed and maintained by systems routines.

3.2.1 Process Descriptors

A process descriptor or process control block (PCB) is constructed at process creation and represents the process during its existence. Process descriptors are used and modified by basic process and resource operations, interrupt routines, and schedulers; they may also be referenced during performance monitoring and analysis. Figure 3-2 shows a possible set of descriptor data for a process in a general-purpose operating system. Each entry may be viewed as an element of a record, where the type of each element is given inside the box. The access to any element of a given descriptor is accomplished through a pointer. For example, $p\uparrow.Main\_Store$ refers to the fourth entry of the descriptor pointed to by pointer p. We have grouped the items comprising the process descriptor into five categories according to their primary purpose as follows:

Identification.   Each process is uniquely identified by the pointer p pointing to its descriptor. These pointers are maintained by the system. In addition, each process has an external identification $p\uparrow.Id$ supplied by the user. Its purpose is to allow convenient and explicit interprocess references. To eliminate conflicts arising from the use of the same external name for more than one process, we impose the convention that the progenies of any process in the tree hierarchy have unique names and define a complete reference from process p_1 to p_2 as the ordered concatenation of Ids of processes on the path connecting p_1 to p_2 (including $p_2\uparrow.Id$); for example, in Figure 3-1, process q can reference process s by the name $B.C$, where $r\uparrow.Id = B$ and $s\uparrow.Id = C$. (More details on this type of referencing may be found in Chapter 6, where a similar scheme is used for naming files in file directories.)

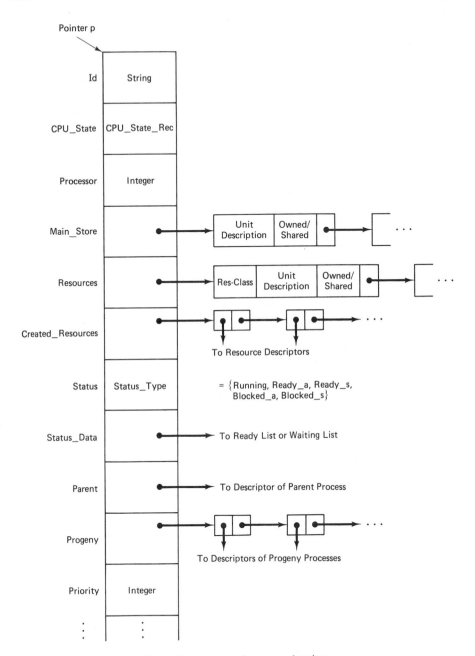

Figure 3-2 Structure of a process descriptor.

Since all pointers to process descriptors are maintained by the system, we assume the existence of a function

$$p := Get\_Pointer(ep)$$

that takes an external process name *ep* as argument and returns the pointer *p* to the process's descriptor.

State Vector.   The execution of a process *p* can be described as a sequence of *state vectors* s_0, s_1, . . . , s_i, . . . , where each state vector s_i contains a pointer to the next program instruction to be executed, as well as the values of all intermediate and defined variables of the program. It also contains the state and capabilities of the processor executing *p*, the allocated address space, and any other resources currently associated with *p*. In other words, a state vector of a process *p* is that amount of information required by a processor in order to run *p*. The state vector can be changed either by the execution of *p* or by the execution of other processes that *share* some state vector components with *p*.

The state vector part in Figure 3-2 consists of the five different components following *Id. p↑.CPU_State* contains the process's capabilities and protection data, as well as the current instruction counter and register contents in the case where *p* is ready or blocked but *not* running. The type of this component is *CPU_State_Rec*, indicating that *p↑.CPU_State* is a record. In general, *p↑.CPU_State* is equivalent to the information contained in the typical third- or fourth-generation machine state word (i.e., the data saved by hardware when an interrupt occurs). When a process *p* is running, *p↑.CPU_State* is undefined. Instead, *p↑.Processor* identifies, by number, the processor executing *p*.

p↑.Main_Store is the main storage map, which describes the real address space of the process and, in case of a virtual memory (Section 5.4), the mapping between the virtual name space and physical memory locations. Thus, *p↑.Main_Store* could contain upper and lower bounds registers for a contiguous partition in main memory, a list of memory blocks allocated to the process, or a pointer to a page or segment table. We have assumed that individual units of main memory resources are maintained in the form of a linked list pointed to by this field. Each unit consists of the unit description and a flag indicating whether this unit is *shared* or *owned*.

The next component *p↑.Resources* is a pointer to a list of all other serially reusable resources allocated to *p*. These might be such resources as peripherals, secondary storage space, or files. Each element on this list contains three main parts: (1) identification of the resource class (type) to which this unit belongs; (2) a unit description, including the details of allocation; for example, the sector addresses of disk space; and (3) an owned or shared flag similar to that used with main memory units.

The *p↑.Created_Resources* list is a linked list of all resource classes created by the process. Each element on this list is a resource descriptor (defined in Section 3.2.2).

Status Information.   The status of a process p is described by an indicator $p\uparrow.Status$ and a data item $p\uparrow.Status\_Data$ pointing to a list associated with the resource responsible for the current status. In general, the status of a process p may be one of the following:

running:	p is running on a processor (the one designated by $p\uparrow.Processor$).
ready:	p is ready to run, waiting for a processor.
blocked:	p cannot logically proceed until it receives a particular resource or message.

These three states can handle many situations, but there are some applications for which a finer division of status types is desirable. Consider the following two examples:

1. A user is interactively debugging or running a program. Often, the user will wish to suspend execution to examine the state of computation, possibly make some changes, and either continue or terminate execution.

2. An internal process might wish to suspend the activity of one or more other processes to examine their state or perhaps modify them. The purpose of the suspension may be, for example, to detect or prevent some kinds of deadlocks, to detect and destroy a runaway process, or perhaps to swap the process out of main memory temporarily.

In both cases one could block the process to achieve the suspension. However, a process could be already blocked when suspension is desired. Unless we wish to allow a process to be blocked on more than one condition, a new suspended status is required.

A process will be either *active* or *suspended*. If active, it may be running, ready, or blocked, denoted by a $p\uparrow.Status$ value of *running*, *ready__a*, or *blocked__a*, respectively. When suspended, $p\uparrow.Status$ is *ready__s* or *blocked__s*. (The possible state changes are shown later in Figure 3-5 and will be discussed in Section 3.3.)

$p\uparrow.Status\_Data$ contains the following additional status information:

$p\uparrow.Status$	$p\uparrow.Status\_Data$
1. *running* *ready* $\binom{s}{a}$	Pointer to ready list (RL) of processes used by the scheduler for allocation of the processor resource.
2. *blocked* $\binom{s}{a}$	Pointer to a waiting list associated with the resource r causing the block.

Details of the ready and waiting lists are provided in Section 3.2.2.

Other Information.   At the beginning of this chapter, the concept of spawning hierarchies of processes was briefly mentioned. Each process p has a creator, called *parent*, that created the process and that owns and controls any of its offsprings.[†] The parent of a process is recorded in the field $p\uparrow.Parent$, which contains a pointer to the parent's descriptor. Similarly, every process p may create other processes; the field $p\uparrow.Progeny$ points to a list, which links together the descriptors of all direct offsprings of p.

The priority of a process, $p\uparrow.Priority$, is a static or dynamic entity indicating the relative importance of p; we will use the convention that $p\uparrow.Priority > q\uparrow.Priority$ implies that process p has a higher priority than q. The priority is not necessarily an external priority assigned to a user or to a batch job when it is submitted to the system. The latter may be viewed as a long-term priority used for determining when the job is to be loaded and activated, while $p\uparrow.Priority$ is basically a short-term and possibly dynamic priority employed by the process scheduler when selecting a process to run. $p\uparrow.Priority$ could be a complex function of an external priority, the resource demands of the process, and the current environment (i.e., other processes in the system).

The last part of the process descriptor (not shown in the figure) is used for scheduling, accounting, allocation, and performance measurement purposes. Typical elements include CPU time used by the process, time remaining (according to some estimate), resources used, resources claimed, and the number of IO requests since creation.

3.2.2 Resource Descriptors

This section presents a data structure skeleton that can describe the state of any of a large number of entities called resources; the class is much larger than one would expect. The data structures described here and the basic resource operations of Section 3.3 were developed by Weiderman (1971) to consolidate and generalize many heretofore isolated but widely used notions.

The term resource is commonly applied to a reusable, relatively stable, and often scarce commodity that is successively requested, used, and released by processes during their activity. The term is most frequently used to describe hardware components. It is evident, however, that many types of software (data and programs) satisfy this common definition also. These resources are called *serially reusable* since they are usually (but not always) shared by processes on a serial basis (i.e., by one process at a time). Each resource class requires at least three descriptive components:

1. An *inventory* listing the number and identification of available units of the resource.
2. A *waiting list* of blocked processes with unsatisfied requests for the resource.
3. An *allocator* responsible for deciding which requests should be honored and when.

There is yet another set of entities that shares the same descriptive needs as serially

[†]There will be one ultimate creator, which is created when the system is first loaded.

reusable resources. These appear in synchronization and communication situations where messages, signals, and data are transmitted among processes. For each class of messages at a given time, there is an inventory of messages that have been produced but have not been received (consumed), a waiting list (perhaps empty) of processes that have requested some information, and some allocation mechanism that matches messages to receivers. We will call these resources *consumable*, after Holt (1971), since they are used primarily in producer/consumer applications, individually have a short lifetime in a system, and are not returned to the system after use. Units of serially reusable resources may be released or returned to the resource inventory *only* if they were previously acquired, whereas elements of consumable resources can be released independently of any previous acquisitions.

Consumable and serially reusable resources have one important property in common: A process can become logically blocked due to an unsatisfied request for such a resource. This leads us to a general definition: A *logical resource*, hereafter called a *resource*, is anything that can cause a process to enter a logically blocked status.

The state of a resource class is described by the data structure, called *resource descriptor*, shown in Figure 3-3. If a process p is blocked due to an unsatisfied request for a resource, the entry $p\uparrow.Status\_Data$ will point to the waiting list associated with the corresponding resource descriptor. In general, resource descriptors may be established *dynamically* during execution when a process creates a new resource class. However, like processes, *static* creation of resources (i.e., at systems load time) is most common.

Identification, Type, and Origin.   As in the process descriptor case, each resource class is uniquely identified by a pointer r to its descriptor; all components of a given descriptor are then accessed through this pointer. Recall that these pointers are maintained by the creator processes in the form of a linked list pointed to by $p\uparrow.Created\_Resources$ (Figure 3-2). This includes both serially reusable and consumable resources created by that process.

Each resource class also has an external (nonunique) name, $r\uparrow.Id$, defined by the creator at resource definition time. This provides a more convenient way for users to refer to resources. To transform an external resource name into a unique pointer, we assume that the same function, *Get_Pointer*, introduced for obtaining pointers to process descriptors may be used with resources. That is, the call

$$r := Get\_Pointer(er)$$

takes an external resource name er as argument and returns the pointer r to the corresponding resource descriptor.

The Boolean indicator $r\uparrow.Sr$ denotes whether the resource is serially reusable ($r\uparrow.Sr = true$) or consumable; recall that only allocated resources of serially reusable type are recorded in $p\uparrow.Resources$ of a process descriptor. The field $r\uparrow.Creator$ points to the descriptor of the process that created the resource class r.

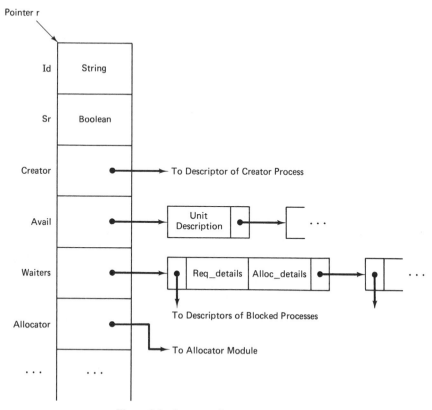

Figure 3-3 Structure of a resource descriptor.

Inventory List.   The reference $r\uparrow.Avail$ points to the head of an availability list or inventory of the resource class r. The list itself could be a single bit indicating the presence or absence of a certain type of interrupt signal, or a table for main storage blocks, or a list of buffers, or some more complex and structured data such as auxiliary storage device addresses that contain availability directories for the particular unit. Figure 3-3 shows the inventory list as a linked list of individual resource units.

Waiting Process List.   All processes blocked on the resource class are found in this list, pointed to by the entry $r\uparrow.Waiters$. Each element on this list contains a pointer to the process descriptor of a blocked process and a description of the request. The description specifies the details of the resource request and might include such things as the size of the request, its type (e.g., a request for a seven- or nine-track tape), and the identification of the process(es) that may give the resource (e.g., send a message) to the requester. It also contains a subfield *Alloc_details*, which identifies (e.g., by a pointer) an area belonging to the calling process. This area is filled by the allocator when the request is satisfied; it describes the details of the resource allocation to the process when it is resumed.

The waiting list can take many forms. In the simplest case, it has a capacity of one element. This occurs in basic signaling applications in which a process is only blocked and waiting for a signal from one other process. It would probably be most efficient to combine all resources of this type into a larger class, since the allocation mechanisms would be the same for each. In more complex applications, the waiting list can have a potentially unbounded number of elements. We account for this situation by assuming a linked list organization.

Allocator.   The allocator of a resource class is a routine that attempts to match available resources to requests of blocked processes. If it decides to satisfy a request, it removes that request from the $r\uparrow.Waiters$ queue, stores the details of the completed allocation in *Alloc_details*, and places the satisfied request on a *List*.

We will allow the allocator to satisfy requests from one or more processes on a single call. This is certainly desirable when resources are added to the availability list, since more than one process may be unblocked as a result of such an action. Less obviously, it may be desirable to defer allocations until some future time, even though resources are available at the time of request. This might be done to prevent deadlock or in anticipation of future requests or for efficiency purposes. We will assume a general call

$$Allocator(r, L)$$

where r and L have the following meaning:

1. r is the pointer to a resource descriptor.
2. L is a linked list of satisfied requests; each element contains a pointer to a process whose request has been satisfied and the details of the resource allocation.

Additional Information.   Additional fields in the resource descriptor can be employed for several purposes. For example, since system behavior depends to a large extent on resource demands and utilization, it may be convenient to maintain some measurement data in the descriptor. The current allocation of the elements of the resource class can also be kept here.

3.2.3 The Processor Resource

There is one resource that must be treated separately, and that is the central processor(s). The reason is that we do not consider a process to be logically blocked if it is waiting *only* for the availability of a processor; rather, we have introduced the special ready state to distinguish such processes. In a system with more than one central processor, a data structure is required to maintain the current state of this special resource. For simplicity, we will assume that all central processors are equivalent in the sense that a ready process may be allocated to any one. In practice, this may not be so since they may vary in speed, the amount and type of internal storage available, and their ability to communicate with other processors, storage devices, and peripherals. Our processor resource descriptor will be similar in structure to those of other resources. There are, however, two important distinctions:

1. The availability list, describing individual processors, is not a linked list; rather, it is an array defined as

$$\textbf{array } Process[1 .. np] \textbf{ of } ptr;$$

   where np is the number of processors in the system and ptr is a pointer to the descriptor of the process currently running on this processor. This pointer may have the value NIL, indicating that the processor is idle. The need for this organization will become apparent when the scheduler is discussed in Section 3.4.2; a scheduler may need to scan all processors quickly in order to test the priorities of currently running processes. If the individual processor element descriptions were distributed throughout the process descriptors, such scan would be too inefficient.

2. Processes waiting for a processor are maintained on a ready list *RL*. Hence *RL* may be viewed as the *Waiters* list associated with the processor resource. Unfortunately, processes are not always scheduled on a first-come/first-served basis, and thus a more complex data structure than just a simple linked list is required. We assume that the selection is based on the process's priority. (Various other strategies for process scheduling will be discussed in Section 3.5.) To facilitate the insertion and deletion of processes, we organize the waiting list as a general priority queue, shown in its simplest form in Figure 3-4. Such a queue consists of a table, where each entry corresponds to one priority level. All processes with the same priority are linked into a list connected to the appropriate priority level by two pointers, one pointing to the first element of the list and the other to the last. This organization permits fast insertion and deletion of elements, as will be discussed in Section 3.2.4.

3.2.4 Implementation of Queues

In the previous sections we have encountered two types of queues, a simple linked list of elements and a priority queue. Examples of the first kind were the queues $p\uparrow.Main\_Store$, $p\uparrow.Resources$, $p\uparrow.Progeny$, or $r\uparrow.Avail$, while the ready list *RL* was organized as a priority queue. To maintain these queues we need at least two operations, one to insert elements into and one to remove elements from a given queue.

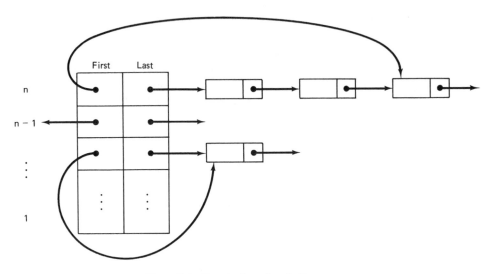

Figure 3-4 Organization of a priority queue.

A simple FIFO queue can be defined and initialized as follows:

```
type   ptr =↑ element;
       element = record
                       data: . . .
                       next: ptr
                end;
       header = record
                       first: ptr;
                       last: ptr
                end

var qh:↑header;
begin
    ⋮
    new(qh);
    qh↑.first := NIL;
    qh↑.last := NIL
    ⋮
end
```

This code creates a new queue header pointed to by *qh*. The two fields in the header are set to NIL, indicating that the queue is empty. Each new element inserted into the queue then consists of two parts: (1) *data*, which could be a simple value or a pointer to some other structure, and (2) a pointer, *next*, to the next element in the queue.

To define a queue of n priority levels, we use the following code:

```
type . . .
n_header = array[1 . . n] of header;
var qh:↑n_header;
begin
    ⋮
    new(qh);
    for i := 1 to n do
    begin
        qh↑[i].first := NIL;
        qh↑[i].last := NIL
    end
    ⋮
end
```

where *header* is the same record type as with a simple queue. This creates an array, pointed to by *qh*, of n such headers, one for each priority level. The two pointers *first* and *last* in each header are set to NIL, indicating that all levels are empty.

To simplify the algorithms presented in subsequent sections, we would like to specify uniformly the insertion and removal of queue elements, regardless of the organization details of the queue. In particular, we do not wish to use different procedure calls for simple queues and for priority queues. For this purpose, we assume the existence of two generic procedures, *Insert* and *Remove*, which operate on any type of queue. Insertion of new elements into a queue is then accomplished by the call

$$Insert(qh, p)$$

which appends the element p to the end of the queue qh. To remove an element from a queue, the call

$$p := Remove(qh)$$

may be used; it detaches the first element qh and assigns p to point to that element.

To implement such generic *Insert* and *Remove* operations, we assume that each queue starts with a *header*, which contains all information necessary to apply the appropriate operations. It then becomes the responsibility of the two procedures to examine the header of a given queue and to invoke the insert/remove operations specific to that type of queue. (Headers are invisible to the callers of *Insert* and *Remove* and thus will not be shown explicitly in figures.)

Using lists with only forward pointers is one of many possible implementations of such structures. Another common approach is to use doubly linked lists, where each element is connected to its left and right neighbor. The resulting circular chains of forward and backward pointers permit a more efficient scanning of the lists since it is possible to move in either direction. The disadvantages are the additional space and time requirements for maintaining backward pointers.

The process and resource descriptors are sufficient to handle a wide variety of multiprogramming applications. However, few commercial systems have such a general structure for these descriptors. Usually each resource class has its own data structure, which is defined at system generation. The process descriptor generally contains fields for each hardware resource that may be allocated and bit strings for indicating the cause of a wait. One pays a price in efficiency for our more general structures: the storage to hold the additional pointers and the extra computing required by the basic process and resource operations. The benefits of such a systematic organization derive primarily from its clarity and uniformity. Changes can be made easily to adapt to new conditions, a system is easier to understand and therefore to analyze and evaluate, and there exists the possibility of implementing primitive operations on these structures in hardware or through microprogramming. The main value of this section is to define a general framework within which specific operating systems data structures of widespread application may be introduced.

3.3 BASIC OPERATIONS ON PROCESSES AND RESOURCES

To implement the high-level concepts of process and resource manipulation, a set of primitive kernel operations is specified. The state of the hypothetical operating system, given by the process and resource descriptors described in Section 3.2.4, is maintained through these primitives. We will take the point of view that each primitive represents a procedure that is executed within the invoking process rather than treating each as a separate process. The primitives are considered indivisible and are protected by a common "busy wait" type of lock; for clarity, we omit the locks in the following descriptions. Error and protection checking are also omitted. These issues are discussed separately in Chapter 6.

3.3.1 Process Control

Five operations on processes are defined:

1. *Create:* Establish a new process.
2. *Destroy:* Remove one or more processes.
3. *Suspend:* Change process status to suspended.
4. *Activate:* Change process status to active.
5. *Change_Priority:* Set a new priority for the process.

To create a new offspring p, the parent process will call the *Create* primitive with the arguments: external name ep, initial CPU state s_0, initial main storage m_0, initial inventory of other resources r_0, priority k_0, and perhaps accounting information and limits. The initial status will be *ready_s* (*ready* because the new process p should be in position to proceed logically and *suspended* because it may be desirable to create a process well before its activation). The *Create* primitive is

```
procedure Create(ep, s₀, m₀, r₀, k₀, accounting);
begin
    new(p);   {Create new instance of process descriptor}
    p↑.Id := ep;
    p↑.CPU__State := s₀;
    p↑.Main__Store := m₀;
    p↑.Resources := r₀;
    p↑.Priority := k₀;
    p↑.Status := 'ready__s';
    p↑.Status__Data := RL;
    p↑.Parent := *;
    p↑.Progeny := NIL;
    Set Accounting Data;
    Insert(*↑.Progeny, p);
    Insert(RL, p)
end
```

The first instruction creates a new instance of the process descriptor record (Figure 3-2) with p pointing to that instance. Subsequent instructions then fill the individual fields of the descriptor using the given parameters. We assume that any process is able to obtain the pointer to its *own* descriptor, either through an agreed upon register or through a kernel call; the asterisk * designates this pointer. *Create* adds p to *'s *Progeny* list using an *Insert* operation and also inserts p on the ready list *RL*. The initial resources, including main storage, are defined as *shared* resources for the new process and must be a subset of those belonging to the parent process; the parent may share any of its resources with other progeny processes in a similar manner. The created process, in turn, can share its resources with its children and can also obtain further resources (using the *Request* primitive presented in Section 3.3.2), which it then *owns*.

A process is permitted to suspend only its descendants. The operation of suspension could be treated in two different ways. A call, *Suspend(ep, p)*, where *ep* is an external process name and p is a pointer to the process descriptor (returned by *Suspend*), could suspend only *ep*, or it could suspend *ep* and all its descendants; both these options may be desirable. The latter possibility is somewhat tricky, since some descendants may already have been suspended by their ancestors (which are descendants of *ep*). For example, the RC4000 system (Brinch Hansen, 1970) suspends in this manner, but, as a consequence, requires more complex process status types (see Exercises 3.2 and 3.3). Our solution is to permit suspension of only one process at a time, but to return enough information to the suspending process so that some or all of the further descendants may also be suspended if desired. This is accomplished by returning to the caller the pointer to the descriptor of the process being suspended; this pointer is the parameter p of the *Suspend* operation.

```
procedure Suspend(ep, p)
begin
  p := Get__Pointer(ep);
  s := p↑.Status;
  if s = 'running' then Stop(p);
  if s = 'blocked__a' then p↑.Status := 'blocked__s' else p↑.Status := 'ready__s';
  if s = 'running' then Scheduler
end
```

This procedure first obtains a pointer p to the descriptor of the process with the external identifier ep and then saves the value of p's Status field in s. The purpose of $Stop(p)$ is to interrupt the processor, c, executing p, store the state of c in p's descriptor, and set the corresponding pointer in the *Process* array (constituting the processor resource) to *NIL*, thus freeing the processor:

```
procedure Stop(p)
begin
  c := p↑.Processor;
  Interrupt(c);
  Store__State(c, p↑.CPU__State);
  Process[c] := NIL
end
```

The last two instructions of *Suspend* then change the status of p and, if p was running at the time *Suspend* was invoked, call the scheduler to allocate the processor to some other *ready__a* process. The suspended process remains linked within the list it occupied prior to its suspension.

Process activation is straightforward, involving a status change to active and a possible call on the scheduler. This call permits the option of preemption scheduling if the activated process becomes *ready__a*. A process may activate any of its known descendants, in particular, its progeny. Thus, the normal sequence for introducing a new process into the system is a *Create* followed by an *Activate*.

```
procedure Activate(ep);
begin
  p := Get__Pointer(ep);
  if p↑.Status = 'ready__s'
  then p↑.Status := 'ready__a' else p↑.Status := 'blocked__a';
  if p↑.Status = 'ready__a' then Scheduler
end
```

For destroying a process, the same alternatives are available as in the *Suspend* operation: one can either remove a single process (a descendant) or remove that process and all its descendants.[†] If the first policy were selected, the process hierarchy could easily fragment and disappear, potentially leaving isolated processes in the system with no control over their behavior. We therefore require that *Destroy* remove a process and *all* its descendants. There remains a question of what to do with the resources of the destroyed processes. The simplest policy here, and the one we choose, is to destroy all resource descriptors created by each destroyee and to return all *owned* serially reusable resources to their respective inventories. If the destroyer wishes detailed descriptor information on the destroyees, it could precede the *Destroy* by one or more *Suspend* operations.

    Destroy is invoked by the call *Destroy(ep)*, where *ep* is the external name of the "root" process of the tree to be removed. The procedure obtains the pointer to this process and calls the procedure *Kill(p)*, which recursively eliminates the entire tree. For each process *p* in the tree, *Kill* deletes *p* from the list pointed to by $p\uparrow.Status\_Data$; this is the ready list if *p* was running or ready, and the *Waiters* list of a resource if *p* was blocked. *Kill* then returns all owned resources to their availability lists and destroys all resource descriptors created by *p*; the latter is accomplished using the primitive *Destroy__RC* discussed in Section 3.3.2. The last instruction of *Kill* then eliminates the process descriptor itself. The process scheduler is called if at least one of the destroyed processes was running, which is recorded in the Boolean variable *sched*.

```
procedure Destroy(ep);
begin
    sched := false;
    p := Get__Pointer(ep);
    Kill(p);
    if sched then Scheduler
end;

procedure Kill(p);
begin
    if p↑.Status = 'running' then begin Stop(p); sched := true end;
    Delete(p↑.Status__Data, p);
    for all q in p↑.Progeny do Kill(q);
    for all r__unit in (p↑.Main__Store ∪ p↑.Resources) do
        if owned(r__unit) then
        begin r := Find__Descriptor(r__unit); Insert(r↑.Avail, r__unit) end;
        for all r in p↑.Created__Resources do Destroy__RC(r);
        Delete__Process__Descriptor(p)
end
```

    The final primitive, *Change__Priority(ep, k)*, changes the priority of process *ep*

[†]We will not permit a process to destroy itself directly; it can commit suicide by sending an appropriate message to a parent process.

to the value *k*. In general, this also requires that *ep* be moved to a different place in whatever list it resides to reflect the new priority. If processor preemption is desirable, the scheduler is called on a priority change.

In all the primitives, it is important that error checking also be included. For example, the last four operations require a test to assure that the named process is in fact a descendant of the caller; this check could be incorporated in the procedure *Get__Pointer*. There is also a problem related to duplication of external names; the direct progeny of each process must have distinct external names, and path names must be given as arguments to the primitives if the possibility of ambiguity exists.

3.3.2 Resource Primitives

As emphasized earlier, all process communication and resource allocation occurs through operations on resource classes. Four such primitives are defined:

1. *Create__RC:* Create the descriptor for a new resource class.
2. *Destroy__RC:* Destroy the descriptor of a resource class.
3. *Request:* Request some units of a resource class.
4. *Release:* Release some units of a resource class.

Following a description of these operations, we present several examples of their use and consider their implementation efficiency.

Create__RC and *Destroy__RC* are concerned with dynamically establishing and removing, respectively, resource descriptors from the system. Descriptors for most of the hardware resources are created at systems generation and at systems load time, while the other resources are created dynamically by systems and users' processes. *Create__RC* requires the initialization and definition of both the inventory and waiting lists, the specification of insertion and removal routines for these lists, and the definition of the allocator for the resource. Upon creation of the descriptor, an entry is made in the resource part of the creator's process descriptor that identifies the process as the creator of the resource.

As in the process case, a resource can be destroyed only by its creator or by an ancestor of the creator. The *Destroy__RC* primitive only names the resource class to be eliminated. It removes the named resource descriptor from the system and wakes up (changes from blocked to ready and inserts on the *RL* list) all processes waiting on that resource. The internal details of *Create__RC* and *Destroy__RC* will not be specified here.

A process requesting resources issues the command *Request(er, Req__details, Alloc__details)*, where *er* is the external name of a resource class, *Req__details* specifies the details of the request, and *Alloc__details* points to a record for storing the results of a satisfied request (i.e., the description of the particular allocation). Processes can be blocked only by their own actions and *only* through this operation. Blocking occurs if the allocator for the resource class cannot or will not satisfy the request immediately. The *Request* primitive is

```
procedure Request(er, Req__details, Alloc__details)
begin
    r := Get__Pointer(er);
    Insert(r↑.Waiters, (*, Req__details, Alloc__details));
    Allocator(r, L);
    self := ¬ on__L;
    while L ≠ NIL do    { for all elements on L}
    begin
        if  L↑.proc ≠ * then begin    {If process is not my own then . . .}
            p := L↑.Proc;   {. . . point p to process . . .}
            Insert(RL, p);
            p↑.Status__Data := RL;
            if p↑.Status = 'blocked__a'
            then p↑.Status := 'ready__a' else p↑.Status := 'ready__s'
        end else self := on__L;   {Remember that own process was on L}
        L := L↑.next;   {Go to next element of L}
    end;
    if self = ¬ on__L then begin    {Own process * must block itself }
        *↑.Status = 'blocked__a';
        *↑.Status__Data = r↑.Waiters;
        Process[*↑.Processor] := NIL;   {Release processor}
        Delete(RL, *)
    end;
    Scheduler
end
```

The strategy within *Request* is to form a request package consisting of the pointer to the calling process, *, the request details, and the allocation details pointer, insert that package on the waiting list, $r\uparrow.Waiters$, associated with the resource class *er*, and then call the allocator; this strategy ensures that the allocator need not distinguish between a *Request* and a *Release* operation. The allocator returns a list *L* of zero or more processes (see Section 3.2). *Request* then changes the status of all processes on *L*, with the exception of its own (*) status, to *ready__a* or *ready__s* and inserts these processes on the ready list, *RL*. The process * requires special attention: if it was on *L*, then *Request* simply exits and the process continues execution; if, however, * was not on *L*, it changes its status to *blocked__a* and sets the processor entry to *NIL*, indicating that it wishes to give up the processor as soon as the procedure (including *Scheduler*) terminates. *Scheduler* is always called at the end of the *Request* to determine any new processor allocations. This is perhaps too general for some situations where the request can be immediately satisfied, but the implementation price is not too high, and the system has the additional flexibility of making new scheduling decisions at that time.

When the allocator assigns resources to a waiting process, it stores the allocation information in the record pointed to by *Alloc_details*; if the resource is serially reusable, the allocation is also stored in the *Resource* list of the process descriptor. The first is needed so that the requesting process can identify the resource; the latter is necessary for resource sharing, process removal, and record keeping.

If a process no longer requires a previously obtained serially reusable resource or if it wishes to add units of a consumable resource to the inventory, it does so by means of the *Release* primitive. The call is *Release(er, Rel_details)*, where *er* is the name of a resource class and *Rel_details* defines the specifics of the freed resource units; *Rel_details* contains the same type of information as the *Alloc_details* parameter of *Request*. *Release* adds the *Rel_details* to the resource inventory and calls the allocator, which tries to satisfy outstanding requests of blocked processes. If allocations are made, the relevant processes are awakened and the scheduler is called:

```
procedure Release(er, Rel_details);
begin
    r := Get_Pointer(er);
    Insert(r↑.Avail, Rel_details);
    Allocator(r, L);
    if L ≠ NIL then begin    { for all elements on L }
        repeat
            p := L↑.Proc;    {Point p to process}
            Insert(RL, p);
            p↑.Status_Data := RL;
            if p↑.Status = 'blocked_a'
            then p↑.Status = 'ready_a' else p↑.Status = 'ready_s';
            L := L↑.next;    {Go to next element of L}
        until L = NIL;
        Scheduler    {Called only when L was not empty}
    end
end
```

Process status thus can be changed as a result of the *Request/Release* operations or any of the process primitives. Figure 3-5 summarizes the possible status changes and the operations causing these changes. Note that only the operation *Request* is performed by the process itself; the operations *Create*, *Suspend*, and *Activate* are issued by one of its ancestors, while the operation *Release* may be executed by any other running process.

The primitives *Request* and *Release* can handle all the resource and synchronization situations that we have encountered. The most variable part of their internal structure lies in the allocator routine. The following examples illustrate some common applications:

Semaphore Operations. *Request* and *Release* can implement the P and V operations, respectively. For a semaphore s, the corresponding calls are defined as *Request(s, Ω, Ω)* and *Release(s, Ω)*, where $Ω$ indicates undefined parameters. The inventory

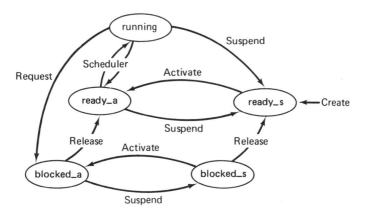

Figure 3-5 Process status changes.

is the value of s; *Insert* and *Remove* for the availability list merely increment and decrement, respectively, the value of s. The allocator determines if an allocation is possible by comparing the length of the waiting list with s. The P and V operations can be generalized to request and release any positive number of units, that is, *Request*(s, n, Ω) and *Release*(s, n), $n \geq 1$; in this case the allocator is considerably more complicated (see Exercise 3.8).

Message Passing.   Let us assume that a message producer sends messages to particular named processes and that message consumers (receivers) can request messages from known processes, that is, selective sends and receives (see Section 2.6.1). Then a message m may be transmitted to a process p by the call

Release(M, (p, m));

where M is the message resource class. A receiver requests a message from a process p by issuing

Request(M, p, m);

where m is a data area that will contain the message. The allocator matches messages to receivers. Other possibilities, for example when the receiver does not specify the sending process, can easily be implemented.

Main Storage Allocation.   For allocation and freeing of contiguous variable-length blocks of main storage, the calls might be

Request(Main__Storage, Number__of__Words, Base__Address);

and

Release(Main__Storage, (Base__Address, Number__of__Words));

Possible forms for the allocator and resource data structure are discussed in Chapter 5.

    With such a general set of primitives, it is appropriate to examine the questions of efficiency and implementation. To maintain our convention that a process can logically block only as a result of the *Request* primitive, the operations are protected by a common busy-wait lock; the same lock is used for all primitives that reference the system descriptors. The critical sections must not only be short, but there must also be a centralized control and responsibility for the allocators and list manipulation routines to assure their correctness and efficiency. This can be accomplished by maintaining a systems library of tested routines and data structures that may be referenced by users when resources are created. Weiderman (1971) has compared assembly and higher-level language implementations of similar *Request* and *Release* operations and common allocators and data structures with similar kernel operations available in several commercial systems; execution times were within the same order of magnitude. A comprehensive operating systems kernel, based on the ideas of Sections 3.1 and 3.2 and also including input/output driver processes and interrupt handlers has been implemented and used for constructing several experimental subsystems (Shaw et al., 1975).

    Details of error checking and analysis have been omitted in our discussion. The process tree structure and access conventions simplify this problem considerably. However, more extensive error tests would generally be required to validate and enforce restrictions on resource requests; for example, it would be desirable in many instances to limit the amount of a resource (e.g., storage) that a particular process can request or even forbid certain processes access to some resources.

    Our final remarks relate to noncritical and delayed requests. A process might wish more units of a resource immediately *if* it were available, but otherwise it could, and may want to, continue processing; similarly, a process may wish to enter a request that need not be satisfied immediately. The first case can be handled by specifying a pair $(0, n)$ in the data field of the request; the allocator is then designed to allocate 0 units (always possible) if n units are not available. The simplest implementation of the second type of request is to send a message to another process, which requests the resource in the normal fashion and releases an answer back to the original process when the resource has been allocated.

3.4 ORGANIZATION OF PROCESS SCHEDULERS

One major task performed by an operating system is to allocate ready processes to the available processors. This task may usefully be divided into two parts, frequently performed by different modules of the system. The first part, referred to as *process sched-*

uling, embodies decision-making policies that determine the order in which active processes should compete for the use of processors. The actual binding of a selected process to a processor, which involves removing the process from the ready queue, changing its status, and loading the processor state, is performed by a *process dispatcher*. In the following sections, unless explicitly distinguished, we will refer to both components jointly as the *scheduler*.

This section is concerned primarily with the *organization* of schedulers, as opposed to particular scheduling strategies; these will be discussed separately in Section 3.5.

3.4.1 Autonomous Versus Shared Schedulers

A process scheduler may be shared by processes in the system in the same manner that the kernel developed in this chapter is shared; that is, the scheduler is invoked by a subroutine call as an indirect result of a kernel operation. The kernel and the scheduler are then potentially contained in the address space of all processes and execute within any process. A second method is to centralize the scheduler (and possibly the kernel). Conceptually, this type of scheduler is considered a separate process running, possibly, on its own processor; it can continuously poll the system for work, or it may be driven by wakeup signals. The autonomous and the shared alternatives are illustrated in Figure 3-6. UNIX is an example of a system where the scheduler (dispatcher) is a separate process. It runs every other time (i.e., between any two other processes). (It also serves as the dummy process that runs when no other process is ready; see the footnote in

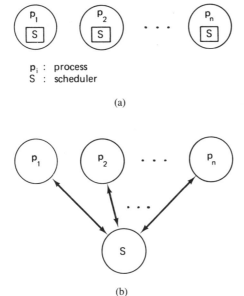

p_i : process
S : scheduler

(a)

(b)

Figure 3-6 Organization of schedulers:
(a) Shared scheduler (b) Master scheduler.

Section 2.4.4.2.) An example of a shared scheduler will be presented in detail in Section 3.4.2.

In multiprocessor systems where one processor is permanently dedicated to scheduling, kernel, and other supervisory activities such as IO and program loading, the autonomous process approach is preferable. In such an organization, referred to as a master/slave organization, the operating system is, at least in principle, cleanly separated from user processes.

Even if a separate processor is not dedicated exclusively to executing parts of the operating system, the autonomous scheduler approach is still possible in both single- and multiprocessor configurations. A logical difficulty, however, arises in these situations: who dispatches the scheduler process? One solution is to transfer control to the scheduler whenever a process blocks or is awakened; the scheduler exists at a higher level than the remaining processes.

Object-oriented Scheduling. The concept of an autonomous scheduler has been extended into a more general scheduling/dispatching framework in object-oriented systems, such as Intel's iAPX-432, where processes as well as processors are viewed as objects.

Scheduling involves moving a process between various process queues, whereas dispatching actually binds selected processes to a processor for execution. On a single-processor system, dispatching is accomplished by a context switch. On a multiprocessor system the dispatcher loads the status information of the process to be started into the free processor and initiates its execution.

Object-based systems permit scheduling and dispatching to be viewed in a more uniform way. Both are implemented using the same basic mechanisms as interprocess communication. Since a process is viewed as an object, it may be passed among other processes like any other object using the **send/receive** primitives. Dispatching is then accomplished by providing a special port, called the *dispatching port*, into which process objects may be queued using the **send** primitive. Processors are viewed as servers: using the **receive** primitive they remove process objects from the dispatching port and start their execution.

For scheduling, another port, the *scheduling port*, is provided. When a processor determines that the currently executing process should be rescheduled, it sends it to the scheduling port, from which it is eventually removed by a scheduler process, using the **receive** primitive. Hence the scheduler views other processes as objects on which certain scheduling operations are to be performed. When it decides that a process should be permitted to run again, it sends it to the dispatching port, from which it will eventually be removed by the dispatcher.

Figure 3-7 illustrates in simplified form the principles of scheduling and dispatching as they are implemented in the iAPX-432 architecture. Let's assume that the physical processor, represented by a *processor objects*, becomes idle. To obtain more work it performs an (implicit) **receive** operation on the dispatching port at which processes are queued while awaiting execution. As a result of this operation, a process, represented

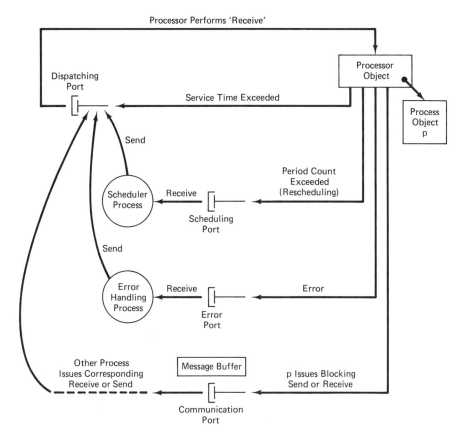

Figure 3-7 Scheduling and dispatching in an object-oriented system.

by a *process object p*, is dequeued and begins execution on the processor. It continues using the processor until one of the following events occurs:

1. Each process has a time quantum, called the *service time*, assigned to it by the scheduler. When this time is exceeded, the process is removed from the processor and is returned to the end of the dispatching queue. This action is performed automatically by the underlying hardware.

2. In addition to its service time, each process also has a *period count*, which specifies how many times the process may be dispatched to the processor. When this count is exceeded, the hardware automatically places the process into the scheduling rather than the dispatching port. A scheduler process eventually retrieves the process from the scheduling port and, treating it as a data object, reevaluates its state for future processing. When the scheduler decides the process should be permitted

to continue (with its newly set attributes), it places it back into the dispatching
port using a **send** primitive.

3. If the process causes an error, it is sent to a special *error port*, from which it is
   eventually dequeued and analyzed by an appropriate error-handling process. Depending on the result of this analysis, it may be terminated or sent back for dispatching.

4. The process may wish to communicate with some other process through a communication port using the **send/receive** primitives. When it issues a **send** operation
   on a port whose message buffer is full, or when it executes a **receive** operation on
   an empty port, it is suspended and placed on a queue associated with the named
   communication port. When some other process performs the corresponding **receive** or **send** operation, the suspended process is reactivated by the hardware and
   placed back into the dispatching port.

The object-oriented point of view offers a number of advantages due to its uniform
structure. Most importantly, it provides for an elegant separation of scheduling and dispatching and permits both to be treated as special cases of interprocess communication.
In addition, it allows other process management functions such as error handling or
various diagnostic tasks to be incorporated into the general framework by using the same
mechanisms of sending and receiving messages.

The uniform view of scheduling, dispatching, and handling of other process-related events as a form of interprocess communication is specially suitable for multiprocessor systems, since there is no need for a centralized scheduling/dispatching authority
responsible for assigning work to idle processors; rather, each processor obtains a new
task from the appropriate port as soon as it terminates its current work or is interrupted.

3.4.2 An Example of a Priority Scheduler

Having discussed some general ideas of scheduling and dispatching, we now present a
concrete example of a relatively complex priority scheduler/dispatcher. Following this,
we discuss a number of simplifications that may be made in common practical situations.

A shared scheduler approach was selected in this example for the following reasons. Because shared kernel components are automatically included in every process,
they are independent of the number of available processors and need not be permanently
associated with any particular one. The view that the kernel really defines a set of machine operations necessary to transform a standard computer into an operating systems
machine naturally leads to such a shared organization. A final point is that different
processes may in principle have different types of operating systems controlling them;
for example, a variety of different schedulers may coexist simultaneously, each attached
to (shared by) a different set of processes. When the kernel code is pure and single-copy
shared, the difference between the shared organization and the one providing an autonomous scheduler process running on nondedicated processors is more a difference of
point of view and less one of implementation strategy.

In the following, we assume that both scheduling and dispatching are performed by the same module or subroutine named *Scheduler*, which is called only within the kernel primitives of this chapter (i.e., within *Suspend*, *Activate*, *Destroy*, *Change__Priority*, *Request*, and *Release*). The ready list *RL* is structured on a priority basis as in Figure 3-4 and contains all processes p such that $p \uparrow.Status$ contains one of the values *running*, *ready__a*, or *ready__s*. A *preemptive* scheduling/dispatching policy is used. That is, the scheduler ensures that, at all times, the priority of any *running* process is greater or equal to that of any *ready__a* process.

The task of the *Scheduler* can be succinctly defined. At any time, let S_r be the set of running processes and S_{ra} be the set of *ready__a* and *running* processes in the system. Define S_a as the set of processes that *should* be running at a given time. S_a is the largest subset of S_{ra} with the properties

$$|S_a| = np \text{ (number of processors)}$$

and for all p in S_a and q in $(S_{ra} - S_a)$, where $p \neq q$,

1. $p \uparrow.Priority \geq q \uparrow.Priority$.
2. If $p \uparrow.Priority = q \uparrow.Priority$, then p precedes q in the *RL*.

The *Scheduler* guarantees that $S_a = S_r$ by allocating all members of $S_a - S_a \cap S_r$ to processors; it allocates these to inactive processors when $|S_r| < np$ and to preempted processors of all members of $S_r - S_r \cap S_a$. (For $|S_a| = np$, we also assume the existence of an idle process for each processor, with priority lower than any working process.)

An implementation, however, requires some care. One source of difficulty lies with the process, designated $*$, within which the *Scheduler* is called. If $*$ is being blocked, as a result of issuing a *Request*, or if $*$ is preempted from its processor, it is necessary to *defer* the transfer of control to some other process until *all* other allocations have been accomplished; otherwise, the *Scheduler* will not be able to complete these allocations since it is executing in the processor of $*$.

When a processor c, including $* \uparrow.Processor$, is reallocated, the state of c must be saved in the process descriptor component $p \uparrow.CPU\_State$. This can be tricky in the case of $*$; the instruction counter stored in $* \uparrow.CPU\_State$ must point to an instruction that allows $*$ to properly continue upon its later resumption (i.e., to return from the *Scheduler*). (Recall that the *Scheduler* is only invoked at the end of a primitive.) We accomplish a switch from process p to q by the procedure

```
procedure Switch(p, q);
begin
    c := p↑.Processor;  {Find processor of p }
    if p ≠ * then Interrupt(c);
    Store__State(c, p↑.CPU__State);
    if p = * then Adjust__Instr__Counter(*↑.CPU__State);
    Load__State(c, q↑.CPU__State);
end
```

Interrupt(c) interrupts processor c unless the process p to be stopped is the one executing *Switch* (i.e., the process *). The function of *Adjust__Instr__Counter* is to set the return address of * to point to the end of *Switch* (and thus to the end of *Scheduler*). This is necessary when * is the process being preempted. Finally *Load__State* transfers control to the new state by loading its state into the processor *c*. The details of *Switch* are highly dependent on the characteristics of the given computer architecture.

The global algorithm of the *Scheduler* for *n* priority levels (*n* being the highest) is then as follows:

```
procedure Scheduler;
begin
    cur__prio := n;    {Set cur__prio to highest priority}
    deferred := NIL;    {No process is initially deferred}
    loop
        Find__Highest(cur__prio, p);
        if p = NIL then Wrap__Up(deferred);    {terminate Scheduler}
        Allocate__Idle__CPU(p, found, q__min, deferred);
        if ¬ found ∧ q__min↑.Priority < p↑.Priority
        then Preempt(q__min,p, deferred);
    end {loop}
end
```

The variable *cur__prio* is global throughout the *Scheduler*; it steps through the priority levels from *n* to 1 whenever the *Scheduler* is invoked. The first procedure, *Find__Highest*, searches for the highest-priority *ready__a* process *p* on the ready list *RL*, starting with the priority level *cur__prio*. If *p* is not *NIL*, the scheduler calls *Allocate__Idle__CPU*; this searches for an inactive processor on which to start *p*. If all processors are busy, *Allocate__Idle__CPU* returns a pointer, *q__min*, to the lowest-priority running process. This is used by the scheduler to test if *p* should preempt that process; if this is the case, the procedure *Preempt* is called, which replaces the lowest-priority process with the process *p* on the appropriate processor.

This cycle is repeated until the ready list is exhausted, as indicated by *p* = *NIL*. At this time, the scheduler exits by calling the procedure *Wrap__Up*. To understand the significance of the parameter *deferred*, we must first consider the other procedures called by *Scheduler* in more detail:

```
procedure Find__Highest(cur__prio, p);
begin
    p := NIL;
    found := false;
    while (p = NIL) ∧ (cur__prio > 0) do
    begin
        cur := RL↑[cur__prio].first;    {Point cur to first process at level cur__prio}
        while ¬ found ∧ (cur ≠ NIL) do    {Scan level cur__prio}
            if cur↑.proc↑.Status = 'ready__a' then
```

```
        begin
            p := cur↑.proc;
            found := true;
        end else cur := cur↑.next;
        cur_prio := cur_prio − 1;   {Move to next lower priority level}
    end
end
```

Find_Highest searches the linked list of processes at each level of *RL*, starting with *cur_prio*. If a process is found, *p* is assigned to point to that process; otherwise, *p* remains *NIL*.

```
procedure Allocate_Idle_CPU(p, found, q_min, deferred);
begin
    found := false; cpu := 1; q_min := p;   {Initial assignment of q_min}
    while ¬ found ∧ (cpu ≤ np) do   {Scan all processors}
    begin
        if Process[cpu] = NIL then   {If processor is idle ...}
        begin   {... start p on that processor}
            found := true;
            Process[cpu] := p;
            p↑.Processor := cpu;
            p↑.Status := 'running';
            if cpu = *↑.Processor   {If own processor is "idle" ...}
            then deferred := p   {... then remember p ...}
            else Load_State(cpu, p↑.CPU_State);   {... else start p}
        end else
        if Process[cpu]↑.Priority < q_min↑.Priority
        then q_min := Process[cpu];   {Remember lowest priority process}
        cpu := cpu + 1
    end
end
```

Allocate_Idle_CPU scans all processors (1 through *np*); if one is found idle, indicated by the corresponding *Process* entry being *NIL*, then the *Process* entry is changed to *p* and the *Processor* and *Status* entry in *p*'s descriptor are set accordingly. If the found processor is not the one running the scheduler process itself, it is loaded with the *CPU_State* of *p*; otherwise, the process *p* is only "remembered" as *deferred*. Note that the latter condition can occur if the scheduler is called from the primitive *Request*; recall that this primitive sets that *Process* entry to *NIL* if it does not find itself on the list *L*. It, however, continues execution and enters the scheduler. Hence, finding *Process[cpu]* = *NIL*, where *cpu* is the processor executing the scheduler, means that the current process * is to be blocked as soon as the scheduler terminates. While searching for an idle processor, *Allocate_Idle_CPU* also memorizes the lowest-priority running process, *q_min*, used by the procedure *Preempt*.

```
procedure Preempt(q__min, p, deferred);
begin
    q__min↑.Status := 'ready__a';   {Change status}
    p↑.Status := 'running';
    p↑.Processor := q__min↑.Processor;   {Reassign processor}
    Process[q__min↑.Processor] := p;
    if q__min = *   {If own process is being preempted ...}
    then deferred := p   {... then remember p ...}
    else Switch(q__min, p)   {... else perform preemption}
end
```

This procedure preempts the process *q__min*, the lowest-priority running process, from its processor and starts the process *p*, which was found previously to be the highest-priority *ready__a* process. Special care must be taken if the process to be preempted is the one currently running the scheduler. In this case, the actual preemption must be postponed in order to permit the scheduler to complete its task, which is accomplished by "remembering" the process *p* as the process *deferred* while the scheduler continues.

```
procedure Wrap__Up(deferred);
begin
    if *↑.Status ≠ 'running' then Switch(*, deferred);
    exit Scheduler
end
```

This procedure exits from the scheduler. Prior to exiting, however, a final process switch may take place between the process *, currently running the scheduler, and the *deferred* process. Recall that a value might have been assigned to *deferred* for two reasons: (1) when a process issues a request that cannot be satisfied, it blocks itself; this block, however, must not become effective until the scheduler, invoked at the end of *Request*, runs to completion; (2) when the process currently running the scheduler has a lower priority than some process on the ready list, preemption must be performed; the actual process switch, however, must be postponed until the scheduler has run to completion. This final switch must be performed as the last operation of the scheduler.

The scheduler, while manageable, can nevertheless be considerably simplified if some of the underlying assumptions are relaxed. Consider first the elimination of preemption. The scheduler then need not be called on a *Change__Priority* operation and about half of the code (and time) is eliminated. The very common situation in which only a single central processor is available ($np = 1$) leads to a much less complex scheduling algorithm. In this case, *Suspend* would never invoke the *Scheduler* and at most one process switch could occur. Another possibility is to limit allocators so that at most *one* process is ever taken off a blocked list (awakened) at any time. Various combinations of the methods are also widely used (see Exercise 3.9).

3.5 SCHEDULING METHODS

In a typical state of execution, the number of active processes able to run exceeds the number of available processors. The task of a scheduler, when invoked, is to examine the current allocation of processes to CPUs and, when appropriate, perform a reallocation according to some scheduling policy. It is usually desirable to employ different strategies for different types of processes. For example, we might wish to discriminate between processes associated with batch jobs and those of interactive users, between system and user processes, or between processes dealing directly with IO and those for purely internal activities. With a general priority mechanism and the careful use of timers, a uniform organization can be designed to handle a broad spectrum of such strategies. In this section we will present a general framework for possible scheduling strategies and discuss a variety of common schemes within this framework. Such strategies then could be incorporated into actual schedulers, such as the one presented in Section 3.4.2, depending on the systems requirements.

3.5.1 The Universal Scheduler

Following the approach of Ruschitzka and Fabry (1977), we introduce a *universal scheduler*, which is specified in terms of the following three concepts:

1. A decision mode
2. A priority function
3. An arbitration rule

At certain times specified by the *decision mode*, the universal scheduler evaluates the *priority function* for all active processes in the system; for each of these processes the priority function yields a value, referred to as the *current priority*. The processes with the highest priorities are assigned to the existing CPUs. The *arbitration rule* is applied in case there are multiple processes with the same priority.

Depending on the particular decision mode, priority function, and arbitration rule, different scheduling disciplines may be defined. We will show that most existing schedulers may be expressed in terms of the universal scheduler.

The Decision Mode.   The decision mode specifies the instants in time, or *decision epochs*, at which process priorities are evaluated and compared and at which processes are selected for execution. The allocation of processes to CPUs cannot change between two consecutive decision epochs.

We can distinguish between two basic types of decision modes: *nonpreemptive* and *preemptive*. In the first case, a process, once started, is always allowed to run when logically possible; that is, scheduling decisions are made only when a process terminates or blocks itself by requesting some service from the operating system or when a newly arriving process finds an idle CPU. Although they are more economical, nonpreemptive algorithms are usually not adequate in real-time or time-shared systems. Rather, a preemptive decision mode must be used, which permits a currently running process to be stopped and the CPU assigned to some other process with equal or higher priority. The decision as to whether a preemption should be attempted may be performed when a new process arrives, when an existing process is awakened as a result of a message or interrupt, or periodically each time a process has executed for a period of q seconds. In the latter case, the algorithm is usually called *quantum oriented*, with q as its quantum size. Another possible strategy would be to perform a preemption whenever the priority of a ready process rises above the priority of a currently running process. This could occur in systems that dynamically change the relative priorities of existing processes.

Preemptive scheduling policies are usually more costly than nonpreemptive policies due to process switching times, the additional logic in the scheduler itself, and swapping of programs and data between primary and secondary memories. Between the two extremes of preemption versus nonpreemption lies another set of possibilities, which we label *selective preemption*.

One such selective policy would assign a bit pair, say (u_p, v_p), to each process p with the interpretation

$$u_p = \begin{cases} 1, & \text{if } p \text{ may preempt another process} \\ 0, & \text{otherwise} \end{cases}$$

$$v_p = \begin{cases} 1, & \text{if } p \text{ may be preempted by some other process} \\ 0, & \text{otherwise} \end{cases}$$

Thus u_p defines the preemptive capability of a process and v_p is really a running priority. (u_p, v_p) would be another component of the process state vector, used in an obvious way by the scheduler. Proceeding in the direction of even more generality, the priority of a process p may be changed to a pair (Π_p, Φ_p), where Π_p represents the ready status priority of p and Φ_p is the priority of p when it is running. Different levels of control are then possible over the preemption power of one process relative to another. Finally, a universal, and probably impractical, scheme requires a preemption matrix with entries (i, j) indicating whether or not a process i can preempt process j. Many of the preceding effects, however, can be obtained through the judicious use of the *Suspend* and *Change_Priority* operations called by high-priority controlling processes, in conjunction with the preemption mechanisms presented earlier.

Example

In a simple batch operating system, most processes can be mutually nonpreemptive. The main exceptions are IO driver processes that service the various peripheral devices, and timer processes that control CPU allocation time. IO processes must be able to preempt most others for two primary reasons. First, the servicing of some devices is time critical; if not handled within a certain period of time, data could be lost. Second, devices should not be left idle for extensive periods of time in order to guarantee their efficient utilization.

Thus, when an interrupt is issued by a device requesting service, the appropriate IO-handling process must be able to preempt any other user or system process. This could be accomplished by setting the (u_p, v_p) bits to $(1, 0)$ for time-critical processes and to $(0, 1)$ otherwise.

The Priority Function.   The priority function is an arbitrary function of process and system parameters. At any time, a process's *priority* is defined as the value of the priority function applied to the current values of the parameters. Some of the parameters on which priorities may be based are as follows:

Memory requirements
Attained service time
Real time in system
Total service time
External priorities
Timeliness
System load

Memory requirements serve as a major scheduling criterion in batch operating systems. In interactive systems, they are also important since they are a good measure of swapping overhead; but the *attained service time*, which is the time during which the process was using the CPU, is usually the most important parameter. The *real time in system* is the actual time the process has spent in the system since its arrival. It is composed of the attained service time and the waiting time during which the process was idle. Note that the attained service time increases at the rate of the actual (real) time when the process is running and remains constant when the process is waiting for the CPU.

The *total service time* is the amount of CPU time the process will consume during its lifetime; it is equal to the attained service time at the point the process terminates. Some systems assume that the total service time is known in advance. This is usually true of batch processes where the programmer is asked to specify a limit on the total service time in order to prevent 'infinite' execution in the case of a program error. If the total service time is known, an appealing philosophy adopted by many installations is to assign higher priority to shorter processes. We give two arguments leading to this philosophy. The first is that users will not be satisfied unless they receive fast service for short tasks; otherwise, they may choose to take their business elsewhere. (Supermarkets have long recognized this elementary fact by providing special checkout counters for customers with few items.) The second reason derives from a theoretical consideration: the order in which processes are executed has no effect on the total time required to complete all processes; the preferential treatment of shorter processes, however, reduces the average time a process spends in the system. (We will return to this issue in Section 3.5.3.)

External priorities may be used to differentiate between various classes of user and system processes. For example, the highest priorities may be assigned to real-time processes, the next lower priorities to interactive processes, and the lowest to batch processes. A cost, based on the type of resources employed, is frequently associated with each priority level; this permits users to select the priority for their processes that will provide adequate service (response) at a price they can afford. For example, a process at priority Π could be charged $\$f_1(\Pi)/sec$ for processor time, $\$f_2(\Pi)/word/sec$ for main memory, $\$f_3(\Pi)/sec$ for terminal connect time, and $\$f_4(\Pi)/line$ for IO.

Timeliness takes into account the fact that the urgency of completing a task may vary with time. A possible strategy would be to increase priority with the time a process spends in the system to minimize the accrued cost resulting from managing delayed processes. The need for such a philosophy also arises in situations where the results of certain computations are time sensitive in that their usefulness or value decreases with time. For example, the results of a weather forecast are useless after the date for which the prediction was made. In such situations, *deadlines* may also be imposed to guarantee the completion of time-sensitive computations.

System load is another important parameter owing to its significant effect on system response. Under heavy load, some schedulers attempt to maintain good response to high-priority processes by discriminating more strongly among external priorities; thus the distinction between the "rich" and the "poor" becomes even more pronounced when resources become scarce. Others take a more "socialistic" point of view by attempting to increase the overall system throughput, for example by reducing swapping overhead through the use of larger quantum sizes; this improves the general conditions for all participants uniformly.

The Arbitration Rule.   This rule resolves conflicts among processes with equal priority. If the likelihood of two or more processes having the same priority is low due to the nature of the priority function, the choice may be performed at *random*. In quantum-oriented preemptive scheduling algorithms, processes with equal highest priority are usually assigned quanta in a *cyclic* (round-robin) manner. In most other schemes, a *chronological* ordering (FIFO) of process arrivals is maintained to serve as an arbitration rule.

3.5.2 Time-based Scheduling Algorithms

The universal scheduler presented in Section 3.5.1 provides a general framework for process scheduling: any scheduling algorithm may be expressed by specifying a decision mode, a priority function of various parameters, and an arbitration rule. A large class of important scheduling algorithms requires a priority function of only three arguments: $P(a, r, t)$, where a is the attained service time, r is the real time that the process has spent in the system, and t is the total service time required by the process. We will refer to these as *time-based* algorithms since all parameters are related to time. A subset of this class of algorithms is independent of the required service time t and thus can be characterized by a priority function of only two parameters: $P(a, r)$. Algorithms in this class are of particular interest in interactive systems where advance knowledge of a process's time requirements is not available.

In the following, we will demonstrate that most of the well-known scheduling algorithms used in existing systems may be defined in terms of a decision mode, a time-based priority function, and an arbitration rule. These are summarized in Table 3-1.

First-in/First-out.   The first-in/first-out (FIFO) strategy dispatches processes according to their arrival time: the earlier the arrival, the higher the process's priority. Hence the priority function depends only on the real time r a process has spent in the system and may be expressed as $P(r) = r$. The decision mode of FIFO is nonpreemptive while its arbitration rule assumes a random choice among processes arriving at exactly the same time.

Last-in/First-out.   The last-in/first-out (LIFO) strategy assigns priorities in the reversed order of process arrival (i.e., a process's priority decreases in real time). The corresponding priority function has the form $P(r) = -r$. The decision mode and the arbitration rule are the same as with FIFO, that is, nonpreemptive and random. While LIFO is not common in contemporary computer systems, it represents an important policy used in operations research. We have included it in our considerations primarily to demonstrate the expressive power of the universal scheduler framework.

Shortest Job Next.   The shortest-job-next (SJN) policy (sometimes also referred to as shortest job first, or SJF) assumes that the total service time t is known in advance. For that reason it is usually applicable only to batch processes. SJN is a nonpreemptive strategy that dispatches processes according to their total service time; thus the priority function may be expressed as $P(t) = -t$. A chronological or random ordering is normally assumed as an arbitration rule among processes with the same time requirements.

Shortest Remaining Time.   The shortest-remaining-time (SRT) policy may be viewed as the preemptive version of the SJN policy; it assigns the highest priority to

TABLE 3-1 CHARACTERISTICS OF SCHEDULING ALGORITHMS.

Scheduling Algorithm	Priority Function	Decision Mode	Arbitration Rule
FIFO	r	Nonpreemptive	Random
LIFO	$-r$	Nonpreemptive	Random
SJN	$-t$	Nonpreemptive	Chronological or random
SRT	$a - t$	Preemptive (at arrival)	Chronological or random
RR	Constant	Preemptive (at quantum)	Cyclic
MLF	(see text)	Preemptive (at quantum)	Cyclic or chronological (within queues)
PD	$r - f^{-1}(a)$	Preemptive (at quantum)	Random

processes that will need the least amount of time to complete. Thus the priority function has the form $P(a, t) = a - t$. The same decision mode and arbitration rule as in SJN are usually employed.

Round Robin.   The round-robin (RR) scheduling discipline imposes a fixed time quantum q, also referred to as _time slice_, on the amount of _continuous_ processor time that may be used by any process. If a process has run for q continuous time units, it is preempted from its processor and placed at the end of the list of processes waiting for the processor. Thus a cyclic ordering is enforced as the arbitraton rule. Note that all processes always have the same priority. The RR behavior is enforced by assuming a quantum-oriented decision mode that causes the assignment of processes to processors to be reevaluated every q time units. Since the priorities of all processes are the same, the cyclic arbitration rule is applied at that time.

The time quantum q may be constant for long periods of time, or it may vary with the process load. If the time Q for one complete round robin of all active processes is to be kept constant, then q can be computed dynamically every Q seconds as $q = Q/n$, where n is the number of active processes competing for the CPU. Methods based on the RR scheme are used by most time-sharing systems for handling interactive processes.

Multilevel Feedback.   The multilevel feedback (MLF) scheduling policy provides n different priority levels. At each priority level Π, there is a corresponding time T_{Π}, which is the maximum amount of processor time any process may receive at that level; if a process exceeds T_{Π}, its priority is decreased to $\Pi - 1$. One possible scheme is to let $T_{\Pi} = 2^{n-\Pi} \times T_n$, where T_n is the maximum time on the highest-priority queue and n is the number of priority levels. With this scheme, a process will spend a time T_n at level n, $2 \times T_n$ at level $n - 1$, $4 \times T_n$ at level $n - 2$, and so on. Thus a process migrates to lower-priority levels as it consumes more CPU time. When it reaches the lowest level 1, it remains there for a period of $2^{n-1} \times T_n$ time units. Exceeding this time may either be interpreted as error (i.e., a runaway process), or this period could explicitly be set to infinity, allowing processes to remain at the lowest level indefinitely.

The organization of the MLF queues is shown in Figure 3-8. A newly arrived process or a process awakened as a result of an IO completion is usually queued at the highest priority level n, where it must share the processor with all other processes at the same level. When it has received the maximum of T_n units of CPU time, it is moved to the next lower priority queue. The CPU is always serving the highest nonempty queue. Thus a process at a level Π receives service only when the queues at levels n through $\Pi + 1$ are empty.

The arbitration rule for the MLF discipline can be either a chronological or a cyclic ordering within each queue. In the first case, each level may be viewed as following a FIFO discipline: the process at the head of the highest-priority nonempty queue Π is assigned a processor, and it executes until it runs to completion or exhausts the maximum time T_{Π}, at which time it is moved to the next lower priority queue $\Pi - 1$. If the cyclic arbitration rule is employed, processes at each level are sharing the processor in a round-

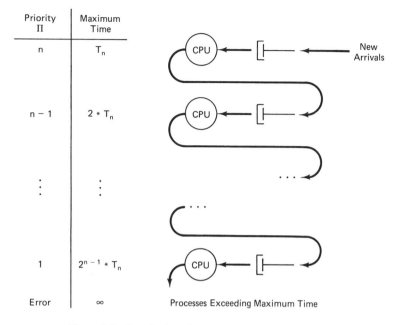

Figure 3-8 Organization of queues with MLF scheduling.

robin fashion. Usually, each of the times T_Π is a multiple of the basic quantum q; thus a process at level Π receives T_Π/q time quanta before it is moved to the next lower priority queue.

The priority function $P(a)$ for the MLF scheduling discipline is derived as follows. The priority of a process changes from Π to $\Pi - 1$ whenever its total attained service time exceeds the sum of all times attained at each of the levels n through Π. Assuming the scheme where $T_\Pi = 2^{n-\Pi} \times T_n$, the attained time a satisfies the following relation:

$$T_n * \sum_{i=0}^{n-\Pi-1} 2^i \le a < T_n * \sum_{i=0}^{n-\Pi} 2^i, \qquad 0 \le \Pi < n$$

By substituting $2^{x+1} - 1$ for $\Sigma_{i=0}^x 2^i$, where x may be any value, we obtain

$$T_n * (2^{n-\Pi} - 1) \le a < T_n * (2^{n-\Pi+1} - 1), \qquad 0 \le \Pi < n$$

This relation may be used to determine a process's priority, given its attained service time a. Specifically, $P(a) = \Pi$. By substituting $n - i$ for Π, we can express the priority function for the MLF scheduling discipline as follows:

$$P(a) = n - i, \quad \text{where } i \text{ is a function of } a \text{ that satisfies the relation}$$

$$T_n * (2^i - 1) \le a < T_n * (2^{i+1} - 1), \qquad 0 \le i < n$$

The latter can be transformed into the form

$$2^i \le \frac{a}{T_n} + 1 < 2^{i+1}, \qquad 0 \le i < n$$

When $a < T_n$, i is zero, resulting in the highest priority level n. As a increases, i steps through the values 1 through $n - 1$, which yields the corresponding priority levels $n - 1$ through 1. When a exceeds the value $T_n * (2^n - 1)$, the priority becomes less than 1, which can be interpreted as an error.

Policy-driven Scheduling.   A policy-driven (PD) scheduling discipline is based on a function $f(r)$, called the *policy function*, which prescribes the correlation between the real time, r, that a process has spent in the system and the *desired* amount of services the process should have received at that time. In the original proposal (Bernstein and Sharp, 1971), services were measured in terms of time units during which a particular resource was used by the process. That is, at time r, the total amount of services $s(r)$ received by a process may be expressed as

$$s(r) = \sum_{j=1}^{n} w_j * \text{units}_j(r)$$

where units_j gives the number of time units the resource j was used by the process up to the time r, w_j is the weight associated with the resource, and n is the number of distinct resources to be considered by the scheduler. For example, if the resources to be considered were the CPU and an IO processor, the total services received by a process at time r would be calculated by the formula

$$s(r) = w_{cpu} * \text{units}_{cpu}(r) + w_{iop} * \text{units}_{iop}(r)$$

where $\text{units}_{cpu}(r)$ corresponds to the attained service time, as defined earlier, and $\text{units}_{iop}(r)$ gives the service time attained by the process on the IO processor.

The priority of a process is based on how closely the process's execution behavior follows the prescribed function (i.e., on the distance between the policy function f and the attained services function s). To simplify the presentation, we will assume that the CPU is the only resource to be considered. Hence the total services received by a process are expressed exclusively by the attained service time: $s(r) = a$. Similarly, the policy function gives the desired correlation between real time and attained service time: for each point in real time, r_t, $f(r_t)$ prescribes the amount of service time a process *should* have received up to that point. Alternately, $f^{-1}(a_t)$, where f^{-1} is the inverse of f, may be interpreted as specifying the real time, r_t, at which the process should have attained a_t of service time.

Assume that r_t is the real time of a process at time t and a_t is the attained service time at that time. Ideally, a_t should be equal to $f(r_t)$ for any t. Unfortunately, when the computing demand exceeds the available capacity, some processes receive less than their fair share of processor time. Similarly, when a process is running, it may actually exceed the prescribed attained time. These deviations from the prescribed behavior automatically change the process's priority, which is defined as the difference between the real time r_t *actually* spent in the system and the real time *prescribed* for a_t by the policy function f. That is, the priority function has the form

$$P(a_t, r_t) = r_t - f^{-1}(a_t)$$

From this definition it follows that the current priority of a process increases with real time when the process is not receiving any service. Consequently, a process should be running as long as its current priority is positive and should stop when this value falls below zero. (Note that when the process is running, its priority may be increasing, decreasing, or remain the same, depending on the slope of the policy curve.)

To illustrate this principle, consider Figure 3-9. Assume that at time r_i the process has received a_i units of service time. The priority function yields the positive value $P(a_i, r_i) = r_i - f^{-1}(a_i)$, indicating that more service time should be granted to the process. If the process continues running until the real time r_j and, as a result, attains a_j units of service time, its priority $P(a_j, r_j) = r_j - f^{-1}(a_j)$ will decrease to a negative value. When the process remains inactive for a period of time, its priority will grow with r until the process is again resumed. Ideally, each process should always follow the prescribed policy function f, thus maintaining a priority value equal to zero.

3.5.3 Comparison of Scheduling Methods

The first four algorithms discussed, FIFO, LIFO, SJN, and SRT, have primarily been developed for batch processing systems. The first two are the simplest to implement

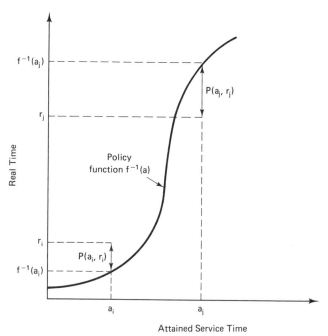

Figure 3-9   A policy function for PD scheduling.

since processes are maintained on a list (a queue in the case of FIFO and a stack in the case of LIFO) in the order of their arrival. SJN, on the other hand, requires that processes be kept sorted according to their time requirement, implying that the queue must be searched each time a new process arrives. In the case of SRT, similar comparisons of times needed to complete the active processes must be performed and, in addition, preemption of the currently running process may have to be performed.

One major criterion used to compare these four scheduling algorithms is the *average turnaround time* (*att*) of all processes, defined by the expression $(\Sigma_{i=1}^{n} r_i)/n$, where r_i is the real time each process i spent in the system, and n is the total number of active processes. The following example illustrates that the SJN and SRT algorithms yield an improvement in average turnaround times over the FIFO discipline.

Example

Consider three batch processes, p_1, p_2, and p_3, with the following arrival times and total service times:

	Arrival	Service
p_1	t	4
p_2	t	2
p_3	$t + 3$	1

Figure 3-10 shows the timing diagram for completing the three processes under FIFO, SJN, and SRT scheduling disciplines.

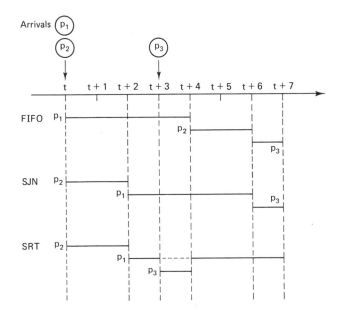

Figure 3-10 Process completion under different scheduling disciplines.

FIFO: Since both p_1 and p_2 arrived at the same time, we assume that p_1 is started first; p_2 and p_3 then follow in the order of their arrival.

SJN: p_2 has a shorter service time than p_1 and thus is started first. When it terminates, p_1 is the only process waiting and thus is started. Finally, p_3, which arrived in the meantime, is processed.

SRT: p_2 and p_1 begin at the same respective times as under SJN. However, when p_3 arrives, its remaining time is only 1 unit of time, whereas the remaining time of p_1 is 3. Thus p_1 is preempted and must wait for the completion of p_3.

Table 3-2 shows the turnaround times for each process, computed as the sum of the waiting time and the total service time. The last column shows the average turnaround time for all three processes.

In time-shared systems, where a number of users interact with the system in the form of a dialog, a scheduler should guarantee an acceptable *response time* for each user. This implies that a preemptive algorithm must be used, which permits the preemption of processes at definite time intervals predetermined by the system. Of the seven algorithms presented, only the last three (RR, MLF, and PD) satisfy this requirement. RR is the simplest to implement and therefore it is relied on heavily in most existing systems. It divides the CPU time evenly among all active processes according to the quantum size q, which becomes the most important parameter of this class of algorithms. If q is large, process switching is less frequent and thus overhead is reduced; response time will of course deteriorate as well. In the extreme case, where $q \to \infty$, processes are never preempted and thus the RR algorithm turns into a FIFO discipline. At the other extreme, where $q \to 0$, all processes may be viewed as running simultaneously at a speed divided by the number of currently active processes. This, however, is only of theoretical interest since the overhead with process switching grows toward infinity as the quantum size approaches zero.

Frequently, more sophisticated preemption schemes that discriminate among different groups of processes based on priorities are needed. The criteria for assigning priorities may be based on a variety of parameters, including external values; more often, they are based on measurements of process behavior rather than a priori declarations. Most of the dynamic schemes are designed to move interactive and IO-bound processes to the top of the priority queues and to let CPU-bound processes drift to lower levels. The MLF policy accomplishes this objective by always placing new processes and those

TABLE 3-2 CALCULATION OF PROCESS
TURNAROUND TIMES.

	p_1	p_2	p_3	Mean
FIFO	0 + 4	4 + 2	3 + 1	14/3 = 4.66
SJN	2 + 4	0 + 2	3 + 1	12/3 = 4.00
SRT	3 + 4	0 + 2	0 + 1	10/3 = 3.33

awakened as a result of IO completion into the highest-priority queue. Processes with short computation phases between IO operations do not exhaust the maximum times associated with the top levels and thus tend to retain higher priority over processes with few IO operations.

The PD algorithm is the most general of the three algorithms that do not depend on the total service time t, since it permits an arbitrary policy function to be specified as part of its priority function. By selecting different policy functions, the algorithm can be made sensitive to the needs of different types of processes. For example, a function that begins with a nonzero value (at the process's starting time) and remains constant for the lifetime of the process guarantees immediate attention by the CPU but prevents an overloading of the system when longer service periods are required; such a function could be used with short real-time processes. A function that rises sharply for the first few milliseconds but has only a moderate increase rate thereafter is designed for normal interactive computing; it offers fast response to short interactions, but deteriorates quickly when longer service periods are needed. Finally, a batch process could be assigned a priority function with a constant rate of increase, which would attempt to keep the process's turnaround time in proportion to its length.

Example

The VAX/VMS operating system provides an elegant scheduling algorithm, which combines the principles of several disciplines discussed earlier (Digital Equipment Corp., 1982). There are 32 priority levels divided into two groups of 16. Priorities 31 to 16, where 31 is the highest, are reserved for *real-time* processes. Other processes, referred to as *regular*, occupy priority levels 15 to 0.

The priority assigned to a real-time process is fixed for the duration of that process. Priorities of regular processes, on the other hand, float in response to various events occurring in the system. A *base* priority is assigned to each such process when it is created; this specifies its minimum priority level. The process's *current* priority then varies dynamically with its recent execution history according to the following rules. Each system event has an assigned priority *increment* that is characteristic of the cause of that event. For example, terminal read completion has a higher increment value than terminal write completion, which, in turn, has a higher value than disk IO completion. When a process is awakened due to one of these events, the corresponding increment is added to its current priority value and the process is enqueued at the appropriate level. When the process is preempted, after receiving its fair share of CPU usage, its current priority is decremented by 1, which places it into the next lower priority queue. Thus the priority of a regular process fluctuates between its base priority and the value 15, which is the maximum priority for any regular process. This concept is illustrated in Figure 3-11.

Processes are always dispatched strictly according to their current priority. This guarantees that real-time processes have precedence over regular processes; only when no real-time process is awaiting execution will a regular process be scheduled.

Preemption of a currently running process from the CPU may be caused by a number of events. A real-time process is preempted only when it blocks itself, for example by issuing an IO instruction, or when a higher-priority process arrives or is awakened; otherwise, it is permitted to run to completion. A regular process is preempted for the same reasons; in addition, it is also preempted when it exceeds its time quantum. When this

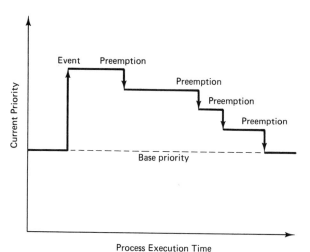

Current Priority

Event   Preemption

Preemption

Preemption

Preemption

Base priority

Process Execution Time

Figure 3-11 Priority changes of a process in VAX/VMS.

occurs, the process is stopped and placed into the next lower priority queue. Thus regular processes are prevented from monopolizing the CPU.

We note that the scheduling algorithm for normal processes (levels 15 to 0) is a variant of the MLF discipline described in Section 3.5.2. The two main distinctions are that (1) under MLF, processes always start at the highest priority level and, if not blocked, propagate toward the lowest level. The VMS scheduler restricts the priority range within which a process may float; the lowest level is given by the process's base priority, whereas the highest level depends on the type of event that caused the reactivation of the process. (2) A quantum is associated with a process rather than with a priority level, which permits the scheduler to discriminate among individual processes.

EXERCISES

3.1. There are four processes p_1 through p_4 in a single-processor system. p_1 has created p_2 and p_3; it also has created two resource classes r_1 and r_2, each consisting of only one unit of that resource. The process p_3 has created the process p_4. Presently, p_1 is *running*, p_2 is *ready__a*, and p_3 and p_4 are both *blocked__a* on the resource r_1. Show the details of all process and resource descriptors and their interconnections (pointers) reflecting the system state described.

3.2. Suppose that the *Suspend* and *Activate* operations are similar to *Destroy* in that they also apply to all descendants of the named process. Also assume that *Suspend* and *Activate* may name only a direct progeny as their argument process. Modify *Suspend* and *Activate* so that a process p invoking *Activate* only activates those descendant processes that were *previously* suspended by p, and *Suspend* suspends only those processes that are active. (*Hint:* Devise additional suspended status types to indicate the source of suspension.)

3.3. In Exercise 3.2 it was assumed that the *Suspend* and *Activate* operations may name only a *direct* progeny (i.e., a child process) as their argument. Extend the solution so that *any* progeny (i.e., child, grandchild, grandgrandchild, etc.) may be named. Assume that processes are well behaved; that is, a process will not attempt to activate processes it has not previously suspended.

3.4. Consider the *Request* procedure of Section 3.3.2. Assume that a different allocator is used, which attempts to satisfy the request of *only* the invoking process; that is, instead of the list *L*, it returns a Boolean variable *satisfied*, which is *true* if the request is granted and *false* otherwise. Show the modified *Request* procedure.

3.5. Assume there are only three process states: *running*, *ready*, and *blocked* (i.e., the distinction between *active* and *suspended* processes is eliminated). Simplify the process and resource primitives of Section 3.3 accordingly. Show also the new forms of the process and resource descriptors.

3.6. Implement *P* and *V* with *Request* and *Release* operations, respectively; in particular, define the data structures of the appropriate lists, the *Insert* and *Remove* procedures, and the allocator.

3.7. Repeat Exercise 3.6 for the bounded semaphore operations defined in Exercise 2.18.

3.8. Repeat Exercise 3.6 for the generalized *P* and *V* operations described at the end of the first example (Semaphore Operations) of Section 3.3.2.

3.9. Give a complete *Scheduler* for each case when the following restrictions are imposed on the system:
(a) Processes are never directly preempted from their processors.
(b) $np = 1$ (i.e., a uniprocessor system).
(c) A *Release* operation wakes up at most one process.
(d) Restrictions (a), (b), and (c) combined.

3.10. Consider a system with a separate processor dedicated entirely to the scheduling of other processors. Let the *Scheduler* poll the other processors for work on a cyclic basis. Assume that the *Scheduler* is invoked indirectly through our nucleus primitives. However, instead of a subroutine call, a special processor register, say R_i for the ith processor, is first set by the primitive and then, in a separate operation, a busy loop on R_i is executed until it is reset by the *Scheduler*. Give an algorithm for a general priority *Scheduler* with preemption in this type of computer system.

3.11. Suppose the following jobs arrive for processing at the times indicated and run the specified amount of time. Calculate the *average turnaround time* for the four scheduling disciplines listed:

Job	Arrival Time	Length
1	0.0	8
2	0.4	4
3	1.0	1

(a) FIFO
(b) SJN
(c) SJN; however, the CPU is left idle for the first time unit.
(d) Round robin

3.12. There are five jobs in a queue waiting to be processed. Their respective total service times are 10, 1, 2, 1, and 5.

  (a) For the following scheduling policies, draw a time chart showing when each of the five jobs will be executed:

  - FIFO
  - Round robin (quantum = 1)
  - SJN

  (b) Assuming that the jobs arrived at the same time but were queued in the given order, determine the turnaround time for each job under each of the policies of part (a).

  (c) Which policy yields the minimum average waiting time (over all jobs)?

3-13. There are three processes, p_1, p_2, p_3, in the system. For each scheduling policy listed in the tables give the numerical priority (as defined by the appropriate priority function) of each of the three processes at time t.

  (a) FIFO

  (b) SJN

	Arrival	Attained	Total
p_1	$t_0 - 25$	30	50
p_2	$t_0 - 15$	0	60
p_3	$t_0 - 5$	0	30

  (c) SRT

	Arrival	Attained	Total
p_1	$t_0 - 20$	20	50
p_2	$t_0 - 10$	0	60
p_3	t_0	0	20

  (d) PD with $f^{-1}(a) = a^2$

	Arrival	Attained	Total
p_1	$t_0 - 25$	15	50
p_2	t_0	0	60
p_3	$t_0 - 10$	10	30

3.14. Consider n processes sharing the CPU in a round-robin fashion. Assuming that each process switch takes s seconds, what must be the quantum size q such that the overhead resulting from process switching is minimized but, at the same time, each process is guaranteed to get its turn at the CPU at least every t seconds?

3.15. Consider a system with an MLF scheduling policy, where $n = 10$, $T_n = 2 * q$ (q is the

quantum size) and, at each priority level, T_{Π} is twice as large as at the next higher level. There are three processes in the highest-priority queue; their respective times until the next IO request are 3, 8, and 5 time units (1 time unit = q). All other queues are empty. As execution progresses, the five processes migrate to lower-priority queues. When a process reaches its IO request, it remains blocked (not competing for the CPU) for 5 time units, after which it reenters the highest-priority queue. The required CPU times until the next IO request are again 3, 8, and 5. Using a timing diagram, show
(a) which process will be running, and
(b) which processes will be in which queue during each of the first 30 time units of execution.

3.16. Repeat Exercise 3.15 assuming that $T_{\Pi} = 2 * q$ (i.e., is constant) for all priority levels.

3.17. There are two processes p_1 and p_2 in a system using policy-driven scheduling. The following table gives the attained service time, the real time spent in the system, and the policy function $f^{-1}(a)$ for each process at a given point in time:

	Attained	Real	$f^{-1}(a)$
p_1	2	2	$a/2$
p_2	3	5	$a/6$

(a) Which process should continue running at this time?
(b) After what period of time will the priorities of the two processes be equal?

4

The Deadlock Problem

The notion of deadlock was informally introduced in the dining philosophers example of Section 2.7.2; the unrestricted competition for the available resources (the forks in this example) led to the undesirable state wherein each philosopher acquired one of the forks and was blocked indefinitely, waiting for the second fork to be released. When some processes are blocked on resource requests that can *never* be satisfied unless *drastic* systems action is taken, the processes are said to be *deadlocked.* This condition normally occurs because the producers of the requested resources are themselves blocked on the same resources. The drastic systems action may consist of involuntary preemption of resources or liquidation of processes.

Why are deadlock studies important? The problem was certainly considered in the design of many present systems, but it has received significant attention in only a few. Deadlock has not been of major concern in the past because in most multiprogramming operating systems, parallel programming and process interaction facilities were restricted to systems processes only, and even then often on a limited basis, and because resources were allocated statically to user processes at creation time. In modern computer systems, however, dynamic resource sharing, parallel programming, and communicating processes are common operating characteristics at many levels of systems and user programs. Hence, the possibilities of deadlock have increased accordingly. The problem is also critical in a number of real-time applications, such as computer control of vehicles or monitoring and control of life-supporting systems, (e.g., during human surgery). There are other reasons why we should examine deadlock in some detail. The work in this area represents one of the few successful examples of a theoretical and realistic treatment of some aspect of operating systems and gives some idea about the possible form of a theory of operating systems. Finally, deadlock studies attempt to partially answer one of the fundamental questions in computer science: Can a process progress to completion?

This chapter contains a relatively formal treatment of the deadlock problem, based primarily on the research and the model of Holt (1971b, 1972). Dijkstra (1965, 1968b) was one of the first and most influential contributors in the deadlock area. More recently, deadlock problems have also been studied in the context of distributed operating systems and database management systems (Gray, 1976). Following some examples and definitions, deadlock detection, prevention, and recovery are discussed with respect to both conventional (serially reusable) and messagelike (consumable) resources.

4.1 EXAMPLES OF DEADLOCK IN COMPUTER SYSTEMS

Examples of different types of deadlocks that can arise with serially reusable (SR) and consumable (CR) resources are presented. The purpose is to illustrate the variety of situations in which deadlock is possible and to motivate the subsequent formal model.

File Sharing.   Suppose processes p_1 and p_2 both update a file D and require a *scratch* tape (i.e., a temporary tape) during the updating. Let T be the only tape drive available for scratch purposes. Assume further that p_2 needs a scratch tape immediately prior to the updating for some other reason, for example to reorganize the input data for the update. Let D and T be SR resources representing permission to update the file and permission to use the tape drive, respectively. Assume that a process is blocked on a *Request* operation until the resource is allocated and that a *Release* operation returns the resource to the system. Then p_1 and p_2 may have the following forms:

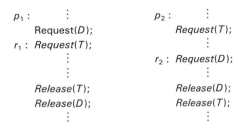

It is possible for p_1 and p_2 to reach r_1 and r_2, respectively, at the "same" time; for example, p_2 first gets T, then p_1 gets D, then p_1 is at r_1, and finally p_2 reaches r_2, in a purely sequential manner. The two processes become deadlocked immediately after this point. Process p_1 blocks on T holding D, while p_2 blocks on D holding T; p_1 cannot proceed unless p_2 proceeds, and vice versa, and the processes are locked in a "deadly embrace." Figure 4-1a graphically portrays the deadlock condition. Boxes denote re-

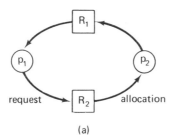

(a)

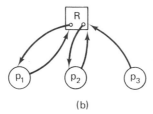

(b)

Figure 4-1 Deadlock with SR resources: (a) Simple example of deadlock (b) Single resource sharing.

sources, and circles represent processes. An arrow (directed edge) from a resource to a process indicates an allocation, while an arrow from a process to a resource is a request. Substitute D for R_1 and T for R_2. (Note that this example would be even more realistic if T were another data file; p_1 and p_2 are then requesting the same data files but in the opposite order.)

Single Resource Sharing.   A single SR resource R, such as main or auxiliary storage, contains m allocation units and is shared by n processes $p_1, \ldots, p_n, 2 \le m \le n$. Let each process use elements of R in the sequence

$$Request(R); Request(R); Release(R); Release(R);$$

where each *Request* and *Release* is for one unit of R. Then a deadlock can easily result when *all* units are allocated; all processes holding units of R could be forever blocked on their second *Request*, while some processes could be similarly blocked on their first *Request*. Such a system state is illustrated in Fig. 4-1b for the case $n = 3$ and $m = 2$. This type of deadlock is relatively common. For example, it may arise in an IO subsystem in which several input and output processes share a pool of buffers; if the space becomes completely allocated to (1) input data for processes currently performing output or (2) output data of processes requiring some input, the system deadlocks.

Locking in Database Systems.   In a database environment, queries or transactions are implemented as relatively short processes that search and/or modify various parts of the database. Since requests arrive at unpredictable times and thus may arbitrarily be interleaved, *locking* must be used to guarantee integrity of the stored data. This may be performed at different levels of granularity, ranging from locking the entire database for the duration of a request to locking each individual data record. If locking is done at any level lower than the entire database, deadlocks may occur. This is because different processes need to work with, and thus lock, different elements of the database. Consider, for example, a system with locking at the record level, where two processes p_1 and p_2 both wish to update two records R_1 and R_2. If p_1 first locks R_1 and then requests a lock on R_2 while p_2 performs the locking in a reversed order, the same deadlock situation as shown in Figure 4-1a may occur.

SR and CR Resources.   A compute process p_c communicates with an IO process p_{io} by requesting and releasing messages describing IO operations and their results. Assume that p_c requests all available storage blocks from the system, say by the operation *Request(M, all)*. The IO process, however, occasionally requires a storage block for buffering purposes, which it acquires through a *Request(M)*. The two processes p_c and p_{io} might be synchronized as follows:

p_c : *Request(M, all)*; p_{io} : *Request(IO__request)*;
    Release(IO__request);   ⋮
r_c : *Request(IO__completion)*; r_{io} : *Request(M)*;
    ⋮   ⋮
    Release(M, all);   *Perform__IO*;
    ⋮   *Release(IO__completion)*;
    ⋮   ⋮

The two processes will *always* deadlock at the *Request*s at r_c and r_{io}. The compute process p_c cannot acquire an "IO completion" signal until p_{io} receives its buffer, but the system has no memory to allocate to p_{io} until p_c receives its "IO completion" and subsequently releases M. The deadlock state is shown in Figure 4-2a; for CR resources, such as *IO__completion*, an arrow is directed from the resource to the producer. (The producer *owns* an unlimited number of units of the resource, as will be explained in Section 4.4.)

Message Passing.   Let process p_1 produce messages S_1, p_2 produce messages S_2, and p_3 produce messages S_3; S_1, S_2, and S_3 are CR resources. Suppose that p_1 receives messages from p_3, p_2 from p_1, and p_3 from p_2. If the message communication for each process occurs in the order

$$p_i : \ldots Release(S_i); Request(S_j); \ldots$$

where for $i = 1,2,3$, $j = 3,1,2$, respectively, then no difficulties arise. However, reversing the two operations causes deadlock (Figure 4-2b):

$$p_1 : \ldots Request(S_3); Release(S_1); \ldots$$

$$p_2 : \ldots Request(S_1); Release(S_2); \ldots$$

$$p_3 : \ldots Request(S_2); Release(S_3); \ldots$$

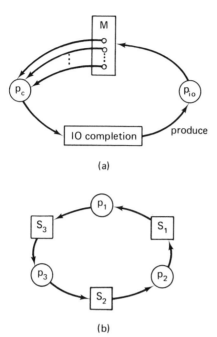

Figure 4-2 Deadlock with CR resources: (a) SR and CR resource sharing (b) Message passing.

An Extreme Example in PL/I.   Holt (1971b) gave the following program to illustrate how easily a user can deadlock a process:

```
revenge: procedure options(main, task);
           wait(event);
         end {revenge}
```

The *wait(event)* is equivalent to *Request(event)* in our notation. The *event* never occurs and *revenge* blocks forever, theoretically.

Effective Deadlock.   A mild form of deadlock is the indefinite postponement of processes competing for a resource, leading to a "starvation" of one or more of these processes. An example was given with the dining philosophers problem in Section 2.7.2.

Suppose that a system allots 200K of main storage to user processes (jobs) and that a job requires either 100K or 200K for its duration. Assume that two 100K jobs are loaded initially and that the job queue *always* contains some 100K jobs. Then, if a new job is selected for loading immediately after a job completion and storage availability is used as the selection criterion, a 200K job will *never* be run. It is possible to prevent this without drastic action by delaying the allocation to 100K jobs if a 200K job has been waiting for a sufficiently long time. This kind of situation, in which a scheduler or allocator can prevent a process from going to completion even though it is logically possible to do so, has been called *effective deadlock* by Holt. Effective deadlock could also occur, for example, in a system that gives highest priority to short jobs and keeps long (heavy compute) jobs waiting until all short jobs are completed. Such deadlocks will be ignored in the rest of this chapter.

As illustrated by these examples, deadlock involves the interaction of potentially many processes and resources; therefore, it must be treated as a global systems problem. The deadlock problem can be divided into three principal parts:

1. *Detection.* Given a system of processes sharing resources and communicating with one another, how can it be determined if some subset of them is deadlocked? One clue obtained from the first five examples is the existence of a cycle (a directed path from a node to itself) in the process-resource graphs.

2. *Recovery.* What are the "best" ways to recover from deadlock? Drastic systems action is necessary, but we want to disrupt the operation as little as possible.

3. *Prevention.* How can deadlock be avoided in the first place? For example, changing the order of *Requests* and *Releases* in the first, third, and fifth examples makes deadlock impossible. We are interested in some general prevention techniques. The first six examples consist of simple sequential code with *no* conditional branching; consequently, there is a fixed sequence of resource operations for each process, which can be determined easily by inspection. However, in the general (and still practical) case, the best that one could do would be to enumerate all the paths through the code; one of these paths might lead to deadlock in combination with other processes, but it is impossible to know a priori for an arbitrary process whether a particular path will in fact ever be taken. (This is the famous halting problem in disguise.)

One can also find examples of deadlock in systems other than computers, such as transportation systems or ecological systems. The same three problems, prevention, detection, and recovery, are present regardless of the domain.

4.2 A SYSTEMS MODEL

For the model of this chapter, the *state* of an operating system will represent the allocation status of the various resources in the system (free or allocated). The system state is changed by processes when they *request*, *acquire*, or *release* resources; these will be the *only* possible actions by processes, since no other operation can affect the system with respect to deadlock. If a process is not *blocked* in a given system state, it may change that state to a new one. However, because it is generally impossible (undecidable) to know a priori which path an arbitrary process may take through its code, the new state may be any one of a finite number of possibilities; processes are therefore modeled as nondeterministic entities. These notions lead to the following formal definitions:

1. A *system* is a pair $\langle \sigma, \pi \rangle$, where σ is a set of *systems states* $\{S, T, U, V, \ldots\}$ and π is a set of *processes* $\{p_1, p_2, \ldots\}$.

2. A *process* p_i is a partial function from systems states into nonempty subsets of systems states; this is denoted

$$p_i: \sigma \rightarrow \{\sigma\}$$

Informally, this expresses the idea that a process can change the current system state into one of several possible states, depending on the operation it executes. Hence the target domain of the function is a *set* of states. If p_i executes an operation in a state S that results in a new state T, we say that p_i can change the state from S to T and use the notation $S \overset{i}{\rightarrow} T$. Finally, the notation $S \overset{*}{\rightarrow} W$ means that there exists a finite sequence of operations that transforms the system from state S to state W. Formally, $S \overset{*}{\rightarrow} W$ means the following:

(a) $S = W$, or

(b) $S \overset{i}{\rightarrow} W$ for some p_i (i.e., p_i can change the system state from S to W), or

(c) $S \overset{i}{\rightarrow} T$ for some p_i and T, and $T \overset{*}{\rightarrow} W$ (i.e., p_i can change the system state from S to T and there exists a sequence of operations that transforms T to W).

Each operation may be performed possibly by a different process of the system.

Example

Define a system $\langle \sigma, \pi \rangle$ with $\sigma = \{S, T, U, V\}$, $\pi = \{p_1, p_2\}$, $p_1(S) = \{T, U\}$, $p_1(T) = \Omega$, $p_1(U) = \{V\}$, $p_1(V) = \{U\}$, $p_2(S) = \{U\}$, $p_2(T) = \{S, V\}$, $p_2(U) = \Omega$, and $p_2(V) = \Omega$, where $p_i(S)$ gives the set of states the system may enter as a result of executing p_i in state S, and Ω indicates undefined. Figure 4-3a represents this system. Some possible sequences of state changes are

$$S \overset{1}{\rightarrow} U, \quad T \overset{2}{\rightarrow} V, \quad S \overset{*}{\rightarrow} V, \quad (\text{e.g., } S \overset{1}{\rightarrow} T \overset{2}{\rightarrow} V \text{ or } S \overset{2}{\rightarrow} U \overset{1}{\rightarrow} V)$$

3. A process is blocked in a given state if it cannot change the state of the system in any way (i.e., the process can neither request, acquire, or release resources in that state). Formally, a process p_i is *blocked* in state S if there exists no T such that $S \overset{i}{\rightarrow} T$.

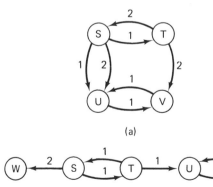

(a)

(b)

Figure 4-3   Examples of systems: (a) System with deadlock states (b) System with deadlock and safe states.

4. A process is deadlocked in a given state S if it is blocked in S and if, no matter what operations (state changes) occur in the future, the process remains blocked. Formally, process p_i is *deadlocked* in state S if, for all T such that $S \xrightarrow{*} T$, p_i is blocked in T. In Figure 4-3a, p_2 is deadlocked in both U and V; p_1 is blocked but not deadlocked in T, because there is no transition from T to any other state using p_1. However, since the transitions $T \xrightarrow{2} V$ and $T \xrightarrow{2} S$ are possible, and p_1 is not blocked in either V or S, p_1 is not deadlocked in T.

5. S is called a *deadlock state* if there exists a process p_i deadlocked in S.

6. Deadlock is prevented, by definition, by restricting a system so that each possible state is not a deadlock state. A state S is a *safe state* if, for all T such that $S \xrightarrow{*} T$, T is not a deadlock state.

The system of Figure 4-3b, where $\sigma = \{S, T, U, V, W\}$ and $\pi = \{p_1, p_2\}$, has both deadlock and safe states. U and V are safe; S, T, and W are not safe because W is a deadlock state and S and T may lead into W.

Example

Consider the file sharing example of Section 4.1 and assume that p_1 and p_2 are cyclic processes. If we sequentially scan through the code of p_1 and p_2, the following *process* states can be easily derived:

States for p_1	States for p_2
0. Holds no resources	0. Holds no resources
1. Requested D, holds no resources	1. Requested T, holds no resources
2. Holds D	2. Holds T
3. Requested T, holds D	3. Requested D, holds T
4. Holds T, holds D	4. Holds D, holds T
5. Holds D (after release of T)	5. Holds T (after release of D)

Let the system state where p_1 is in process state i and p_2 is in state j be S_{ij}. Then the system can be represented by the diagram of Figure 4-4. State changes (operations) by process p_1 are graphed horizontally; those by process p_2 appear vertically. Processes p_1 and p_2 are deadlocked in $S_{3,3}$; p_1 is blocked but not deadlocked in $S_{1,4}$, $S_{3,2}$, and $S_{3,5}$; p_2 is blocked but not deadlocked in $S_{2,3}$, $S_{4,1}$, and $S_{5,3}$. No state is safe. (Note that the states $S_{3,2}$ and $S_{2,3}$ always lead to deadlock.)

With this model of a system, we next examine the components of a system state, the operations for changing state, and the deadlock problem when the resources are serially reusable only.

4.3 DEADLOCK WITH SERIALLY REUSABLE RESOURCES

A *serially reusable* resource (SR) is a finite set of identical units with the following properties:

p_1

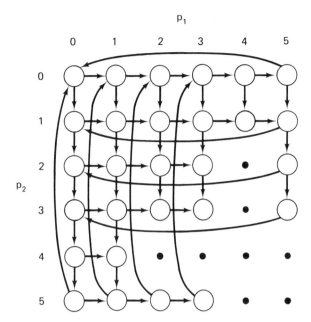

Figure 4-4 System state changes in file sharing example.

1. The number of units is constant.
2. Each unit is either available or allocated to one and only one process (no sharing).
3. A process may release a unit (make it available) only if it has previously acquired that unit.

The definition abstracts those essential features of conventional resources necessary for our deadlock studies; in particular, it is not necessary to identify each unit of such a resource explicitly. Examples of SR resources are hardware components such as main storage, secondary storage, peripherals, and perhaps processors and software such as programs, data files, or tables.

4.3.1 Reusable Resource Graphs

The state of an operating system is represented by a process-resource graph, called a *reusable resource* graph in the SR case. A *directed* graph is defined as a pair $\langle N, E \rangle$, where N is a set of *nodes* and E is a set of *edges*, represented as ordered pairs (a, b), where a and b are in N. A reusable resource graph is a directed graph with the following interpretation and restrictions:

1. N is divided into two mutually exclusive subsets, a set of process nodes $\pi = \{p_1, p_2, \ldots, p_n\}$, and a set of resource nodes $\rho = \{R_1, R_2, \ldots, R_m\}$. Graphically, processes are represented as circles and resources as squares. (Refer, for example, to Figure 4-1.) Each resource node R_j in ρ denotes an SR resource.

2. Each resource consists of one or more units represented graphically as small circles within the resource node. The number of units for each resource R_j in ρ will be given by a nonnegative integer t_j. When $t_j = 1$, the circle may be omitted from the graph. (Compare, for example, the resources of Figure 4-1a and b.)

3. The graph is bipartite with respect to π and ρ. That is, each edge e in E is directed between a node of π and a node of ρ; it never connects two processes or two resources. If $e = (p_i, R_j)$, that is, is directed from p_i to R_j, then e is a *request* edge and is interpreted as a request by p_i for 1 unit of R_j. If $e = (R_j, p_i)$, that is, is directed from R_j to p_i, then e is an *assignment* edge and indicates an allocation of 1 unit of R_j to p_i.

4. Let $|(a, b)|$ be the number of edges directed from node a to node b. The system must always work within the following limits:
   (a) No more than t_j assignments (allocations) may be made for R_j, where t_j is the number of units of R_j; formally, $\Sigma_i |(R_j, p_i)| \le t_j$, for all j. In the graphical representation, the number of edges emanating from R_j must not exceed the number of units of R_j.
   (b) The sum of the requests and allocations of any process for a particular resource cannot exceed the available units; that is, $|(R_j, p_i)| + |(p_i, R_j)| \le t_j$ for all i and j. Graphically, the number of edges between any process p_i and a resource R_j (regardless of their orientation) must not exceed the number of units of R_j.

Example

1. Figure 4-1a is a reusable resource graph.

$$\rho = \{R_1, R_2\}; \quad \pi = \{p_1, p_2\}; \quad N = \rho \cup \pi; \quad t_1 = t_2 = 1$$

$$E = \{(p_1, R_2), (R_2, p_2), (p_2, R_1), (R_1, p_1)\}$$

2. The second example of Section 4.1 is represented by the graph of Figure 4-1b.

$$\rho = \{R\}; \quad t = 2; \quad \pi = \{p_1, p_2, p_3\}$$

$$E = \{(p_i, R) | i = 1, 2, 3\} \cup \{(R, p_1), (R, p_2)\}$$

The systems state is changed to a new state only as a result of requests, releases, or acquisitions of resources by a single process.

1. *Request.* If a system is in state S and process p_i has *no* requests outstanding (no request edges), then p_i may *request* any number of units of any of the resources, subject to the limitations of restriction 4. The system then enters a new state T, which differs from S only in the additional request edges from p_i to the requested resources. The prerequisite that p_i has no outstanding requests is essential. It reflects the assumption that a process cannot execute *any* operations from the time it issues a request until acquisition takes place.

2. *Acquisition.* A system can change from state S to state T by an *acquisition* operation of p_i, that is, $(S \xrightarrow{i} T)$, if and only if p_i has outstanding requests and *all* such

requests can be satisified. Formally, for *all* resources R_j such that (p_i, R_j) is in E, the graph must satisfy the condition

$$\left|(p_i, R_j)\right| + \Sigma_k \left|(R_j, p_k)\right| \leq t_j.$$

The first term gives the number of units of r_j requested by p_i, and the second term gives the number of units of R_j currently allocated to other processes p_k. The graph of T is identical to S, except that all request edges (p_i, R_j) are reversed to (R_j, p_i) to reflect the allocations.

3. *Release.* p_i can cause a state change from S to T by a *release* operation if and only if p_i has *no* outstanding requests and some allocations, that is, if there exist no edges (p_i, R_j) for any j and there exist some edges (R_j, p_i) for some j in the reusable resource graph of state S. p_i may release *any* nonempty subset of its resources in this operation. The resulting state graph is identical to that of state S, except that each unit of R_j released by p_i has its corresponding edge (R_j, p_i) deleted.

Example

Figure 4-5 illustrates these operations for a system with one resource (3 units) and two processes. Initially, p_2 holds one unit of R. The first operation is a request by p_1 for two units of R. The second operation shows the acquisition of these units. Finally, the third operation is a release of one of the units by p_1.

Note that processes are nondeterministic; subject to the preceding restrictions, *any* operation by *any* process is possible at *any* time. Unless execution time traces are available or processes are restricted in their operations and use of resources, this nondeterministic feature is necessary, because there is no way of knowing precisely which resource a process will request or release at any time. Also, in a multiprogramming environment, there is no general way of knowing a priori which process is allocated a given resource at any time, and which process is running on the CPU and therefore able to effect a state change. After treating the general case, we examine the effects of restricting some of the process operations and resources.

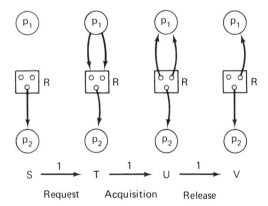

Figure 4-5 Process operations.

4.3.2 Deadlock Detection

To detect a deadlock state, it is necessary to determine whether each process *can* ever progress again. (It *may* be *possible* for a process to perform an operation in some present or future state, but this does *not* assure us that the process *will* in fact ever move again; a resource allocator or process scheduler might prevent it from doing so, either deliberately or inadvertently. This effective deadlock was discussed in the seventh example of Section 4.1.) Because we are looking at the possibility of process progress rather than the certainty of it, it is sufficient to examine only the most favorable state changes. In other words, we wish to find out whether, in a given situation, there exists a sequence of operations such that the system will not deadlock. The strategy for detecting deadlock will be to simulate the most favorable execution of each unblocked process in a non-multiprogrammed (sequential) mode, as follows.

An unblocked process acquires any resources it needs, releases *all* of its resources, and remains dormant thereafter; the released resources may wake up some previously blocked processes. We continue in this fashion until there are no remaining unblocked processes. If there are some blocked processes at the termination of this execution sequence, the original state S is a deadlock state; otherwise, S is not a deadlock state. We now formally develop and prove these notions.

Reduction of Reusable Resource Graphs.   A process p_i is blocked if it is unable to perform any of the three operations defined in Section 4.3.1. This can only arise if p_i has outstanding requests that exceed the available resources; that is, there must exist at least one resource R_j such that

$$\left|(p_i, R_j)\right| + \Sigma_k \left|(R_j, p_k)\right| > t_j$$

Note that this prevents not only the acquisition of R_j but also any new requests or releases of other resources by p_i; the latter two operations may be performed only when the process is not blocked. The most favorable operations for an unblocked process p_i can be represented by a *reduction* of the reusable resource graph, defined as follows:

1. A reusable resource graph is *reduced* by a process p_i, which is neither blocked nor an isolated node, by removing all edges to and from p_i. This is equivalent to p_i acquiring all resources for which it has pending requests and then releasing all its resources; the acquisition is possible because p_i is not blocked, and the subsequent release is possible because p_i has no outstanding requests at that time. p_i then becomes an isolated node.

2. A reusable resource graph is *irreducible* if the graph cannot be reduced by any process.

3. A reusable resource graph is *completely reducible* if there exists a sequence of reductions that deletes *all* edges of the graph.

Figure 4-6 illustrates a sequence of reductions; the graph in the initial state S is completely reducible, since $S \overset{*}{\to} U$ and U contains no edges. Note that p_2 is blocked in S on R_1 but becomes unblocked after the reduction by p_1.

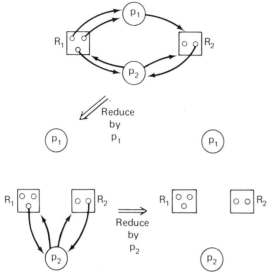

Figure 4-6 A sequence of reductions.

For SR resources, the order of reductions is immaterial; all sequences lead to the same irreducible graph. This is proved in the following lemma.

Lemma 1.   *All* reduction sequences of a given reusable resource graph lead to the *same* irreducible graph.

Proof. Assume that the lemma is false. Therefore, there must exist some state S that is reduced to an irreducible state T_1 by a reduction sequence seq_1 and to an irreducible state T_2 by seq_2, such that $T_1 \neq T_2$ (i.e., all processes in T_1 and T_2 are either blocked or isolated). We will now derive a contradiction whose only resolution is that $T_1 = T_2$. Suppose seq_1 consists of the ordered list of processes $(q_1, q_2, \ldots, q_k)$. Now seq_1 must contain a process q that is not contained in seq_2. If not, T_1 had to be equal to T_2, because a reduction only deletes edges already present in state S; consequently, if seq_1 and seq_2 contained the same process set (in a different order), exactly the same set of edges would be deleted. An inductive proof will now show that $q \neq q_i$ for all $i = 1$, $2, \ldots, k$, resulting in our contradiction:

1. $q \neq q_1$, since S can be reduced by q_1 and seq_2 must therefore also contain q_1. This is because q_1 is unblocked in S and will remain unblocked regardless of what reductions are performed.
2. Assume now that $q \neq q_i$ for $i = 1, \ldots, j$. Since a reduction by q_{j+1} is possible in seq_1 after reduction by q_i, $i = 1, \ldots, j$, the same must be true for seq_2 regardless of the ordering of q_i or other intervening processes; the same set of edges is deleted by the q_i. Thus $q \neq q_{j+1}$.

Therefore, $q \neq q_i$ for $i = 1, \ldots, k$; that is, q cannot exist, contradicting the assumption that $T_1 \neq T_2$. Therefore, $T_1 = T_2$.

Algorithms for Deadlock Detection with SR Resources. With the aid of Lemma 1, we can prove a simple necessary and sufficient condition for the existence of a deadlock, expressed by the following theorem.

Theorem 1. The Deadlock Theorem. S is a deadlock state if and only if the reusable resource graph of S is not completely reducible.

Proof. To prove the necessity of the condition, assume that S is a deadlock state and process p_i is deadlocked in S. Then, for all T such that $S \xrightarrow{*} T$, p_i is blocked in T. Since the graph reductions are identical to a series of process operations, the final irreducible state of a reduction sequence must leave p_i blocked. Therefore, the graph is not completely reducible. This proves that the preceding condition for deadlock is *necessary*.

To show that the condition is also *sufficient*, suppose that S is not completely reducible. Then there exists a process p_i that remains blocked on all possible reduction sequences by Lemma 1. Since any reduction sequence terminating in an irreducible state assures that all SR resources that can ever possibly be made available are in fact released, p_i is blocked forever and therefore deadlocked. Hence the preceding condition for deadlock is sufficient.

The deadlock theorem directly yields algorithms for deadlock detection. One simply attempts to reduce the graph in an efficient manner; if the graph is not completely reducible, the original state was a deadlock state. Lemma 1 permits the reductions to be ordered in any convenient way. A reusable resource graph can be represented by either matrices or lists; in both cases, storage is conserved by compressing several acquisition edges or request edges between a particular resource and a given process into a single edge and an associated *weight* giving the number of units:

1. *Matrix representation.* The graph is represented by two $n \times m$ matrices;
   (a) An *allocation* matrix A, where rows represent processes and columns represent resources, and each entry A_{ij}, $i = 1, \ldots, n, j = 1, \ldots, m$, gives the number of units of resource R_j allocated to process p_i; that is, $A_{ij} = |(R_j, p_i)|$.
   (b) A *request* matrix B, analogous to A, where each entry B_{ij} gives the number of units of resource R_j requested by process p_i; that is, $B_{ij} = |(p_i, R_j)|$.
2. *Linked list structure.* Four types of lists are used. The resources *allocated* to any process p_i are linked to p_i as follows:

$$p_i \rightarrow (R_x, a_x) \rightarrow (R_y, a_y) \rightarrow \cdots \rightarrow (R_z, a_z)$$

where each R_j is a resource node and a_j is the number of units of R_j allocated to p_i; that is, $a_j = |(R_j, p_i)|$. The resources *requested* by a process p_i are linked together using a similar list. Analogous allocation and request lists are used for resources. For each allocated resource R_j, an allocation list and a request list are maintained. The allocation list for each allocated resource R_j links all processes currently holding any units of that resource:

$$R_j \to (p_u, b_u) \to (p_v, b_v) \to \cdots \to (p_w, b_w)$$

where each p_i is a process node and b_i gives the number of units of R_j allocated to p_i; that is, $b_i = |(R_j, p_i)|$. The request list for each resource is similar; it contains processes requesting units of R_j.

For both representations, it is also convenient to maintain an *available units* vector $(r_1, \ldots, r_m)$, where r_j gives the number of available (unallocated) units of R_j; that is, $r_j = t_j - \Sigma_k |(R_j, p_k)|$.

A straightforward detection method is to loop through the process request lists (or matrices) in order, making reductions where possible, until no more reductions can be made. The worst-case situation occurs when the processes are ordered $p_1, \ldots, p_n$ but the only possible order of reductions is $p_n, \ldots, p_1$, and when every process is requesting all m resources. Then the number of process inspections is $n + (n - 1) + \cdots + 1 = n(n + 1)/2$, each inspection requiring the examination of m resources; thus the worst-case execution time is proportional to mn^2.

A more efficient algorithm can be obtained at the expense of maintaining some additional information about requests. A *wait count* w_i is defined for each process node p_i consisting of the number of resources (not resource units) that cause the process to be blocked at any time; we also keep the requests for each resource ordered by size. Then the following reduction algorithm has maximum execution time proportional to mn. (Curly braces are used here to denote sets rather than program comments.)

```
L := {p_i | w_i = 0};
for all p in L do
begin
    for all R_j such that |(R_j, p)| > 0 do
    begin
        r_j := r_j + |(R_j, p)|;
        for all p_i such that 0 < |(p_i, R_j)| ≤ r_j do
        begin
            w_i := w_i - 1;
            if w_i = 0 then L := L ∪ {p_i}
        end
    end
end;
Deadlock := ¬(L = {p_1, . . . , p_n});
```

L is the current list of processes that can perform a graph reduction. The program selects a process p from L, reduces the graph by p by incrementing the available units r_j of all resources R_j allocated to p, updates the wait count w_i of each process p_i that can have its request satisfied for a particular resource R_j, and adds p_i to L if the wait count becomes zero. A deadlock is detected if, at the termination of the algorithm, L does not contain *all* processes.

Related Results Derived from the Deadlock Theorem. Two important results can be derived from the deadlock theorem. First, when we apply the deadlock detection algorithm and detect that a given state S is a deadlock state, we know that at least one process is deadlocked in S; the algorithm, however, does not specify which one. In many situations, we may be interested in determining only whether a specific process is deadlocked, rather than testing the entire system state. In this case, we can apply the following rule: *A process p_i is not deadlocked in a state S if and only if a series of reductions produces a state in which p_i is not blocked.* The existence of such a series is found by successively reducing the given state and testing, for each new state, whether p_i is blocked. The algorithm stops when a state is found in which p_i is not blocked (hence not deadlocked in S) or when no more reductions are possible.

The second important result derivable from the deadlock theorem is concerned with the *number* of processes deadlocked in a given state S. From the definition of the deadlock state, we know that at least one process must be deadlocked in S. We can, however, strengthen this statement by showing that *at least two* such processes must exist. In other words, a single process can never become deadlocked; rather, mutual blocking of two or more processes is necessary for deadlock to occur.

Other Conditions for Deadlock Detection. The graph structure representing a given system state provides a simple necessary, but not sufficient, condition for deadlock. Before stating this condition, we must introduce the notion of a *cycle* in a graph. For any graph $G = \langle N, E \rangle$ and node a in N, let *Reach*(a) be the set of nodes "reachable" from a. Formally,

$$Reach(a) = \left\{ b \mid (a, b) \text{ is in } E \right\} \cup \left\{ c \mid (b, c) \text{ is in } E \wedge b \text{ is in } Reach(a) \right\}$$

Then G has a cycle if there exists some node a in N such that a is in *Reach*(a). The necessary condition for deadlock is then given by the following theorem.

Theorem 2. The Cycle Theorem. A cycle in a reusable resource graph is a necessary condition for deadlock. (The proof is left as an exercise.)

The deadlock theorem and the cycle theorem are the most general statements one can make about deadlock detection when no restrictions are made on the use of the SR resources. The deadlock test can be accomplished more efficiently, however, if it is done on a *continuous* basis. That is, if we know that the current state S is not deadlocked, the testing of the next state T may be simplified considerably; it is only necessary to examine the one process that caused the transition from S to T. The following theorem provides the formal basis for continuous detection.

Theorem 3. If S is not a deadlock state and $S \xrightarrow{i} T$, then T is a deadlock state if and only if the operation by p_i is a request and p_i is deadlocked in T. (The proof is left as an exercise.)

The implication of Theorem 3 is that a deadlock can be caused only by a request that cannot be granted immediately. In terms of continuous deadlock detection by graph reductions, this means that one need only apply reductions after a request by some p_i. Furthermore, one should attempt to reduce the graph by p_i first; if p_i can be reduced, no further reductions are necessary.

4.3.3 Special Cases of Reusable Resource Graphs

In previous sections we studied deadlock detection in unrestricted reusable resource graphs. Restrictions imposed on the allocators, the number of resources requested simultaneously, and the number of resource units lead to simpler conditions for deadlock. For some of these special cases, another graph theoretic concept is useful.

A *knot* in a directed graph $\langle N, E \rangle$ is a subset of nodes $M \subseteq N$ such that, for all a in M, $Reach(a) = M$. That is, every node in a knot is reachable from every other node in the knot, and a node outside a knot is not reachable from one inside the knot. Figure 4-7a illustrates the general idea of a knot. Note that a cycle is a necessary but not sufficient condition for a knot. In Figures 4-7b and c the nodes b, c, d, and e form a cycle; hence each is reachable from any other within that cycle. However, only the graph in (b) forms a knot because none of the four nodes has an edge directed to the outside; in (c), the node b violates this requirement. (A knot-detection algorithm is given at the end of this section in the discussion of single-unit requests.)

Immediate Allocations.   If the system state is such that all satisfiable requests have been granted, a simple sufficient condition for deadlock exists. This situation occurs if resource allocators do not defer satisfiable requests but grant them immediately when possible; most allocators follow this policy. The resulting states are called *expedient*. That is, an expedient state is one in which all processes having requests are blocked. Such states offer the following simple condition for deadlock detection: *If a system state is expedient, then a knot in the corresponding reusable resource graph is a sufficient condition for deadlock*.

To verify the validity of this condition, consider a graph containing a knot K. Then all processes in the knot must be blocked *only* on resources in K, since no edges may be directed out of K by definition. Similarly, all allocated units of resources in K are held by processes in K for the same reason. Finally, all processes in K must be blocked because of the expediency condition and the definition of a knot. Hence, all processes in K must be deadlocked.

Single-Unit Resources.   In many situations, resources are limited to only one unit; that is, $t_j = 1$ for $j = 1, \ldots, m$. With this restriction, *a cycle becomes a sufficient and necessary condition for deadlock*.

The necessity of a cycle for deadlock to occur is proved directly by Theorem 2. To show that a cycle is also sufficient, let us assume that the graph contains a cycle C and consider only those processes and resources that are part of C. Since each such

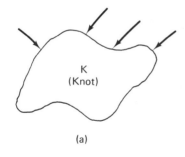

(a)

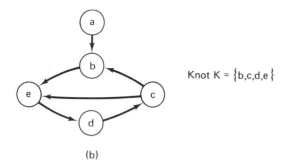

Knot K = {b,c,d,e}

(b)

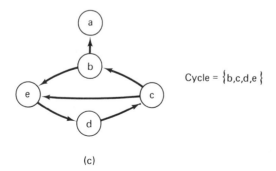

Cycle = {b,c,d,e}

(c)

Figure 4-7 Illustrations of cycles and knots: (a) General knot structure (b) Example of a knot (and a cycle) (c) A cycle but not a knot.

process node must have an entering and exiting edge, it must have an outstanding request for some resource in C and must hold some resources in C; similarly, every (single unit) resource in C must be held by some process in C. Therefore, every process in C is blocked on a resource in C that can be made available only by a process in C. Hence, the processes in the cycle are deadlocked.

    Based on this result, we have merely to test the reusable resource graph for cycles in order to detect deadlock in the single-unit resource case. Let a *sink* be any node that does not have edges directed from it. One efficient cycle-detection algorithm is based on the successive deletion of edges directed into sinks; if the resulting graph contains only sinks, then no cycle was present in the original graph.

    Let w_i denote the number of edges directed from node i; formally, $w_i = \Sigma_k |(i, k)|$.

Our cycle detection algorithm for a graph $\langle N, E \rangle$ then has the following form:

```
S := {i | node i is a sink};
for all i in S do
begin
    for all j such that (j, i) is an edge do
    begin
        w_j := w_j - 1;    {delete edge (j, i)}
        if w_j = 0 then S := S ∪ {j}
    end
end;
Cycle := ¬(S = N);
```

The algorithm first collects all sinks into a set S. During the subsequent nested loops, all nodes j connected to any node i in S are considered. Each of the edges (j, i) is "deleted" by decrementing the counter w_j; if this was the only edge emanating from j, then j becomes a sink and is included in S. A node on a cycle will never be included in the set S because, initially, it is not a sink and, during subsequent execution, its w_i is always greater than zero. Hence a cycle exists if S does not contain all nodes of the graph N when the algorithm terminates, as reflected by the Boolean variable *Cycle*. The execution time of the algorithm is proportional to the number of edges in the graph, which in the worst case is *mn*.

For continuous detection, we can take advantage of Theorem 3. Then it is necessary only to test whether the requesting process p_i is on a cycle. This can be accomplished by tracing all paths starting with p_i, looking for the reappearance of p_i.

Single-Unit Requests.   Assume that a process may request only one unit at a time; that is, at most one request edge can be connected to any process node. Then, *for expedient states, a knot becomes a necessary and a sufficient condition for deadlock.*

We have already seen that a knot is a sufficient condition in such a situation (see the first special case, immediate allocation). Hence only the necessity of a knot needs to be shown. Assume that the graph is in a deadlock state yet does not contain a knot. We will show that, for any process node p_i, there exists a sequence of reductions involving p_i; this will contradict the preceding assumption that a deadlock exists. Consider any process node p_i that is not an isolated node. (The latter can clearly be ignored.) Since there is no knot in the graph, p_i is either (1) a sink or (2) on a path leading to a process node that is a sink. The sink node in case 1 cannot be a resource, since the state is expedient. In case 2 a reduction by p_i is obviously possible. For case 2, let the processes on the path be $p_i, p_j, p_k, \ldots, p_x$, where p_x is the sink node. The graph may be reduced by processes $p_x, \ldots, p_k, p_j, p_i$ in that order; a simple inductive argument based on single-unit requests will establish this fact. Therefore, a reduction by an arbitrary process p_i can always be made eventually, and, by Lemma 1, the graph is completely reducible.

Knot detection can be accomplished in a similar but simpler manner than cycle detection. From the definition of a knot we know that a sink can never be part of a knot.

Hence, we begin with the set of sink nodes S and incrementally include all nodes j that have edges leading into S; these also cannot become part of a knot. When the algorithm terminates, a knot has been detected if there are some nodes in N that have not been included in S. The algorithm for a graph $\langle N, E \rangle$ is

$$S := \{i \mid node\ i\ is\ a\ sink\};$$
for all i **in** S **do**
    for all j **such that** (j, i) *is an edge* **do**
        if j **is not in** S **then** $S := S \cup \{j\};$
$Knot := \neg (S = N);$

If continuous detection is desired, Theorem 3 can again be used. It is necessary only to test whether or not the requesting process p_i is on a knot. We can do so by tracing all paths from p_i looking for a sink.

4.3.4 Recovery from Deadlock

There are two general approaches for recovering from deadlock states. The first relies on process *terminations*. Deadlocked processes are successively terminated (destroyed) in some systematic order until enough resources become available to eliminate the deadlock; in the worst case, all but one of the originally deadlocked processes must be liquidated. The second approach is based on resource *preemption*. A sufficient number of resources are preempted from processes and given to deadlocked processes to break the deadlock; processes in the former set are left with outstanding requests for their preempted resources.

Perhaps the most practical and straightforward technique is a termination strategy that destroys lowest-termination-cost processes first. The termination cost of a process may be, for example:

1. The priority of the process.
2. The cost, according to the normal system accounting procedures, of restarting the process and running it to its current point.
3. A simple external cost based on the type of job associated with the process (e.g., student jobs, administrative jobs, production jobs, research jobs, and systems programming jobs may each have fixed termination costs).

The recovery algorithm would terminate the least expensive process by destroying the process and releasing its resources, and then reduce the graph as far as possible; these steps are repeated until the graph contains only isolated nodes. After recovery, the initial systems state is the original deadlock state with the terminated processes removed. This method has the virtue of simplicity, but unfortunately also indiscriminately destroys those processes that have little effect on the deadlock.[†]

[†]We have ignored one important practical problem in this discussion: a process that is executing inside a critical section must, in general, be permitted to leave the critical section before it is terminated; otherwise, common data areas may be left in incorrect or "unstable" states.

A more satisfying but less efficient termination scheme performs a *minimum-cost* recovery. Let C_i be the cost of destroying process p_i. Then a minimum-cost policy terminates a proper subset π' of the process set π such that

1. The termination of all members of π' eliminates the deadlock.
2. For all other subsets $\tilde{\pi} \subset \pi$ whose liquidation would remove the deadlock condition, the recovery cost is greater than that of π'; that is,

$$\Sigma_{p_i \text{ in } \pi'} C_i \le \Sigma_{p_i \text{ in } \tilde{\pi}} C_i$$

The cost of recovery from a deadlock state S is defined recursively as the sum of (1) the cost of destroying a process p_i and (2) the cost of recovery from the next system state resulting from eliminating p_i. Note that the latter depends on the choice of the process p_i. Hence, the minimum cost for recovering from deadlock state S, $rc\_min(S)$, satisfies the relation

$$rc\_min(S) = minimum(C_i + rc\_min(U_i)),$$

$$\begin{pmatrix} All\ p_i \\ deadlocked \\ in\ S \end{pmatrix}$$

where U_i is the state following S upon the termination of p_i.

An algorithm for obtaining $rc\_min(S)$ and the corresponding destroyed processes can be derived directly from this relation. The algorithm systemically produces new states by process destruction until a nondeadlocked state appears. It does so recursively for all possible combinations of process destruction.

```
procedure rc__min(S: state; var d: set__of__processes, rc: real);
begin
    if deadlocked(S) then
    begin
        rc__curr := ∞;
        for all p_i deadlocked in S do
        begin
            terminate p_i to create state U_i from S;
            rc__min(U_i, d_i, rc_i);
            rc_s := rc_i + C_i;
            d_s := d_i ∪ {p_i};
            if rc_s < rc__curr then
            begin
                rc__curr := rc_s;
                d__curr := d_s
            end
        end;
        d := d__curr; rc := rc__curr
    end else d := {}; rc := 0
end
```

S is the input to the procedure; d and rc are output parameters. d is the set of processes that must be destroyed to recover from the initial deadlock in S, and rc is the corresponding recovery cost. The first test, *deadlocked*(S), can be done by reducing the graph. When *true*, the procedure considers all processes p_i deadlocked in S; for each, it creates a new state U_i, and it recursively calls itself to determine the cost rc_i and the set of processes d_i to recover from U_i. The cost of destroying p_i is then added to rc_i, and p_i is included in the set of processes to be destroyed. At each iteration, the loop remembers the currently lowest recovery cost, rc_curr, and the corresponding set of processes to be destroyed, d_curr. At the end of the loop, these two values are returned by the procedure as the result.

The exhaustive-search nature of the minimum-cost algorithm makes it impractically inefficient for complex deadlock situations. For example, if C_i is a constant, all m resources are single-unit resources, $n = m$, each resource R_i is assigned to p_i, and each p_i requests all resources except R_i, then the minimum-cost deadlock recovery requires time and space proportional to at least $n!$. However, if the system is restricted to single-unit requests, an efficient and more practical recovery method exists.

Assume that the system states are expedient and that requests may only be of the single-unit type. Then, by the condition of deadlock derived for single-unit requests (third special case in Section 4.3.3), a minimum-cost recovery need merely eliminate knots in the serially reusable resource graph in a minimal-cost manner. To eliminate a knot, it is sufficient to delete all edges directed *from any* selected node in the knot, thus making the node a sink. This leads to the following algorithm:

1. Find all knots in the graph.
2. For each knot, select a resource node R_i such that the cost of deleting processes p_k holding units of R_i is a minimum; that is, select R_i such that, for all $R_j \neq R_i$ in the knot,

$$\Sigma_{|(R_i, p_k)| > 0} C_k \leq \Sigma_{|(R_j, p_k)| > 0} C_k$$

3. Eliminate each knot by terminating all processes having allocations of the selected R_i; that is, terminate all p_k such that $|(R_i, p_k)| > 0$.

One way to identify the knots in a graph (step 1 in the algorithm) starts by grouping all nodes in common cycles into the same *equivalence* class as follows. All paths from a given node are systematically traced until the node repeats or the graph has been searched. In the former case, a cycle has been detected and all nodes in the cycle are replaced by a single node representing the equivalence class; edges entering or leaving any node in the cycle similarly enter or leave the equivalence class node. This process is repeated until no further cycles are found. The knots in the original graph then correspond to those equivalence classes that are sinks and contain at least two nodes. For a reusable resource graph with single-unit requests, the knot identification and the remainder of the algorithm have execution times proportional to $(n + m)^2$ in the worst case.

The two previous minimum-cost algorithms presented could also be based on resource preemptions. A preemption cost may be associated with each unit of a resource. Instead of terminating deadlock processes, a minimum-cost set of resources is preempted to break the deadlock. When a resource is preempted by a process, the process receives an assignment of the resource, and the preempted process has its assignment changed to a request. A practical version of this technique is used in database operating systems, where deadlock is often permitted on database elements because of improved performance through concurrency (Gray, 1976). The recovery method is to preempt resources (database elements) and restart the preempted process (transaction) at an earlier checkpointed operation.

If deadlock detection is done on a continuous basis, Theorem 3 offers a simple recovery technique. The deadlock can be removed by either terminating the requesting (deadlocked) process or by preempting resources and assigning them to the requesting process.

4.3.5 Prevention Methods

Recall that a *safe* state was defined in Section 4.2 as one that cannot ever lead to deadlock. The general approach to deadlock prevention is to restrict the system so that all states are safe. For serially reusable resources, this can be accomplished trivially by permitting only one process at a time to hold resources; in practice, a policy of this type essentially produces a single-programming rather than multiprogramming operation and can therefore be dismissed as impractical except in isolated situations.

A more practical restriction is to insist that every process request and acquire at *one* time all resources it may conceivably need; normally, this will be the first operation that a process performs. Processes with allocated resources will never be blocked because they cannot make any further requests, and will eventually release all their resources, not necessarily at the same time. Thus a given process will either have assignments or requests, but never the two together. Deadlock is therefore impossible and every state is safe. From another point of view, it is impossible for the reusable resource graph to contain a cycle, a necessary condition for deadlock (Theorem 2 in Section 4.3.2). The principal disadvantages of such a policy are that resources may have to be allocated well ahead of their actual use and thus become unavailable to other processes for possibly extensive periods of time. Resources may also be requested unnecessarily in anticipation of a possible use that does not materialize.

An *ordered resource* policy, originally devised by Havender (1968) for the IBM operating system OS/360, prevents deadlock with less drastic restrictions than the above "collective" request scheme. Reusable resources are divided into k classes, K_1, K_2, $\ldots$, K_k. A process is permitted to request resources from any class K_i *only* if it has no allocations from classes K_i, K_{i+1}, $\ldots$, K_k. (If $k = 1$, the last method and this method are identical.) It can be proved by induction on k that no state with these restrictions can be deadlocked. The key part of the proof is that a request for the highest class K_k will always be honored eventually. This must be true, since no process with allocations from K_k can make any further requests until it releases its resources in K_k; thus all allocations from K_k are guaranteed to be released.

Example

In IBM OS/360, a batch processing system, job initiator processes obtain and release resources for a user job and each step within the job using an ordered resource strategy.
$k = 3$ and the resource classes are

$$K_1 = \{\text{data sets or files}\}, \quad K_2 = \{\text{main storage}\}, \quad K_3 = \{\text{IO devices}\}$$

Figure 4-8 illustrates a systems state within this policy. It shows four processes competing for three different resource classes. Process p_1 has no outstanding requests; process
p_2 is requesting a unit each of R_1, R_2, and R_3; process p_3 holds a unit of R_1 and is requesting
units of R_2 and R_3; process p_4 holds units of R_1 and R_2 and is requesting a unit of R_3.

By assigning the most expensive or scarce resources to the highest classes, the
requests of the most valuable resources can be deferred until they are actually needed.
However, the same disadvantages of the first collective scheme are present here also;
some resources must be allocated well in advance of their need.

Deadlock Prevention Based on Maximum Claims.   Deadlock prevention is

also possible in the important case where the *maximum claim* of all resources is known
a priori for each process. The maximum claim for any process is the largest number of
units of each resource that the process will need at one time. It can be represented as a
claims matrix c_{ij} with $i = 1, \ldots, n, j = 1, \ldots, m$, similar to the allocation and request matrices of Section 4.3.2, where c_{ij} gives the maximum claim of process p_i for
resource R_j. A system of this type has the following additional restriction on the serially
reusable resource graph: *the sum of all allocations and requests of any process cannot
exceed its maximum claims.* This is expressed formally by the condition

$$\left|(p_i, R_j)\right| + \left|(R_j, p_i)\right| \leq c_{ij} \leq t_j$$

which must hold for any process p_i and resource R_j.

A serially reusable resource graph of a state S is extended into a *claim graph* of S
by adding to it n_{ij} *potential* request edges (p_i, R_j) for each process p_i and resource R_j.
Each potential request edge may, in the future, be transformed into an actual request
edge and, subsequently, into an assignment edge. The maximum claim c_{ij} is the sum of

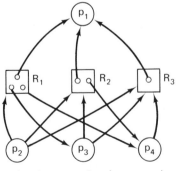

$$K_1 = \{R_1\} \quad K_2 = \{R_2\} \quad K_3 = \{R_3\}$$

Figure 4-8 System state using an ordered
resource policy.

the potential request edges, the actual request edges, and the assignment edges between the process p_i and resource R_j; that is,

$$c_{ij} = n_{ij} + |(p_i, R_j)| + |(R_j, p_i)|$$

The claim graph obtained from S represents a *worst-case* future state T derivable from S; it would occur when all processes requested the maximum number of resources permitted by their claims. Figure 4-9 shows examples of claim graphs for several states. Regular request and allocation edges are shown as before; the added claim edges are dashed. The graph shows that process p_1 may request at most two units of R at any given time, while p_2 may request all three.

There is no simple way to determine whether a state in a general unrestricted maximum-claim system is safe. One could test a state for safeness by an exhaustive search procedure, but this approach, while guaranteed to terminate, is inordinately time and space consuming. However, there is a way to prevent deadlock in maximum-claim systems. This is achieved by not allowing any *acquisition* operations unless the resulting claim graph is completely reducible. The complete reducibility of the claim graph means that the worst future state can be handled: If all processes successively request the remainder of their claim, the requests can be satisfied. This prevention policy can be restated as the following theorem.

Theorem 4.   If acquisition operations that do not result in a completely reducible claim graph are prohibited, any system state (which is not already deadlocked) is safe. Furthermore, any policy that permits acquisitions that result in nonreducible claim graphs (and makes no further restrictions on request or release operations) will produce some system states that are not safe. (The proof is left as an exercise.)

The reduction procedure that determines whether the claim graph is completely reducible should attempt to reduce by the acquiring process p_i first. If the claim graph was completely reducible before the acquisition, it is completely reducible after that operation if and only if an eventual reduction by p_i is possible. This result is analogous to the continuous detection theorem (Theorem 3 in Section 4.3.2).

Maximum-claim systems were introduced and studied by Dijkstra (1965) and Ha-

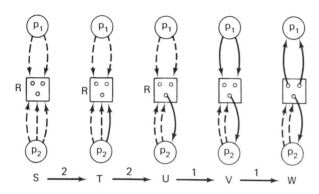

Figure 4-9 Examples of operations on claim graphs.

bermann (1969). Dijkstra employed an interesting analogy to banking systems, where resource classes correspond to currencies, allocations are analogous to loans, and maximum claims are considered as credit limits. Deadlock prevention is accomplished by a Banker's Algorithm, which is an implementation of the ideas embodied in Theorem 4.

Maximum-Claim Graphs with Single-Unit Resources. When resources are of the *single-unit* type, a more efficient method of testing the reducibility of the claim graph exists: *an acquisition yields a completely reducible claim graph if and only if the acquiring process p_i is not on a cycle in the claim graph;* therefore, a simple path-tracing algorithm from p_i can be employed for deadlock prevention.

Safeness of states in maximum-claim graphs can also be easily tested when only single-unit resources exist. Consider the *undirected* claim graph obtained by treating each edge of the claim graph as an *unordered* pair. An *undirected cycle* is defined as a sequence of unordered edges (a, b), (b, c), . . . , (r, s), (s, a) in which no edge appears more than once; note that the edge (a, b) is the same as the edge (b, a) in the undirected graph. Then, safeness can be determined by testing for cycles: *a state S in a maximum-claim system with single-unit resources is safe if and only if the undirected claim graph contains no undirected cycles.*

Consider first the sufficiency of the preceding condition. If the undirected claim graph contains no cycles, the directed claim graph also does not contain any cycles. The reusable resource graph is a subgraph of the claim graph, and hence it also contains no cycles. We have already shown (Section 4.3.2) that the absence of cycles in a reusable resource graph with single-unit resources implies that the system is not in a deadlock state. Since no edges are ever added to the claim graph, a cycle cannot be created and hence no future state will be deadlocked.

To verify the necessity of the condition, let the undirected claim graph contain a cycle. The edges can now be changed to directed edges as follows: each undirected edge can become either (1) an allocation edge, pointing from a resource to a process (subject to the usual restriction that this is the only allocation of the resource), (2) a request edge, pointing from a process to a resource, or (3) a potential request edge (dashed), pointing also from a process to a resource. By an obvious choice of successive edges in the cycle, this transformation can yield a particular state S' of the system, where the graph contains a directed cycle. (Note that, in general, many legal states can be obtained, depending on the kind of directed edges selected.) Thus a reusable resource graph containing a cycle (a sufficient condition for deadlock in single-unit resource systems) can be constructed from the undirected claim graph. Either the original state S can eventually be transformed to the deadlock state S' represented by the preceding graph, or the system deadlocks before reaching S'. In both cases, the original state S is not safe.

This reasoning proves that a cycle is a necessary and sufficient condition for the safeness of a given state S. Note, however, that the undirected claim graph is identical for *all* states that the system can ever reach. Hence, we have really proved a stronger result: *all states in a maximum claim system with single-unit resources are safe if and only if the (unique) undirected claim graph contains no undirected cycles.*

When users are required to specify their (reusable) resource needs in the beginning of each job, maximum claim information is readily available. Deadlock prevention based on maximum claims, however, still potentially wastes resources, since a process might not ever need its maximum claim of all resources simultaneously.

A systems designer thus has two options with respect to SR resources: (1) permit deadlock and employ some detection and recovery techniques, or (2) prevent deadlock, sacrificing some potential resource use. A realistic approach taken in many systems is to prevent deadlock on some classes of resources and processes for which recovery is difficult and to permit its occurrence on other classes; for example, a deadlock prevention policy may be implemented for systems processes while detection and recovery are limited to user processes.

The deadlock problem with respect to reusable resources has been studied extensively. Similar approaches, which we have not presented here, have been used for deadlock studies in distributed operating systems and in database systems (Gray, 1976).

4.4 CONSUMABLE RESOURCE SYSTEMS

A *consumable resource* (CR) can be distinguished from an SR in several important ways:

1. The number of available units of a CR varies as elements are acquired (consumed) and released (produced) by processes and is potentially unbounded.
2. A producer process increases the number of units by releasing one or more units it has "created."
3. A consumer process decreases the number of units by first requesting and then acquiring one or more units. Units that are acquired are not, in general, returned to the resource but are consumed by the acquiring process.

Many signals, messages, and data generated by both hardware and software have these characteristics and may be treated as CR resources for deadlock studies. These include IO and timer interrupts, process synchronization signals, messages containing requests for various services or data, and structures such as a job descriptor that may be passed from one process to another as a user job is handled by an operating system.

We first informally consider *unrestricted* CR systems. As in the SR case, the system changes state when any *unblocked* process p_i executes one of the three operations: *request*, *acquisition*, and *release* of CR resources. Note that there are no theoretical limits on the number of units requested or released, provided that they remain finite.

Two important deadlock properties of such a system are easily deduced. First, a *state is deadlocked if and only if all processes are blocked*. If there is one unblocked process in a given state, it can acquire its requested resources, if any, and then release enough units of all resources to wake up every blocked process. The second property is that *no state is safe*; all unblocked processes can always request, in succession, an amount of resources exceeding the current supply. More practical and interesting results can be derived when some additional information about the process interactions is available. Two such cases are systems where (1) the producers of all resources are known a priori, and (2) both producers and consumers of all resources are known a priori. The corresponding CR systems can then be modeled and analyzed by using techniques similar to those developed for SR resources.

4.4.1 Consumable Resource Graphs with Known Producers

Assume that the *producer* processes for each resource are known a priori; that is, the set of processes that may execute *release* operations is specified. Then the state of a system containing only CR resources can be represented by a directed graph $\langle N, E \rangle$, called a *consumable resource graph*, with the following characteristics:

1. Analogous to the SR case, $N = \pi \cup \rho$, where π is a set of process nodes $\{p_1, \ldots, p_n\}$ and ρ is a set of CR nodes $\{R_1, \ldots, R_m\}$.
2. The graph is bipartite with respect to π and ρ; that is, each edge is directed between one node of π and one node of ρ.
3. If an edge e is directed from a process to a resource, that is, $e = (p_i, R_j)$, then e is a *request* edge and is interpreted as a request by p_i for one unit of R_j.
4. For each R in ρ, there is a nonempty set of *producer* processes $\pi_R \subseteq \pi$. The graph contains a *producer edge* (R, p), directed from R to p, for all p in π_R. (Producer edges are similar to assignment edges in SR graphs; they are, however, permanent fixtures of the graph and are never removed.)
5. A nonnegative integer r_i, specifying the number of *available units*, is associated with each R_i in ρ. (This is analogous to the t_j counter in the SR case.)

Figure 4-2b contains a consumable resource graph; $\pi_{S_i} = \{p_i\}$ and $r_i = 0$, for $i = 1, 2, 3$. Another example is given in Figure 4-10a, where $\pi_{R_1} = \{p_1\}$, $\pi_{R_2} = \{p_2\}$, $r_1 = 2$, and $r_2 = 0$. Process p_2 has outstanding requests for three units of R_1 and one unit of R_2.

The rules for performing the *request*, *acquire*, and *release* operations are as follows. A process p_i, with no outstanding requests, may perform a *request* for any finite number of units of any number of resources; the new state has the appropriate request edges added. If p_i has outstanding requests, it can perform an *acquisition*, provided that it is not *blocked* (i.e., there is a sufficient number of resource units to satisfy the request). Formally, p_i can perform the acquisition if, for all R_j such that (p_i, R_j) is in E, $|(p_i, R_j)| \leq r_j$. The acquisition updates the available units of each acquired resource R_j by the appropriate number of units: $r_j := r_j - |(p_i, R_j)|$.

A process p_i that has no outstanding requests and is a producer of one or more resources may execute a *release* operation in which any finite number of units are added to one or more of the resources; the corresponding available units counters (r_j) are increased accordingly. Figure 4-10b illustrates these operations and the resulting states.

Deadlock Detection in Consumable Resource Graphs.   Graph reductions are central to our deadlock studies for CRs also. A CR graph can be *reduced* by a process

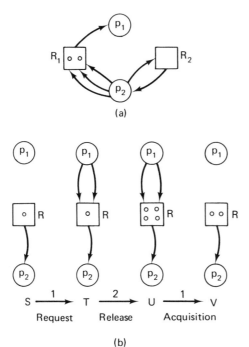

(a)

$S \xrightarrow{\ 1\ } T \xrightarrow{\ 2\ } U \xrightarrow{\ 1\ } V$

Request   Release   Acquisition

Figure 4-10   Consumable resource
graphs: (a) Example of a CR graph (b)
Operations on CR graphs.

(b)

p_i that is neither blocked nor an isolated node. The reduction consists of the following
two operations:

1. Satisfy any outstanding requests of p_i by deleting its request edges and decrementing the appropriate available units counters.
2. For each R_j such that p_i is a producer of R_j, release enough units to satisfy all
   outstanding requests for R_j and delete the producer edge (R_j, p_i). We avoid keeping
   track of available units of R_j by setting r_j to a special "number" ω with the property that, for any integer i, $\omega > i$ and $\omega + i = \omega - i = \omega$. In other words, ω
   represents any number of units requested by a process.

Example

Figure 4-11 illustrates a sequence of reductions by p_1, p_2, and p_3. First, S is reduced by p_1,
the producer of R_1, resulting in the generation of ω units of R_1. Next, the new state T is
reduced by p_2, resulting in the generation of ω units of R_2. Finally, p_3's requests are satisfied. This shows that the original state S was completely reducible, since all edges are
deleted in the *irreducible* state V. (See Section 4.3.2 for definitions.)

Note that, while a reduction in an SR graph never decreases the available units,
the CR graph reduction may in fact leave a smaller r_j; thus, in Figure 4-11, $r_2 = 1$ in
state S and $r_2 = 0$ in state T. The preceding example also illustrates another important

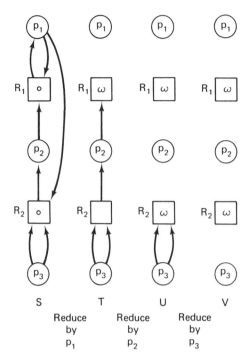

Figure 4-11 Reductions of a CR graph.

difference in CR systems: the *order of reductions is significant*. If S is first reduced by p_2, it is no longer possible to reduce the new state by p_1. Lemma 1 of Section 4.3.2 does *not* hold here.

Theorem 1 of Section 4.3.2, which states that S is a deadlock state if and only if the graph of S is not completely reducible, is also *not* true here, as shown by Figure 4-12; the illustrated state is not a deadlock state because either process may continue by consuming the two available resource units, yet the graph is not completely reducible. However, we can still employ graph reductions to determine if a particular process is deadlocked. This is formalized in the following theorem:

Theorem 5:   A process p_i is not deadlocked in a state S of a CR system with known producers if and only if there exists a sequence of reductions producing a state T in which p_i is not blocked.

Proof. To show that the condition is sufficient is simple: if there exists a sequence of reductions that leaves p_i not blocked in T, then there must exist a sequence of oper-

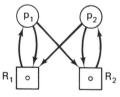

Figure 4-12 A state which is not deadlocked and not completely reducible.

ations (each corresponding to one or more reduction) that leads from S to T. Hence p_i is not deadlocked in S.

The proof of the condition's necessity is more difficult; it is based on the following idea. If p_i is not deadlocked in state S, then there must exist a sequence (possibly empty) of operations producing a state T' in which p_i is not blocked. From this sequence of *operations*, I, a sequence of *reductions*, J, is derived; this produces a state T in which p_i is not blocked. The derivation of the sequence J from I is accomplished as follows. The sequence of processes performing the operations in I is scanned from left to right and only the *first* occurrence of any process is retained; all repetitions are removed. The resulting sequence is the sequence J, which transforms the state S into the state T. It is easy to show that the reductions prescribed by the sequence J can all be performed. The final step is to show that, since p_i is not blocked following the sequence of operations I, it is also not blocked following the sequence of reductions J.

To detect deadlock, one must search for a *different* reduction sequence for each process, a very inefficient task in general. Whereas a deadlock can be caused only by a request operation in SR systems, both requests and acquisitions can result in deadlocks in the CR case. An example appears in Figure 4-12, where the acquisition by p_1 of one unit of R_1 and one unit of R_2 puts p_2 in deadlock. In a manner similar to the proof of Theorem 2, it can be shown that *a cycle is a necessary condition for deadlock*. It can also be shown that, similar to SR graphs (Section 4.3.2), *a knot is a sufficient condition for deadlock in expedient states*.

Deadlock detection is considerably simplified if the system is restricted to *single-unit requests*; that is, at most *one* request edge may be directed from any process node. Then the results obtained for SR graphs are valid here also: *A CR graph with known producers and single-unit requests in an expedient state is a deadlock state if and only if the graph contains a knot*. The knot-finding algorithm in Section 4.3.2 can then also be employed for deadlock detection in this important special case.

Recovery from Deadlocks in CR Systems.   The only practical way to recover from deadlock is by termination of the deadlocked processes. Liquidation of non-deadlocked processes does not help, since their CR resources have been consumed; preemption of resources is not possible, because there is nothing to preempt. Process termination is more complex than in the SR case, since the candidate for liquidation might well be a producer of resources required by other processes; that is, other processes might eventually need the messages produced by the deadlocked process. This problem can be solved by releasing appropriate error messages when an attempt is made to interact with the destroyed process or, in the worst case, also by terminating the interacting processes, if known. For example, if a process associated with a user job or job step is deadlocked, then the entire job or job step may be aborted.

When only the producer processes are known a priori and any process is a potential consumer, no system state is safe, by the same argument presented at the beginning of this section for unrestricted systems. However, knowledge of consumers as well as producers permits one to test for safeness and establish a simple prevention policy.

4.4.2 Consumable Resource Graphs with Known Producers and Consumers

Assume that both producers and consumers of each resource are known a priori; that is, for each resource R, there exists a nonempty set of producer processes π_R^P and a non-empty set of consumer processes π_R^C. A process p may request and acquire units of R *only* if p is in π_R^C, and it may release units of R only if p is in π_R^P. A system state is again represented by a consumable resource graph. Within each such system, there is one state, called the *claim-limited* state, that has a special role. It is a state where each consumer of a resource is requesting exactly *one* unit of that resource and there are currently *no* units of any resource available. Formally, the claim-limited state is defined as follows:

1. A process p has an outstanding request for one unit of a resource R_j if and only if p is in $\pi_{R_j}^C$. No other requests appear.
2. All resources have zero available units; that is, $r_i = 0$ for $i = 1, \ldots, m$.

The corresponding graph is called the *claim-limited consumable resource graph* for the system. An example appears in Figure 4-13; $\pi_{R_1}^P = \{p_1, p_2\}$; $\pi_{R_1}^C = \{p_2\}$; $\pi_{R_2}^P = \{p_1\}$; $\pi_{R_2}^C = \{p_2\}$. The principal result is given in the following theorem:

Theorem 6.   All states in a consumable resource system in which producers and consumers of each resource are known are safe if and only if the claim-limited consumable resource graph is completely reducible.

Proof. To show the necessity of the condition, assume that all states are safe. Then the claim-limited state is safe and is completely reducible, since the reductions correspond to a possible sequence of operations by processes.

To show that the condition is sufficient, assume the claim-limited state V is completely reducible by the sequence of processes $p_{v_1}, p_{v_2}, \ldots, p_{v_k}$. It is relatively easy to show that *any* sequence of reductions of a claim-limited consumable resource graph leads to the same unique irreducible graph. (This is analogous to Lemma 1 of Section 4.3.2.) Therefore, V is a safe state. We now demonstrate how any state S can be reduced by the same sequence that reduces V. The first process in the V reduction, p_{v_1}, cannot be blocked in state S. (p_{v_1} cannot be a consumer of *any* resources, because it would then be blocked in V.) Let S be reduced by p_{v_1} to state S_1. The second process, p_{v_2}, cannot be

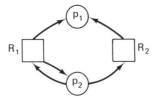

Figure 4-13 A claim limited CR graph.

blocked in S_1, since p_{v_2} must be a consumer *only* of resources produced by p_{v_1}. (If p_{v_2} is an isolated node in S, we ignore it.) Otherwise, p_{v_2} would not be able to perform the second reduction from V. Continue in this manner, terminating after the reduction by p_{v_k}. The resulting state, S_k, say, must consist of isolated processes, because the V sequence includes *all* producer and consumer processes. Thus S is completely reducible. Since S is an arbitrary state, no state in the system is deadlocked. Therefore, all states are safe.

Theorem 6 provides a scheme for preventing deadlocks: the claim-limited graph is tested for complete reducibility. If it is completely reducible, the system can be run without worrying about deadlock; otherwise, the systems designer attempts to modify the process interactions to achieve reducibility. The latter may not be feasible, however. For example, the claim-limited graph is not completely reducible unless there exists at least one process that consumes no resources; if a system is designed so that every process must both receive and send messages, then this property is not satisfied. Deadlock can also be prevented by eliminating any cycles in the claim-limited graph; the absence of cycles is an even stronger restriction than complete reducibility. Note that lack of safeness does not necessarily mean that a given system will ever, in fact, deadlock; the logic of the code of each process might be such that deadlock "paths" are never taken during execution.

4.5 GENERAL RESOURCE GRAPHS

The models of Sections 4.3 and 4.4 can be combined to represent systems containing both serially reusable and consumable resources. The state of an operating system is represented by a *general resource* graph $\langle N, E \rangle$, where

1. $N = \pi \cup \rho$. π is a nonempty set of process nodes $\{p_1, \ldots, p_n\}$, and p is a nonempty set of resource nodes $\{R_1, \ldots, R_m\}$.
2. $\rho = \rho_s \cup \rho_c$. ρ_s is a set of serially reusable resources, and ρ_c is a set of consumable resources.
3. Each edge e in E is directed between one node of π and one node of ρ. If $e = (p_i, R_j)$, then e is a *request* edge and is interpreted as a request by p_i for one unit of R_j. If $e = (R_j, p_i)$, then (a) if R_j is in ρ_s, then e is an *assignment* edge and indicates an allocation of one unit of R_j to p_i, or (b) if R_j is in ρ_c, then e is a *producer* edge and indicates that p_i is a producer of R_j. A producer edge is permanently directed from each resource to all its producer processes.
4. For each R_j in ρ_s, there is an associated positive integer t_j denoting the *total units* of R_j; $r_j = t_j - \Sigma_i |(R_j, p_i)|$ then gives the number of available units of R_j.
5. For all R_j in ρ_s and processes p_i, the following must always hold:
   (a) $\Sigma_i |(R_j, p_i)| \le t_j$; that is, the total number of allocations of units of R_j to the various processes must not exceed t_j.

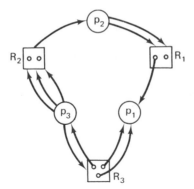

Figure 4-14 A general resource graph.

(b) $|(R_j, p_i)| + |(p_i, R_j)| \leq t_j$; that is, the sum of requests and allocations of units of R_j to a process p_i must not exceed t_j.

6. For each R_j in ρ_c, there is a nonnegative integer r_j giving the *available* units of R_j.

Figures 4-2a and 4-14 contain examples of general resource graphs; in Figure 4-14, ρ_s = $\{R_1, R_3\}$, $\rho_c = \{R_2\}$, $t_1 = 2$, $t_3 = 3$, $r_1 = 1$, $r_2 = 2$, and $r_3 = 0$.

Request, acquisition, and release operations are defined as in Sections 4.3.1 and 4.4. Reductions are similarly defined. The following basic deadlock theorem is easily proved by using the results of the two previous sections.

Theorem 7. A process p_i in a general resource system is not deadlocked if and only if there exists a sequence of reductions producing a state in which p_i is not blocked.

The following results also hold for a general resource graph:

1. A cycle is a necessary condition for deadlock.
2. If the systems state is expedient, a knot is a sufficient condition for deadlock.
3. With single-unit requests, if the system state is expedient, a knot is a necessary and sufficient condition for deadlock

Deadlock can be detected by graph reductions but, because the order of reductions is significant, this method is quite inefficient. For single-unit requests, the knot-detection algorithm permits fast testing for deadlock. Few additional results for the general resource case are known.

4.6 DYNAMIC ADDITION AND REMOVAL OF PROCESSES AND RESOURCES

The models developed in this chapter assume a constant set of processes and resources in a system. This is the case for most serially reusable resources. However, processes are often being created and destroyed continually, and some resources may also be dynamic. Examples of the latter are synchronization constructs such as mailboxes or monitors, which could be created at execution time. In this section, we briefly examine systems deadlocks in an environment allowing the dynamic creation and termination of processes and resources.

Consider first the effects of allowing processes to enter and leave a system containing a *constant* set of SR resources. The removal of a process is essentially equivalent to a reduction by that process and can only help the deadlock situation, since the number of available units of SR resources may increase. On the other hand, the introduction of a new process increases the competition for resources in general; it thus becomes easier to reach a deadlock state. In both cases, the deadlock detection algorithms presented in Section 4.3.2 are immediately applicable to the new set of processes. Two new operations are added to the system:

1. *Create* a process. This adds either an isolated process node or, possibly, a process node with some initial allocation to the graph.
2. *Destroy* a process. A process node and all its assignment and request edges are deleted from the graph.

The discussion on deadlock prevention with SR resources (Section 4.3.4) is also applicable to the dynamic situation. The addition or deletion of a process in a system following an ordered resource policy still leaves a safe system. If deadlock prevention is based on maximum-claim information with the acquisition restriction of Theorem 4, the removal of processes only simplifies the testing of acquisition operations; the addition of a new process to a system in a safe state still results in a safe state, since the new process can clearly be reduced *last* in the reduction of the claim graph.

Dynamic processes working with CR resources have slightly more complex effects. If only the producers are known, then either the creation or termination of a process can cause deadlock. Deletion of a producer process may produce a deadlock, while the deletion of a process that produces no resources can in some cases prevent a future deadlock (Figure 4-15). In the former case, some processes may be waiting forever for a message from the deleted producer if only one producer process was associated with the message resource; this can be easily handled in practice by providing a message to the requesting processes stating that the producer no longer exists. Similarly, the introduction of a new producer process can prevent a possible deadlock (or even break a deadlock), whereas the addition of a consumer may aggravate the situation (Figure 4-16). If both producers and consumers are known, the same effects can be observed. However, the results of Section 4.4 remain valid and can be employed for deadlock detection and prevention in a straightforward manner.

The dynamic addition and removal of resources can also be handled within the graph models. Removal of an SR resource will, at worst, have no deadlock effect and, at best, may prevent or even break a deadlock; in the latter case, a cycle or knot in the SR graph could disappear as a result of the resource liquidation. (Of course, in a practical sense, removal of an SR resource, such as a data file or buffer area, might be disastrous

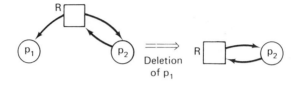

(a)

Figure 4-15 Deletion of processes: (a) Process deletion producing a deadlock (b) Preventing future deadlock by process deletion.

for a process assigned or requesting the resource, making it also necessary to terminate the process.) The definition of a new SR resource has the sole effect of complicating the deadlock-detection methods. For deadlock prevention using maximum-claim information of SR resources, the addition of a new resource makes sense only if all processes claiming that resource are introduced *after* the new resource has been defined. If the system is safe before the new resource is established, it remains safe, provided that the acquisition restriction of Theorem 4 is not violated thereafter. Removal of a CR resource is similarly beneficial only with respect to deadlock. The deadlock effects of adding a new CR resource are left as an exercise.

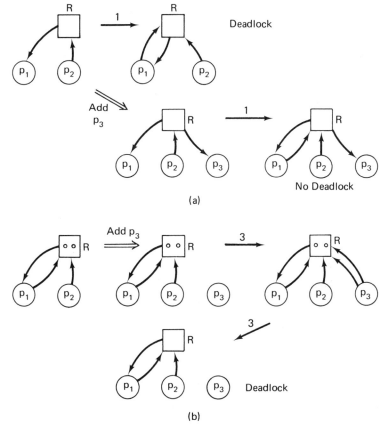

(a)

(b)

Figure 4-16 Effects of adding processes: (a) Addition of a producer process (b) Addition of a consumer process.

EXERCISES

4.1. Consider the following reusable resource graph:

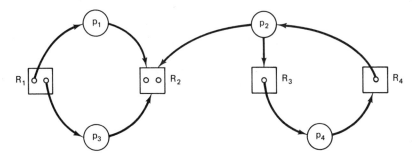

(a) Which processes are blocked?
(b) Which processes are deadlocked?
(c) Is the state a deadlock state?
(d) Does the graph contain a knot? If so, list the nodes constituting the knot.

4.2. Consider three processes p_1, p_2, and p_3 executing asynchronously the following sequences of code:

p_1	p_2	p_3
$\vdots$	$\vdots$	$\vdots$
$P(x)$	$P(y)$	$P(z)$
$\vdots$	$\vdots$ $\leftarrow$	$\vdots$
$P(z)$ $\leftarrow$	$V(y)$	$P(x)$ $\leftarrow$
$\vdots$		$\vdots$
$V(x)$		$V(z)$
$\vdots$		$\vdots$
$V(z)$		$V(x)$

The arrow in each column indicates which instruction the corresponding process is currently executing. All semaphores were initially set to 1.

(a) Draw a reusable resource graph describing this situation where each semaphore is interpreted as a resource, and P and V operations represent *requests* and *releases* of the resources.
(b) Reduce the graph as much as possible, showing that it represents a deadlock state.
(c) If you could increase the number of units of any of the three resources, which increase (if any) would resolve the deadlock?

4.3. Using the definitions of Section 4.2, prove that "S is not a deadlock state" does *not* imply that "S is a safe state." Safeness and deadlock are not complementary.

4.4. (Holt, 1971a) Let two processes p_1 and p_2 share a SR resource R containing two identical units. Each process can be in one of the following states:

0. Holds no resources.
1. Requested 1 unit of R, holds no resources.
2. Holds 1 unit of R.
3. Holds 1 unit of R, requested 1 unit.
4. Holds 2 units.

Each process can change from state 0 to 1 by a request, from 1 to 2 by an acquisition of a unit of R, from 2 to 3 by a request, from 3 to 4 by an acquisition, from 4 to 2 by releasing one unit, and from 2 to 0 by releasing one unit; these are the only state changes possible. Let the system state be S_{ij} where i is the state of p_i and j is that of p_2. Derive a state diagram for this system similar to Figure 4-4. In what state(s), if any, is the system deadlocked and/or blocked?

4.5. (Holt, 1971) Consider a system consisting of three processes and a SR resource class with 4 units. Each process needs at most 2 units. Show that the system is deadlock free (i.e., all states are safe).

4.6. (Holt, 1971) Consider a system consisting of n processes and a SR resource class with m units. Show that the system is deadlock free if the sum of all maximum needs of each process is less than $n + m$ units.

4.7. Prove that the second deadlock-detection algorithm (using wait counts) has maximum execution time proportional to mn.

4.8. Prove Theorem 2. (*Hint*: Use the following property of directed graphs: if a directed graph does not contain a cycle, then there exists a linear ordering of the nodes such that, if there is a path from node i to node j, then i appears before j in that ordering.)

4.9. Prove Theorem 3.

4.10. Prove the following by counterexamples.
  (a) A cycle is not a sufficient condition for deadlock.
  (b) A knot is not a necessary condition for deadlock in expedient state graphs.

4.11. Prove that the successive deletion of edges directed into sinks will result in a graph containing only sink nodes if and only if the graph contains no cycles.

4.12. Describe an algorithm for continuous deadlock detection in a system with the following:
  (a) Single-unit resources
  (b) Single-unit requests

4.13. Develop a minimum-cost recovery algorithm that uses resource preemption rather than process terminations.

4.14. Prove that the serially reusable resource graphs never contain cycles in the following two cases:
  (a) Every process must request all resources at one time.
  (b) The ordered resource policy of Section 4.3.5 is employed.

4.15. Consider the following SR graph in a state S, with maximum claims shown by dashed lines:

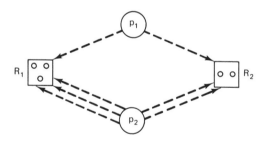

  (a) Show a sequence of operations leading from state S to a deadlock state.
  (b) Show how deadlock could have been prevented, in your example of part (a), by using the policy stated in Theorem 4 (Section 4.3.5).

4.16. Prove Theorem 4. Note that the safeness or lack of safeness must result only from the acquisition restriction; requests and releases may be made in any order and quantity, subject only to the maximum-claim limitations.

4.17. For any single-unit resource maximum-claim system, prove that an acquisition operation produces a safe state if and only if the acquiring process is not in a cycle in the resulting claim graph.

4.18. Consider again the three record-locking modes I, S, and X, presented in Exercise 2.28, and assume that all records are ordered in a tree structure. Let each process (database transaction) obey the following locking protocol:

- Before a process requests an I, S, or X lock on a given record, all ancestors of that record must be locked by that process in I mode.
- At the end of a transaction, a process releases its locks starting from the leaf nodes and proceeding toward the root of the tree.

    (a) Show how two processes obeying this protocol can become deadlocked.
    (b) Give and prove necessary and sufficient conditions for processes to be deadlocked in such a system.
    (c) State and prove a deadlock-prevention policy in such a system, where the policy still allows a reasonable amount of parallel access to the database.

4.19. Prove the following in a CR system with known producers:
    (a) A cycle is a necessary condition for deadlock.
    (b) If a system state is expedient, a knot is a sufficient condition for deadlock.

4.20. Work out the details of the proof of Theorem 5.

4.21. Prove that *all* possible reduction sequences of a given consumable resource graph with known producers and consumers lead to the *same* irreducible graph.

4.22. Consider the system state given by the general resource graph of Figure 4-14. Show that the system is not deadlocked by exhibiting a sequence of reductions that completely reduces the graph.

4.23. Prove Theorem 7 and the subsequent three conditions for the general resource case.

5

Main Storage Management

Main storage, the memory that may be directly accessed as data or instructions by a central processor, is usually a critical and limiting resource in a computer system. In this chapter, we examine the principal software techniques and hardware support for the allocation and administration of main memory.

5.1 PREPARING A PROGRAM FOR EXECUTION

Most application, operating system, and utility programs are written in some user-oriented high-level language or, less frequently, in assembly language. Each such program must undergo a series of transformations before it can be executed by the machine hardware. The first step in such a series, as shown in Figure 5-1, is a translation of the *source program* into a machine-specific version in which all symbolic instructions, operands, and addresses are converted into numerical values. In the case of high-level languages this translation process is referred to as *compilation*, while the term *assembly* is used with lower-level languages that represent a more convenient form of the underlying machine language. The resulting program is called the *object module*.

Software systems of any substantial size cannot be developed as one monolithic entity. Instead, modules reflecting different functions of the system are designed separately, possibly by different programmers, and then interconnected into one complex

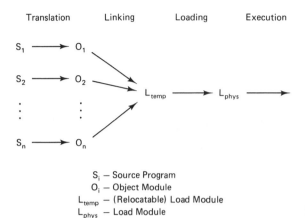

S_i — Source Program
O_i — Object Module
L_{temp} — (Relocatable) Load Module
L_{phys} — Load Module

Figure 5-1 Transformations of programs.

system using a technique called *linking*. The main task to be performed during linking is to resolve external references; these are operand or branch addresses referring to data or instructions within some other module. The resulting module, denoted as L_{temp} in Figure 5-1, is referred to as the (*relocatable*) *load module*—relocatable because its absolute starting address in memory may still be unknown at this time. Only when the program is ready to execute must this address be known and the program brought into main memory. At this stage, it is referred to as the *load module*, L_{phys}.

5.1.1 Relocation

A main task that must be performed before a program can be executed is the assignment of the physical memory locations in which machine instructions and data values are to reside during execution. This assignment may not be known until the time the module is actually loaded into memory. Hence the programmer, the language translator, and the linker have to work with some *assumed* logical addresses when creating or transforming a program. Typically, symbolic names are used by programmers to refer to data or branch locations, which the translator and linker transform into numerical values, assuming some hypothetical starting address (e.g., zero). When the actual physical locations are assigned, all operand and branch addresses within the program must be adjusted according to this assignment. This operation, which moves the program from the assumed hypothetical storage space starting at zero into the space starting at the assigned memory address is referred to as *relocation*. It may take place at different times during a program's life span, including the time of translation, linking, loading, or even execution. Let us examine these various possibilities in turn.

5.1.1.1 Static Relocation

The earliest possible time to assign a physical address to an instruction or a data word is at the time of writing a program. Some assemblers permit the specification of an absolute (physical) address, thus providing for this possibility. With symbolic references, the binding must be carried out at some later time. We can distinguish between *internal* references, which refer to locations within the same source program, and *external* references, which address locations in other programs. With *internal* references, the earliest possible moment to perform the binding is at the time of translation; in this case, the assembler or compiler must be given the actual starting address of the object module. Such early binding of programs to physical memory locations is very restrictive and thus rarely used. It is more practical to postpone the binding until the time of linking. At this time, all modules to be linked together are known, which permits both internal and external references to be resolved. With this approach, the load module is not relocatable ($L_{temp} = L_{phys}$), and the task of the loader is reduced to simply copying the load module into memory. The linker and the loader may usefully be combined into one subsystem called the *linking loader*. This approach is used widely in single-user microcomputer systems.

Separating the linker from the loader offers more flexibility in that the starting address need not be known at the time of linking. Only when the module is actually to be executed are physical addresses bound by relocating the complete load module. Hence the load module may be loaded into a different region of memory without relinking each time.

To permit relocation of a module (at the time of linking or loading), language translators produce instruction records that generally consist of some variation of the form

$$Loc \ oc \ a_1 a_2 \ldots a_n$$

where *Loc* is the relative address of the instruction, *oc* is the operation code, and the a_i are the instruction operand fields. *Loc* can be eliminated except when the $(i + 1)$st instruction does not have a relative address immediately succeeding the *i*th. If the object module is to be loaded into contiguous storage starting at location α and the program has been translated relative to β, then the instruction will be stored in $Loc + k$, where $k = \alpha - \beta$ is referred to as the *relocation constant*.

Now consider the operand fields. Each a_i can be a register name, an immediate operand, the storage address of an operand, or the storage address of an instruction. In the latter two cases, relocation may be necessary, depending on the structure of the machine and the original source program. (We are simplifying the situation somewhat, since other information, such as indirect addressing flags, may be present.) When addresses are always relative, for example by using base registers, no relocation is required. However, when address fields are treated as absolute by the machine, an address a_i must be changed to $a_i + k$ by the linker or loader. The instruction records produced by the translator can be augmented by indicators specifying which a_i are to be relocated, or a global relocation dictionary associated with the program may be used to point to these operands.

Data records are treated in a similar manner. They have the general form

$$Loc \ d_1 d_2 \ldots d_m$$

where *Loc* is the relative address of the data and the d_i are data items. As before, the data items will be loaded starting at storage location $Loc + k$. If a field d_i contains a relative address, it must also be relocated by k.

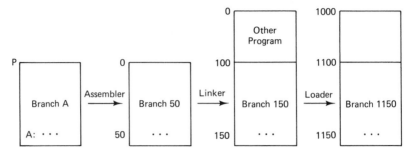

Figure 5-2 Transformation of a sample program under static relocation.

Example

Figure 5-2 shows the successive transformation of an internal reference as a program is prepared for execution. In the source program *P*, the hypothetical branch instruction uses the symbolic name *A* to refer to another statement in the program. The assembler assumes zero as the starting address for the object module and transforms the name *A* into the corresponding offset, say 50. The linker, assuming a starting address 0 for the load module, combines *P* with some other object module, whose length we assumed to be 100; the branch address is now changed to 150 to reflect the new starting address of *P*. Finally, when the actual starting address, 1000, is known, it is added to all relocatable addresses.

It is worth noting that the program in this example has been relocated *twice*: once to reflect the starting address zero assumed by the linker and a second time when the physical address was known. With a linking loader, the two phases would have been combined, resulting in a single relocation.

5.1.1.2 Dynamic Relocation

When all address transformations are completed *before* execution of a program commences, the relocation is referred to as *static*. More flexibility is gained when relocation occurs at run time *immediately* preceding *each* storage reference. With such *dynamic* relocation, programs are bound to the machine at the latest possible moment.

Dynamic relocation is normally accomplished by hardware (for reasons of efficiency) and is invisible to all users except some systems programmers. To illustrate the concept, we consider the instruction cycle of a simple one-address machine both with and without dynamic relocation. Let $M[0..m]$ represent main storage, *reg* be a general purpose register, *ic* be the instruction counter, *Address(w)* a function to compute the operand address of the instruction *w*, and *Opcode(w)* a function to select the operation code *oc* from *w*, where $oc = 1$ indicates addition, $oc = 2$ is a store register operation, and $oc = 3$ designates an unconditional branch. Without dynamic relocation, the basic hardware instruction cycle for such a machine is typically

```
loop
    w := M[ic];   { fetch instruction}
    oc := Opcode(w);
```

```
adr := Address(w);
ic := ic + 1
case oc of
1 : reg := reg + M[adr];   {plus}
2 : M[adr] := reg;      {store}
3 : ic := adr;          {branch}
⋮
end
end {loop}
```

With dynamic relocation hardware, the addresses *ic* and *adr* are treated as relocatable addresses and *mapped* (transformed) into real storage addresses at the time of reference. We designate the mapping function as *NL__map*, for *Name Location map* (Dennis, 1965); for each address in the program, referred to as the *effective* or *virtual address (va)*, *NL__map* produces the corresponding *physical address (pa)*.

> *NL__map*: {relocatable (virtual) addresses} ⇒ {real (physical) storage addresses}

The basic instruction cycle algorithm is changed as follows to make it describe a similar machine with dynamic relocation:

```
loop
w := M[NL__map(ic)];   {fetch instruction}
oc := Opcode(w);
adr := Address(w);
ic := ic + 1
case oc of
1 : reg := reg + M[NL__map(adr)];   {plus}
2 : M[NL__map(adr)] := reg;      {store}
3 : ic := adr;                   {branch}
⋮
end
end {loop}
```

NL__map can be viewed as a hardware box placed between the CPU and main storage through which all storage addresses must pass. Figure 5-3 illustrates the hard-

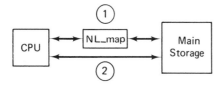

① : Dynamic Address Relocation

② : Read or Write

Figure 5-3 Storage references with dynamic relocation.

ware mapping; a memory access consists of two steps after virtual address is extracted from the instruction: (1) the address is dynamically relocated by *NL_map*, and (2) the actual read or write operation is performed. During the mapping, *NL_map* may reference main storage for tables and the CPU for special registers.

Example

> Figure 5-4 shows the transformations of a program in a system with dynamic relocation. The tasks performed by the assembler and linker are the same as in Figure 5-2. The loader, however, does *not* change the program in any way when it loads it into memory; the branch instruction still shows the address 150. The necessary relocation constant of 1000 is added to this address by *NL_map* each time the instruction is executed.

The storage system as seen by the typical user (i.e., the space of relocatable addresses) is called *name* space or *virtual* memory. The physical address space is sometimes termed *location* space. If programs or data are relocated in main storage, only *NL_map* need be changed; name space addresses remain invariant to location space assignment. This forms the basis of the *virtual storage* concept, which will be discussed in Section 5.3.

The main advantages of dynamic relocation are that, in principle, it permits a flexible and efficient use of main storage and, at the same time, offers a convenient (virtual) memory interface to users. With the more sophisticated relocation hardware, storage allocation can be performed dynamically *on demand* rather than statically before execution; that is, the system has the option of delaying the storage assignments up to the time of the first address reference to a block of code or data. Consequently, linking and loading of a particular procedure is similarly delayed, and storage that has not been referenced in the recent past can be released if necessary. Fragmentation (checkerboarding) of storage may decrease because a contiguous allocation policy for each user is not necessary and the units of allocation may be small. During a single run, a procedure may easily be swapped in and out of different areas of memory. With dynamic relocation, it is also easier for several processes to share a single copy of a procedure. Finally, it is possible to present to the user a large contiguous virtual storage space and to relieve him of any management tasks resulting from the limited physical space.

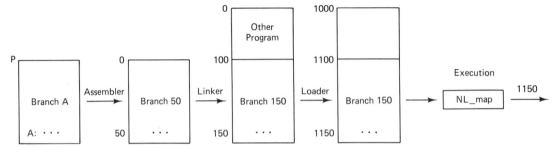

Figure 5-4 Transformation of a sample program under dynamic relocation.

5.1.2 Linking

Linking is used to permit independent development and translation of modules. These may be combined at some later time into more complex systems by resolving external references used by the individual program modules.

At the time a source program is translated into an object module, external references cannot normally be resolved; instead, the translator only records where such references occur in the program to facilitate the subsequent task of the linker. For that purpose, the translator generates an *external symbol table* for each module, which lists all external references used in that module.

Two different linking methods are in common use. The first of these *links* all locations containing a particular external reference into a chain headed by the corresponding entry in the external symbol table. When the address of the external symbol becomes known, it can be easily inserted in the correct locations by tracing through the chain.

Example

Figure 5-5a shows the skeleton of a source program containing calls to two other procedures, *SUB*1 and *SUB*2. The corresponding object module is shown in Figure 5-5b. All instructions referring to the same external name are linked into a chain that starts in the

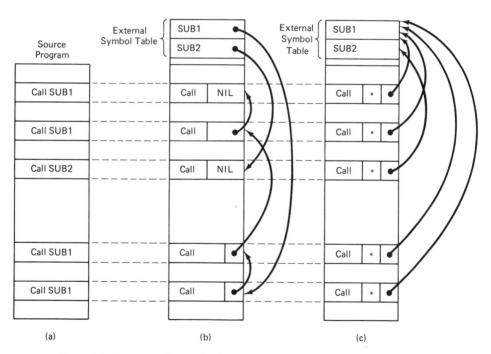

Figure 5-5   Treatment of external references: (a) A sample source program (b) Object module with chaining methods (c) Object module with indirect addressing.

corresponding entry of the external symbol table; the last element in the chain is denoted by *NIL*.

The second method avoids changing locations at linking time by using *indirect addressing* for all external references. Each such reference is set up by the translator to point to the appropriate entry in the external symbol table. When the actual address is known, only the external symbol table entry is changed. Each external reference then passes indirectly through this table, also referred to as the *transfer vector*. Linking is faster and simpler than with the chaining method, but at execution time two memory accesses instead of one are required to complete the reference. With indirect addressing, the external symbol table becomes a *permanent* part of the program, whereas with the chaining method it may be discarded after linking is completed.

Example

Figure 5-5c shows the object module for the source program of Figure 5-5a when indirect addressing is used; the asterisk denotes indirection.

When all external references are resolved before execution of the program begins (using either of the two methods), the linking is referred to as *static*. When, on the other hand, external references are kept in their *symbolic* form and are resolved during execution, the linking is called *dynamic*. Resolving an external reference does not necessarily imply binding that reference to a physical location. Rather, it implies that a common name space has been assigned to all modules linked together and that all references, internal and external, refer to locations within that space. Assume, for example, that the program P in Figure 5-2 contained a reference to the first instruction of the program labeled ''other program''; the linker would transform this into the address zero, which would be subject to relocation (static or dynamic) when the load modules were actually transferred into memory for execution.

5.2 SIMPLE MEMORY MANAGEMENT SCHEMES

Even though the cost of random-access memory has been decreasing dramatically in recent years, there is still shortage of main memory in most computer systems. Two main problems result from this limitation. One is caused by the sheer size of many applications, which simply exceed the amount of physical memory available in a given system. To solve this problem, programs must somehow be divided into smaller blocks and loaded into memory only as needed. The second problem arises in multiprogramming systems, where several active processes need to share main memory at the same time. In this section we introduce some simple schemes for partitioning main memory to permit such sharing and for coping with its limited size.

5.2.1 Fixed Partitions

In multiprogrammed operating systems, memory management may be quite complex since it has to arbitrate among the needs and desires of many processes simultaneously competing for this resource. The simplest scheme, found in some early systems, is that of *fixed memory partitioning*. As the name suggests, memory is divided into a number of separate spaces, called partitions. Typically, partitions have different sizes to accommodate different programs; however, the sizes are fixed at system initialization and may not be changed while the system is operating.

The determination of partition sizes has a strong impact on the system's efficiency. Unfortunately, it is very difficult to estimate the demands that will be placed on a system at future times; bad choices may lead to a severe underutilization of main memory or other resources. A related problem is process scheduling for each of the partitions. Two possible schemes, depicted in Figure 5-6a and b, can be devised. In the first, a separate queue of processes exists for each partition. Typically, a process would be scheduled for the smallest partition that satisfies its memory requirements. This scheme is very simple to implement provided the requirements are specified a priori by each process. The obvious disadvantage is that partitions may remain unused if no processes of the appropriate sizes are available.

The second scheme, depicted in Figure 5-6b, employs a single queue for all arriving processes. The assignment to partitions is then made by the operating system dynamically. While more complicated to implement, this scheme offers greater flexibility for the system to adapt to the current workload. For example, when no process with the appropriate size is available for a given partition, the operating system may decide to assign to it some other process with smaller memory requirements, rather than leaving it completely idle.

The main advantage of fixed partitioning is its simplicity; the partitions are set up at the time the system is generated, and only a minimum amount of software is needed

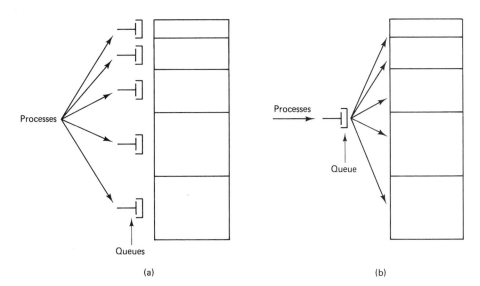

Figure 5-6 Scheduling of processes into fixed partitions: (a) using a separate queue for each partition (b) using a common queue for all partitions.

to perform the necessary scheduling at run time. Examples of systems using this approach include IBM DOS and IBM OS/MFT (multiprogramming with fixed number of tasks).

5.2.2 Variable Partitions and Compaction

Instead of determining the partition sizes at system initialization, a variable partition scheme may be employed. As new processes arrive, the operating system assigns to each the exact amount of space required. Since processes do not normally terminate in the order of their arrival, memory will consist of a number of variable-sized blocks, only some of which will be occupied by active processes. Hence the main task of the operating system is to keep track of the free spaces and to assign these to newly arriving processes. It must also coalesce adjacent free spaces released by terminating processes into larger blocks to prevent *fragmentation* of main memory into spaces too small for any process to use. Theoretically, contiguous assignment is not necessary, and individual procedures and data may be allocated separately; this, however, complicates the storage management and protection procedures considerably. (Fragmentation occurs in different forms and with different degrees of severity, regardless of the allocation policy; we will return to this problem in succeeding sections.) An example of a system using a variable-partitioned memory scheme is the IBM OS/MVT (multiprogramming with variable number of tasks).

A question related to fragmentation is: what should be done in a situation where an arriving process is too large to fit into any single free space currently available, but the total of two or more existing spaces would be sufficient. Figure 5-7 illustrates this situation in a simple case. In the figure, H_i represents a hole, and $|X|$ is the quantity of storage occupied by program or hole X. Suppose program B finishes, creating a hole between A and C; if program D is now ready to be loaded, there is not enough contiguous

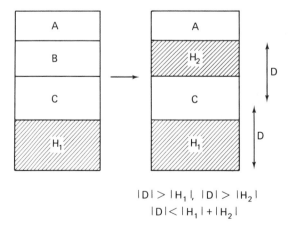

$$|D| > |H_1|, \ |D| > |H_2|$$
$$|D| < |H_1| + |H_2|$$

Figure 5-7 Storage fragmentation.

storage available, even though the total amount of unused memory is ample. One possible solution is to let the process wait until a free space of sufficient size is created as other processes terminate. Another solution is to rearrange the current memory allocation to create sufficient contiguous space for the process. Obviously, a dynamic relocation scheme is required here, since the rearranged storage contains linked programs and data. Several such strategies, called *memory compaction*, could be envisioned.

To illustrate the principles, assume that memory is occupied as shown in Figure 5-8a and that a request for a block of size 10 is to be satisfied. One possible way to accomplish this is to move all currently occupied blocks to one end of the memory, thus creating a single free space of size 20 (Figure 5-8b). Note that the entire memory need not be reorganized in order to create a free space of size 10. Instead, the compaction procedure could start moving occupied blocks to one end of the memory, as in the previous case, but stop when a free space of sufficient size is created, as illustrated in Figure 5-8c.

Finally, more sophisticated versions of these strategies could be devised in an attempt to minimize the total amount of work to be performed. For example, in Figure 5-8d, only the block *p2* had to be relocated to free the necessary space. Such algorithms, however, are quite complex. Only the simpler versions are usually implemented on existing machines.

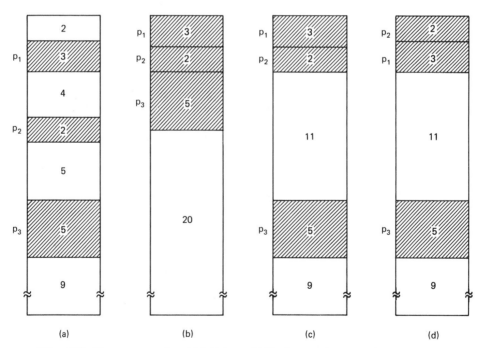

Figure 5-8   Memory compaction: (a) Initial state (b) Total compaction (c) Partial compaction (d) Partial compaction under minimization of moved data.

5.2.3 Overlays

The actual size of main memory imposes severe limitations in both single- and multi-programmed systems; in the former, the largest possible space for programs or data is the entire physical memory; in the latter, it is the largest partition. For computations that exceed the given limit, programs must be divided into smaller segments and loaded into memory separately. In the simplest case, a technique called *overlaying* is employed, in which program segments replace (overlay) each other in memory as execution proceeds. The programmer is required to specify those parts of the program that must reside in memory simultaneously. Such a specification may be obtained from the calling structure (tree) of a program, which describes the dependencies among procedures.

Consider, for example, a program consisting of five procedures A, B, C, D, and E. The calling structure depicted in Figure 5-9a shows the procedure A as the parent (caller) of the two procedures B and C, and C as the caller of D and E. Since B and C do not call each other, they need not reside in memory at the same time. The same is true of the procedures D and E; furthermore, their presence is needed only when C is resident. Based on this information, the operating system can allocate memory as shown graphically in Figure 5-9b. The two procedures B and C have the *same* starting address $k1$, while $k2$ is the common starting address of D and E. Each time A calls either B or C, the operating system is invoked; it determines which of the two procedures is to be executed, loads that procedure into memory starting at location $k1$, and completes the call by transferring control to that location. The same principle applies when C calls D or E.

The last three subsections have addressed two major issues in memory management: (1) sharing of main memory among different processes, and (2) execution of programs larger than the available physical space. (These two issues are related to one another in that increasing the number of programs that share the same memory necessarily reduces the portion available to each.) With the memory management schemes discussed so far, possible solutions to both problems have been offered. However, the existing memory limitations were directly *visible* to the programmer and thus required that all programs be planned and designed according to the available physical storage space. In the following section we present the concept of virtual memory, which liberates the programmer from the limits of physical memory by shifting the burden of memory management to the operating system.

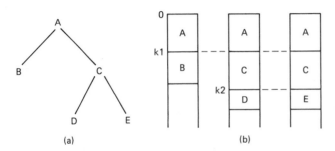

Figure 5-9 Program overlays: (a) Procedure calling structure (b) Address assignment.

5.3 PRINCIPLES OF VIRTUAL MEMORY

The basic idea of virtual memory is to hide the features of the real memory system from the user. In particular, virtual memories conceal the fact that physical memory is limited and, in the case of multiprogrammed systems, shared among different processes. The underlying implementation creates the *illusion* that a process has one or more contiguous "private" name spaces, each beginning at address zero. The sizes of such virtual address spaces may, for most practical purposes, be assumed unlimited. The principle is illustrated in Figure 5-10, which shows how different portions of two virtual spaces VM1 and VM2 are mapped onto physical storage.

The organization of virtual memory or name space is dependent on the mapping hardware, *NL_map*, that performs the translation to location space. However, it is convenient to describe the two principal virtual memory organizations before we consider their implementation.

The simplest and most obvious form of virtual memory is a contiguous linear space corresponding to our conventional view of storage. Virtual memory is a large, linearly addressed sequence of cells (words, bytes, or other units) with addresses typically sequenced: $0, 1, 2, \ldots, n - 1$, where $n = 2^k$ and $k \geq 1$. We call this a *single segment* name space.

A *multiple segment* virtual memory divides the name space into a set of segments S_i, where each S_i is a contiguous linear space. A *segment* is a user-defined entity that can be treated as a logical and independent unit, for example a procedure or an array of data. One may also view a program segment as that code which constitutes a relocatable object module. Addresses can be put in the form of a pair (s, w), where s represents a segment identifier and w is a word identifier (name or number).

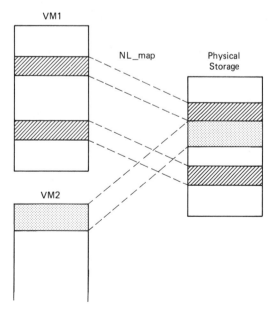

Figure 5-10   Principles of virtual memory.

Example

The following represent possible virtual memory addresses:

1. (5, 927): word 927 in segment 5. This could be the result of an address computation immediately prior to dynamic relocation.
2. (*Matrix*, 315): the 315th word in the segment named *Matrix*. The addresses in relocatable object code normally take this form.
3. (*Compiler*, *Entry__point*3): This is a typical reference to an external segment and may appear in a relocatable procedure or data segment prior to static or dynamic linking.

The organization of virtual memory as a set of logical segments is appealing for a number of reasons. First, what constitutes a segment is usually determined by a user when defining a program and its data areas; they are thus the natural units by which a user refers to information. As a consequence, operating systems can conveniently access user information on a segment basis. Information sharing (i.e., sharing of programs and data), protection against invalid access and addressing errors, storage allocation, and language translation may all be treated by the system in units of segments. Because segments are largely independent of one another, it is often possible in dynamic storage systems to permit them to grow and shrink as execution progresses, provided the virtual memory is large enough.

To implement a virtual memory, three main storage management decisions must be resolved. These are *placement*, *replacement*, and *load control* strategies.

The *placement* strategy determines *where* in executable storage to load all or part of virtual memory. For example, one could either assign the first free block (hole) that fits a given request or the smallest hole that fits.

A *replacement* strategy is necessary in systems that employ dynamic memory allocation policies. Here we must decide *what* to remove from executable storage when not enough room is available for a program or data that must be loaded; the intuitive solution is to select that area of storage with the least likelihood of being referenced in the near future. We will consider various solutions to this problem in the context of specific dynamic relocation hardware.

The third problem, *load control*, is concerned with the policies of *when* to load portions of virtual memory and *how much* of it to load at any given time. At one extreme, a static linking loader loads all of a process's virtual memory prior to execution; this automatically restricts the number of processes that can be active simultaneously. A policy at the other extreme is to load portions of virtual memory at the last possible moment (i.e., at the time of reference to a segment or part of a segment). In this latter case of *demand loading*, only the "how much" decision has to be made. The disadvantages of static loading are the limited degree of multiprogramming and the possible waste of main storage and IO time when only a small part of virtual memory is accessed within a given time interval. On the other hand, demand loading can incur much system overhead and consume an inordinate amount of IO time, especially in a nearly saturated situation, where the same code may be loaded and replaced many times during a single run. Section 5.4 discusses the various solutions and trade-offs.

5.4 IMPLEMENTATION OF VIRTUAL MEMORY

5.4.1 Single-segment Name Space

5.4.1.1 Contiguous Storage Allocation

In one of the earliest methods for dynamic relocation, a single-segment name space is mapped into a contiguous region of main storage. This can be accomplished through a relocation register, RR, which always contains the base address of the location space for the process currently running on the CPU. The mapping, NL_map, is simply a hardware implementation of the basic relocation principles described in Section 5.1.1:

```
function NL_map(va): pa;
begin
    NL_map := va + RR
end
```

where va is a virtual address and pa is a physical address. Location spaces (or portions thereof) for several different processes may reside concurrently in main storage for multiprogramming purposes. The state vector of each process p must minimally contain the following:

1. The virtual storage instruction counter ic_p.
2. The base address ba_p of p's real memory (location space).

A switch from process p_1 to p_2 then includes the following actions:

$$ic_{p_1} := ic; \qquad \text{(Store state of } p_1\text{)}$$
$$ic := ic_{p_2}; \ RR := ba_{p_2} \qquad \text{(Load state of } p_2\text{)}$$

where ic is the machine instruction counter (Figure 5-11).

The limitation of this simple virtual memory scheme is that each name space must be smaller than or equal to main storage in size. The main advantage of using the relocation register is that programs may be swapped in and out of different areas of memory easily; only the base address of the location space need be changed. Programs and data are still statically linked and relocated in virtual memory prior to initial loading. As one example, the IBM 7090, a once popular second-generation machine, was modified for the MIT Project MAC time-sharing system to perform dynamic relocation with a single relocation register (IBM, 1963).

If there is more than one relocation register, the contiguous location space requirement is no longer necessary and a more general segmented virtual memory organization can be implemented. For reasons of protection, the relocation registers must *not* be accessible to regular user programs.

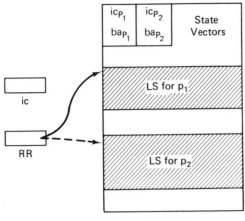

Main Storage

Figure 5-11 Process switching with
simple dynamic relocation.

LS: Location Space

5.4.1.2 Paging

The term *paging* is used to describe a particular implementation of virtual memory and
organization of main storage. The latter is divided into a number of equal-sized contiguous *blocks* or *page frames* $f_0, f_1, \ldots, f_{F-1}$; the most common block size is 512 or
1024 words. A physical memory address *pa* is considered a pair (f, w), where f is the
page frame number and w is a word number (i.e., an offset or displacement within the
frame f). Usually, when *pa* is a string of k bits (resulting in a physical memory of 2^k
words), the first n bits are interpreted as the frame number f, while the remaining $m =
k - n$ bits give the word number w. For example, a 16-bit address could be divided into
$f = 7$ and $w = 9$, resulting in 128 frames of 512 words each.

Similarly, a name space is divided into a number of equal-sized contiguous *pages*
$p_0, p_1, \ldots, p_{P-1}$, where page size is identical to page frame size. (The last page,
p_{P-1}, may have to be padded at the end to have the size of a frame.) An address *va* in
virtual memory is treated as a pair (p, w), where p is a page number and w is a word
number within that page; the correspondence between *va* and (p, w) is obtained in the
same manner as that between *pa* and (f, w). The *NL_map* then associates a virtual
memory page with a physical memory page frame, as illustrated in Figure 5-12.

The *NL_map* translates a virtual memory address (p, w) into a real address
$(f, w) = f \times 2^m + w$, where 2^m is the page size. One approach to implementing
NL_map is to maintain a table of length F that gives the correspondence between every
frame and page. Let this table be an array $pn[0..F - 1]$, where $pn[f]$ contains either
the number of the page stored in frame f for the current process or some indication that
frame f is not allocated to the current process. Assuming that each addressed page is in
main storage, the *NL_map* could (conceptually) be written as follows:

```
function NL_map((p, w)): pa;
begin
```

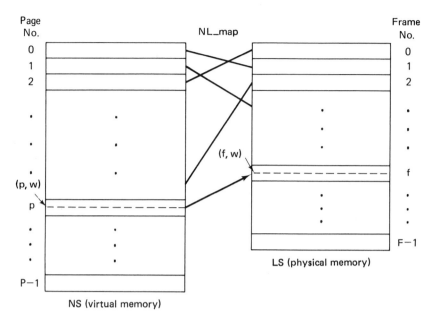

Figure 5-12 A paged virtual memory.

$$f := 0;$$
$$\textbf{while } pn[f] \neq p \textbf{ do}$$
$$\qquad f := f + 1$$
$$\textbf{end};$$
$$NL\_map := f \times 2^m + w$$
$$\textbf{end}$$

Unfortunately, a sequential search such as this is extremely inefficient, even if accomplished through hardware since, on the average, $F/2$ comparisons would have to be made at *every* storage reference. To make this approach practical, the table is stored in *associative memory*, and the search is effectively performed in parallel.

An associative memory is one in which cells are referenced by their *content* rather than their address. A familiar example will clarify this concept. Each entry in a telephone book may be found easily when addressed by a triple: (*page, column, line*). To find a phone number for an individual, it is necessary to search the directory for a (*last name, first name*) match; this task is not difficult *only* because the entries have been sorted in alphabetical order by name. If, however, one starts with a phone number and wishes to find the name or address of the party with that number, the task is hopelessly time consuming. Storing the telephone book in a general associative memory would permit access of any entry using either a name or an address or a phone number as the search key; that is, any field in an entry can be used and the search occurs by content. Sorting is then not required. Hardware implementations of associative memories are not quite this general and normally only provide one search field for each entry.

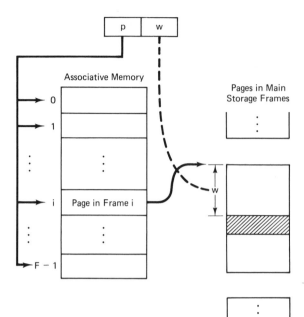

Figure 5-13 Address translation using associative memory.

Paging can be credited to the designers of the ATLAS computer, who employed an associative memory for the *NL_map* (Kilburn et al., 1962). The virtual address (p, w) is an $n + m$ bit number where the high-order n bits correspond to page number and the low-order m bits to word number. The page number is transformed by a parallel hardware search through an associative memory of F page registers into a frame number f. The concatenation of f onto w yields the physical storage address (Figure 5-13). For the ATLAS computer, $m = 9$ (resulting in 512 words per page), $n = 11$, and $F = 32$; thus a 2^{20}-word virtual memory was provided for a 2^{14}-word (16K) machine. The original ATLAS operating system employed paging solely as a means of implementing a large virtual memory; multiprogramming of user processes was not attempted initially.

More recent schemes maintain a *page table* in main storage for *each* process, instead of an associative memory. The ith entry in each page table identifies the page frame, if any, that contains page number i for that process. A page table register (*PTR*) contains the base address of the page table corresponding to the process currently executing on the CPU. The address computation performed by the *NL_map* is

function *NL_map*((p, w)): *pa*;
begin
   NL_map := $M[PTR + p] \times 2^m + w$
end

where M represents main storage. Figure 5-14 presents the mapping in graphical form. For example, suppose that the page table for the current process were located starting at

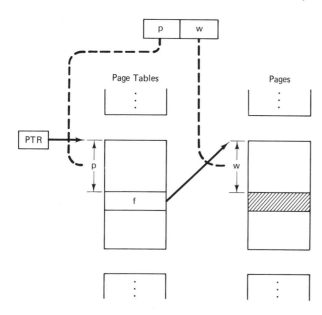

Figure 5-14 Address translation using a page table.

address 1024 and had the following contents:

$$1024: 21 \qquad 1025: 40 \qquad 1026: 3 \qquad 1027: 15 \quad \ldots$$

Assuming a page size of 1024 words, a virtual address (2, 100) would dynamically map into $M(1024 + 2) \times 1024 + 100 = 3 \times 1024 + 100 = 3172$. Note that *two* memory accesses must be made in order to read or write any storage word during a virtual memory operation, one access to the page table and the second to the actual page. To avoid the first access most of the time, it is common to use either an associative memory or a set of registers for all or part of the page table of the current process.

Systems that employ paging have two main advantages over nonpaged systems. The first is a very simple *placement* policy. Since the basic unit of storage allocation is a page, programs and data need not occupy a contiguous area of memory but can be scattered through it on a page basis. Thus, if a demand for k pages of storage is made and there are at least k free frames, the placement decision is straightforward; any frame may be allocated for any page. One might conclude erroneously that paging eliminates the fragmentation problem occurring in variable memory partition schemes. It is certainly true that the specific difficulty illustrated in Figures 5-7 and 5-8 cannot occur. However, because the sizes of programs and data are rarely multiples of the page size, the last page of each virtual memory space is generally only partially filled. Thus we now have an *internal* fragmentation problem.

The second major virtue of paging systems is that programs larger than the available main storage may be executed without requiring the programmer to specify an overlay structure. This is accomplished by implementing dynamic storage allocation, where pages are loaded at their first reference rather than statically. This policy is called *demand paging.* It requires a mechanism that signals a ''missing page'' when reference is made to a page currently not resident in main memory. This event, called *page fault*, invokes the operating system, which loads the desired page into a selected frame (possibly after removing from that frame a currently resident page) and reactivates the process that caused the page fault. The following extension of the *NL_map* function illustrates this principle; the function *resident(m)* returns the value *true* if *m* designates a currently resident page and the value *false* if the page is missing from memory:

```
function NL_map((p, w)): pa;
begin
    if resident(M[PTR + p])
    then NL_map := M[PTR + p] × 2^m + w
    else page fault
end
```

With this feature, an operating system can provide name spaces larger than main storage. (We postpone the detailed discussions of different placement and replacement policies until Section 5.5.2.)

Example

The paging hardware available on the XDS Sigma 7 computer permits a large virtual memory of up to 132K words for each user. It has 256 fast registers that implement the virtual-to-physical address mapping. The page frame number entries in a user page table are loaded into these registers prior to execution; the mapping occurs dynamically through these registers rather than main storage. Page size is 512 words in the Sigma 7.

Another example of a system that employs pure paging is DEC's VAX 11/780. The virtual space of each process is divided into four regions as shown in Figure 5-15 (Digital Equipment Corp., 1982). The first region is referred to as the *program region*; it contains all executable code and user data comprising the current process. The second region, referred to as the *control region*, contains process control structures, such as stacks and the IO database, and other process-related information maintained by the system. The program

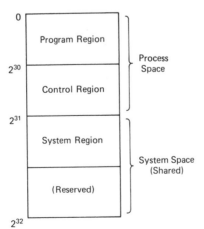

Figure 5-15 Memory organization in VAX 11/780.

and the control regions are private to the process; they constitute the *process space*. The remaining two regions constitute the *system space*, which is shared by *all* processes. The first of these, the *system region*, contains the VAX/VMS executive (i.e., the operating system itself) and those data structures required to control the processes and to maintain the status of all physical and virtual pages within the system. The last region is reserved for future expansion.

All four regions are divided into pages of 512 words each, which can be moved between secondary and primary memory as necessary. Each virtual address consists of 32 bits; the first 2 bits are used to select a region, the next 21 bits select the page, and the remaining 9 bits select the word within the page. This implies a total virtual address space of 2^{23} pages per process.

5.4.2 Multiple-segment Name Space

There are two different approaches to implementing a multiple-segment virtual memory. The first treats the segment as the basic unit for storage allocation and assumes that storage can be dynamically allocated and relocated in variable-sized blocks. The second employs paging as a means of allocating space for a segment.

5.4.2.1 Contiguous Allocation per Segment

Storage is allocated and addresses are relocated on a segment basis. The most prominent example of this method is found in the Burroughs B5500 and B6500 computers (Burroughs Corp., 1964, 1967). These are stack machines oriented toward the efficient compilation and execution of block-structured languages. Segments correspond to natural source language units such as procedures, arrays, or abstract data types.

A *segment table* is maintained in main storage for each active user process. Each entry in the table contains the base location of the code or data and protection information. A segment table register (*STR*) points to the segment table for the process currently running in the CPU; the *STR* is similar to the *PTR* described in the last section. A virtual address (*s*, *w*) is mapped to a real storage address as follows:

```
function NL__map((s,w)) : pa;
begin
  if resident(M[STR + s])
  then NL__map := M[STR + s] + w
  else segment fault
end
```

We have assumed that segments are numbered sequentially and the *i*th entry in the segment table (*i* = 0,1, . . .) corresponds to segment number *i*. The function *resident* serves the same purpose as with demand paging; if the referenced segment is currently not resident in memory, a *segment fault* invokes the operating system to take the necessary actions. The segmentation scheme is considerably simplified if all segments of an active process are required to reside in memory at all times. In this case, the test may be omitted since no segment fault is possible. The segment table itself is treated as a segment by the system. The mapping may be performed more efficiently by keeping $M[STR + s]$ in a hardware stack for the current segment s.

The main advantage of this organization as compared with paging is that it divides programs into variable-sized components, thus preserving their logical structure. This simplifies linking and sharing of procedures and data, as will be discussed in Section 5.6. The drawbacks of segmentation are a complex placement and, in the case of demand segmentation, a complex replacement policy. Also, the possibility of much unused memory (external fragmentation) exists, because the unit of allocation is variable in size. The decision whether paging or segmentation should be implemented depends largely on the system's environment and its intended domain of applications. In recent years, systems using only paging or paging combined with segmentation have become more common than those using pure segmentation.

5.4.2.2 Paging with Segmentation

To provide a multisegment address space for each user and yet, at the same time, permit a simple placement policy, the principles of paging and segmentation have been combined into one memory management scheme. Storage is organized in fixed-sized blocks that are allocated to programs and data as in the case of pure paging. However, one more level of indirection in the dynamic mapping is introduced. That is, a virtual memory address is considered a triple (s, p, w), where s is the segment number, p is the page number within the segment, and w is the offset within the page. A segment table register STR points to the segment table for the current process; the segment table entries point to page tables (one per segment), which in turn point to pages (frames). The resulting NL_map for a virtual address (s, p, w) is

```
function NL__map((s, p, w)): pa;
begin
    NL__map := M[M[STR + s] + p] × 2^m + w
end
```

as illustrated in Figure 5-16. This is the simplest form of NL_map, which assumes that the segment table, the page tables, and the pages themselves are resident in memory. If this requirement is relaxed (as is frequently done to permit more efficient utilization of main memory), each reference may potentially produce a page fault. Hence, NL_map must be extended to ensure that a page is resident before the access is made.

With the preceding scheme, each segment and page table is considered to be a page. Each process has its own private segment table and may or may not have private page tables. Demand paging is attractive under this organization; it permits an efficient use of storage and allows dynamic changes in segment size. The disadvantages of paging with segmentation are the extra storage required for the tables, the overhead of administrating storage in such a complex system, and the inefficiency of two additional storage references at each mapping. Again, fast associative memories are used to avoid extra references (Section 5.4.2.4).

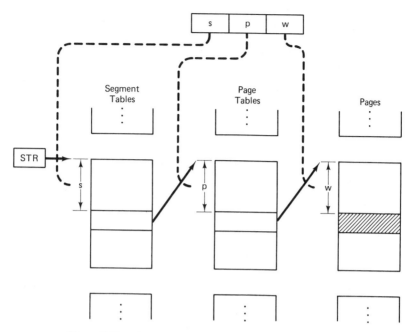

Figure 5-16   Address translation using segment and page tables.

Example

Paging with segmentation has been used primarily in large general-purpose time-sharing systems. The GE 645 (Bash et al., 1967), IBM 360/67 (Comfort, 1965), and RCA Spectra 70/46 (Oppenheimer and Weizer, 1968) are the most prominent examples of such systems. Table 5-1 shows the sizes of the s, p, and w fields for the three machines. From the number of bits in each field, we can easily compute the page size and the maximum number of segments and pages per segment for each virtual space.

TABLE 5-1   EXAMPLES OF s, p, AND w SIZES.

	s	p	w
GE 645			
(word addressing)	18	8	10 bits
IBM 360/67			
(byte addressing)	4 or 12	8	12
RCA Spectra 70/46			
(byte addressing)	5	6	12

5.4.2.3 Paging of System Tables

The sizes of the segment and page tables of a virtual memory system are determined by the lengths of the s and p address components, respectively. In some systems, these tables may become potentially very large and thus it may not be practical to keep them permanently resident in main memory. Rather, each table must itself be divided into pages and loaded only as needed. Let us illustrate how this may be accomplished in the case of a segment table. The s component of the virtual address is divided into two parts, say $s1$ and $s2$. The segment table is then broken into pages of size $2^{|s2|}$, where $|s2|$ is the number of bits comprising $s2$. Normally, the page size for the segment table would be the same as the page size for program and data pages: $|s2| = |w|$.

To keep track of the pages comprising the segment table, we need a new page table, as shown in Figure 5-17. The $s1$ component is used to index this table, which, at run time, is pointed to by the register *STR*; this becomes the *root* of the memory-mapping mechanism. The individual pages comprising the segment table are indexed by $s2$; p and w are used as before. Assuming that all tables are in memory, the *NL__map* for a virtual address $(s1, s2, p, w)$ can be described as

function *NL__map*$((s1, s2, p, w))$: *pa*;
begin
    NL__map $:= M[M[M[STR + s1] + s2] + p] \times 2^m + w$
end

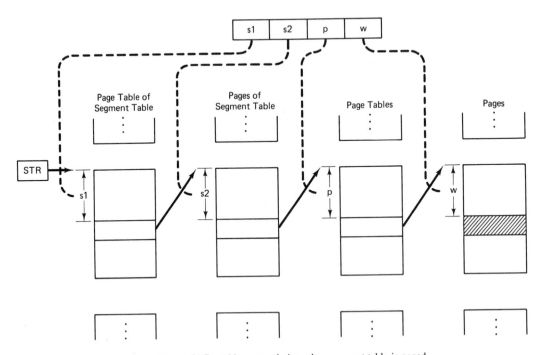

Figure 5-17   Address translation when segment table is paged.

Example

The s component in the MULTICS operating system is 18 bits long (Table 5-1), resulting in a segment table of 2^{18} or 262,144 entries. This table is divided into pages of 1024 words, resulting in $|s2| = 10$ and $|s1| = |s| - |s2| = 8$. Hence the page table of the segment table has 256 entries.

In the VAX/VMS operating system, the p component has 21 bits, resulting in a very large page table of 2^{21} or 2,097,152 entries. VAX/VMS solves this problem by keeping the page tables for the program and control segments in the system space, which is automatically subject to paging. In general, a page of a page table will be resident in memory only when it contains at least one reference to a currently resident page of process space (program or control segment). Only the page table of the system space is kept permanently resident.

5.4.2.4 Address Translation Buffers

The concept of virtual memory offers a number of advantages over approaches that make physical memory visible to programs. Its main drawback, however, is the increased number of memory operations necessary for each reference. In the simplest case of pure paging or segmentation, one additional memory read is necessary to access the page or segment table. If both approaches are combined, two additional memory reads are needed, one to the segment table and a second to the page table. Finally, when segment or page tables are themselves paged, the number of references increases by three, each possibly involving a page fault.

To alleviate this problem, special high-speed memories, sometimes called *translation look-aside buffers*, are often provided to aid the address translation process. The basic idea underlying such buffers is to keep the most recent translations of virtual to physical addresses readily available for possible future use. An associative memory, the principles of which were already explained in Section 5.4.1, is employed for this purpose. When a given virtual page is accessed several times within a short time interval, the address translation is performed only during the first reference; subsequent accesses bypass most of the translation mechanisms by fetching the appropriate frame number directly from the associative buffer.

Figure 5-18 shows the organization of such a translation look-aside buffer for a system with both segmentation and paging. The first column contains entries of the form (s, p), where s is a segment number and p is a page number. When a virtual address (s, p, w) is presented to the memory system, the buffer is searched associatively (in parallel) for the occurrence of the pair (s, p). If found, the number f in the second column of the buffer gives the frame number in which the corresponding page currently resides. By adding the offset w to f, the addressed word is found. Note that only one access to main memory is necessary in this case; the segment and page table were bypassed by searching the buffer. Only when the search for (s, p) fails need the complete address translation be performed. The resulting frame number is then entered, together with the pair (s, p), into the buffer for possible future references to the same page. This normally requires the replacement of a current buffer entry. The most common policy is

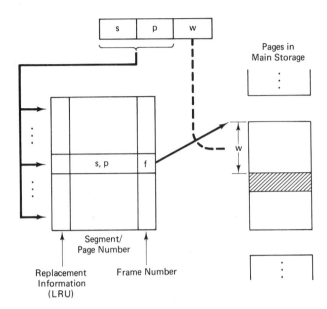

Figure 5-18   A translation look-aside buffer.

to replace the least recently used such entry (LRU), which is determined by a built-in hardware mechanism. (More detail on this policy may be found in Section 5.5.2.3.)

5.5 ALLOCATION STRATEGIES

5.5.1 Storage Allocation in Nonpaged Systems

This section is concerned with the problems of allocating and freeing *variable*-sized blocks of main storage in systems without paging hardware. These operations might be performed by the two commands (see Section 3.3.2):

1. *RequestMain__Store,Size, Base__Addr*, and
2. *Release(Main__Store,(Size, Base__Addr))*,

where *Size* is the number of contiguous units involved in the operation and *Base__Addr*, the first (low-order) address of the block, is an output parameter of *Request* and an input parameter to *Release*.

Given a request for a storage block of size k, we can generally proceed as follows. If there is a hole H of size h such that $h \geq k$, then allocate k units of H to the requesting process. (The criterion for selecting one of several competing satisfactory holes was called the placement strategy in Section 5.3.) If a hole of sufficient size is not available, one can choose from a number of alternative strategies: The requesting process can be placed in blocked status until sufficient free storage becomes available, one or more used blocks may be deallocated to create a hole of adequate size (a replacement policy), or used storage may be compacted (i.e., moved to a single contiguous area) in an attempt to create a large enough hole (Section 5.2.2). We examine two popular placement strategies.

5.5.1.1 First Fit and Best Fit Placement

Let main storage be divided into two sets of variable-sized blocks: a set of empty or unused holes $\{H_i \mid i = 1, \ldots, n\}$ and a set of allocated or full blocks $\{F_i \mid i = 1, \ldots, m\}$. Given a request for a block of size k, a *first-fit* placement strategy searches for the *first* hole H_i, such that $h_i \geq k$, where h_i is the size of hole H_i. A *best-fit* strategy selects that hole H_i with the closest fit (i.e., $h_i \geq k$, and for all H_j such that if $h_j \geq k$ then $h_j \geq h_i$ for $i \neq j$). For both strategies, when $h_j - k$ is small but nonzero, it is preferable to allocate all of H_i rather than just k units; otherwise, the newly created hole of size $h_i - k$ may be too small to be of any future value and may result in wasted time and space during all subsequent storage management activities. First fit is fast but, intuitively, it wastes larger holes by prematurely allocating parts of them. Best fit retains larger holes for future use but is a slower procedure; it also has a tendency to create many small and useless holes. It is easy to devise nonpathological examples in which either of the two methods is superior to the other.

Examples

For simplicity, we just consider a sequence of storage *Requests* and allocations and assume that storage blocks are not *Released*.

REQUEST SEQUENCE WHERE BEST FIT PERFORMS BETTER

Storage Request	Size of Holes in Available Space	
	First Fit	Best Fit
(1) Initial state	2000,1500	2000,1500
(2) 1200	800,1500	2000,300
(3) 1600	Blocked	400,300

REQUEST SEQUENCE WHERE FIRST FIT PERFORMS BETTER

Storage Request	Size of Holes in Available Space	
	First Fit	Best Fit
(1) Initial state	2000,1500	2000,1500
(2) 1200	800,1500	2000,300
(3) 1400	800,100	600,300
(4) 700	100,100	Blocked

Experiments with both these methods over a wide range of simulated data were performed by Knuth (1968). In most cases, the best-fit system terminated earlier (blocked in our simplified examples) because of insufficient storage. The simulations indicate that one cannot always trust intuition. Note also that longest time until termination is not necessarily the best criterion to use; for example, different results might be obtained if processes were placed in blocked status on unsatisfied requests. Extensive experiments should be made using realistic statistical distributions of request size, request arrival times, and the "lifetimes" of allocations before committing an operating system to any particular policy.

The first-fit method of searching available space can be improved with a simple trick (Knuth, 1968). Assume that holes (size and address) are kept in a list. A straightforward search might always start at the top of the list and continue sequentially until a fit is found. Unfortunately, this tends to cluster the smaller holes near the top of the list, since allocations are performed there first if possible; as time proceeds, it would then take longer and longer on the average before obtaining a fit. An efficient scheme that would keep the hole size more uniformly distributed over the list is to start the search at some variable point Q within the list. One possibility for Q is the next item following a selected hole on a successful search. This policy is referred to as *rotating first fit* and has been used, for example, in the INTEL iAPX 432 (see Section 5.7).

5.5.1.2 *Available Space Administration*

We first investigate data structures for maintaining information on available space (holes). The goal is to exhibit a structure in which first-fit and best-fit searches may be done conveniently and new holes can be added as storage is released. Instead of keeping a separate storage area for the data structure, we can use the hole space itself.

Consider the straightforward use of a simple singly linked list (Figure 5-19). The first entries of each hole block contain the length of the block and a pointer to the next hole. A header pointer, say *Avail*, points to the first block of the list; *NIL* indicates the last element. The following difficulty arises. A block that is released can be surrounded by a free or full block on either side, as illustrated in Figure 5-20. It is desirable to coalesce or merge adjacent free blocks on a release, but to do this the allocation of the blocks surrounding the released block must be obtained easily. In the data structure of Figure 5-19, it would be very awkward to determine whether a hole or a full block is adjacent to any given block.

The problems are avoided by tagging the upper and lower boundaries of each full and empty block and by chaining holes using doubly linked lists (Knuth, 1968). We store a single-bit tag (assumed to be a Boolean variable for this discussion) and the block size as both the first two and the last two elements of each block; a *true* tag denotes a hole, and a *false* tag indicates a full block. In addition, a forward and backward pointer is stored at the head of each hole as part of the hole chain (Figure 5-21). The pointer changes on a block release for case d of Figure 5-20 are illustrated in Figure 5-22. New holes are inserted at the head of the list, since this is the most conveniently accessed place. (The list tail would do equally well.)

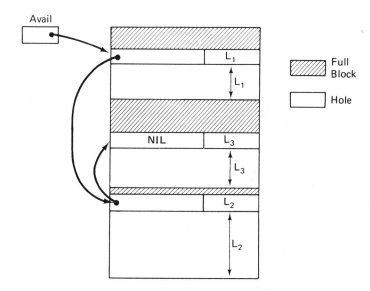

Figure 5-19 Available space administration using a singly linked list.

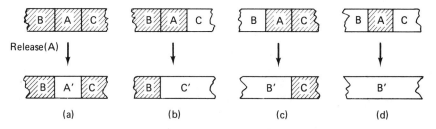

Figure 5-20 Hole coalescing on a release.

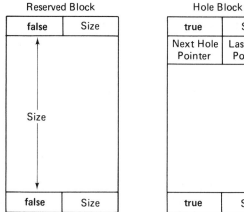

Figure 5-21 Boundary tag data structure.

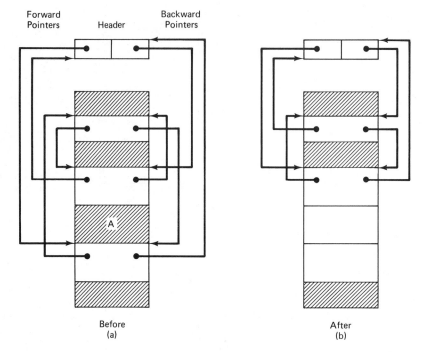

Figure 5-22   Effect of executing *Release (A)*.

Linked lists are not always the best way to keep track of available space. If storage is allocated in contiguous sequences of *fixed-sized* blocks, a separate table containing a bit map may be more efficient. For example, suppose that storage is broken into 32K-word blocks for allocation purposes, and there are 256K words (8×32) of main memory. Then the allocation state of storage can be represented by a bit string, $B = b_0 b_1 \dots b_7$, where $b_i = 0$ or 1, depending on whether block i is free or used. A storage-release operation can be done with a logical AND of B and an appropriate bit mask. For example, the release of blocks 4, 5, and 6 is accomplished by the statement

$$B := B \wedge \text{''11110001''};$$

A first-fit search for k contiguous blocks, $1 \leq k \leq 8$, involves a number of shifts and logical operations as follows:

Mask := ''$0^k 1^{8-k}$'';   {0^k *and* 1^{8-k} *denote strings of k zeros and 8 − k ones*}
Block_start := −1;   {*initially undefined*}
for i := 0 **to** 8 − k **do**
    if (*Mask* $\wedge$ *B*) = *B* **then begin** *Block_start* := *i;* **exit; end**
    else *Mask* := *Right_circular_shift*(*Mask*,1)   {*shift by* 1}
if *Block_start* = − 1 **then** report failure

5.5.1.3 Some Analysis of Storage Fragmentation and Utilization

It is possible to obtain some measures of the fragmentation and utilization of main storage under the preceding strategies for placement and release. We assume that requests and releases are equiprobable and that the system has reached an equilibrium state where the average change per unit time in the number of holes is zero. Let n and m be the average number of holes and full blocks, respectively, at equilibrium. Consider again Figure 5-20, which shows the effect of releasing a block A. There are four possible cases, depending on whether A is surrounded by free or full blocks. Let a, b, c, and d be the average number of full blocks of each type in storage during equilibrium. Ignoring boundary conditions at both ends of memory, we have

$$m = a + b + c + d \tag{1}$$

$$n = \frac{2d + b + c}{2}$$

Since $b = c$, we obtain

$$n = d + b \tag{2}$$

Let q be the probability of finding an exact fit hole on a request and $p = 1 - q$. In Figure 5-20, the number of holes increases by 1 in case a, decreases by 1 in case d, and remains constant in cases b and c as a result of the release. The probability that n increases by 1 at any change in storage allocation is

$$Prob(release) \times \frac{a}{m} \tag{3}$$

The probability that n decreases by 1 is

$$Prob(release) \times \frac{d}{m} + Prob(request) \times (1 - p) \tag{4}$$

where $Prob(release)$ and $Prob(request)$ are the relative probabilities of storage requests and releases.

The equilibrium condition implies that (3) = (4). Since $Prob(request) = Prob(release)$,

$$\frac{a}{m} = \frac{d}{m} + (1 - p)$$

That is,

$$a = d + (1 - p)m \tag{5}$$

Substituting (2) and (5) in (1), we have

$$m = d + (1 - p)m + b + c + d = (1 - p)m + 2b + 2d = (1 - p)m + 2n$$

which gives the final result:

$$n = \tfrac{1}{2} pm$$

This measure of storage fragmentation was originally derived by Knuth (1968), who called it the *50 percent rule*, since n tends to 50 percent of m as p approaches 1.

Denning (1970) obtained the following result on storage utilization. Let the average hole size be $h = kb$, where b is the average full block size and $k > 0$; and let p, the probability used in the 50 percent rule, be 1. Then, the fraction f of storage occupied by holes in an equilibrium state is

$$f = \frac{k}{k + 2}$$

This can be easily derived by using the 50 percent rule with $p = 1$. Let M be the storage size. Then

$$h = kb = \frac{M - mb}{m/2}$$

This leads to

$$M = mb\left(\frac{k}{2} + 1\right)$$

Therefore,

$$f = \frac{(m/2)\,kb}{M} = \frac{(m/2)\,kb}{mb\left[(k/2) + 1\right]} = \frac{k/2}{(k/2) + 1} = \frac{k}{k + 2}$$

Simulations by Knuth (1968) indicate that an average request size $b \le M/10$ is necessary to obtain a hole fraction of $f \approx 0.1$;[†] in this case, hole size is approximately $0.22b$. When b is large, say about $M/3$, f rises to 0.5, and k is then 2. The obvious conclusions are that M must be large relative to b in a dynamic environment or else much storage will remain unused, and that some fraction f of storage will always be wasted.

When a request cannot be satisfied, storage compacting may be considered as a means to produce a large enough hole. However, it is frequently the case that storage utilization is high at this point, and the results are not worth the effort. An alternative policy is to swap out enough full blocks to create the required size of hole. The replacement strategies discussed for paging systems in the next section are also applicable to the swapping case.

5.5.2 Storage Allocation in Paged Systems

5.5.2.1 Static and Dynamic Allocation

Paging hardware can be useful in systems that allocate storage *statically* for each user, as well as in *dynamically* allocated systems. In static allocation, paging permits the

---

[†]A simulation experiment terminated on "memory overflow" (i.e., on a request that could not be satisfied).

assignment of noncontiguous fixed-sized storage blocks (page frames) to a single-name space; no placement decisions, such as first fit or best fit, are necessary, since a given page can reside in any page frame. Available space administration is also simplified considerably; an unordered list of free frames is a sufficient data base for memory requests and releases. The main disadvantage of static allocation is that user name space must be less than or equal in size to real main storage; the degree of possible multiprogramming is also reduced since all pages comprising a process's virtual space must be resident while the process is active. Alternately, a system may permit user-specified overlays in virtual memory.

The arguments for dynamic allocation, for example demand paging, are the conservation of main storage, the reduction of IO time and storage interference between IO and central processors, and the increase in the number of active processes maintained in main memory.

Example

The RCA Spectra 70/46 provides a concrete example of the cost of loading unreferenced pages (Oppenheimer and Weizer, 1968): IO transmission time for one page (4K bytes) between secondary storage and main memory is approximately 12.5 ms. The memory interference rate is 1.44 μs/2 bytes; that is, for every 2 bytes transmitted over a channel, main memory is unavailable to the CPU for 1.44 μs. Thus, about 3 ms are stolen from the CPU by an IO channel for each page read or written. Looking at these figures in another way, there is a degradation of CPU activity by 24 percent (3/12.5) during a page IO; if the page is not referenced, this is a total waste. Similar ratios can be derived for more recent systems as well.

When virtual memories are implemented, the sum of the name space sizes for active processes is generally much larger than the available main storage, which is frequently entirely allocated. Consequently, most storage requests cannot be satisfied immediately. One often has the option of either *replacing* some page(s) in storage to make the requested frame space available, (a resource preemption policy), or delaying the requesting process until space becomes available by natural means. Replacement is commonly used, since much of the allocated storage will not be referenced again in the near future, if at all, and paging allows efficient replacement. The selection of the particular page to replace has been the subject of much research. The results can also be applied to replacement decisions in pure segmented systems. We also observe that, under paging, the placement strategy is determined a priori, leaving only the replacement and load-control strategies as the variables with which to optimize the behavior of a system with respect to its storage management policies. (We are assuming that the page size and the amount of main storage allocated to a program are fixed.) In the remainder of this section, a useful model for studying allocation and replacement policies with paged systems is presented.

We consider a complete execution time trace Z of a particular program with a specific set of input data. Z is given in the form

$$r_0 r_1 \ldots r_k \ldots r_T$$

where r_k is the instruction or data *page* referenced by the program at its kth storage access and r_T represents the last such reference; this type of trace has been called a *program reference string*. The subscripts in the reference string can be treated as time instants. Assume that the program and data corresponding to Z are allocated a main storage area of size m page frames, where $1 \leq m \leq n$ and n is the number of *distinct* pages in Z. An allocation policy P defines for each instant of time k the set of pages p_k that are loaded into memory at time k and the set of pages q_k that are removed or *replaced* at time k during the processing of Z. A common measure of goodness for a policy P is the total number of pages $n_P(Z)$ loaded into memory when Z is processed:

$$n_P(Z) = \sum_{k=0}^{T} |p_k|$$

Example

Let $Z = cadbebabcd$ and $m = 4$. The number of distinct pages is $n = 5$, since Z references the pages $\{a, b, c, d, e\}$. (We will use the same reference string and memory size for all examples in this section).

Consider a policy P that always assures that storage contains one of $\{a, b, c, d\}$, $\{a, b, e\}$, or $\{c, d, e\}$. Initially, memory contains the pages $\{a, b, c, d\}$. Then the storage map could change as shown by the following table:

Time	0	1	2	3	4	5	6	7	8	9	10
Z		c	a	d	b	e	b	a	b	c	d
Frame 0	a	a	a	a	a	a	a	a	a	c	c
Frame 1	b	b	b	b	b	b	b	b	b	d	d
Frame 2	c	c	c	c	c	e	e	e	e	e	e
Frame 3	d	d	d	d	d	—	—	—	—	—	—
Page fault						*				*	
p_P						e				c, d	
q_P						c, d				a, b	

Asterisks indicate the occurrences of page faults; p_P is the set of pages loaded into memory at that time, and q_P is the set of pages removed.

This example illustrates a policy that does *not* use pure demand paging. Rather, more than one page can be brought in (and, as a result, replace more than one currently resident page) at each time instant. For example, at time 5, two pages are removed; at time 9, two pages are brought in.

Mattson et al. (1970) have shown that, for *any* policy P and initial allocation of pages of Z, there exists a *demand* paging policy P_d such that

$$n_{P_d}(Z) \leq n_P(Z)$$

That is, an appropriately selected demand paging policy will yield the minimal $n_P(Z)$. However, one must be very careful in interpreting the results of such analyses, since the model and its assumptions may not be valid for some systems and the criterion of optimality, $n_P(Z)$, may not be appropriate. In particular, the demand paging result does *not* prove that this is the best policy to use; it only says that it brings in the fewest pages. Suppose, for example, that the cost $h(k)$ of loading k pages at a time was equal to $C_1 + C_2 k$, where C_1 and C_2 are constants. This is not an unrealistic cost formula for transmitting from secondary storage to executable storage; C_1 includes housekeeping and waiting costs, and $C_2 k$ assumes that the transmission cost is directly proportional to the number of pages. Then the loading cost for the policy of the preceding example is $2C_1 + 3C_2$. There were two page faults, during which three pages were loaded. The best demand paging policy for this reference string (see Section 5.5.2.2) has the cost $3C_1 + 3C_2$. For *any* $C_1 > 0$, we have $2C_1 + 3C_2 < 3C_1 + 3C_2$, showing that demand paging is more expensive.

In the remainder of this chapter, we will be concerned with only demand paging policies. Since only one page is loaded as a result of a page fault (except for possible prepaging when a process is activated),

$$n_P(Z) = \text{number of page faults}$$

We will use this measure as a quantitative criterion in comparing different page-replacement policies.

5.5.2.2 Page-Replacement Schemes with Fixed Number of Frames

During normal operation of a multiprogramming system, pages belonging to different processes are dispersed throughout the frames of main memory. When a page fault occurs and there is no free frame, the operating system must select one of the resident pages for replacement. Two possible strategies can be employed:

1. The page to be replaced is selected from the resident set of the *faulting* process.
2. The page to be replaced may belong to *any* of the processes in memory.

The two strategies will be referred to as *local* and *global* page-replacement schemes, respectively. The feature common to both is that a fixed set of page frames is provided, the total main memory in the case of global replacement and some constant subset thereof in the case of local replacement, from which pages may be selected. In this section we will examine a set of algorithms that may be employed in both cases.[†]

Optimal Replacement Policy (MIN).   For later comparisons and to provide insight into practical methods, we first describe a theoretically *optimal* but unrealizable replacement scheme. The model and criterion of goodness of Section 5.5.2.1 are assumed. That is, program reference strings are known a priori, and it is required to minimize $n_P(Z)$ for each string Z. Since there exists a demand paging policy with minimal $n_P(Z)$, only this type of policy is considered; the criterion for comparison is then the

---

[†]While both local and global replacement may be used with a fixed number of frames, the latter is more common. With a variable number of frames, the replacement is always local. In the literature, the terms global and local are sometimes used to refer to fixed and variable replacement schemes, respectively.

number of page faults. It can be proved that the following replacement strategy is optimal (Belady, 1966; Mattson et al., 1970; Aho, Denning, and Ullman, 1971): Select for replacement the page that will not be referenced for the longest time in the future. That is, if a page fault requiring a replacement occurs at time k, select the page r such that

$$r \neq r_i, \quad \text{for all } i, k < i \leq T, \text{ (i.e., } r \text{ is not referenced again)} \tag{1}$$

or, if such an r does not exist, select

$$r = r_t, \quad \text{where } k < t \leq T \text{ and } t - k \text{ is a maximum} \tag{2}$$

$$r \neq r_{t'}, \quad \text{for all } t; k < t' < t$$

Example

Let $Z = cadbebabcd$ and $m = 4$, as in the previous example. At time 0, memory contains the pages $\{a, b, c, d\}$. With the optimal replacement policy, the memory allocation changes as follows:

Time	0	1	2	3	4	5	6	7	8	9	10
Z		c	a	d	b	e	b	a	b	c	d
Frame 0	a	a	a	a	a	a	a	a	a	a	d
Frame 1	b	b	b	b	b	b	b	b	b	b	b
Frame 2	c	c	c	c	c	c	c	c	c	c	c
Frame 3	d	d	d	d	d	e	e	e	e	e	e
page fault						*					*
p_{MIN}						e					d
q_{MIN}						d					a

Two page faults occurred while processing Z. The first, at time 5, caused the replacement of page d, since d will not be referenced for the longest time in the future. For the second page fault, at time 10, we assumed that page a will not be referenced again and thus may be replaced.

Random Replacement and the Principle of Locality. Program reference strings are virtually never known in advance. Thus practical page replacement policies must be devised that can make the necessary decisions without an a priori knowledge of the reference behavior. The simplest scheme one might consider is a *random* selection strategy where the page to be replaced is selected using a random-number generator. This strategy would be useful if no assumption about the program's behavior could be made. Fortunately, most programs display a pattern of behavior called the *principle of locality*. According to this principle, a program that references a location n at some point in time is likely to reference the same location n and locations in the immediate vicinity of n in the near future. This statement is quite intuitive if one considers the typical execution patterns of a program:

1. Except for branch instructions, which typically constitute an average of only some 10 percent of all instructions, program execution is sequential. This implies that,

most of the time, the next instruction to be fetched will be the one immediately following the current instruction.

2. Most iterative constructs consist of a relatively small number of instructions repeated many times. Hence computation is confined to a small segment of code for the duration of each iteration.

3. A considerable amount of computation is spent on processing large data structures, such as arrays or sequences of records. A significant portion of this computation requires sequential processing; thus consecutive instructions tend to reference neighboring elements of the data structure. (Note, however, that the way data structures are stored in memory plays an important role in locality behavior. For example, a large two-dimensional array stored by columns but processed by rows might reference a different page on each access.)

Since moving pages between main memory and secondary storage is costly, it is obvious that a random page-replacement scheme will not yield as effective a policy as one that does not ignore the principle of locality.

First in/First out (FIFO).   Assuming a physical memory size of m page frames, an ordered list of resident pages, $P[0]$, $P[1]$, . . . , $P[m - 1]$, and a pointer k are maintained, such that $P[k]$ identifies the most recently loaded page and $P[k +_m i]$, $i = 1, 2, . . . , m - 1$, points to the ith page in chronological order. On a page fault, page $P[k +_m 1]$ is selected for replacement and k is incremented by 1 (mod m); the number of the loaded page is subsequently entered in $P[k]$.

Example

For the reference string $Z = cadbebabcd$ and physical memory size $m = 4$, we obtain the following changes in memory occupancy:

Time	0	1	2	3	4	5	6	7	8	9	10
Z		c	a	d	b	e	b	a	b	c	d
Frame 0	$\to a$	$\to a$	$\to a$	$\to a$	$\to a$	e	e	e	e	$\to e$	d
Frame 1	b	b	b	b	b	$\to b$	$\to b$	a	a	a	$\to a$
Frame 2	c	c	c	c	c	c	c	$\to c$	b	b	b
Frame 3	d	d	d	d	d	d	d	d	$\to d$	c	c
page fault						*		*	*	*	*
p_{FIFO}						e		a	b	c	d
q_{FIFO}						a		b	c	d	e

We have assumed that the pages resident in memory at time 0 were loaded in the order a, b, c, d (i.e., a is the oldest and d is the youngest resident). The arrow next to a page represents the pointer k. This causes a to be replaced first (at time 5) when the first page fault occurs. The algorithm results in a total of 5 page faults.

The main attraction of the FIFO replacement strategy is its simplicity in implementation: a list of m elements and a pointer, incremented each time a page fault occurs, are all that is required. Unfortunately, this strategy assumes that pages residing the *longest* in memory are the least likely to be referenced in the future and, as a consequence, it exploits the principle of locality only to some degree: in particular, it will not remove pages that have been brought into memory in the most recent past and that, according to the principle of locality, are likely to be referenced again in the near future. It does not, however, account for the fact that programs may return to pages referenced in the more distant past and will remove these even if they become heavily used again. Thus the principle of locality is often violated.

Least Recently Used (LRU). The LRU algorithm has been designed to fully comply with the principle of locality. If a page fault occurs and there is no empty frame in memory, it removes the page that has not been referenced for the longest time. To be able to make the correct choice, the algorithm must keep track of the relative order of all references to resident pages. Conceptually, this can be implemented by maintaining an ordered list of references. The length of this list is m, where m is the number of frames in main memory. When a page fault occurs, the list behaves as a simple stack: the page at the bottom is removed and the new page is added to the top. Hence the stack length m remains constant. To maintain the chronological history of page references, the list must, however, be reordered upon each reference: the referenced page is moved from its current position to the head of the list. The CDC STAR-100 implements this principle in its global form.

Example

The following table shows the current memory contents for the reference string $Z = cadbebabcd$ and $m = 4$ as in the previous examples. Below the memory, the stack is shown at each reference.

Time	0	1	2	3	4	5	6	7	8	9	10
Z		c	a	d	b	e	b	a	b	c	d
Frame 0	a	a	a	a	a	a	a	a	a	a	a
Frame 1	b	b	b	b	b	b	b	b	b	b	b
Frame 2	c	c	c	c	c	e	e	e	e	e	d
Frame 3	d	d	d	d	d	d	d	d	d	c	c
page fault						*				*	*
p_{LRU}						e				c	d
q_{LRU}						c				d	e
Top of stack	?	c	a	d	b	e	b	a	b	c	d
	?	?	c	a	d	b	e	b	a	b	c
	?	?	?	c	a	d	d	e	e	a	b
	?	?	?	?	c	a	a	d	d	e	a

At time 0 the stack is empty; during the next four references, it grows to *bdac*, where b is the top element. At time 5, a page fault occurs, which replaces page d, the lowest in the stack, with the new page e. The latter becomes the top-of-stack element. The next three references do not cause any page faults; however, the stack is reordered on each reference by moving the currently referenced page to the top of the stack. The next page fault causes the removal of page d, which, at that time, was the least recently referenced page. Similarly, the page fault at time 10 replaces the least recently referenced page e, thus bringing the total number of page faults produced by this algorithm to 3.

The implementation of LRU as a software stack is impractical due to the high overhead with reordering the stack upon each reference. Several methods implemented directly in hardware to reduce this overhead have been proposed. One suggested scheme employs a *capacitor* associated with each memory frame. The capacitor is charged upon each reference to the page residing in that frame. The subsequent exponential decay of the charge can be directly converted into a time interval that permits the system to find the page that has not been referenced for the longest time.

Another attractive technique uses an *aging register* of n bits for each page frame:

$$R = R_{n-1}R_{n-2} \ldots R_1R_0$$

On a page reference, R_{n-1} is set to 1, and every τ time units R is shifted right one unit. Thus, when interpreted as a positive binary number, the value of each R decreases periodically unless the corresponding page is referenced. Upon page fault, the algorithm selects the page with the smallest value of R to be replaced.

Clock Replacement Algorithm.   Due to the high cost of implementing LRU directly, the clock replacement scheme has been developed; it approximates the LRU scheme at a fraction of its cost. The clock algorithm maintains a circular list of all resident pages and a pointer to the current page in much the same way as the FIFO scheme described earlier. In addition, a bit u, called the *use* bit, is associated with each page frame. Upon each reference, the hardware automatically sets the corresponding use bit to 1. To select a page for replacement, the clock algorithm operates as follows. If the pointer is at a page whose use bit is 0, then that page is selected for replacement and the pointer is advanced; otherwise, the use bit is reset, the pointer is advanced to the next page on the list, and the same step is repeated. The name clock is derived from the fact that the pointer may be visualized as scanning the circumference of a dial, i.e., the circular linked list, until a page with $u = 0$ is found.

Example

For $Z = cadbebabcd$ and $m = 4$, the memory occupancy under the clock algorithm changes as follows:

Time	0	1	2	3	4	5	6	7	8	9	10
Z		c	a	d	b	e	b	a	b	c	d
Frame 0	$\to a/1$	$\to a/1$	$\to a/1$	$\to a/1$	$\to a/1$	$e/1$	$e/1$	$e/1$	$e/1$	$\to e/1$	$d/1$
Frame 1	$b/1$	$b/1$	$b/1$	$b/1$	$b/1$	$\to b/0$	$\to b/1$	$b/1$	$b/1$	$b/1$	$\to b/0$
Frame 2	$c/1$	$c/1$	$c/1$	$c/1$	$c/1$	$c/0$	$c/0$	$a/1$	$a/1$	$a/1$	$a/0$
Frame 3	$d/1$	$d/1$	$d/1$	$d/1$	$d/1$	$d/0$	$d/0$	$\to d/0$	$\to d/0$	$c/1$	$c/0$
page fault						$*$		$*$		$*$	$*$
P_{CLOCK}						e		a		c	d
q_{CLOCK}						a		c		d	e

The current value of the use bit is shown as a 0 or 1 following each page. Initially, we have assumed all pages to have the use bit set. At the time of the first page fault (time 5), the pointer is at the page a. Its use bit is reset and the pointer is advanced to the next page, b. b's use bit is also reset and the pointer is advanced to c. The same operation is applied to c and d, thus reaching page a once more. At this time, a's use bit is 0, causing that page to be replaced by the new page e. The pointer is now at page b. The next page fault at time 7 does not replace b but only resets its use bit and proceeds by replacing the following page c. The last two page faults occur when c and d are rereferenced at times 9 and 10, respectively. The total number of page faults is 4.

The clock algorithm approximates LRU in that frequently referenced pages will have their use bit set to 1 and thus will not be selected for replacement. Only if a page has not been referenced for the duration of a *complete* cycle of the pointer through the list will it be replaced. The IBM VM/370 operating system uses this approach.

The Second-chance Algorithm.   A replaced page must be written back onto secondary storage if its contents have been changed during its last occupancy of main memory; otherwise, the replaced page may simply be overwritten. A page that has been written into is frequently referred to as a *dirty* page. To be able to distinguish between the two types of pages, the hardware provides a *write* bit, say w, associated with each page frame. When a new page is loaded, the corresponding write bit is 0; it is set to 1 when the information in that page is modified by a store instruction. The write bit is sometimes called the *dirty* bit.

The pair of bits u (use bit) and w (write bit) associated with each page frame is the basis for the second-chance algorithm. As was the case with the clock algorithm, a circular list of all pages currently in memory and a pointer are maintained. When a page fault occurs, the pointer scans the list until it finds a page with both bits u and w equal to 0; this page is selected for replacement. Each time the pointer is advanced during the scan, the bits u and w are reset as shown in Table 5-2. If the change is from 01 to 00, the algorithm must also remember that this page is dirty and thus, prior to replacement, must be copied back onto secondary storage. The asterisk in the table indicates this situation.

The name second chance derives from the fact that a page that has been written

TABLE 5-2 CHANGES OF u
AND w BITS UNDER
SECOND CHANCE
ALGORITHM.

Before	After
u w	u w
1 1	0 1
1 0	0 0
0 1	0 0 *
0 0	(select this page)

into is not removed until the pointer has completed *two* full scans of the list. Thus, compared to a page that has not been modified, it has one additional chance to be referenced again before it is selected for removal.

Example

For this policy, in addition to specifying the reference string, $Z = cadbebabcd$, and the memory size, $m = 4$, we also need to know which references are write requests. For the sake of this example, we assume that the references at times 2, 4, and 7 are write requests, as indicated by the superscript w. The memory changes are then as follows:

Time	0	1	2	3	4	5	6	7	8	9	10
Z		c	a^w	d	b^w	e	b	a^w	b	c	d
Frame 0	→$a/10$	→$a/10$	→$a/11$	→$a/11$	→$a/11$	$a/00*$	$a/00*$	$a/11$	$a/11$	→$a/11$	$a/00*$
Frame 1	$b/10$	$b/10$	$b/10$	$b/10$	$b/11$	$b/00*$	$b/10*$	$b/10*$	$b/10*$	$b/10*$	$d/10$
Frame 2	$c/10$	$c/10$	$c/10$	$c/10$	$c/10$	$e/10$	$e/10$	$e/10$	$e/10$	$e/10$	→$e/00$
Frame 3	$d/10$	$d/10$	$d/10$	$d/10$	$d/10$→	→$d/00$	→$d/00$	→$d/00$	→$d/00$	$c/10$	$c/00$
page fault						*				*	*
$p_{2ND CHANCE}$						e				c	d
$q_{2ND CHANCE}$						c				d	b

At the time of the first page fault, the pointer is at page a. The algorithm scans the pages while resetting the u and w bits as follows: reset u bit of a; reset u bit of b; reset u bit of c; reset u bit of d; reset w bit of a and remember that the page is dirty (asterisk); reset w bit of b and remember that the page is dirty. The subsequent page c has now both bits equal to 0 and is replaced by the new page e. The next three references (6 through 8) do not cause page faults but only modify the u and w bits of pages a and b according to the reference type. (Note that the dirty mark on page a is removed since the page has again been written into and thus its w bit was set.) The last two references replace pages d and b, thus bringing the total number of page faults to 3.

5.5.2.3 Page-replacement Schemes with Variable Number of Frames

Measurements of paging behavior indicate that each program requires a certain minimum set of pages to be resident in memory at all times in order to run efficiently; otherwise, the page fault rate becomes unacceptably high. Furthermore, it can be observed that the size of this set changes dynamically as a program executes. These observations lead to the development of several page-replacement methods that attempt to maintain an *optimal* resident set for each active program. As the set size changes, the number of page frames occupied by the program increases or decreases. Hence the name ''page-replacement with *variable* number of frames.'' These schemes are strictly local since the page-replacement algorithm must distinguish between pages belonging to different processes. Thus a page fault caused by a process p will never be resolved by reducing the resident set of any other process q.

Optimal Replacement Policy (VMIN).   Similar to the optimal replacement policy MIN, used with a fixed number of frames, there exists an optimal replacement policy, VMIN, that varies the number of frames according to the program's behavior (Prieve and Fabry, 1976). As with MIN, it is unrealizable because it requires advance knowledge of the reference string. VMIN employs the following page-replacement rule invoked after each reference: Assume that at time t the page $Z(t)$ is referenced. The algorithm then looks ahead in the reference string Z. If that page is *not* referenced again in the time interval $(t, t + \tau)$, where τ is a system constant, the page is removed. Otherwise, it remains in the process's resident set until it is referenced again. The interval $(t, t + \tau)$ is frequently referred to as a *moving* (or sliding) *window*, since at any given time the resident set consists of those pages visible in that window; the window size is the constant τ.

Example

We use the reference string $Z = ccdbcecead$. Instead of specifying the number m of available page frames, however, we must give the size of the working set window; we assume $\tau = 4$. The string Z references five different pages a through e over time. We assume that at time 0 only the page d is resident. The following table shows the working set at each reference; a dash indicates that the page is not in the working set. Note that this table does not show *how* pages are mapped onto physical memory frames; it only specifies *which* pages must be resident at any moment.

Time	0	1	2	3	4	5	6	7	8	9	10
Z	d	c	c	d	b	c	e	c	e	a	d
Page a	—	—	—	—	—	—	—	—	—	a	—
Page b	—	—	—	—	b	—	—	—	—	—	—
Page c	—	c	c	c	c	c	c	c	—	—	—
Page d	d	d	d	d	—	—	—	—	—	—	d
Page e	—	—	—	—	—	—	e	e	e	—	—
page fault		*			*		*			*	*
p_{VMIN}		c			b		e			a	d
q_{VMIN}					d	b			c	e	a

When a page fault occurs, the missing page is loaded. If it is not referenced again during the next four time instants, it is removed. For example, at time 0, page d is referenced. Since it is needed again at time 3, it is retained in memory until that time. The next reference to d is at time 10 and hence d is removed in the meantime. That is, d is not part of the resident set during the time interval 4 through 9. Similarly, b is loaded at time 4. However, since it is not referenced again, it is removed immediately prior to the next reference (to page c). The total number of page faults for VMIN in this example is 5. Note, however, that at most two page frames are occupied at any time. By increasing τ, the number of page faults could be reduced at the expense of using more page frames.

The Working Set (WS) Model.   The WS model (Denning, 1968, 1980) relies heavily on the principle of locality discussed previously. Its underlying philosophy is that, at any given time, the amount of storage required by a program may be estimated based on its recent past behavior. It employs a similar concept of a moving window as

VMIN; however, the algorithm does not look *ahead* in the reference string, but looks *behind*. According to the WS model, each process at a given time t has a working set of pages $W(t, \tau)$, defined as the set of pages referenced by that process during the time interval $(t - \tau, t)$. It is assumed that the working set W, as well as the number of pages in W (the cardinality of W), remains nearly constant over small time intervals.

The storage management strategy is then governed by the following two rules:

1. At each reference, the current working set is determined and only those pages belonging to the working set are retained in memory.
2. A program may run if and only if its entire current working set is in memory.

Example

Let $Z = ccdbcecead$, $\tau = 4$, and the initial resident set at time 0 contain the pages $\{a, d, e\}$, where a was referenced at time $t = 0$, d was referenced at time $t = -1$, and e was referenced at time $t = -2$. The following table shows the working set at each reference. As with the previous example of VMIN, this table does not show a physical memory map but only specifies the set of resident pages.

Time	0	1	2	3	4	5	6	7	8	9	10
Z	a	c	c	d	b	c	e	c	e	a	d
Page a	a	a	a	a	—	—	—	—	—	a	a
Page b	—	—	—	—	b	b	b	b	—	—	—
Page c	—	c	c	c	c	c	c	c	c	c	c
Page d	d	d	d	d	d	d	d	—	—	—	d
Page e	e	e	—	—	—	—	e	e	e	e	e
page fault		*			*		*			*	*
p_{ws}		c			b		e			a	d
q_{ws}			e		a			d			

As with VMIN, the working set size changes dynamically during execution. A page is resident only as long as it is visible in the moving window. For example, at time 1, the working set increases form three to four pages due to the missing page c. At time 2, the set is again reduced to three pages $\{a, c, d\}$ visible in the window $(t - 4, t)$. At time 4, the working set size is still 3; however, page a "fell out" of the window (1 through 4); instead, page b was included. Similarly, at time 7, the page d "fell out" of the window (4 through 7). The total number of page faults for this algorithm is also 5, but the average number of page frames used is 3.

While conceptually very attractive, the WS strategy is difficult to implement in its full generality. One problem is the estimation of the appropriate window size τ, which is the crucial parameter of the policy. This is usually performed empirically by varying τ until the highest performance is achieved. Except for rare cases when anomalous behavior has been observed (Franklin, Graham, and Gupta, 1978), increasing the window size reduces the paging activity of each process. The trade-off is a reduced number of processes that may be run concurrently.

A more serious problem with a pure WS policy is the large overhead in implementation since the current working set can change with each reference. To alleviate this problem, special hardware may be provided as, for example, in the MANIAC II (Morris, 1972). Alternatively, approximations of the WS algorithm have been developed that permit the working set to be reevaluated less frequently.

Example

The virtual memory operating system (VMOS) running on UNIVAC Spectra 70 Series (Fogel, 1974) implements an interesting approximation of the working set model. In a greatly simplified form, the scheme is as follows. Each page frame has associated with it a use bit (reference bit), which is turned on by the hardware when the page is accessed. In addition, a time stamp is provided for each frame. The use bit and the time stamp are examined and possibly changed whenever a page fault occurs, but also at least every 4000 instructions (using a time out). When the use bit is found to be 1, it is reset, and the time of this change is recorded with the frame. When the bit is found to be 0, the time since it has been turned off, denoted as t_{off}, is compared against two system parameters, t_{max} and t_{min}. Depending on the outcome of this comparison, the following actions are taken:

1. If $t_{off} > t_{max}$, the page is removed from the working set (i.e., the frame is released)
2. If $t_{min} < t_{off} < t_{max}$, the page is *tentatively* removed from the working set; this is accomplished by putting the frame on a special tentatively released list, rather than on the list of free frames.
3. If $t_{min} > t_{off}$, the page is retained in the process's working set and the time stamp is reset.

If a new page frame is needed (as a result of a page fault), one of the following alternatives is taken:

1. If the list of free page frames is not empty, one of these is used.
2. If there are no free page frames, but the list of tentatively removed page frames is not empty, the first page on this list is used. This guarantees preferential treatment to pages that have not yet exceeded t_{max} but have not been used for a significant length of time (at least t_{min}).
3. Otherwise, the faulting task is deactivated and its page frames are added to the free page frame list.

Page Fault Frequency (PFF).   One of the main objectives of any page-replacement policy must be to keep the number of page faults to a minimum. In the WS policy described previously, this objective was accomplished indirectly by adjusting the working set size. The PFF policy takes a more direct approach by actually measuring the page fault frequency in terms of time intervals between consecutive page faults. These times are then used to adjust the resident page set of a process at the time of each page fault as follows: if the time between the current and the previous page fault exceeds a critical value τ, all pages not referenced during that time interval are removed from memory. Otherwise, the new page is simply included in the resident page set. More formally, if t_c is the time of the current page fault and t_{c-1} is the time of the previous page fault, then all pages not referenced during the interval $t_{c-1} \le t \le t_c$ are removed if and only if $t_c - t_{c-1} > \tau$, where τ is a system parameter. In other words, the set of resident pages at time t_c, denoted as $R(t_c, \tau)$, is described as

$$R(t_c, \tau) = \begin{cases} Z(t_c, t_c - t_{c-1}), & \text{if } t_c - t_{c-1} > \tau \\ R(t_{c-1}, \tau) + Z(t_c), & \text{otherwise} \end{cases}$$

where $Z(t_c, t_c - t_{c-1})$ denotes the set of pages referenced during the interval $(t_c, t_c - t_{c-1})$, and $Z(t_c)$ is the page referenced at time t_c (and found missing from the resident set). The PFF policy guarantees that the resident set grows when page faults are frequent, and it shrinks when the page fault rate decreases. The main advantage of PFF over the WS model is that the resident set is adjusted only at the time of a page fault instead of at each reference.

Example

We use the same reference string, $Z = ccdbcecead$, as before and set the parameter τ to 2. Let the resident set at time 0 consist of the pages a, d, and e. The following table shows the set of resident pages at each subsequent reference; a dash indicates that the page is not in the working set.

Time	0	1	2	3	4	5	6	7	8	9	10
Z		c	c	d	b	c	e	c	e	a	d
Page a	a	a	a	a	—	—	—	—	—	a	a
Page b	—	—	—	—	b	b	b	b	b	—	—
Page c	—	c	c	c	c	c	c	c	c	c	c
Page d	d	d	d	d	d	d	d	d	d	—	d
Page e	e	e	e	e	—	—	e	e	e	e	e
page fault		*			*		*			*	*
p_{PFF}		c			b		e			a	d
q_{PFF}		?			a, e					b, d	

The first page fault occurs at time 1. Depending on when the previous page fault occurred, pages may or may not be removed at this time as indicated by the question mark. The next page fault occurs at time 4. Since $t_c = 4$ and $t_{c-1} + \tau = 3$ (i.e., less than t_c), all pages not referenced during the time interval $(1, 4)$ are removed; these are the pages a and e. The next page fault occurs at time 6. No pages are removed at this time because 6 is not greater then $4 + \tau$. Pages b and d are removed at time 9. The PFF algorithm produces a total of five page faults for the string Z.

5.5.2.4 Prepaging

In a system with static allocation, all pages belonging to an active process are loaded before the process is permitted to run. In a dynamically allocated system, pages are loaded only as a result of page faults. The latter method works well when the process already has some reasonable set of pages in memory, since page faults do not occur too frequently. Before this set is established, however, the page fault rate is high. This is the case when a newly created process is started or when an existing process is reactivated as a result of a satisfied request. Such program behavior can be captured by a process *lifetime curve*, which plots the mean time between page faults, L, against the mean set, R, of pages resident in memory (Denning, 1980). The typical shape of a lifetime curve is shown in Figure 5-23a. As long as the resident set of pages is small, page faults occur frequently. When the set size is increased, the page fault rate decreases dramatically until it reaches a *knee*, beyond which it decreases only slightly. This suggests that a process should not be started or reactivated with an empty or a very small resident set. Rather, a set of pages should be *prepaged* at the time of activation. This can obviously be done more efficiently than loading one page at a time.

Theoretically, the optimal size of the prepaged set is given by the point at which the lifetime curve reaches its knee. In practice, however, this value is difficult to estimate. For a newly created process, prepaging is rarely used. In the case of an existing process, a good choice for the prepaged set is the set of pages that were resident just

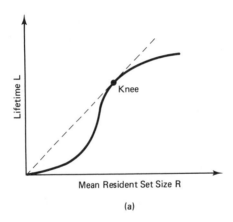

(a)

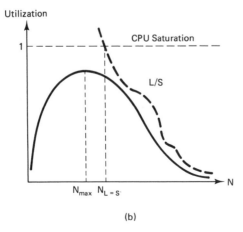

(b)

Figure 5-23 Program behavior under multiprogramming: (a) Lifetime curve of a program (b) CPU utilization.

before the process was suspended. This is particularly attractive with schemes based on the working set model, where a list of currently resident pages is explicitly maintained.

5.5.3 Load Control and Thrashing

When implementing a virtual memory management scheme, one of the main problems is to maintain a balance between the degree of multiprogramming and the amount of paging to be performed. Load control refers to the policy that determines the number and type of processes that should be permitted to execute, thus competing for memory, CPU time, and other critical resources.

In the case of page-replacement schemes with a variable number of page frames, such as WS or PFF, much of the load control is determined by the policy itself. Since each process has a predetermined resident set, the system can increase the degree of multiprogramming only to the point where all memory is allocated. Only if the current resident sets shrink due to changing patterns in process behavior, or when one or more processes are deactivated, can new processes be added to the currently active set. Conversely, if a process's resident set expands, it may be necessary to deactivate one or more of the currently active processes in order to create the necessary space.

In page-replacement schemes with a fixed number of frames (local or global), the degree of multiprogramming is not determined automatically. As a consequence, additional load-control mechanisms must be provided to guarantee that each active process has some minimum number of resident pages. With too many active processes, the page fault rate could increase to the point where most of the system's effort would be expended on moving pages between primary and secondary storage, a condition referred to as *thrashing*.

Two basic questions must be answered when implementing load-control mechanisms:

1. What should be used as a criterion to increase or decrease the level of multiprogramming?
2. Which of the currently active tasks should be deactivated if the degree of multiprogramming must be reduced?

A number of schemes have been proposed and studied for both of these problems. In answering the first question, our objective must be to reduce the amount of paging as much as possible while maintaining a high degree of multiprogramming. Hence most methods for determining an optimal balance are linked to the rate of paging. Two examples are the $L = S$ *criterion* and the *50 percent criterion* (Denning et al., 1976). Using the former, the system maintains a level of multiprogramming such that the mean time between faults, L, is equal to the mean page fault service time, S (i.e., the time it takes to replace a page in primary memory). The rationale behind this criterion is that the CPU usually reaches its maximum utilization when L approaches S (see Section 5.5.4). The second criterion adjusts the level of multiprogramming such that the paging device is busy 50 percent of the time. This is based on the observation that CPU utilization tends to be highest when the utilization of the paging device is approximately 50 percent. Both these criteria are closely related.

Another criterion, called *clock load control*, has been proposed by Carr (1981). It is applicable to schemes that employ a pointer to scan the list of page frames when searching for a page to be replaced. The criterion is based on the rate at which the pointer travels around the page frame list. If this rate is low, at least one of the following two conditions is true:

1. The page fault rate is low, resulting in few requests to advance the pointer.
2. The mean distance traveled by the pointer between page faults is small, indicating that there are many resident pages that are not being referenced and are readily replaceable.

In both cases the level of multiprogramming might usefully be increased. Conversely, if the travel rate of the pointer increases past a certain threshold value, the level of multiprogramming should be decreased.

For the second question, which process to deactivate when more space is needed, many schemes have also been suggested. Some of the possible choices for selecting a replacement candidate are the lowest priority process, the faulting process, the last process activated, the smallest process, and the largest process. In general, it is not possible to determine the superiority of one choice over another since each depends on many other policies and system parameters, in particular the scheduling methods used in a given system. Hence the decision will rest with the intuition and experience of the system's designer.

5.5.4 Evaluation of Paging

Many experiments have been carried out to study the dynamic behavior of programs under paging (Belady, 1966; Fine, Jackson, and McIsaac, 1966; Coffman and Varian, 1968; Freibergs, 1968; Baer and Sager, 1972; Gelenbe, Tiberio, and Boeckhorst, 1973; Rodriguez-Rosell, 1973; Opderbeck and Chu, 1974; Lenfant and Burgevin, 1975; Sadeh, 1975; Spirn, 1977; Gupta and Franklin, 1978). The general method is to execute interpretively a sample set of programs, simulating the paging mechanism; the most significant parameters that are varied are page size and the amount of available storage. The data obtained from these independent studies were generally consistent with one another. The first set of results, shown in Figure 5-24, illustrate the behavior of an individual process under different conditions and can be summarized as follows:

1. Most processes require a high percentage of their pages within a very short time period after activation; for example, about 50 percent of a process's total pages on the average were referenced during a single quantum in a typical time-sharing operation.
2. A relatively small number of instructions within a page are executed before control moves to another page; for page sizes of 1024 words, less than 200 instructions

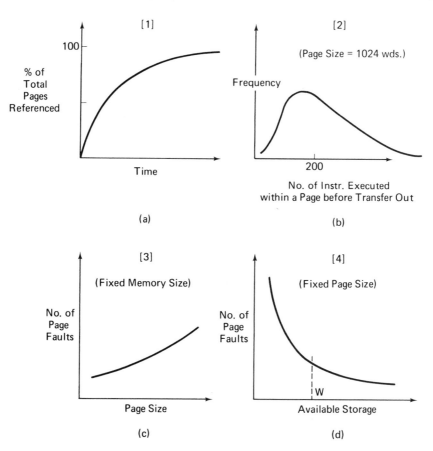

Figure 5-24 Qualitative behavior of programs under paging: (a) Pages referenced over
time (b) Portion of each page actually executed (c) Effect of page size on page faults
(d) Effect of memory size on page faults.

were executed before another page was referenced in most of the samples investigated.

3. In the range from 64 to 1024 words per page, the number of page faults increases
as the page size increases, while available memory is kept fixed.

4. As storage decreases, there is a point at which page faults rise exponentially for a
fixed page size (thrashing).

Figure 5-24 illustrates these effects qualitatively. They reveal several important
aspects of paging systems, some of which we have already mentioned in previous sections. The first curve is a direct consequence of the principle of locality; when a program
is activated, it will need a relatively high percentage of its pages during the first few
moments of its lifetime. After a certain working set is established, additional pages are
demanded at a much slower rate.

Figures 5-24b and c provide evidence suggesting that page size should be *small*. In Figure 5-24b, reducing the page size may eliminate much of the instructions that will not be referenced, but must be brought into memory as part of each page. Similarly, the curve in Figure 5-24c shows that the number of page faults decreases with page size. An additional argument, not reflected in the figures, is the amount of storage wasted due to internal fragmentation; this amount is confined to at most one page per segment and hence internal fragmentation decreases with a smaller page size. There are, however, important counterarguments in support of a relatively *large* page size. First, larger page sizes require smaller page tables to address a given amount of virtual storage, which reduces the software overhead during processing. They also mean that main memory must be divided into a smaller number of physical frames, which reduces its cost. Finally, the physical characteristics of rotating paging devices, which perform most efficiently when transmitting larger blocks of data, favor a larger page size.

Typically, pages in commercial systems range from 128 words (e.g., DEC VAX-11) to 1024 (IBM 360/370). For systems in which the average segment size s_0 is much larger than the page size, z, and all page tables are stored entirely in main memory, an optimal page size can be derived analytically (Denning, 1970; Wolman, 1965).

Theorem.   Let c_1 be the cost of losing a word of main storage to page table use and c_2 be the word cost for internal fragmentation. If $z \ll s_0$ and each segment begins on a page boundary, the optimal page size z_0 is approximately $\sqrt{2cs_0}$, where $c = c_1 / c_2$.

Proof. For each segment, the cost C_z of lost storage with page size z is

$$C_z = C_i + C_t$$

where C_i is internal fragmentation cost and C_t is page table cost. If $z \ll s_0$, then $C_i = c_2 z / 2$ approximately, since on the average, one-half of the last page of a segment is wasted. $C_t = c_1 s_0 / z$ approximately, since each segment requires roughly s_0 / z page table words. Therefore, $C_z = c_2 z / 2 + c_1 s_0 / z$. To find the optimum z_0, we solve $dC_z / dz = 0$; that is, $c_2 / 2 - c_1 s_0 / z_0^2 = 0$, leading to our result.

This result confirms our conclusion on small page sizes. If, for example, we assume $s_0 \leq 5000$ and $c = 1$ (i.e., $c_1 = c_2$), then $z_0 \leq 100$ words. z_0 is even smaller if the typical segment sizes of 100 words (!) as measured on the B5500 (Batson, Ju, and Wood, 1970) are regarded as universal. However, smaller page sizes require larger page tables to address a fixed amount of virtual storage and also mean that main memory must consist of a larger number of blocks.

Figure 5-24d confirms the observation that IO activity resulting from page faults can become intolerably high and unproductive unless each active process has a sufficient amount of storage (e.g., a working set) available for program and data needs. If this is not guaranteed, the CPU devotes much of its time to housekeeping related to paging, the CPU and channels operate sequentially instead of in parallel because all active processes are continually in need of page space, and the same pages continually get swapped in and out; in other words, there is a dramatic decrease in the amount of useful work accomplished. The point labeled W in Figure 5-24d represents a minimum amount of storage required to avoid these thrashing effects. This can be controlled by changing the level of multiprogramming, as was discussed in Section 5.5.3.

Figure 5-23 shows results related to load control in multiprogramming systems. The significance of the lifetime curve (a) was already discussed in Section 5.5.2.4. These results are congruent with the page demand ratio shown in Figure 5-24a. CPU utilization is one of the most important measures of overall performance since it is directly proportional to the system's throughput. Figure 5-23b shows the effect of multiprogramming on CPU utilization for a fixed-sized main memory, regardless of the page-replacement policy used. The abscissa N gives the degree of multiprogramming (i.e., the number of processes sharing main memory) and the coordinate shows the corresponding CPU utilization. The curve rises rapidly toward CPU saturation, but is eventually depressed by the ratio L/S, the utilization of the saturated paging device. To achieve highest overall performance, the multiprogramming level must be adjusted such that CPU utilization is at its maximum. The $L = S$ criterion selects the point $N_{L=S}$ as the desired level of multiprogramming. This is slightly higher than the optimum, N_{max}, but the deviation is usually tolerable for the purposes of load control. The curve is based on extensive measurements in actual computer systems and is valid under general conditions that apply to almost all real multiprogramming systems (Denning, 1980).

5.6 LINKING AND SHARING OF PROCEDURES AND DATA IN MAIN MEMORY

The development of large software systems is greatly simplified if individual modules can be developed separately and later linked together. This also permits the reuse of modules developed previously, thus reducing the total software development cost. Typically, such modules include certain routines provided by the operating system (e.g., input/output procedures, utility programs, or useful subroutines developed by other users). To facilitate the necessary cooperation, a flexible linking mechanism must be provided that does not require individual modules to be recompiled each time they are being included in a user's address space. Additional benefits would result if the *same* copy of a module could be linked into more than one address space at the same time. This concept is referred to as *sharing* of the given module among different processes.

5.6.1 Why Share?

Sharing of computer programs and data is often accomplished by providing users with their own private copy of the shared information. The copy could be incorporated by manually editing it into a program or data file before initiating the computation, or it might be automatically added by a linker/loader referencing a library or utility file. This could be done in a single- or multiprogramming environment. However, several active processes often need the same code or data resident in main storage at the same time. If each process had its own copy, unnecessary systems costs would be incurred; these consist of the IO overhead in loading the excess copies and the memory to store them.

A serious problem occurs when multiple copies of the same data file are updated; it is almost always necessary to have one consistent file that contains *all* updates. The problem here somewhat resembles the familiar critical section problem discussed in Chapter 2, and the same type of errors can appear unless handled carefully. For these reasons, a *single* copy in main storage is frequently shared by more than one process; the sharing occurs in a time-multiplexed fashion when several processes share a single CPU or essentially simultaneously when the processes are running on independent processors with a common memory. The remainder of this chapter is concerned with the structure of the programs (and data to some extent) required to perform single-copy sharing correctly and efficiently. We first look at some typical applications of data and procedure sharing.

Data Sharing

1. *File directories.* Several processes, possibly invoked by interactive users, may simultaneously interrogate a file system. The directories or index of the files would be simultaneously in use.
2. *Status databases.* Systems programs share various databases containing, for example, the status of resources (e.g., which elements of the resources are free or busy); this information is generally continually searched and updated by various systems processes. In addition, a display process might exist that writes the current status on some output device.
3. *Critical sections.* These are primarily used to control data sharing on a sequential basis. (See the application examples in Chapter 2.)

Procedure Sharing

1. *Systems kernel routines.* In a multiprogramming system, all processes share the same set of kernel routines, for example the IO programs.
2. *Utilities and system services.* Widely used routines, such as various debuggers, file manipulation routines, or linkers and loaders, may be single-copy shared.
3. *Language processors and text editors.* Popular compilers, assemblers, and interpreters are often maintained in executable storage to allow their simultaneous use by more than one process. Text editors and interactive language subsystems, such as those for APL or BASIC, are designed in many cases to handle several terminal users at the same time with a single copy of the system.
4. *Applications programs.* Individual users have an increasing need to cooperate by building on the work of others. Thus it is desirable that users be able to make their own programs or data files available for public or selective use. For such sharing, it is often simpler to load a separate copy into main memory for each requesting process. Some more sophisticated systems, however, implement main memory sharing in its full generality (i.e., permit arbitrary programs or data files to be single-copy shared). Another convenient use of code sharing is found in parallel programming, where several processes executing the same code but with different

data sets may be spawned. The examples in Section 2.2 illustrate simple situations in which a single code copy is most convenient.

5.6.2 Requirements for Code Sharing

In the early days of computing, it was often claimed that much of the power and flexibility of computers derived from the ability to modify programs during execution; instructions could be treated as data, and vice versa. The claim was more practical than theoretical. The structure of the first generation of machines made instruction modification necessary in order to produce efficient and practical programs. Looping and subroutine transfer and return were the two principal areas that required programs to modify themselves dynamically. For example, to process an array iteratively in a loop, the address fields of the load/store instructions had to be modified on each iteration to access different elements. Later, the use of index registers to compute addresses made instruction self-modification unnecessary.

Instruction modification during execution is not considered good programming practice today for at least two reasons. Program logic often becomes very obscure and difficult to follow; the result is that programs are hard to explain, debug, and maintain. Uncontrolled program self-modification also makes it impossible to share code; a process may be interrupted after it has changed an instruction (or data item), and another process, sharing the same code and data area, may either change the same instruction (data item) or execute (use) it, incorrectly assuming that no changes have been made. For both these reasons, clarity and sharing, it is desirable to eliminate *store* operations that modify code areas.

Self-initializing Programs.   In serial-sharing situations, it is possible to change code and/or data local to a program if that program is *self-initializing*; that is, initial values of code and data are set by the program itself and the initializing code remains inviolate. Then, a single copy is sufficient as long as each process sequentially uses the copy to completion before another process is allowed entry. The code is thus a critical section and acts as a serially reusable resource. For example, a heavily used subsystem (e.g., a compiler or a linking loader) could be kept permanently in a single partition or block of main memory in self-initializing form. This approach was used in older systems, especially when little or no multiprogramming was needed or desired in the subsystem. For example, the subsystem could have been written very carefully so that IO and computing were well balanced.

Pure Procedures.   *Pure procedures* are programs that do not modify their own instructions or local data; that is, internal store (write) to memory operations are prohibited. Any such program that is execute- and read-only is also called *reenterable* (IBM, 1965), since it may be resumed at any time with the assurance that nothing has been changed. Thus, pure procedures may be shared by more than one process in either a time-multiplexed or multiprocessing mode.

Variable data associated with the process using a pure procedure must be stored in separate private areas. These data normally include arguments, return addresses, and temporaries. In systems using segmentation, the most convenient way is to allocate separate segments to the pure code and to the private data. Sharing of the code segment can then be easily accomplished, as will be discussed in Section 5.6.3.3. In systems using paging (without segmentation) separate pages may be assigned to shared and private program/data sections. This, however, requires more care, since programs and data areas are rarely multiples of the given page size. In systems without paging or segmentation, variable information may be accessed by base registers that point to the private storage area at run time.

Example

Let *ARG* be a symbolic name of a location containing some variable; [*ARG*] designates the contents of *ARG*. To store the contents of a register *Ri* into *ARG*, the following instructions might be employed in a nonpure procedure (the effect of executing the instruction is shown as the assignment statement following the instruction as a comment).

STO Ri, ARG   {[ARG] := [Ri];}

This is not correct in general, however, *if* the instruction is part of a procedure *P* shared by several processes, since each process might be simultaneously storing different values into *ARG*. To correct this situation, *ARG* could be an offset within a private area of any process executing *P*; a base register, say *Rb*, is assumed to contain the base address of this area at run time. Then the correct referencing instruction that keeps *P* pure might be

STO Ri, ARG(Rb)   {[[Rb] + ARG] := [Ri];}

Base registers, which are stored as part of the state vector of a process, thus provide a simple means for linking pure procedures to changeable data. Before a pure procedure is called, arrangements must be made for passing parameters, the return address, and temporary storage locations through the registers.

5.6.3 Static Linking and Sharing

Linking, as introduced in Section 5.1.2, is the process of combining several separately translated programs into one system. The main tasks are the relocation of individual modules and the resolving of external references. In systems that do not employ segmentation, all modules are linked into *one* contiguous name space. This space can be the actual physical space, a contiguous relocatable space, or a paged virtual space. The techniques described in Section 5.4.1 apply equally in all three cases. In systems with segmentation, linking is conceptually much simpler. Each segment to be linked is assigned a segment number. All external references are then simply replaced by a pair (*s*, *w*), where *s* is the segment number of the referenced segment and *w* is the offset within that segment. In all the preceding schemes we have assumed that the linking process is completed (i.e., all symbolic external references are replaced by their corresponding physical or virtual addresses) before execution commences. Such linking is referred to as *static*. Note that static linking may be used in systems with both static or dynamic relocation.

Let us now consider sharing. It may be viewed as linking of the *same* physical copy of a module into *two* or more name spaces. If the links are resolved prior to execution, the sharing is called *static*. Let us consider how static sharing may be accomplished in the three possible memory management schemes: without segmentation or paging, with pure paging, and with segmentation (possibly followed by paging).

5.6.3.1 Sharing in Systems without Segmentation or Paging

In the absence of any dynamic relocation mechanisms, storage must be allocated to programs statically at the time of linking or loading. Several base registers are assumed available for accessing private or shared data and for linking to and from shared procedures. In virtually *all* such systems, a sharp distinction is made between systems and users' programs, often corresponding to privileged (master) and slave hardware modes, respectively. Users invoke shared systems programs and data by executing supervisor call instructions (SVCs), but generally cannot share other users' information. To provide sharing on a more general basis, linking loaders must be modified to search main memory for the occurrence of potentially shared modules. If a module is found, the link to the same physical copy is established; otherwise, it must be brought into memory at the time of loading. This implies that the usual contiguity requirement for process storage space must be abandoned. One major problem is that of assuring adequate protection. Since allocated space is not contiguous, simple bounds or length registers cannot be used (Section 6.3.2). If physical storage keys are associated with memory blocks, the shared information and, consequently, all memory associated with the sharing processes must have the same key, thus fully exposing the sharing processes and their data to one another.

Example

Consider a process p_1 consisting of the modules $Q1$, $Q2$, and $Q3$. While p_1 is active, a second process p_2 wishes to use the modules $Q1'$, $Q2$. A possible memory map is shown in Figure 5-25. If $Q2$ is a procedure, it must be reenterable. Note that p_2's space is not contiguous.

In systems that implement dynamic relocation using a simple relocation register (Section 5.4.1.1), sharing is equally difficult. If only one such register is provided, con-

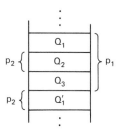

Figure 5-25   Sharing of a module.

tiguous memory allocation is required for each process space. With multiple relocation registers, the problems are similar to those in statically relocated systems (Section 5.5.1). In the following sections we examine how the situation improves when paging or segmentation is used.

5.6.3.2 Sharing in Systems with Paging

Paging permits a noncontiguous allocation of main memory. Each page is pointed to by an entry in the process's page table. Sharing may be accomplished on a page basis by pointing to the same page frame from two different page tables. If the shared pages contain only *data* (i.e., no addresses either to themselves or to other areas), the linker can assign arbitrary page numbers to the shared pages for each process and adjust the page tables to point to the appropriate page frames. The following example illustrates this situation.

Example

Consider two processes p_1 and p_2 whose virtual address spaces are represented by the two page tables PT_1 and PT_2, respectively (Figure 5-26). Assume that page 0 of each process contains a reference to a shared data page. Under p_1, the shared page is assigned the number $n1$ and hence the corresponding reference is adjusted to $(n1, w)$, where w is the offset within the page. Under p_2, the same shared page is assigned the number $n2$, and thus the reference in p_2's page 0 is adjusted to $(n2, w)$. The page numbers $n1$ and $n2$ need not be the same as long as the shared page contains only data. The memory-mapping mechanism (*NL_map*) guarantees that at run time the correct page table is used. (The significance of the *Branch* instruction will be explained shortly; for this example, assume that the shared page will not be executed; it is treated only as data by p_1 and p_2.)

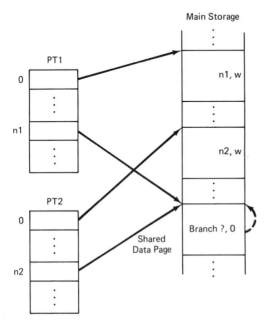

Figure 5-26 Sharing in a paged system.

Sharing procedures requires more care since instructions must contain addresses referring to other instructions or data. For shared procedures to execute correctly under different processes, they must be assigned the *same* page numbers in *all* virtual address spaces. To illustrate why this is necessary, consider again the preceding example. Assume that the shared page is a procedure containing a branch instruction to some other location within that procedure, say to the instruction 0. When executing under process p_1, the branch address must have the form $(n1, 0)$, while under p_2 the same address had to contain $(n2, 0)$. Since a memory cell can hold only *one* value at any time, the two page numbers $n1$ and $n2$ must be the same. In other words, the shared page must be assigned the same entries in *both* page tables. As a consequence, page number conflicts and wasted table space can occur when a new process requires several independent, shared, and already loaded modules (see Exercise 5.19).

One can circumvent this problem, but the methods seem to be quite clumsy. If the total set of sharable modules is known to the system, it might be possible to *permanently reserve* their page numbers; the same page numbers are used for those procedures and data segments that are mutually disjoint (i.e., those that are never used together by the same process).

5.6.3.3 Sharing in Systems with Segmentation

Sharing segments is, in general, simpler and more elegant than sharing pages since the former represents natural logical entities such as procedures or data files. The sharing of a segment in memory by two or more processes may be accomplished by pointing to that segment from entries in different segment tables. These entries point to the absolute locations of the shared segments or, if the memory is also paged, to *shared* page tables.

As in the case of paging, sharing of segments containing only *data* presents no serious problems. A shared segment can have a different segment number assigned to it in each process's segment table. With *procedure* segments, two approaches can be taken to permit each procedure to reference its own content correctly. The first is to require that all shared procedure segments have the *same* segment numbers in all virtual spaces; this was the solution used with paging. The example in Figure 5-26 would apply equally here if segments and segment tables were used instead of pages and page tables, respectively. The second approach is to use base registers that at execution time contain the segment numbers of the currently running process. The base registers are loaded by the system when the process is activated and may not be modified by the user. All references (internal and external) are then relative to a base register. In this way, the segment numbers become part of the invoking process rather than part of the code; the segment tables for different processes may then use different entries for the same procedure. The table entries point to the absolute locations of the (shared) procedure or, if the memory is also paged, may point to (shared) page tables.

Although this latter approach is quite powerful, there are still some problems due to possible conflicts in the assignment of base registers. The dynamic linking method described in the remainder of this section is the most general scheme that permits arbitrary sharing among any procedure or data segments; it applies in the static case also.

5.6.4 Dynamic Linking and Sharing

When external references are kept in their symbolic form and resolved only when actually used during execution, the linking is referred to as *dynamic*. We use the term *dynamic sharing* when the same physical copy of a segment is linked (dynamically) into two or more separate virtual address spaces. This scheme requires that a multiple-segmented virtual name space is used. All name space addresses consist of a segment and a word pair (s, w), as in Section 5.4.2. Relocation takes place through segment tables and a dynamic storage allocation policy is employed. Our discussion will be based on the MULTICS system (Bash, Benjafield, and Gandy, 1967; Daley and Dennis, 1968) because of the elegance and generality of the techniques developed in this pioneering system. (The paging in the MULTICS system will be ignored here because the linking methods are almost independent of this aspect of memory organization.)

Since segment numbers are assigned during execution and may differ for the same procedure or data segment depending on the referencing process, it is imperative that no segment numbers appear explicitly in segments. This applies to both internal (self) and external references. Two different processes sharing the same information segment will, in general, refer to that segment by different segment numbers. The particular numbers assigned depend on the current segment number allocations for the process.

Internal references are handled easily by using a base register for the segment number of the running process; the segment number is then a part of the state vector of the process. Thus, only word numbers appear explicitly in shared code. External references must remain symbolic for two reasons. First, this is the only way to allow dynamic linking, which must permit assignment of different segment numbers to the same shared segment under different processes. The second reason is to ensure that the procedures that refer to shared information are immune to most changes in the latter (e.g., recompilation). On the other hand, if external references were *always* symbolic, accessing time would probably be impractically long because of the need for interpretive execution.

The compromise used in MULTICS is to let only the *first* access by a given process to each external item be performed interpretively with symbolic information; this includes retrieval of the segment by the file system, protection checking, and segment and possibly word number assignment. On *subsequent* references, the interpretive software is bypassed and access is performed through hardware only, using a normal (s, w) address. How this is accomplished and, at the same time, the references are kept symbolic and code pure for potential use by other processes is outlined in the next few sections. We will use capital letters to designate symbolic references and lowercase letters for numerical (resolved) virtual space addresses. For example, $(Sub, Entry)$ might be a symbolic external reference, while $(sub, entry)$ could be a corresponding segment number/word number pair after dynamic linking.

5.6.4.1 Form of a Procedure Segment

The MULTICS solution to the problems of dynamic linking/sharing involves the use of two types of structures:

1. A *linkage section LS* is defined for each potentially sharable or sharing segment. Transfer of control and external data references occur by indirect addressing through linkage sections. *Each* process receives a *private* copy of a segment's linkage section when it uses (links to) that segment.

2. A private *stack* segment is allocated to each process for storing arguments, return addresses, processor states, and temporaries; the segment is organized as a stack for convenient call and return linkages and so that every procedure may be used recursively if desired.

During execution, the stack and linkage section addresses are maintained as (s, w) pairs in two base registers, lp (linkage pointer) and sp (stack pointer), respectively. A procedure base register pbr always contains the segment number of the procedure currently in execution.

Each pure procedure segment P consists of three parts: a *symbol table*, the *pure code*, and the *linkage section*. (For simplicity, we will take some liberties in describing the content and pointer structure within these parts.) The symbol table can be viewed as consisting of an *entry point* table and an *external symbol* table. The first lists all symbolic names and their relative locations within the procedure that may be used by other procedures to enter or otherwise reference P. The second is the list of all external references used by P.

Figure 5-27 shows a skeleton of a hypothetical procedure P. The entry point table defines n symbols $E_1, E_2, \ldots, E_n$, for possible external use; that is, they may be used as (P, E_i) pairs in other segments to reference the appropriate point in P. The names $e_1, e_2, \ldots, e_n$ designate word numbers (offsets) of their respective names E_i in P. This information is used when some other procedure links to P. (The meaning of l_{e_i} will be explained in Section 5.6.4.3.). The procedure P itself refers symbolically to word X in a data segment D and a word E in a procedure segment Q, as shown in the external symbol table.

The pure code part of P is set up by the compiler in such a way that all external references are offsets into the linkage section for P (LS_P); each entry in the linkage section is, in turn, an offset into the external symbol table, where it points to the corresponding symbolic name. For example, the instruction ADD specifies l_{DX} as its operand, which is to be used relative to the beginning of the linkage section; this is indicated by the flag $\overline{lp}$. The corresponding entry in the linkage section contains the value i_{DX}, which is interpreted as an offset into the symbol table; it refers to the symbolic reference (D, X).

For the TRA instructions, the analogous offsets l_{QE} and i_{QE} are specified. The asterisk in both instructions indicates indirect addressing along the respective reference chains. The significance of the *trap tags* in the linkage section, both of which are initially set to *true*, and the code segment at the locations l_{e_i}, will be explained shortly.

When a process p links to P, it is given a *private* copy of the linkage section LS_P, say LS_P^p; the base address of LS_P^p is inserted into the linkage pointer lp so that all external references from P are accessed through P's private linkage section LS_P^p, rather than LS_P

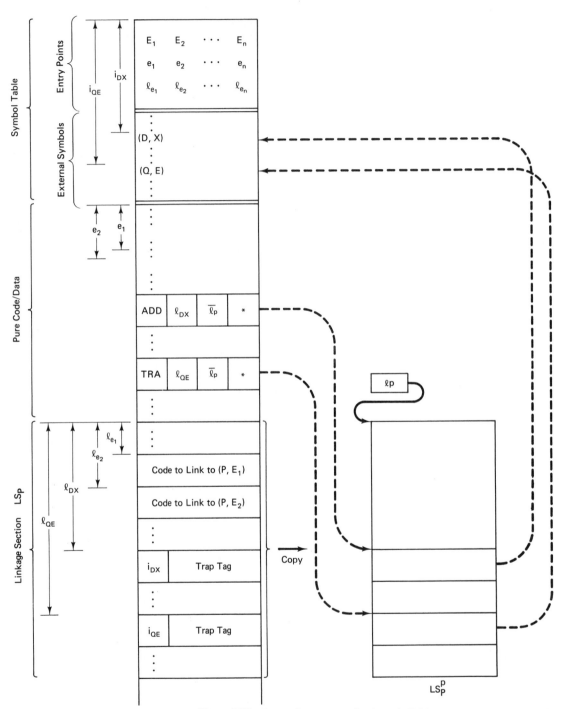

Figure 5-27   A procedure segment for dynamic linking.

itself. The dashed lines in Figure 5-29 show the exact flow of the indirect references when the instructions *ADD* and *TRA* are executed. It should be emphasized that all parts of P, including LS_P, remain invariant; only LS_P^p is ever modified.

5.6.4.2 Data Linkage

We now examine how external data references are resolved during execution. Assume that a process p is executing the segment P of Figure 5-27 and is just starting the operand fetch for (D, X) in the *ADD* instruction; it is the first time that this particular instruction is executed by p. The *pbr* register points to P and *lp* points to the linkage section copy, LS_P^p, associated with p. Initially, LS_P^p is identical to LS_P. Figure 5-28a shows the parts of Figure 5-27 that are relevant to this situation.

The operand, l_{DX}, in conjunction with the *lp* register, first produces the address a. Because of the indirect addressing of the *ADD* instruction, the effective address mechanism fetches the contents of a. Since the *trap tag* is set, an internal trap (interrupt) occurs and control is transferred to the *linker*. The main functions of the latter are to establish the correct linkage to (D, X), that is, to determine the corresponding (d, x), and to ensure that future references by p to (D, X) in P are automatic.

The linker finds the symbolic name of the segment, D, from the linkage section of P, using the pointers in an obvious way (Figure 5-27). The segment management module is then invoked, which makes the segment D known to p by assigning to it a

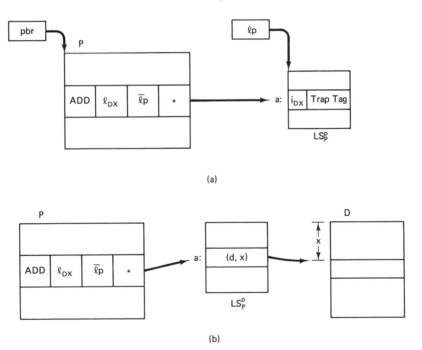

(a)

(b)

Figure 5-28 Data linkage by process p in P to (D, X): (a) First data reference to (D, X) (b) Completed linkage to (D, X).

segment number, say d, and entering that number into p's segment table. This process can be quite complicated, involving calls on the file system, storage allocation for segment (and page) tables, possibly storage replacements, verification of the legality of the access, and much table housekeeping. (Chapter 6 describes the file system functions in more detail.)

The symbol table of D then allows the linker to obtain the word number x of the symbolic name X. The pair (d, x), which now forms a valid virtual address, is inserted at a, replacing i_{DX}, and the *trap tag* is turned off (Figure 5-28b). At this point, p is ready to continue, and the indirect addressing is completed using the inserted (d, x) pair. On all subsequent executions of the *ADD* instruction (or any other instruction pointing to the same location a), the virtual address (d, x) is used without further traps. P still remains intact for use by other processes.

The preceding technique requires two storage accesses to perform an external reference, one for the indirect addressing and the second for the actual data access, in addition to the memory references necessary for implementing the segmentation/paging map. This is the price one must pay for maintaining symbolic information in pure code. External data in the form of arguments and return addresses need not be symbolic, since standard calling sequences and the use of the stack assure that relative locations of this information are known. The stack pointer register provides a sufficient and efficient means for data operand retrieval in pure code. (The MULTICS system also uses an argument register ap to point to a list of arguments.)

5.6.4.3 Procedure References

Transfer of control from one procedure segment to another is more complex than data linking. This is because the system must not only establish the link upon the first reference but also arrange for insertion of the appropriate new contents of the *pbr* and the *lp* pointers each time the transfer is performed. The loading of the *pbr* register is done automatically by the hardware as part of the *TRA* instruction. The loading of the *lp* register, however, must be done explicitly. This is particularly difficult during the second and subsequent transfers to the same procedure since the operating system is *not* invoked (the trap mechanisms have been turned off).

The solution adopted in MULTICS is to incorporate the code necessary to switch the *lp* pointer into the linkage section of the called procedure. That is, for each name E_i in the entry point table there exists a piece of code in the linkage section (at the offset l_{e_i}) that is executed whenever the procedure is to be entered via that entry point (Figure 5-27). The overall strategy is then to move from P through LS_P^p to LS_Q^p and finally to Q when executing the instruction *TRA*.

Assume that p is executing P and is just starting the operand fetch for (Q, E); it is the first time that the *TRA* instruction is executed by p, and no changes have been made to LS_P^p. The instructions preceding the call to Q must, of course, provide for argument and return address linkage and for temporary stack space that Q might need.

As in the case of data linkage, the indirect addressing in *TRA* and the current content of *lp* cause a trap to the operating system. The linker invokes a segment management module, providing it with the symbolic name Q. The segment Q is made known

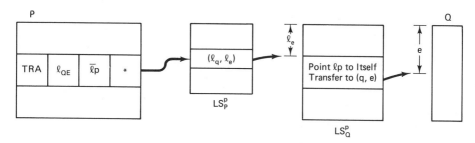

Figure 5-29   Procedure linkage by process p in P to Q.

to p by allocating a private copy, LS_Q^p, of its linkage section and assigning segment numbers to Q and LS_Q^p; we assume these to be q and l_q, respectively. The links are then set up as shown in Figure 5-29. The entry in LS_P^p pointed to from TRA is set to (l_q, l_e), where l_q is the segment number assigned to LS_Q^p and l_e is the offset at which the code for completing the transfer, that is, the code to link to (Q, E), has been placed originally by the compiler of Q.

When the links are established as described, the original TRA instruction is resumed, which transfers control to the word l_e in LS_Q^p. At this time, pbr actually points to this new linkage section. The code executed in LS_Q^p consists of essentially two instructions; the first changes the contents of lp by pointing it to itself (using the current pbr), and the second completes the transfer to Q, using the virtual address (q, e), and automatically sets pbr to point to Q.

The linking is now complete. Further execution of the TRA instruction in P by p will automatically proceed through the linkage sections without any traps, as illustrated in Figure 5-29. The procedure Q can return to its caller P by branching through the stack segments of p to the return address.

In addition to the work in initially performing the linking, two extra instructions and two indirect address fetches are the price of the full generality of procedure sharing. The techniques described in these last sections can also be employed in statically allocated systems, with a static linking loader performing the functions of the dynamic linker; the *trap tag* is then not required.

5.7 OBJECT-ORIENTED MEMORY MANAGEMENT

In all the memory management schemes described so far, main storage was organized as one or more linear spaces of elements, called segments. There are essentially three types of operations an instruction can apply to a given segment: it can *read* (load) data from the segment, it can *write* (store) data into the segment, or it can *branch* (transfer control) to the segment. Object-oriented systems raise the level of abstraction by organizing storage into more general collections of information called *objects*.

The basic concept of an object, which combines into one package a particular data structure and the set of permissible operations applicable to that data structure, was already introduced in Section 3.4. Examples of such objects were processes, processors, or ports. The main advantage of this approach is that objects hide the details of the underlying implementation of the data structures and the associated operations and provide only a simple and concise interface to the user. In general, objects incorporate more semantic meaning than the simple linear spaces provided by conventional approaches. The latter could, in fact, be viewed as a specific type of object, with the operations read, write, and execute associated with them.

The INTEL iAPX 432 is an example of a system that provides extensive hardware support for the object-oriented point of view. We will use it to illustrate some of the concepts in object-oriented memory management. We restrict our discussion to only the simplest case, where objects consist of one or more segments; the latter are simple linear memory spaces as in other segmented memory systems. For each object *type*, an object *manager* is defined that incorporates all knowledge about the objects' internal organization and their operations. Given an object type, an arbitrary number of *instances* of that object may be created, using operations provided by the manager. When an object instance is created, it is not made directly accessible to the creator; only a pointer (capability) is returned. To manipulate the object in any way, one of the procedures defined as part of the corresponding manager must be called. The pointer to the object to be manipulated is passed to the manager as a parameter. The manager performs all operations on that object on behalf of the caller.

In addition to providing an elegant structuring technique for the development of software, the object-oriented point of view has another major advantage over a conventional organization: the ability to handle dynamic allocation and deallocation of main storage in a uniform and elegant manner. The actual physical memory cells are hidden inside a collection of *storage resource objects* (SROs). These can be *global* (i.e., shared by all processes) or *local*. Objects created from a local SRO are relatively short-lived; they are automatically released when the creating procedure returns to its caller. Their primary use is for dynamic data structures created and modified during execution. If the object is to remain in existence beyond the lifetime of its creator, the global SRO must be used.

The structure and internal organization of a storage resource object are shown in Figure 5-30. It has two main components. The first is a *physical storage object*, which describes the current physical memory allocation. It contains pointer pairs, each delimiting a currently free block of main memory. For a global SRO, many such blocks may be recorded. In the case of a local SRO, only one block exists for each process. The second component of any SRO is an object table, which points to individual objects created from the space managed by the SRO; these would reside in the allocated areas of physical memory (shown as shaded areas in Figure 5-30).

When a process wishes to create a new object, it uses a special Create_Segment instruction to obtain the necessary segment(s). Three parameters must be specified with each Create_Segment instruction: (1) the length of the new segment, (2) a free location (slot) into which the pointer to the segment should be inserted after creation, and (3) a storage resource object. The latter could be the process's own local SRO or the global SRO. With the former, storage allocation is very simple: the necessary space is taken from the one free block pointed to by the corresponding physical storage object; the

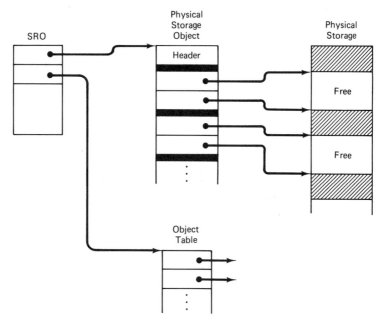

Figure 5-30 Object-oriented storage management.

pointers are updated, and the object is recorded in the object table of the SRO. If the global SRO is used, space is allocated using a *rotating first-fit* algorithm (see Section 5.5.1), which searches the list of free blocks in the physical storage object for the first free block large enough to hold the new segment.

Main storage is thus viewed as a collection of SROs operated on by the Create__Segment instructions. Hence a very simple interface to the storage management subsystem is provided for each process. This approach may actually be carried one step further by including the management of secondary storage into the general object-oriented framework. We can distinguish two types of information kept on secondary storage. The first includes segments belonging to existing processes (i.e., their virtual address spaces). These are moved between main and secondary storage as needed, for example, using demand paging or segmentation strategies. The second type of information kept on secondary storage is files, which exist independently of any process. By providing generic mechanisms for transferring objects between primary and secondary memory, *both* the virtual space management and the filing of objects may be accomplished in a uniform manner. (We will return to this topic in Section 7.3.4 after the basic principles of access control have been discussed.)

EXERCISES

5.1. The following modules are produced by a compiler using the address chaining method described in Section 5.1.2.

```
                Main                    SUB1                    SUB2
External   | SUB1 | 30 |           | SUB2 | 60 |           |      |      |
Symbol     |------|----|           |------|----|           |      |      |
Table      | SUB2 | 50 |           |  .   |  . |           |  .   |  .   |
           |  .   |  . |           |  .   |  . |           |  .   |  .   |
           |  .   |  . |           |  .   |  . |           |  .   |  .   |

    0:  |          |          0:  |          |          0:  |          |

   20:  | Call  NIL|                                     20:  | Branch  30 |

   30:  | Call  20 |                                     30:  |          |

                                  40:  | Call  NIL|      40:  | Branch  0 |

   50:  | Call  NIL|

                                  60:  | Call  40 |

   70:  | Branch  0|

                                  80:  | Branch  0 |
```

Consider each of the following cases for linking the modules together:

(a) There is no virtual memory; starting location of load module is 100.

(b) A single relocation register is provided.

(c) Pure paging is used.

(d) Pure segmentation is used.

Show the resulting load module for each case with the resulting address fields of the call and the branch instructions.

5.2. Consider a system with 4200 words of main memory using variable partitions. At some time, the memory will be occupied by three blocks of code/data as follows:

Starting Address	Length
1000	1000
2900	500
3400	800

When loading a new block into memory, the following strategy is used:

- Try the best-fit algorithm to locate a hole of appropriate size.
- If this fails, create a larger hole by shifting blocks in memory toward address zero; this always starts with the block currently at the lowest memory address and continues only until enough space is created to place the new block.

Assume that three new blocks with the respective sizes 500, 1200, and 200 are to be loaded (in the order listed). Show the memory contents after all three requests have been satisfied.

5.3. Consider the following four systems A through D:

	A	B	C	D
Page size (in words)	512	512	1024	1024
Word size (in bits)	16	32	16	32

For each system determine (a) the size of the page table (number of entries) and (b) the size of the virtual memory (number of pages). Assume that only one page table exists for the entire system and each virtual address (p, d) occupies one word (16 or 32 bits).

5.4. A pure paging system has a page size of 512 words, a virtual memory of 512 pages numbered 0 through 511, and a physical memory of 10 page frames numbered 0 through 9. The current content of physical memory is as follows:

```
                 Physical
                 Memory
        0   ┌──────────┐
            │    ·     │
            │    ·     │
     1536   ├──────────┤
            │ Page 34  │
     2048   ├──────────┤
            │ Page 9   │
            │    ·     │
            │    ·     │
     3072   ├──────────┤
            │Page Table│
     3584   ├──────────┤
            │ Page 65  │
            │    ·     │
            │    ·     │
     4608   ├──────────┤
            │ Page 10  │
            │    ·     │
            │    ·     │
            └──────────┘
```

(a) Assuming that page tables contain frame numbers (rather than physical memory addresses), show the current content of the page table.

(b) Show the content of the page table after page 49 is loaded at location 0 and page 34 is replaced by page 12.

(c) What physical address is referenced by the virtual addresses 4608, 5119, 5120, and 33300?

(d) What happens when virtual address 33000 is referenced?

(e) If the page loaded at page frame 9 is a procedure and another process q wants to share it, where must it appear in q's page table? (Give the page table entry.)

5.5. You are given the following information about a virtual memory system that employs both paging and segmentation:

- Word size is 32 bits.
- Page and segment table entries each occupy one word.
- Page size is 512 words.
- A page table occupies at most one page.

- Virtual addresses have the form $(s1, s2, p, w)$, where $|s1|$, $|s2|$, $|p|$, and $|w|$ denote the lengths (in bits) of each of the four address components.

(a) What is the value of $|w|$?

(b) What is the maximum number of pages per segment and what is the corresponding value of $|p|$?

(c) Using the determined values of $|p|$ and $|w|$, which of the following choices for $|s1|$ and $|s2|$ is preferable? Explain.
  i. $|s1| = |w|$ and $|s2| = 32 - |s1| - |p| - |w|$.
  ii. $|s2| = |w|$ and $|s1| = 32 - |s2| - |p| - |w|$.

(d) Would either choice under part (c) result in a larger virtual address space? Explain.

5.6. The following diagram is a memory dump (snapshot) of a hypothetical computer that uses paging and segmentation similar to the Multics system.

Main Memory

Address	0	1	2	3	4	5	6	7	10	11	12	13	14	15	16	17
Content	4	10	-2	–	17	24	100	3	-1	3	16	0	–	–	–	–
Comment																

	20	21	22	23	24	25	26	27	30	31	32	33	34	35	36	37
	64	-1	–	–	–	–	–	–	3	-2	44	47	0	14	–	–

	40	41	42	43	44	45	46	47	50	51	52	53	54	55	56	57
	34	60	–	74	70	–	–	–	30	–	–	–	50	24	–	–
		PT of ST														

	60	61	62	63	64	65	66	67	70	71	72	73	74	75	76	77
	20	–	–	44	120	16	16	27	64	47	-1	3	54	–	–	–

Secondary Memory

Disk Address	0				1				2				3			
Content	7	11	14	16	3	16	13	25	-11	4	-2	3	4	106	10	0

The following basic rules apply:

- All addresses are given in octal.
- The page table of the segment table is at address 40 (PT of ST).

- A dash (—) denotes a nonexistent page.
- Negative numbers denote out-of-memory pages, with their absolute value being their location on disk.
- Accessing a page not in memory causes a page fault and a free page frame, if available, is used up.

(a) In the comment line, describe each page (e.g., "page table of segment table," "page 0 of segment table," "page table of segment 0," etc.).

(b) Determine the content of the virtual address 161_8? (*Hint*: Translate the octal number into an equivalent 8-bit binary number and interpret each 2-bit component as $s1$, $s2$, p, and w.)

Consider the following additional rules:

- To facilitate the search for free page frames, a list of these is maintained by the operating system. In our example, segment 12 is dedicated to this purpose. That is, pages constituting segment 12 contain physical addresses of free page frames. [Verify this by comparing the contents of segment 12 with the page frames marked "free" under part (a).]
- If a page fault occurs and there are free page frames, the first frame from the list in segment 12 is used and the list is updated.
- If a segment is deactivated, then all the freed page frames are added to the free page frame list in segment 12.

(c) What is the content of the virtual address 104_8? (In case a page fault occurs, show all changes.)

(d) Deactivate segment 7 (i.e., free the corresponding pages and the page table).

5.7. Suppose, along with the diagrammed memory of Exercise 5.6, a translation look-aside buffer with the following contents is included:

$s1$, $s2$, p	Frame Address
0_8	4_8
20_8	64_8

(a) Which of the following virtual addresses will be translated using the buffer, i.e., bypass the page and sequent tables: 0_8, 1_8, 2_8, 3_8, 4_8, 20_8, 21_8, 64_8, 100_8, 101_8, 104_8?

(b) How many page faults occur for each of these cases?

(c) Assume that each reference to main memory takes 1 microsecond. How long does it take to resolve a virtual address if, on the average, 60 percent of all program references find a match in the translation look-aside buffer. (Assume that access to the latter is instantaneous.)

(d) Repeat part (c) for a match ratio of 85 percent.

5.8. Extend the *NL__map* procedures of Sections 5.4.2.2 and 5.4.2.3, assuming the following:

(a) Segment and page tables are always resident, but individual pages may not be.

(b) Only the segment table is permanently resident.

(c) Only the page table of the segment table (Section 5.4.2.3 only) is permanently resident.

5.9. The following sequence of requests is issued to the memory manager:

- Allocate block b_1 of size 100.
- Allocate block b_2 of size 500.
- Allocate block b_3 of size 60.
- Allocate block b_4 of size 100.
- Release block b_1.
- Release block b_3.
- Allocate block b_5 of size 50.
- Allocate block b_6 of size 90.

Assuming a total memory size of 1024, list the *starting addresses* and the *sizes* of all free spaces for the following two memory management schemes after all requests have been processed.

(a) First fit

(b) Best fit

5.10. Consider a system with 64KB of main memory. The following blocks are to be requested and released:

Block	A	B	C	D	E	F
Size (in KB)	20	20	15	8	8	24

Obviously, not all blocks may be reserved at the same time. We say an allocation failure occurs if a request is made that cannot be satisfied (i.e., no free memory fragment is large enough to hold the requested amount of memory). Give a sequence of requests and releases that results in an allocation failure (a) under the first-fit policy, but not the best-fit policy, and (b) under the best-fit policy, but not the first-fit policy. For each of the two situations, draw a diagram that shows what parts of memory are allocated at the time of failure.

5.11. Three procedures, A, B, and C, are to be linked together into one process and loaded into memory. The length of each procedure is 600 words. Consider the following memory management schemes:

(a) Paging (no segmentation)

Page size: 1000 words

Page table occupies 1 page

(b) Segmentation (no paging)

Segment table size: 1000 words

(c) Paging and segmentation: combined information from parts (a) and (b)

Assume that all procedures and all tables are in memory. For each of the three systems, what is the total occupied memory space (i.e., the space that cannot be used by another process)? This includes the space occupied by the procedures and the various tables, as well as space wasted due to the fixed page size.

5.12. Consider three procedures with sizes 700, 200, and 500 words, respectively. If pure segmentation is used, the total memory requirement (ignoring the space for segment tables) is the sum of the three sizes. With pure paging, on the other hand, some amount of space is generally lost, because procedure sizes are rarely exact multiples of the page size (internal fragmentation). For each of the following page sizes, determine the total amount of storage

wasted due to internal fragmentation when the three procedures are loaded into memory:
(a) 200; (b) 500; (c) 600; (d) 700 words.

5.13. Assuming a physical memory of four page frames, give the number of page faults for the
reference string *abgadeabadegde* for each of the following policies. (Initially, all frames
are empty.)

(a) MIN

(b) FIFO

(c) Clock replacement algorithm

(d) Second-chance algorithm (assume that all accesses to page *b* are write requests)

(e) LRU

(f) WS with $\tau = 3$

5.14. Consider the following sequence of virtual memory references generated by a single program in a pure paging system:

$$10, 11, 104, 170, 73, 309, 185, 245, 246, 434, 458, 364$$

(a) Derive the corresponding reference string, assuming a page size of 100 words.

(b) Determine the number of page faults for each of the following page-replacement strategies, assuming that two page frames are available to the program:

(i) FIFO

(ii) Clock

(iii) LRU

5.15. Consider the reference string *abcdebcdcbddbddd*. Assuming the working-set replacement
strategy, determine the minimum window size such that the string generates at most five
page faults. Show which pages are in memory at each reference. Mark page faults with an
asterisk.

5.16. Devise data structures and algorithms for

(a) Maintaining the working set of a process.

(b) Selecting a replacement page using working-set principles.

5.17. A two-dimensional 512 × 512 matrix is stored in row order in a paged virtual memory
system with page size 512 and 16 frames of physical storage. Assuming the FIFO page-
replacement discipline, how many page faults will be generated in order to sequentially
process the entire matrix (a) by row? (b) by column? Would the results be different under
the LRU policy?

5.18. Consider two processes p_1 and p_2 in a purely segmented system. Their current segment
tables contain the following entries (segment lengths are not shown):

	ST1		ST2
0	4000	0	2000
1	6000	1	6000
2	9000	2	9000
3	2000		
4	7000		

(a) Which segments are shared, if any?

(b) Which of the following virtual addresses would be illegal when used by the segment
at location 6000: (0, 0) (1, 0) (2, 0) (3, 0) (4, 0) (5, 0)? Explain.

(c) The segment at location 7000 is swapped out and later reloaded at location 8000. Similarly, the segment at location 2000 is swapped out and reloaded at 1000. Show the new segment tables.

(d) A third process, p_3, wishes to share the segments at locations 2000, 4000, and 6000. Which of these must be data segments (as opposed to procedures) to make this possible?

5.19. Examine the problems of static sharing in a purely paged system (no segmentation) by considering the following situation: A process p_a requires programs Q_1 and Q_2, temporary storage T_1, and data D_1, of size q_1, q_2, t_1, and d_1, respectively, in pages. These are combined and linked into a virtual space program of size $q_1 + q_2 + t_1 + d_1$ pages in that order and loaded into memory. While p_a is still active, another process p_b requests loading of information Q_1', Q_2, T_1', and D_1 with page sizes q_1', q_2, t_1', and d_1, respectively, where $q_1' > q_1$ and $t_1' < t_1$. Q_2 and D_1 are to be shared between p_a and p_b. Describe possible contents of the page tables for p_a and p_b. What problem arises if a new process p_c now enters the system and wants to share Q_1' and Q_1?

5.20. Consider two processes p_1 and p_2 sharing the same procedure P, which references a data segment D. After all links to P have been resolved, main memory is occupied as follows:

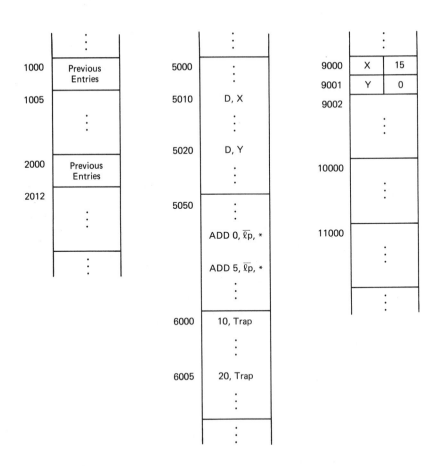

- Segment table for p_1: 1000 (the next free entry is at 1005)
- Segment table for p_2: 2000 (the next free entry is at 2012)
- Symbol table for P: 5000
- Code for P: 5500
- Linkage section LS_p: 6000
- Symbol table for D: 9000
- Data segment D: 9002

Complete the preceding diagram by showing the linkage sections for p_1 and p_2 starting at locations 10000 and 11000, respectively, before execution of the ADD instructions. Show all changes that occurred in memory due to dynamic linking after execution of the ADD instructions.

6

File Systems and Input/Output Processing

In addition to the main processors and primary memory, any computer installation must be equipped with devices that permit the user to interact with the system and secondary (or auxiliary) storage units on which the user may keep information for indefinite periods of time. By far the most popular device for interactive communication with a system is the CR terminal, consisting of a screen and a keyboard. These terminals have almost completely replaced noninteractive devices such as punch card and paper tape units, used extensively in past decades. For hard-copy output, a variety of printers, ranging from simple dot-matrix devices to the most sophisticated laser printers, exist. We will refer to communication and secondary storage devices jointly as *input/output (IO) devices*. The control of all these units to perform the desired data transfers is called *input/output (IO) processing*.

Secondary storage has already been discussed briefly in the context of virtual memory; there, however, the devices were transparent to the user. To provide permanent storage for each user, most contemporary systems offer extensive services for managing data, organized into *files*, on secondary storage. A *file* is defined as a collection of data elements grouped together for purposes of access control, retrieval, and modification. Traditionally, each data element is considered a *record*, which is a linear list of information items. Some modern systems define a file simply as a sequence or *stream* of basic data units (e.g., characters).

Examples of files are source and machine language programs, application data, file directories, and systems accounting and performance data. In fact, virtually all program and data information accessed by a computer system (i.e., all computer software) is treated as a file at some point during processing. Files may reside on any of a large variety of storage media including disks, drums, magnetic tape, main memory, and paper; associated with each kind of storage is a processing unit that permits reading or writing data on that storage device, as well as control and testing operations. The same file often occupies different storage media during its lifetime. For example, a file containing a user program could successively appear on tape, disk, and main storage as the program moves from an archive to a loaded state.

A *file system* is that software responsible for creating, destroying, organizing, reading, writing, modifying, moving, and controlling access to files and for management of the resources used by files. Without a file system, efficient computing would essentially be impossible. It is this component that permits the use of many language processors, on-line user libraries of programs and data, spooling operations in batch systems, and practical interactive computing. This chapter discusses the organization of file and IO subsystems and the tasks to be performed by the different software levels comprising these.

6.1 ORGANIZATION OF THE FILE AND IO SUBSYSTEMS

6.1.1 Basic Issues in Device Management

The functions performed by a typical file system in collaboration with the IO services can be divided into three basic classes, according to their purpose:

1. Present a logical or *abstract view* of files to the users by hiding the physical details of IO devices.
2. Facilitate the *sharing* of physical IO devices and *optimize* their use.
3. Provide *protection* mechanisms for data being transferred or managed by the IO devices.

In this chapter we are concerned primarily with the first two functions, which indicate the need for making programs independent of the operational or organizational details of physical devices; the problems of protection will be treated separately in Chapter 7.

The first function addresses the fact that device interfaces are very complex. Each logical command must typically be decomposed into long sequences of low-level signals to trigger the actions to be performed by the device and to supervise the progress of the operation by testing the device's status. For example, to read a single word from a moving-head disk, a sequence of instructions must be generated to move the read/write arm to the track containing the desired word, await the rotational delay until the sector containing the desired word passes under the read/write arm, transfer the data, and check for a number of possible error conditions.

The user should not have to deal with such low-level details of the system's operation, especially since these are usually of no interest to the computation at hand. The problem is further aggravated because one must cope with a multitude of different IO interfaces, not only for different device types but even for different models within the same class of devices. Considering the rapid development of new increasingly sophisticated IO units, it would not be practical to require that each programmer know the operational details of each device to be employed by a program. Furthermore, the number and type of devices may change as the computing facility is reconfigured. It is essential that such changes remain transparent to all but a few special system programs.

To satisfy the preceding requirements of device independence, an operating system usually provides an *abstract interface* that presents to the user a greatly simplified view of the computing environment. Our definition of a file as a set of related data records imposes little structure on a file, only subdivision into records, and is almost independent of the medium on which a file is stored. Thus at the most abstract and unstructured level, we will consider a file to be an ordered sequence of *logical records*, $R_0, R_1, \ldots, R_n$. Such a file will be referred to as a *logical file* and will be identified by a symbolic name, F. The logical record is the smallest addressable unit within a logical file. The purpose of the logical file concept is to provide users with one simple, uniform, linear space for their files. These then may be manipulated by a simple set of read and write operations provided by the abstract user interface; the actual implementation of each of these operations is hidden from the user by the file system and IO modules.

Communication devices may be viewed abstractly as *sources* and *sinks* of sequential streams of data. Each user is presented a collection of virtual devices that may be controlled by a set of simple generic operations similar to those provided for the manipulation of files. In fact, if sequential access to files is assumed, there is little difference between a virtual device and a file, and hence virtual devices may be manipulated using the same instructions as those provided to access files.

The second reason for device independence is the desire to share devices and, at the same time, optimize their use. Most devices are electromechanical and hence their operation is slow compared to the speed of processing. To maximize their utilization, the system may attempt to schedule operations globally according to the characteristics of each device. For example, requests to read from or write to a moving-head disk unit may be ordered such that the distance the read/write head must travel between operations is as short as possible.

When devices are shared among different processes, the file/IO subsystem must also take into consideration the device type. For example, read/write operations issued by different processes to the same disk unit can in general be interleaved freely. Other devices, on the other hand, may only be shared in a serial fashion; that is, a process must be granted exclusive access to a particular device for possibly a significant length of time. Printers are a good example, since they must complete the processing of one output task before attempting to serve another process. Before discussing the various levels comprising the file and IO subsystems, we first present a hypothetical abstract interface provided to the user.

6.1.2 The Abstract User Interface

We introduce a simple abstract interface consisting of six generic operations that establish connections between files (or virtual devices) and users and transfer data to and from these files. Each of these operations must be interpreted by the underlying file system and IO processing modules and transformed into the necessary device specific commands. The following two commands are used to establish and to terminate a connection between a program and a file or a device.

Open (F, op__type). Since a file may usually be accessed in several different ways, most operating systems require that a logical connection be established between a process and the file prior to performing any data transfers. The *Open* command, which is widely used for this purpose, specifies the file *F* to be opened for the type of operation specified by *op__type*, for example, read, write, or both. In the case where *F* is not a file but an IO device, such as a printer or a terminal, a similar connection must be established, which reserves the named device for the user and performs the mapping of the symbolic name *F* onto the actual hardware device. The command is then usually called *Attach* or *Allocate*, instead of *Open*.

Close (F). This command reverses the effect of *Open*; that is, it disconnects the file *F* from the current process, thus making it inaccessible to the latter. In the case of IO devices, the commands *Detach* or *Deallocate* usually perform the analogous functions of *Close*.

Once a connection is established between a process and a file (device), data may be transferred in the appropriate direction using one of the following commands. (A record-oriented point of view is assumed here. If, instead, files are organized as linear sequences of bytes, without any superimposed record structure, the commands would specify the starting byte number or pointer and the number of bytes to be transferred, instead of a record number.)

Read__d (F, rec__no, buf). This command performs a *direct* read operation; it causes the transfer of the logical record specified by the record number (*rec__no*) of the file *F* into the memory area starting at location *buf*. The latter will be called the input buffer.

Write__d (F, rec__no, buf). Analogous to a direct read operation, the direct write operation performs a transfer from the memory area starting at address *buf* (the output buffer) to the logical record specified by *rec__no* of the file *F*.

Read__s (F, buf). The sequential read operation makes use of an internal pointer, maintained by the system, that refers to the next logical record to be read. One such pointer is maintained for each file *F* opened for sequential access. Each time a sequential read operation is issued, the contents of the current record are copied into the memory area designated by the address *buf*, and the pointer is updated to point to the next logical record.

Write__s (F, buf). Analogous to a sequential read, the sequential write operation transfers the contents of the memory area at address *buf* into the current logical record of the file *F* and updates the current-record pointer accordingly.

The task of the file and IO subsystem modules is to map the abstract user interface onto lower-level commands and control signals interpreted by the underlying hardware.

6.1.3 A Hierarchical Model of the File and IO Subsystems

The file system, together with the IO processing modules, forms a layer of software that accomplishes the mapping of the abstract user interface onto the actual collection of hardware. We take the position that the average user need be concerned with only logical files and devices, structured and accessed according to a given application, and that he or she should be isolated from machine-dependent details, such as the particular device, storage allocation algorithms, software accessing mechanisms, blocking (i.e., combining of several logical records into one physical record for the purposes of more efficient data transfers), and buffering. All these should be made invisible by the underlying file and IO processing modules.

While some functions may be labeled as typical file system functions and others as typical IO functions, it is, in general, difficult to draw a line between the two subsystems. Instead, we will present a unifying view by decomposing both subsystems into several major parts and showing the interactions among individual modules. The assumed organization is a modification of the model presented originally in Madnick (1968) and Madnick and Alsop (1969), where the file and IO subsystems are decomposed into a number of levels in a hierarchical structure that bridges the gap between the abstract user interface and the various hardware device interfaces. Each level represents a successively more abstract machine in that a module at level k may communicate directly with only modules at the same level k or at the immediately adjacent levels, $k + 1$ and $k - 1$. The hierarchical organization is useful because it permits us to understand the rather complex file and IO subsystems incrementally by studying each level in isolation.

The model consists of five functional levels, as illustrated in Figure 6-1. Next we briefly outline the tasks within each level, proceeding from the abstract user interface down to the hardware. The remainder of this chapter is then devoted to discussing the functions of each level in more detail.

L5. *Directory retrieval.* The primary function of the procedures at this level is to convert symbolic file names to identifiers, which, in turn, point to the precise location of either the file, its descriptor, or perhaps a table containing this information. To accomplish this, the directory structure is searched for an entry to the referenced file.

L4. *Basic file system.* This part activates and deactivates files by invoking opening and closing routines and is responsible for verifying the access rights of the caller on each file request, if necessary. The primary task is to retrieve the descriptor for the file when it is being opened.

L3. *Physical organization methods.* The original user request for access to certain logical file addresses is translated into physical secondary storage address requests, reflecting the actual locations and organization of the desired records. Allocation

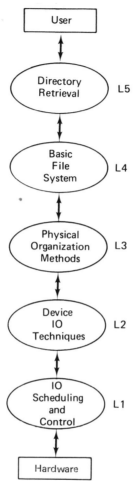

Figure 6-1 A hierarchical file systems model.

of secondary storage and main storage buffers is conveniently treated in this level also.

L2. *Device IO techniques*. The requested operation(s) and physical record(s) are converted into appropriate sequences of IO instructions, channel commands, and controller orders. Various buffering schemes may be employed to better utilize the available devices. Local optimizations, for example the minimization of rotational delays of disks, may also be performed here or at the next lower level.

L1. *IO scheduling and control*. The actual queuing, scheduling, initiating, and controlling of all IO requests occur at this level, which directly connects to the IO hardware of the computer system. Basic IO interrupt servicing and reporting of device, controller, and channel status are also done here.

One reason for this particular choice of levels and functions is the simple communication that exists between levels. The information passed down from the user through successive levels is basically requests for work and the following data:

$$\text{user} \xrightarrow[A_5)]{\text{(symbolic file name,}} \text{L5} \xrightarrow[A_4)]{\text{(file identifier,}} \text{L4} \xrightarrow[A_3)]{\text{(file descriptor,}}$$

$$\text{L3} \xrightarrow[A_2)]{\text{(physical record list,}} \text{L2} \xrightarrow[A_1)]{\text{(IO sequences,}} \text{L1}$$

where each A_i represents other parameters such as type of operation, length, and memory address.

The information passed upward in the hierarchy would be essentially completion messages. Parts of the hierarchy may often be bypassed within a given system by special classes of users and/or for certain files; for example, some supervisory routines might access the basic file system or the IO scheduling and control modules directly.

Example

In UNIX, all data transfers are accomplished by reading and writing files. This is because all devices, including the user's terminal, are viewed as files. Before a file may be accessed it must be opened using the following command:

$$fp = fopen(F, mode)$$

where F is the file's symbolic name, *mode* specifies whether the file is to be used for reading, writing, or appending data, and *fp* is a pointer returned by the call. This pointer is then used to access the file using one of several possible commands (system procedures). Let us consider the implementation of the *fopen* command and the following simple character-oriented read operation,

$$c = readc(fp)$$

which sequentially accesses the file pointed to by *fp*. Each time *readc* is called it copies the next character of that file into the variable c.

The main purpose of *fopen* is to locate the file with the symbolic name F and to record information describing the current status of the file in the appropriate system tables. Two such tables, referred to as open file tables (OFT), are primarily affected by this process. The first, which is private to a user, contains information such as the pointer to a buffer used in conjunction with the open file, the position of the next character to be read or written, the number of characters left in the buffer, and the access mode. It also contains an integer, referred to as the file descriptor *fd*, that is used as an index into the second, system-wide OFT. The corresponding entry in this table contains the data necessary to locate the file and to perform the read or write operation. This includes the device number, an index for locating the description of the file, and the current read/write pointers. (In UNIX terminology, the term file descriptor is used to refer to the index *fd*, rather than the descriptive information itself; the latter is called an *i-node*.) Figure 6-2 shows the relationship between the two OFTs and the corresponding *i*-node. (The purpose of the directory

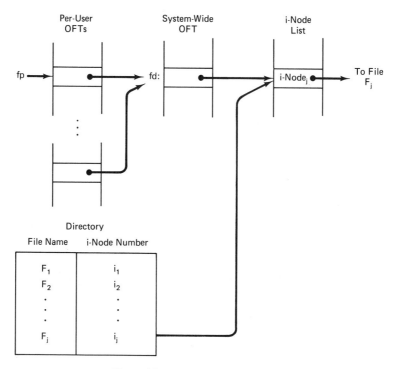

Figure 6-2   File system tables in UNIX.

structure will be explained in Section 6.2.) The value of *fd* is used as argument with any low-level read or write operation on the file.

When a file is to be opened for reading, it must already exist in the file system. The operation *fopen* verifies this fact by calling on a lower-level *open* procedure, which creates a new entry in the system-wide OFT and returns the corresponding index value *fd*, if the file already exists in the file system; otherwise, the value −1 is returned. This involves searching the file directory for the existence of the file name *F* and verifying that the requested access type is permitted. If the test is positive, *fopen* makes a new entry in the private OFT, fills in the appropriate values of the descriptive data, and returns the pointer *fp* to the user. The file is now ready for reading.

The functions described correspond to those associated typically with the two highest levels L5 and L4 (Figure 6-1). Assume now that the user issues the first *readc* command. This is directed at the modules of level L4, which expect a file identifier (pointer) as argument. The underlying procedure finds that no buffer has yet been assigned to the file and attempts to correct that situation by calling a memory-allocation routine that resides at level L3. Assuming that this is successful, the buffer is allocated and filled with the first set of data by issuing a low-level unbuffered *read* command, directed also at level L3. This command has the following form:

$$stat = read(fd, buf, n)$$

where *fd* is the integer file descriptor (found in the per-user OFT), *buf* is the pointer to the newly created input buffer, *n* is the number of characters to be read, and *stat* indicates the status of the read operation upon completion; it returns the number of characters actually read or a −1 if an error occurred. If the read was successful, the first character in the buffer is copied to the variable *c* specified with the *readc* command and the current character pointer is incremented. Subsequent *readc* operations access only the buffer until the last character is used. At that time, another *read* operation is invoked to fill the buffer with the next set of data from the file.

Each *read* operation must be transformed into a physical record address and, subsequently, into device-specific commands, by the next lower levels L3 and L2 of the file/IO subsystems. This results in the forming of a request packet, called a *transaction record*, which specifies the type of operation (read), a main memory address (buffer), a physical device address (cylinder, track, sector), and the amount of data to be transferred. This packet is placed in a queue, from which it is eventually removed by the appropriate device driver process, executing at level L1. A possible reordering of packets in the queue for the purposes of access optimization could precede the selection of the packet. Once the selection is made, the instructions contained in the packet are transmitted to and processed by the device controller. When all data transfers terminate, the original *read* operation is considered completed and execution proceeds with the next operation.

6.2 DIRECTORY MANAGEMENT

All systems have a set of *directories* (*dictionaries*, *catalogs*), which identify and locate all files accessible to user and systems processes. Minimally, a directory entry contains the name and physical address of a file or of its descriptor; at the other extreme, a complete file descriptor may be stored in each entry. UNIX, for example, takes the first approach (Figure 6–2). Each directory entry contains a symbolic file name together with an index (*i*-node number), that locates the file's descriptive information (*i*-node). Since directories are themselves data objects that are searched and modified, they are often treated as files, albeit with a special role; then the operations of the file system can also be used for directory management. We now examine methods for organizing directories and for naming files.

The most general practical directories organization is a *tree* structure, where each node of the tree is a directory (file) and each branch is a directory entry that points to either another directory or a data file. If data files are added to the tree, they will occupy all the *leaves*. The *root* of the tree is called the *master* directory. These concepts are illustrated in Figure 6-3. (Ignore the dashed connections for the moment.)

If we require that all files (data and directory) with the *same* parent node have unique symbolic branch names in the parent, then an unambiguous name for each file exists: the name formed by concatenating all branch identifiers found along the path from the master directory to the desired file. Each such name is referred to as a *path name*; it uniquely identifies one file in a tree-structured hierarchy. (Since we have assumed a tree structure, a given file is pointed to by one and only one directory branch; otherwise, for example, in an acyclic tangled graph hierarchy, more than one possible path name for any given file may exist.)

Example

1. In Figure 6-3, data file 14 has the name *Root.C.E.G.K*, where *Root* refers to the master directory. Similarly, directory 8 has the name *Root.C.D.*

2. A typical example of a file directory tree is given in Figure 6-4. The master directory has six entries, pointing to the directories for the operating systems routines (*OS*), authorized (paying) users (*Account*), basic utilities such as file manipulation programs (*Utilities*), language processors (*Language*), public libraries of programs and data submitted by external users (*Pub__Lib*), and individual user libraries (*User__Lib*). The unique identification for the run-time library associated with the FORTRAN system, starting from the root node, is *Language.Fortran.Runtime*, while the compiler is accessible by *Language.Fortran.Compiler.Phase__i.*

The naming scheme avoids any file identification conflicts among users while permitting an almost arbitrary assignment of branch names. The branch name can be interpreted as the name given to a file by a user while working within a given file context. The tree path name can be employed as a search argument to find any data or directory file. Since the directories are files, access control restrictions can also be defined for

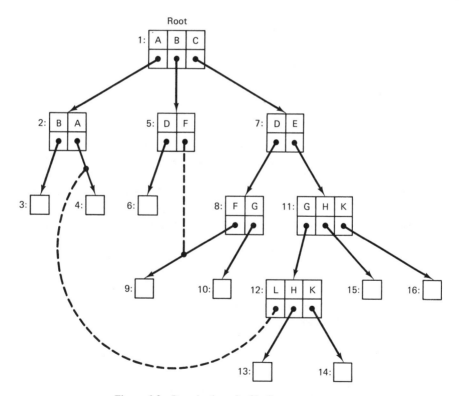

Figure 6-3 Organization of a file directory structure.

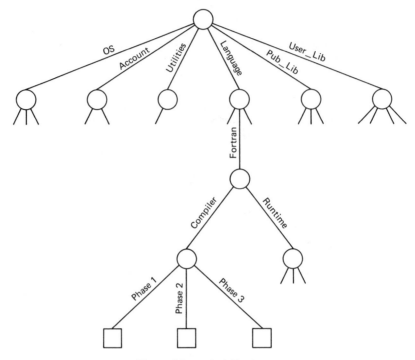

Figure 6-4 Typical file directory.

them, thus controlling the set of users capable of modifying and retrieving directory information.

   While path names uniquely identify any file within the directory structure, their use would be extremely tedious if the user had to specify the full path name each time a file were to be accessed. A number of schemes have been developed to alleviate this problem. In many systems, for example MULTICS or UNIX, each user (process) is assigned a *working directory*; files are then referenced *relative* to the current working directory. For example, if the working directory of some user U is directory 7 in Figure 6-3, U would identify file 16 by the path name $E.K.$ A convention for moving up the tree permits the identification of both ancestral and other groups of files that are not descendants of the working directory. Assume that an asterisk (*) indicates the *parent* of a given file. Then file 6 in Figure 6-3 is referenced by $*.B.D.$, assuming file 7 to be the current working directory; if the working directory were file 12, then file 9 would be located as $*.*.D.F.$

   Links may be established between directory entries to increase the efficiency of cross-directory references. A link is an entry in a directory that points directly to another directory *entry*, rather than a file. This is illustrated by the dashed lines in Figure 6-3; links exist from directory 12 to the A entry of directory 2 and from directory 5 to the F entry of directory 8. Links are assigned names in the same manner as branches. Then, the name of file 9 with respect to working directory 5 is either $*.C.D.F$ or, using the link, just *F*; as another example, file 4 could be referenced with respect to directory 11 by either *.*.*A.A* or by *G.L*. One must be careful with links because they destroy the basic tree organization and can lead to inconsistencies; for example, if file 4 and the corresponding branch *A* of directory 2 were deleted, then the link *L* in directory 12 would point to a nonexistent entry.

To further decrease the need for specifying long path names and thus improve user friendliness, most modern systems provide *directory search routines* that attempt to find the unique file ID for a given symbolic name (not a path name). One possible strategy could be as follows. Assume that a program *P*, recorded in a directory *D*, specifies a symbolic name *S* of a file to be accessed; since *S* is not a unique path name, it could designate different files depending on the current context. The search routines could proceed according to the following rules to locate the desired file:

1. Search the parent directory of the calling program *P*, that is, the directory *D*. If unsuccessful then:
2. Search the current working directory *W*. (Frequently, this would be the same directory as the parent directory *D*.) If unsuccessful, then:
3. Search the system library. If unsuccessful, then report an error.

The following example shows the effect of this strategy in different situations:

Example

Consider again the directory structure of Figure 6-3 and assume the following conditions:

- File 2 (path name *Root.A*) is the system library.
- File 1 (path name *Root*) is the current working directory.
- File 6 (path name *Root.B.D*) is the currently executing program; it uses the two symbolic names, *F* and *A*, to refer to two other files.

The two references are resolved as follows:

1. *F* refers to file 9, since the name *F* is found in the caller's parent directory (file 5).
2. *A* is not found in the caller's parent directory; hence the search continues in the current working directory. *A* is found there and thus it refers to file 2.

Assume now that the current working directory is some other file (e.g., file 5). The reference to *F* will be resolved to the same file 9. The reference to *A*, however, will fail in both the parent and the current working directory, and the search will resort to the systems library. Thus *A* will refer to file 4 in this case.

Most directories are stored on secondary memory, because each one can contain many entries and a potentially large number of these directory files may be defined. For removable libraries and self-contained systems of files, the "local" directories are often on the same storage device as the files to which they point. It is normal for part or all of the master directory to reside in main storage, temporarily or permanently; in either case, the descriptor for the master directory is permanently maintained in main memory so that file searching can be initiated.

6.3 BASIC FILE SYSTEM

For each file, there must exist some amount of descriptive information required by lower levels of the file and IO subsystems in order to perform the desired read and write operations. The main purpose of the basic file system is to retrieve that information and to invoke the opening and closing routines that associate the appropriate access procedures and data structures with the desired file.

6.3.1 File Descriptors

The descriptive information about each file is usually contained in a record called the *file descriptor*. If a given file may be addressed by only *one* directory entry in the system, then the necessary descriptive information may be kept within the directory itself as part of each entry. In practice, it is often stored in a separate area of the storage device containing the corresponding files.

Three basic data items appear in descriptors in virtually all file systems: the file identification, information about its physical location, and access control information.

File Identification   This item normally consists of a symbolic name N and an internal identifier I. N could be a nonunique character string, such as the branch names in the directories tree discussed in the last section, or it could be a unique symbolic name, such as the path name from the master directory to the named file; one advantage of the second scheme is that the name information is then helpful both in reconstructing the directory after a system crash and in testing the file system for consistency. The purpose of I is to provide a unique, simple identifier for each file so that the descriptor can be easily located and the file may be conveniently referenced. This identifier might be the actual location of the descriptor; or a pair (i, d) indicating the ith file on device d; or the result of some straightforward counting method, for example file number 325; or something more esoteric, such as the time the file was created.

Physical Address Information.   The location and extent of a file are defined here. For files that are not stored sequentially, the address and length of each physical record must be specified either directly by a list or indirectly, for example by a pointer to an index table or to the first record of a linked set of records. The mapping between logical records and the corresponding physical record addresses appear in this component either implicitly through the physical address information or explicitly, for example by a table.

Access Control Information.   The facility to control *who* can access a given set of files and in what manner is one of the central and most important services provided in multiuser, resource-sharing systems. This information is usually stored in the file descriptor. The file system must rigorously enforce these access control specifications and keep them tamperproof. We will postpone the discussion of access control until Chapter 7, which is dedicated exclusively to issues of protection and security.

A variety of other useful data can appear in the descriptor, such as the following:

1. *Historical and measurement information.* This may include date of creation, date of last change or last read, number of times the file has been opened, and other use data.

2. *Disposition.* A file could be *temporary*, to be destroyed at "closing" time or at the termination of the process for which it was created; or it may be stored indefinitely as a *permanent* file.

3. *Coding of information.* File data may be coded as uninterpreted *binary* strings meant to be directly loaded into the machine or as *characters* (e.g., in EBCDIC or ASCII code) that must be decoded and encoded or unpacked and packed during input and output, respectively.

4. *Physical organization.* Examples are sequential, linked, or indexed organizations with fixed- or variable-length records; this information could also be part of the *physical address* component of the descriptor.

Example

Figure 6-2, discussed in the example of Section 6.1.3, illustrates the use of descriptors as it is implemented in the UNIX file system. The descriptors, called *i*-nodes, are kept on a list accessed only by the file system. Each *i*-node contains, among other information, the following entries:

1. Identification of the owner
2. File type (directory, special file, regular file)
3. Protection information
4. Mapping of logical records onto physical blocks of storage
5. Time of creation, last use, and last modification
6. Number of directories sharing (pointing to) the file

Directories refer to files via the *i*-node list; to access a file F_j, the corresponding *i*-node number, i_j, is found in the directory and submitted to the system, which uses it as an index to locate the *i*-node in the list. This convention permits the use of relatively large descriptors and allows the contents of an auxiliary storage device to be directly identified within the storage itself; also, several directory entries can then conveniently point to the same file. The descriptor is normally kept resident in main storage from the time the file is opened until it is closed; during this time, it is usually augmented by processing dependent information, such as buffer locations and accessing routines.

6.3.2 Opening and Closing Routines

When a process wishes to use or create a particular file, it must declare its intent by issuing the *Open* command presented in Section 6.1.2. As a result, a set of *opening routines* is invoked to perform a number of initialization activities. Many systems permit the *Open* command to be omitted, in which case it is generated implicitly by the system itself. At the termination of a file's processing, *closing routines* are invoked, either in response to an explicit *Close* command or implicitly as the result of a process's termination. The closing routines essentially release the resources used for accessing the file and render the file inactive for the particular user.

The opening routines are responsible for associating with the file the necessary resources that enable data transfers to and from the file and for making the file active. This includes the following tasks:

I. For *old* files (i.e., those already recorded in the directory structure):
  1. Locate the file specified by the unique identifier found by the directory search routines (level L5) and make it available for processing. If the file is off-line, for example on magnetic tape or removable disk, allocate a unit and physically mount the file.
  2. Use the access control information in the descriptor to check that the user has authority to access the file in the manner requested.

II. For *new* files that are to be created:
  1. Allocate secondary storage and/or device(s) for the file. A block of secondary storage or a tape or disk unit might be reserved.

III. For old and new files:
  1. Obtain any main memory needed for IO buffers.
  2. Load routines for accessing the file and effecting the virtual to real space mappings.
  3. Possibly generate a skeletal form for the IO command sequences to be employed.
  4. Insert the data of (I), (II), and (III) and the descriptor into an open (or active) file directory (OFT); an OFT entry is sometimes called a *file control block* or a *data control block*. Each user may have a private OFT, or the OFT could be consolidated into one system-wide structure; a combination of both alternatives is often used.

Example

As already pointed out in Section 6.1, the UNIX operating system implements both private and system-wide OFTs (Figure 6-2). Each entry in the per-user OFT points to the corresponding file by an entry in the system-wide OFT. This organization permits many of the preceding steps to be bypassed if the file is already active as a result of a previous opening by some other user; in particular, only the appropriate entry in the private OFT must be made.

The closing routines reverse the opening work. Specifically, closing of a file involves the following operations:

I. For *temporary* files, created solely for the current tasks, and for files that will *never* be referenced again:

    1. Destroy the file by releasing its secondary (and off-line) storage resources and deleting its directory entry.

II. For *new* files that are to be retained (i.e., *permanent* new files):

    1. Insert an appropriate entry in the directory structure.

III. For *permanent* old and new files:

    1. Update the file descriptor with any new data resulting from its most recent use; these could include changes to the file, such as length, and historical information, such as time of last reference or time of last change.

    2. If necessary, insert end-of-file markers after the last record in the file.

    3. Store the file identification and location so that the file may be copied later for back-up purposes. (These procedures are discussed more fully in Section 6.7.)

IV. For *all* files:

    1. "Rewind" the file and possibly unmount the storage device.

    2. Remove the file entry from the OFTs.

    3. Release any buffer space and reserved devices to their respective resource pools.

6.4 PHYSICAL ORGANIZATION METHODS

The file descriptor discussed in Section 6.3.2 contains information that specifies the mapping of the logical file onto physical storage. The collection of modules constituting the layer L3 (Figure 6-1), termed physical organization methods, uses this information to locate the actual data corresponding to the device-independent request issued by the user. An important part of this task is the management of free space; for example, space must be allocated if the file expands due to a write operation.

6.4.1 Logical File Organization

Let us first review the details of the logical organization of files as seen by the user through the abstract interface and then discuss possible mappings onto physical storage devices. (We will use the terms virtual and real as synonyms for logical and physical, respectively.) A virtual file is perceived as an ordered collection of *records*, R_0, R_1, . . . , R_n, where a record is a contiguous block of information transferred during a logical read or write operation. Typically, a file may be opened for *sequential* or for *direct* access. In the first case, the file must be accessed in sequence according to the ordering. If the *i*th record R_i was last read or written, the next record accessed is automatically R_{i+1}. The operations *Read_s* and *Write_s* presented in Section 6.1.2 enforce this discipline by internally maintaining a pointer to the current record. This is the oldest type of structure and has been employed for magnetic tape files since the earliest days of computing.

    If a file is opened for direct access, records may be accessed in arbitrary order. In this case, each record R_i must have a logical identification or *key* given by *i*. The keys could simply form an integer sequence, for example, 1, 2, . . . , *number_of_records*, where each integer, *i*, designates the *i*th record. In general, keys could be the result of some transformation or sorting procedure on more complex alphanumeric keys. To access a record, the corresponding key is supplied as a parameter to one of the operations *Read__d* or *Write__d* that locate the record and perform the necessary data transfers.

Whether a file may be opened for sequential or direct access depends on how it is physically organized on the underlying storage device. Normally, files that may be opened for direct access may also be opened for sequential access; the converse is, however, not always true.

Records constituting a logical file may be of *fixed* or *variable* length. In the fixed-length record file, each record has the same length; in the variable-length case, each record may have a different length. At the abstract interface level, we assume the existence of a logical pointer, which always points to the next record to be accessed when sequential read/write operations are performed. The underlying implementation must take into account the possibly different record lengths when advancing the pointer after each operation. The details of this implementation are transparent to the user.

6.4.2 Physical File Organization

Space on secondary storage devices is organized into sequences of blocks called *physical records*; the record size is determined by the characteristics of the storage medium. Several logical records may be mapped onto one physical record, or, conversely, one logical record may be spread over a number of physical records. A collection of physical records containing a logical file will be called a *physical* file. We will describe four common organizations of physical files: *contiguous*, *linked*, *index-sequential*, and *B-tree structured*. Depending on the particular organization, the read and write operations of the abstract user interface must follow different strategies in determining the physical record(s) that contain the logical record to be accessed.

6.4.2.1 Contiguous Organization

A logical file may be mapped onto a sequence of adjacent physical records. The resulting physical file may be viewed as a contiguous sequence of secondary storage locations starting at some address s. The mapping of a logical file of fixed-length records onto such a physical file is shown in Figure 6-5a. In the variable-length case, a length field n_i directly precedes each record R_i, as shown in Figure 6-5b.

The read and write operations of the abstract user interface are implemented as described next, where r is the pointer to the beginning of the next logical record to be accessed, n is the logical record length, *buf* [j] refers to the jth word in the memory buffer *buf*, and $F[j]$ denotes the jth word in the file F. Under direct access, *rec__no* is an integer between 0 and (*number__of__records* $-$ 1) designating the desired record.

1. Fixed length
   (a) *Read__s* (*F, buf*) or *Write__s* (*F, buf*): The transfer occurs between $F[r + j]$ and *buf* [j], where $j = 0, \ldots, n - 1$. The pointer r is incremented by n (i.e., $r := r + n$).

File Space Addresses

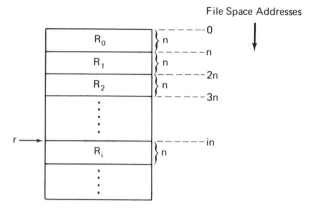

(a) Fixed Length

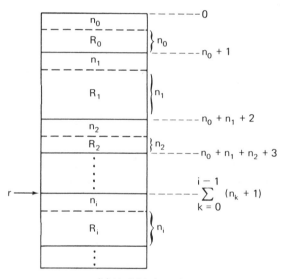

(b) Variable Length

Figure 6-5 Sequential files: (a) Fixed-length records (b) Variable-length records.

    (b) *Read__d(F, rec__no, buf)* or *Write__d(F, rec__no, buf)*: The transfer occurs between $F[rec\_no * n + j]$ and $buf[j]$, where $j = 0, \ldots, n - 1$. The pointer r is set to $(rec\_no + 1) * n$.

  2. Variable length

    (a) *Read__s(F, buf)* or *Write__s(F, buf)*: In the case of read, the logical record length must be read first; this could be accomplished by first reading $F[r]$, which contains the record length n_i. The subsequent transfer then occurs between $F[r + 1 + j]$ and $buf[j]$, with $j = 0, \ldots, n_i - 1$. The pointer r is set to $r + n_i + 1$. The write operation is similar; the record length is stored in the file location $F[r]$ and the subsequent data transfer occurs between $F[r + 1 + j]$ and $buf[j]$, with $j = 0, \ldots, n_i - 1$. (This operation only makes sense if the new record has the same or smaller length as the old one, or if it is a new record being appended to the end of the file; otherwise, the file must be rewritten after record r.)

(b) *Read_d(F, rec_no, buf)* or *Write_d(F, rec_no, buf)*: In the absence of any additional data structures to facilitate access, a sequential scan of the length fields of all logical records preceding the record to be accessed is necessary. This would make direct reading or writing of variable-length records under this storage organization prohibitively expensive. To handle this type of access more efficiently, an *index table* may be added, as shown in Figure 6-6. The table is ordered so that the *i*th entry contains the length and the address of record R_i. Two operations are then required to read or write R_i; the first is a read of the appropriate entry i of the index table. This yields the record length n_i and the starting address (pointer), r, of the desired record. The subsequent data transfer is then between $F[r + j]$ and $buf[j]$, with $j = 0, \ldots, n_i - 1$. Note, however, that the addition of the index table makes it no longer necessary to maintain the records in a physically continuous sequence. In fact, the organization of Figure 6-6 represents a special case of the index-sequential organization discussed in Section 6.4.2.3.

The main attraction of a contiguous organization of physical files is the simplicity with which both sequential and direct access (with fixed-length records) may be accomplished. It is particularly applicable to read-only (input) or write-only (output) files, where the entire file is sequentially read or written; it is also widely used in applications that involve a complete scan of a file, for example a weekly payroll run. One can also easily *backspace* over the records; for variable-length records, however, the length field must then also appear at the *end* of each record. In the case of devices that permit only sequential access, such as magnetic tapes, contiguous organization is the only scheme that may be implemented efficiently.

The major problem with contiguous allocation of physical records is its inflexibility in deleting, inserting, and, in the case of variable-length records, changing the length of a record. In all three cases, it is generally necessary to physically move all records

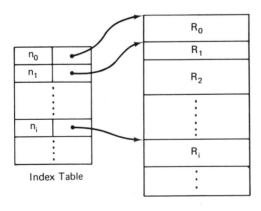

Index Table

Figure 6-6 Organization of index table.

following or preceding the location of the modification to preserve the contiguity of allocation. Alternatively, insertions and deletions may be permitted only at the end of a file. A related problem is the need to declare the maximum file length a priori. If too little space is allocated, the file may not be able to expand; too much space, on the other hand, results in wasted resources.

6.4.2.2 Linked Organization

The logical records of a physically linked file are not, in general, stored in contiguous physical records. Instead, they may be scattered throughout the secondary storage device. Each record is linked to the logically next one by a forward pointer, as illustrated in Figure 6-7. If backspacing is also desired, an additional backward pointer may be used; then a record R_i would contain a pointer to R_{i+1} and another pointer to R_{i-1}. With a linked organization, sequential access is very simple; a pointer to the current record, similar to that used with a contiguous organization, is maintained. The pointer is set to refer to the next logical record each time a record is read or written. The list of physical records to be accessed by each operation is determined in the same way as with the contiguous organization.

    The main advantage of a linked organization is the ease with which records may be inserted, deleted, and modified within the structure, thus expanding and contracting the file. Consequently, no upper limit must be imposed on the file length a priori, and the sizes of individual records can be easily changed during execution.

    To access a record directly requires that the read or write operation follow the chain of pointers until the desired record is found. If the links are maintained on secondary storage as part of each record, the resulting overhead is unacceptable. A much more efficient implementation is to maintain all pointers as a separate linked list in main memory. The length of this list corresponds to the number of records R_i comprising the file. Each element of the list then contains two pointers: one to the logically next element of the list and the other to the actual record on secondary storage.

    To further improve direct access to a linked-structured file, an index in the form of a B^+-tree (Section 6.4.2.4) may usefully be employed.

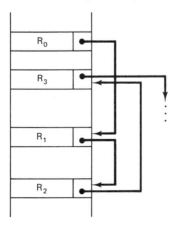

Figure 6-7 Linked file organization.

6.4.2.3 Index-sequential Organization

The purpose of this organization is to permit direct access to records while eliminating the problems of insertion and deletion inherent to schemes with contiguous allocation of storage. This implies that logical records may be scattered throughout the secondary storage device. However, some mechanisms must exist for locating each record efficiently without scanning long chains of pointers. This is accomplished by dividing the file into groups of n logical records and providing an index table of the form shown in Figure 6-8.

Each record group is stored on a contiguous sequence of secondary storage locations. Individual groups, however, may be scattered throughout the storage device arbitrarily. Typically, a group could consist of a sector or track on a disk. The index table is ordered so that each entry contains the key of the first record within the group, a pointer to the first record, and the number of records comprising the group. Due to insertions and deletions, this number may vary. To find a record R_i, the index i is used to search the index table for an entry with the largest ij (index of first record), such that ij is less than or equal to i. Following the pointer found in that entry, the group containing the record i is located and scanned sequentially until the desired record is reached.

The advantage of this method is that, for direct access to a record, the necessary sequential search is limited to only one group of records, rather than the entire file, as would be the case with a purely contiguous organization. Sequential access to records can also be implemented easily with the index-sequential organization. The process simply moves through the index table and, for each entry, accesses all records pointed to by the corresponding pointer.

When the index table becomes large, it can be organized as a fixed-length record file I in the form of a tree (Madnick and Alsop, 1969). For example, if the record length is m and there are $k \leq m$ records in the file F indexed by the table, then one record in I is sufficient. For $m < k \leq m^2$ records in F, each entry in the first record I_0 of I potentially points to another table of length m, which, in turn, contains the address of records of F. For $k = m^2$, we have $m + 1$ tables: I_0 at the first level and $I_1, \ldots, I_m$ at the second tree level. The address of the ith record of F is obtained from the entry at offset ($i \bmod m$) of the record I_r, where $r = i/m + 1$. For example, with $m = 4$, record

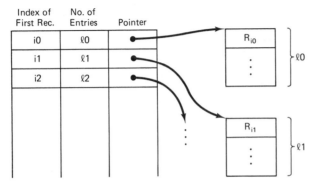

Figure 6-8 Index-sequential organization.

7 is found in I_2 at offset (7 mod 4) = 3. The tree structure is extended to further levels for $k > m^2$.

Example

A variation of this scheme has been implemented in the UNIX operating system. Each file descriptor, or *i*-node in UNIX terminology, contains 13 entries describing the mapping of the logical file onto physical blocks of storage (Figure 6-9). The first 10 entries point directly to blocks holding the contents of the file; each block consists of 512 bytes. The

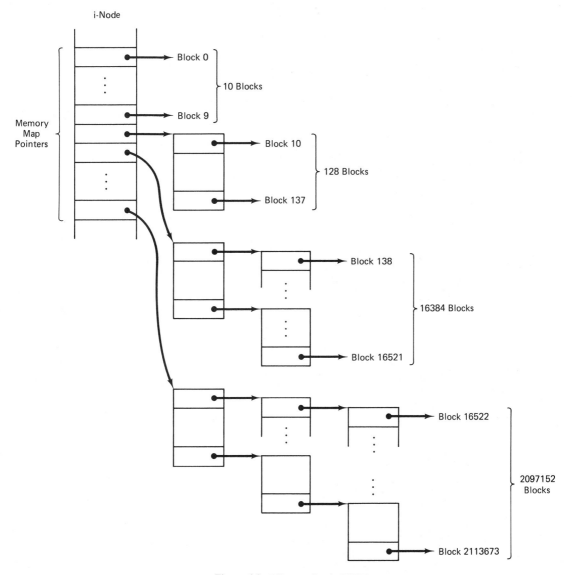

Figure 6-9 File mapping in UNIX.

number of blocks is allocated according to the file length. If more than 10 blocks are needed, the eleventh entry of the index table is used to point to an indirection block that contains up to 128 pointers to additional blocks of storage. This yields a total of (10 + 128) blocks to hold the file's content. If this is still insufficient, the twelfth entry of the index table points by a twofold indirection to an additional 128^2 blocks of storage. Finally, for files exceeding the total of (10 + 128 + 128^2) blocks, a threefold indirection starting in the thirteenth entry of the index table provides 128^3 blocks of additional storage to hold the file. The main advantage of this scheme is that the file descriptor is very small and remains constant regardless of the size of the file. Small files, which constitute the majority of existing files, are accessed efficiently without indirection; yet it is possible to implement extremely large files at the cost of additional indirect accesses.

The main difficulty with the index-sequential file organization is the need for periodic massive *reorganization* of the index structure, since the numbers of records, lj, comprising each group change as insertions and deletions are performed. When a group size becomes too large, performance deteriorates due to the increased sequential scan of the group. It may also be necessary to move the entire group to a different set of locations; this would occur when a record is to be inserted and there is not enough space for the group to expand. When, on the other hand, the group becomes too small, the relative overhead of using the index structure increases. The B-tree organization eliminates these problems.

6.4.2.4 B-Tree Organization

B-trees and their many derivatives have become one of the most common techniques for organizing files on secondary storage. The basic assumption underlying this organization is that index files are generally too large to be kept in main storage. Consequently, the primary objective is to minimize the number of accesses to the index structure. This is true for both sequential and direct access to files.

A *regular B-tree* is organized as follows. Every node may be viewed as containing s slots, each capable of holding one record key (together with the address of the corresponding record on secondary storage) and $s + 1$ pointers to nodes at the next lower level of the tree. At any given time, each node must be at least half-full (i.e., contain at least $s/2$ keys and the corresponding number of pointers).

Figure 6-10a shows an example of a B-tree with $s = 2$. The nodes are organized according to the following rule: for any given key k, the subtree pointed to by the left-hand pointer contains only keys whose value is *less* than k; the subtree pointed to by the right-hand pointer contains only keys whose value is *greater* than k. This determines a simple rule for locating a record given a key k: Starting with the root node, k is compared to the keys recorded in that node. If a match is found, the corresponding record is accessed. Otherwise, the search follows the pointer immediately succeeding the smallest key k' found in that node, such that $k' < k$. If no such k' exists, the leftmost pointer in that node is used. This is repeated until the desired record is found. The cost of the search operation is proportional to the depth of the tree (i.e., the logarithm of the file size). For example, to locate the record with $k = 35$, first the pointer to the right of key

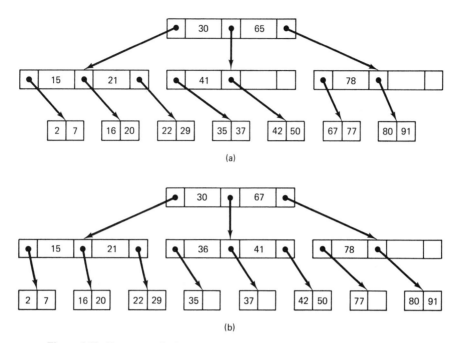

Figure 6-10   B-tree organization: (a) Example of a B-tree (b) Effect of insertion and deletion.

30 is followed and then the pointer to the left of key 41 is followed. The desired key 35 is found in the leaf node.

An important property of B-trees is that they are *balanced*; that is, the distance between the root and any leaf is constant. The insertion and deletion operations defined on B-trees are guaranteed to preserve this property. Each of these operations may require the splitting or collapsing of nodes on the path between the root and the affected node. The cost of these, however, may at most double the cost of a search; hence, the total cost of insertion/deletion is still proportional to the logarithm of the file size. Figure 6-10b shows the result of inserting the key 36 and deleting the key 65 in the tree of Figure 6-10a. (For more detailed descriptions of algorithms for insertion and deletion in B-trees, the reader may refer to Comer (1979).)

So far, only the cost of direct-access operations was considered. Unfortunately, the performance of sequential operations on simple B-trees is not very satisfactory. This is because logically adjacent keys may be stored arbitrarily far apart in the tree structure, and there is no easy way of determining the location of the logically next key, given a key k. In fact, accessing the logically next key is as costly as performing a direct access.

To improve the performance of sequential access, variations of the simple B-trees have been proposed, the most popular of which are B^+-*trees*. The main distinction between the B- and B^+-tree is that keys (and the corresponding pointers to file records) are kept only in the leaf nodes in the B^+-tree. The leaves are linked together as illustrated

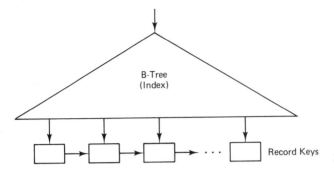

Record Keys   **Figure 6-11**   A B$^+$-tree.

schematically in Figure 6-11. The nodes above the leaves may be viewed as a restricted simple B-tree, whose sole purpose is to serve as index for locating the desired leaf nodes As in the case of simple B-trees, the search for a given key starts with the root node and proceeds along the pointers toward the leaves. Insertions and deletions are also similar as in the case of simple B-trees, resulting in the same logarithmic cost. The main advantage of B$^+$-trees, however, is an efficient sequential access; given a key k, the logical successor (in ascending or descending order) is found either in the same leaf node immediately adjacent to the key k, or, if k is the rightmost (leftmost) key in that node, by following the appropriate pointer to the neighboring leaf node.

Example

> The VSAM (virtual storage access method) developed by IBM (Keehn and Lacy, 1974) is based on the principles of B$^+$-trees. The basic organization is as in Figure 6-11; the leaf nodes, however, do not point to individual records. Rather, records are grouped into larger blocks according to the physical characteristics of the underlying storage devices. Information is then read in units of blocks, instead of individual records, to improve the utilization of the devices.
>
> VSAM supports both sequential and direct access for retrieval, insertion, and deletion of records. The use of the B$^+$-tree algorithms eliminates the need for periodic reorganization of the index structure inherent to systems based on an index-sequential organization; with the B$^+$-tree organization, the index structure is modified dynamically in response to insert and delete operations.

6.4.3 Management of Auxiliary Storage Space

Important parts of the physical organization methods (level L3 in Figure 6-1) are the allocation strategies and schemes for keeping track of space on direct-access secondary memory; the space on a device is assumed to be *shared* among several files rather than entirely dedicated to one file. Not surprisingly, some of the techniques for main storage administration described in Chapter 5 are also applicable here.

The basic function of the storage allocator is to satisfy requests for *fixed*-size blocks. This is because of the fixed-length physical record organization of many storage media, the large amount of available storage, and the relative simplicity of such a policy. Efficiency of IO is often the main criterion for deciding which of several possible free blocks to select; one wishes to minimize rotational delays and seek times (where applicable) when the acquired blocks are later accessed. Thus, it is desirable to allocate all storage for the same request and same file ''close'' together. However, the fixed-size blocks need not be allocated contiguously, but could be linked or indexed in some fashion, as described in Section 6.4.1; the allocation and retrieval of blocks is then analogous to that for *paged* main memory, but without the continual need for dynamic replacements. Blocks of secondary storage are freed when a file is moved off-line either as a result of a user request or because of its inactivity, or when a file is purposely destroyed or shrunk in size.

Arguments for and against static versus dynamic allocation are also present here but in somewhat different form than in the main memory case. File size is often not known in advance, so a static allocation policy must frequently rely on upper-bound size estimates. Unless much wasted space can be tolerated, a dynamic method seems necessary for many types of files.

There are several ways to keep track of *available* space. The most obvious method is to link all free blocks together by pointers stored in each free space block. It suffices to maintain in main storage a pointer to the first such block. This has the advantage of simplicity but is severely inefficient. To add or remove free space from the lists, extensive IO operations must be executed to find the appropriate number of blocks and to modify the pointers.

For this reason, it is more common to employ index table techniques, similar to those outlined in Section 6.4.2. A separate table or set of tables containing all free space is maintained on a device basis. The tables can be organized internally as linked lists or as bit arrays. In the former case, one word is allocated for each fixed-size block of secondary storage, and all free blocks are linked together. It is relatively easy to release and allocate blocks with this organization, but it consumes a large amount of storage. Much less table space is necessary if each block is represented by a *single* bit in the table: a 1 is interpreted as a free block and a 0 as unavailable. Retrieval of free blocks and the efficient representation make the bit method generally preferable. With the possible exception of the bit table method, it is usually necessary to store most of the available space records on secondary storage because of their large size; only the currently active records are kept in main memory.

Available and used space records provide an opportunity for some useful redundancy. Two separate sets of tables can be maintained, one for free space and the other for used space. This permits some elementary file system consistency checks when hardware and software errors occur; the tables can be matched against each other and the directory entries. These tables are conveniently treated as files; they thus can be accessed through the file system commands and appear in the file directory.

One other component of the secondary storage administration subsystem must be carefully designed. Since the storage is limited in capacity, facilities must be provided for moving inactive files off-line, for example onto magnetic tape, and for transferring files through a hierarchy of storage devices when one exists. Typically, the bases for moving include the current filing load on the system, the priorities of the file users, the relative activities of the files, and the file sizes. In addition to file movement routines, there is a need for file *copying* to provide back-up capability.

6.5 THE IO SUBSYSTEM

The functions of the two remaining levels in the hierarchy presented in Section 6.1.3, the device IO techniques and IO scheduling and control, are highly interrelated, thus making it difficult to describe one without the other. For the time being, we will refer to both jointly as the *IO subsystem*; the differentiation will be made in Section 6.5.3. The primary function of this portion of the operating system is to translate read and write requests generated by the physical file organization level into low-level commands interpreted by the device controllers or specialized IO processors and to interpret the devices' responses. The read and write requests to be translated are for physical records and thus are device dependent.

The IO subsystem must generate the necessary device-specific commands to prepare the device for a data transfer (e.g., position a read/write arm of a disk to the desired cylinder), to initiate the transfer of each physical record, and to supervise the progress of these operations. The type and granularity of such commands varies greatly with the device types and with the type of connection (controller, channel) responsible for their operation. In this section, we consider only commands that directly effect the transfer of data and status information; the necessary setup commands, which may precede the actual transfer, will not be shown explicitly.

The basic schemes for communicating between the CPU and various devices were introduced briefly in Chapter 1. In this section, we review and elaborate on the different approaches and show typical examples to illustrate how they affect the programming of input and output routines.

6.5.1 Programmed IO

The simplest type of processor/device interface, used primarily with slow, character-oriented devices such as printers or user terminals, requires that all data be explicitly transferred between main memory and the device by the CPU. For example, to effect the printing of a character, the CPU must read the data from memory and store it into a specific register or data buffer associated with the device. It then initiates the device to print the supplied data. To input a character, a similar protocol is followed: The CPU initiates an input device and waits until an appropriate register or data buffer is filled.

To inform the CPU of the completion of an IO operation, a special flag is raised by the device. This flag may be tested in one of three possible ways, depending on the hardware provided: (1) the test is part of the IO instruction itself, (2) the CPU may test the flag explicitly using a special programmer-accessible instruction, or (3) the test could be performed as part of every instruction executed by the CPU.

Let us examine the impact of these three possible schemes on the type of IO routines necessary to service a device. Assume that a sequence of characters is to be written to a printer. To accomplish that, the CPU must repeatedly perform the following three tasks: (1) move a character between memory and a device buffer, (2) initiate the device, and, using one of the three possible IO completion schemes, (3) await the termination of the data transfer. For input, for example, to read a sequence of characters from a terminal, a similar protocol is obeyed. In this case, each character operation begins with tasks 2 and 3, while the transfer from a device buffer into memory is done last. We consider the three possible device completion schemes in turn:

1. In the simplest case, the testing of the device flag is performed as part of the IO instruction hardware itself. The following algorithm shows the hardware actions comprising an IO instruction:

> *Read/Write Instruction:*
>   *device__flag := 1;* *{set device flag}*
>   *Initiate Input/Output Device;*
>   **while** *device__flag = 1* **do** ; *{wait loop}*

To obtain data, the CPU issues the *Read* instruction, which fills the input hardware buffer or register, say *in*, with the next character from the device. To perform output, the program must store the data in an output buffer, say *out*, and then issue the *Write* instruction. In both cases, the IO instructions wait for the device to complete and thus may be used in the same way as reading from or writing to main memory. For example, to input or output a sequence of characters, simple loops of the following form may be used:

> *Input:*
>   *i := 0;*
>   **repeat**
>   *Read;*
>   *in__area[i] := in;*
>   *Increment i;*
>   *Compute;*
>   **until** *all__data__in*

> *Output:*
>   *i := 0;*
>   **repeat**
>   *Compute;*
>   *out := out__area[i];*
>   *Increment i;*
>   *Write;*
>   **until** *all__data__out*

Read and *Write* are the machine IO instructions issued by the CPU. *in__area[i]* represents the main memory area into which data are transferred from the input device buffer *in*; analogously, *out__area[i]* is the main memory area from which data are moved into the buffer *out* during output. The *Compute* statements represent the consuming of a character in the case of input and producing a character in the case of output.

Instructions that simply wait for devices to complete are sometimes called *direct* IO instructions; they were used in most earlier computers and are still common in many smaller microprocessor-based systems. The resulting interface is very simple but also extremely inefficient; the CPU is not available for the entire duration of an IO operation and hence no overlap is possible between the CPU and IO devices. Consequently, the time t_p for a program p to run to completion is $t_p = t_{io} + t_c$, where t_{io} is the time required to complete the IO operations requested in p and t_c represents the compute time (the time for execution of the internal non-IO operations of p).

2. The second IO completion scheme provides a special test-device-flag instruction, which permits the programmer to explicitly test the status of the device. The CPU may issue this instruction at any time and, depending on its outcome, restart the device or continue doing some other useful work while the device is busy. In this case, the IO instructions have the following form. (Assume that the *Initiate* command simply waits if the device is busy at the time it is issued):

Read/Write Instruction:
device__flag := 1;
Initiate Input/Output Device;

The following simple algorithms illustrate how such *Read* or *Write* instructions could be used in a program to input/output a sequence of characters using a loop.

```
Input:
    i := 0;
    repeat
        Read;
        while device__flag = 1 do Compute__only;
        in__area[i] := in;
        Increment i;
        Compute
    until all__data__in

Output:
    i := 0;
    repeat
        Compute;
        out := out__area[i];
        Increment i;
        Write;
        while device__flag = 1 do Compute__only
    until all__data__out
```

where *in__area* and *out__area* are the main memory areas, *in* and *out* are the hardware device buffers, and *Compute* is the statement that consumes/produces characters, as described with the previous scheme. The *Compute__only* statement represents computation not requiring any new input or output. This computation may be performed by the CPU while waiting for a device to complete, thus overlapping its operation with that of the device. For example, in the case of input, the next *Read* instruction is always issued as soon as the *in* buffer is copied into the *in__area*. This permits the CPU to work with the current content of *in__area* (during the statement labeled *Compute__only*), while the *in* buffer is being filled with new data by the device. In this way, the input device always reads one set of data ahead of the program. An analogous scheme is used with the output scheme.

The main limitation of this approach is that programs must be carefully organized with respect to the spacing of IO commands and compute-only sections of code if a reasonable overlap of the two is to be obtained. If the test–device–flag instruction is issued too sparsely, devices will be underutilized; executing it too frequently, on the other hand, results in wasted CPU time.

3. The third and most sophisticated approach to detecting IO completion is the use of *interrupts*. This requires special hardware that performs the testing of the device flag (and other possible conditions) automatically as part of each instruction execution cycle. When the test is positive (i.e. the device has completed its task), the normal stream of instruction execution is interrupted and diverted to some predefined location associated with the cause of the interrupt. Starting at this location is a routine called the *interrupt handler*, which determines the cause of the interrupt and decides on the appropriate actions to be taken next. In the case of IO interrupts, it would analyze the state of the devices and controllers involved in the operation and, prior to returning control to the interrupted program, issue the commands necessary to initiate the next IO operation.

The input and output instructions cause the same basic hardware actions as with the previous scheme, where the device flag is explicitly tested by the CPU. Their use in a program, however, follows a very different pattern. The following algorithms illustrate the principles:

```
Input:
     i := 0;
     repeat
         Read;
         wait__for__interrupt;
         in__area[i] := in;
         Increment i;
         Compute
     until all__data__in

Output:
     i := 0;
     repeat
         Compute;
         out := outarea[i];
         Increment i;
         Write;
         wait__for__interrupt
     until all__data__out
```

The *Read/Write* instructions initiate the appropriate device but do not wait for its completion. The statement "wait_for_interrupt" indicates that the program suspends itself while waiting for the data transfer to be completed. In a multiprogramming system, this permits other processes to utilize the CPU in the meantime. When the device completes the transfer, it causes an interrupt that invokes the suspended process and permits it to issue the next IO instruction.

The main advantage of this scheme is its flexibility: the interrupt handling routine may be programmed in a variety of ways to best utilize the available resources. It eliminates the need for explicitly testing the device flag, and thus a careful interleaving of IO instructions and compute-only phases is not needed; the next IO instruction may be invoked as soon as the previous instruction completes.

6.5.2 Direct Memory Access (DMA) Interface

A programmed IO interface without interrupts is usually found only in small, microprocessor-based systems. In larger systems, a programmed IO interface with interrupts would typically be employed to service slow, character-oriented devices. No serious degradation of performance is usually observed in this case, since the CPU is capable of executing thousands of instructions between any two IO commands.

For fast, block-oriented devices, such as disks, it is desirable that the CPU be liberated from the task of having to explicitly transfer all data between main memory and the device. This is accomplished by permitting the device controller to access memory directly. The CPU only initiates the IO operation and continues with the next instruction while the controller supervises the operation of the device. This necessarily requires higher intelligence on part of the controller than with programmed IO. In the most general case, a specialized *IO processor* or *channel*, capable of executing programs directly out of main memory, may be provided. Programs executed by such processors are usually referred to as *channel programs*. When executing a channel program, the channel is responsible for issuing the appropriate signals to the devices, counting the number of blocks transferred, calculating the memory address for each new block, and testing for possible errors, without any involvement of the CPU.

The CPU only initiates the execution of a channel program using a general instruction of the form

Startio(ch, channel_prog)

where *ch* identifies the particular channel or DMA controller, and *channel_prog* designates a main storage area containing a channel program or some other IO-request specification used by the channel to perform the desired operation. For read/write operations, the channel program specifies a main storage address and the amount of data to be sent to or from that address; it will also, in general, contain orders to select and activate the desired IO device. Both the channel and central processor compete for storage cycles during concurrent operation, with the channel normally having the highest priority; the CPU is idle until the channel storage request has been honored. If the channel is busy when a *Startio* call is issued, we assume that the CPU *waits* until the channel can accept the IO request.†

To avoid unnecessary complexities in subsequent discussions on IO programming, we will assume that IO commands issued by the CPU to start a channel are of the form

Read(ch, p_rec, buf)

and

Write(ch, p_rec, buf)

instead of the general *Startio* instruction, where *ch* designates a channel, *p_rec* is the address of the physical record to be transferred, and *buf* is the starting address of a memory buffer into/from which the record is to be transferred. *Read* and *Write* represent *initiation* of the channel, if possible, by the CPU; the CPU is immediately released, thus operating *in parallel* with the channel.

The status of a channel may be interrogated at any time by the CPU. A flag, either in storage or in a register, is set when the channel is busy and reset when it is free. We will use the Boolean variable *busy[ch]* to test the busy status of channel *ch*; *busy[ch]* is *true* if channel *ch* is busy and *false* otherwise. Usually, other channel and device status information, such as the occurrence of IO errors or whether a unit is busy or even connected, is also available, but will be ignored here.

A more common method of communicating between a channel and the central processor is through interrupts in much the same way as with programmed IO described previously. Here the channel interrupts the CPU on termination of a given channel program or the occurrence of some error condition, which causes control to be transferred to a predefined location. The routine starting at that location normally restarts the channel with the next IO request, if there is one, prior to returning control to the interrupted program.

The type of IO completion scheme (i.e., channel interrogation versus interrupts) strongly influences the way IO routines are organized and structured. To illustrate the fundamental distinctions, we consider several possible implementations of a program whose task is to input a sequence of physical records from a disk and store these sequentially in a predefined memory area. We assume that some modest amount of processing is to be performed with each record, for example formatting it for use by some other process. (The schemes for output are analogous; see Exercise 6.16).

6.5.2.1 DMA with Interrogation of Channel

We first implement a procedure *Get(loc)*, which waits for the channel to terminate and then transfers the contents of *buf*, used by the channel as its input buffer, to some other

---

†This CPU behavior on a busy channel is not commonly found. More frequently, one always gets an immediate return from the *Startio* accompanied by some status information indicating the reason for not starting the IO.

memory location *loc*. Prior to exiting, *Get* restarts the channel to begin transferring the next record into *buf*; the function *next (p__rec)* represents the computation necessary to determine the next physical record to be read.

```
procedure Get(loc);
begin
    while busy[ch] do ; {wait loop}
    loc := buf;
    Read(ch, next(p__rec), buf )
end
```

Using this procedure, the input routine for a sequence of records may then be written as follows:

```
Read(ch, first(p__rec), buf )   {Initial read}
repeat
    Get(loc);
    Compute(loc);
until all__records__in
```

Initially, *buf* must be loaded by executing *Read (ch, first (p__rec), buf)*, where the function *first* determines the first physical record to be read. The procedure *Compute* represents the tasks of formatting the given record and transferring it to its final destination in memory. Note that this scheme is very similar to the second scheme used with the programmed IO, which explicitly tests the device flag (Section 6.5.1); the program is always reading one record ahead of its demand. Figure 6-12a illustrates the possible overlap between computation and IO graphically.

Let t_c represent the time to execute *Compute (loc)*, t_{io} the time the channel is busy, and t_b the time to copy the buffer into *loc*. Then, assuming that all three times are constant at every call, the time to read and process one record is $\max(t_c, t_{io}) + t_b$.

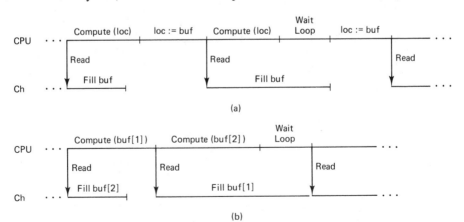

Figure 6-12 CPU/IO overlap: (a) Using a single buffer (b) With buffer swapping.

The primary overhead in the *Get* routine is the time to move the buffer contents into the storage location *loc*, where it is processed. To eliminate this potentially lengthy buffer transfer, it is possible to use several buffers and do the processing directly in the buffer area. Let there be two buffers, *buf* [1] and *buf* [2], each containing one record. While a read operation is using *buf* [1], a compute operation may reference *buf* [2], and vice versa. The roles of the buffers are reversed at the completion of an IO. We change the *Get* routine so that, at return, its argument will contain a buffer index:

```
procedure Get(i);
begin
    while busy[ch] do ; {wait loop}
    Read(ch, next(p__rec), buf[i]);
    if i = 1 then i := 2 else i := 1
end
```

The program to input a sequence of records then could have the form:

```
i := 2; Read(ch, first(p__rec), buf[1])    {Initial read}
repeat
    Get(i);
    Compute(buf[i]);
until all__records__in
```

Figure 6-12b illustrates the possible overlap between computation and IO. The time to read and process one record is then $\max(t_c, t_{io})$, where t_c and t_{io} have the same meaning as before. This is the best that we could ever hope to do for this type of program structure. The technique is termed *buffer swapping*.

Unfortunately, timing sequences in real-world situations are rarely that simple. Programs often contain sequences of IO "bursts," followed by much computing. Also, the times for executing *Compute(loc)* and for copying the buffer usually depend on the data and thus vary from call to call. Similarly, the time that the channel is busy varies because different physical records may be accessed on each call. Furthermore, in a multiprogramming environment, the speed with which a given program is executed and the current availability of devices are unpredictable. Consequently, the *Get* routine frequently waits at the *Read* operation or, conversely, the device remains idle for excessive periods of time. The obvious solution is to add more buffers and try to distribute the IO operations more uniformly throughout the program without distributing the program structure by reading even farther ahead than just one record.

A Circular Buffer with a Coroutine Structure.[†]   Let there be a set of *n* buffers, *buf* [0], *buf* [1], . . . , *buf* [$n - 1$], $n \geq 1$, implicitly linked in a circular list so that *buf* [*i*] is followed by *buf* [$i +_n 1$], $i = 0, 1, \ldots, n - 1$. The main program (i.e., the routine to input and preprocess a sequence of records) will ask for a buffer by call-

---

[†]The treatment in this section follows approximately the model described by Knuth (1968), pp. 214–221.

ing the routine *Get__buf*, then compute with the buffer returned by *Get__buf*, say *buf* [*current*], and finally release *buf* [*current*] by the call *Release__buf*. The *buf* data structure and routines *Get__buf* and *Release__buf* are precursors to the bounded buffer data type as presented in Chapter 2.

It is assumed that the execution sequence of the main program can be put in the following form:

```
repeat
    Compute__only;
    Get__buf (current);
    Compute(buf [current]);
    Release__buf;
until all__records__in
```

where *Compute__only* represents computation involving no buffer reference. Since we are dealing with input operations only, *Get__buf* will retrieve the next *input-full* buffer, and *Release__buf* will designate *buf* [*current*] as free, that is, available for more input. (In the case of an output application, *Get__buf* would return an empty or free buffer and *Release__buf* would return an *output-full* buffer.)

At the same time as the main program, henceforth termed the *Compute program* because it does not directly interface to the channel, is executing, we will try to keep the channel busy filling up buffers. This is accomplished by means of an *IO Driver program* that controls the channel and runs in a quasi-concurrent manner to the *Compute* program. Two pointers to the buffers are necessary: one, *next__get*, which points to the next available buffer for the *Compute* program, and the other, *next__io*, which indicates the next free buffer for the IO routine. A typical situation is illustrated in Figure 6-13a. Here $n = 5$ and no buffer requests have been made; the *G* buffers are filled with anticipated input, while the *R* buffers are empty and available for a *Read* operation. Figure 6-13b gives the buffer status after the normal processing of a *Get__buf*; that is, the effect is

$$current := next\_get; \; next\_get := next\_get +_5 1;$$

C designates the current buffer. A *Read* operation would normally be filling up *buf* [*next__io*] concurrently; when the *Read* completes, a new *G* buffer then exists and we have

$$next\_io := next\_io +_5 1;$$

The release of *buf* [*current*] by *Release__buf* changes the *C* buffer into type *R*. Figure 6-13c contains the new buffer situation after the completion of both the *Read* and *Release__buf* call.

The two pointers continually "chase" each other around the buffer circle. The algorithms must be carefully designed so that one pointer does not overtake and pass the other. If *next__get* overtakes and passes *next__io*, then the buffers retrieved by *Get__buf*

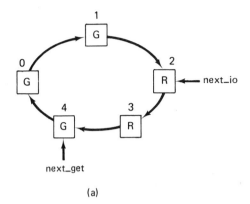

(a)

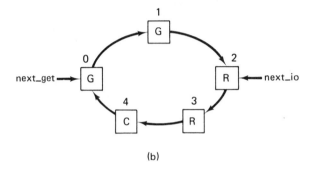

(b)

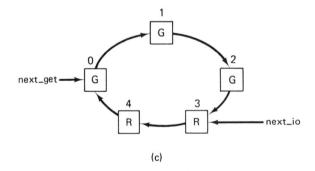

(c)

Figure 6-13 A circular buffer structure: (a) No buffer is assigned (b) After *Get__buf* (c) After *Release__buf* and IO completion.

will no longer be input-full buffers; this can be prevented by not allowing *Get__buf* to proceed when *next__get=next__io*. A system is said to be *IO bound* if the compute program part is asking for IO faster than the IO part can produce it. Similarly, if *next__io* overtakes and passes *next__get*, the system will overwrite input-full buffers that have not been used (i.e., there must be an empty buffer available before an IO command is issued). The system is *compute bound* if the IO Driver program produces IO faster than the compute program can consume it.

The *Compute* and *IO Driver* programs are designed as almost independent routines that, conceptually, run in parallel. We simulate this parallelism by means of a *coroutine* program structure. Coroutines are explained by contrasting them with more familiar subroutines. In a *subroutine* program structure, there exists an asymmetric master/slave relationship between a calling program and its subroutine; generally, a subroutine is entered at one of a fixed number of entry points (usually one), and all variables that are neither global nor parameters are undefined at entry.

Coroutines, on the other hand, are programs that may call each other but do not have this master/slave organization; the relationship is symmetric, with each coroutine being both master and slave. On exit from a coroutine, its state is saved; the next time the coroutine is called, it *resumes* at exactly the point where it left previously with all of its internal variables unchanged (i.e., the previous state is restored). The call on a coroutine C is designated "**resume** C" (Wegener, 1968). The arrows in the example in Figure 6-14 show the flow of control between two coroutines, A and B, where A is started initially. (Before a coroutine can be "resumed" for the first time, its state must be initialized.) Note that a low-level coroutine mechanism can be used to simulate and implement processes.

The *Compute* program, *CP*, and *IO Driver* program, *IOP*, will each be a coroutine. To keep both the CPU and channel active, *CP* normally resumes the *IOP* if the input channel ch is not busy and *IOP* resumes *CP* if the channel is busy. In addition, **resume**'s are invoked if the required buffer type is not available. Let n be the total number of buffers and r be the number of R buffers. The two procedures *Get_buf* and *Release_buf*

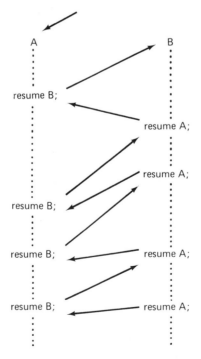

Figure 6-14 Coroutine flow of control.

within *CP* are

```
procedure Get_buf(current);
begin
    repeat
        if ¬busy[ch] then resume IOP
    until r ≠ n;   {At least one buffer is full}
    current := next_get;
    next_get := next_get +ₙ 1
end {Get_buf}


procedure Release_buf;
begin
    r := r + 1;
    if ¬busy[ch] then resume IOP
end {Release_buf}
```

Finally, throughout the *Compute_only* portions of *CP* we liberally intersperse the statement

```
if ¬busy[ch] then resume IOP
```

We thus attempt to keep the channel busy whenever logically possible. The *IOP* co-routine is

```
loop
    while r = 0 do resume CP;   {All buffers are full}
    Read(ch, next(p_rec), buf[next_io]);
    resume CP;
    next_io := next_io +ₙ 1
    r := r − 1;
end [loop}
```

Initially, all buffers are set to R ($r = n$), and *next_get* and *next_io* are both set to the same buffer index, say 0. The same routines could be employed to buffer output: the *Read* in *IOP* is changed to a *Write*; all buffers are set to G ($r = 0$) initially, since the *Get_buf* routine now retrieves empty buffers and *Release_buf* returns full buffers.

How large should n, the number of buffers, be? Let t_{c1} be the time taken for the *Compute_only* phase of *CP*, t_{c2} the time for *Compute*(*buf*[*current*]), and t_{rio} be the IO time for one record. If either $t_{c1} + t_{c2} < t_{rio}$ or $t_{c1} + t_{c2} > t_{rio}$ for all cases, then $n = 2$ will allow maximum CPU/channel overlap. (Execution times of *Get_buf* and *Release_buf* have been ignored.) This just reduces to the buffer swapping situation described earlier. In fact, $n = 1$ might be adequate if $t_{c1} + t_{c2}$ is always either *very* much less or *very* much greater than t_{rio}. It is only when the sum $t_{c1} + t_{c2}$ (i.e., the time between two successive *Get_buf*'s) is scattered on both sides of t_{rio} that $n > 2$ becomes beneficial.

Although the preceding techniques based on the CPU interrogating the channel are employed in some systems and are useful for explaining the principles of buffering, the most common approaches take advantage of interrupts and avoid most of the resume-type calls.

6.5.2.2 DMA with Channel Interrupts

It is assumed that a channel will interrupt the CPU at the termination of an IO operation; possible interrupts from other causes will be ignored here. Interrupts allow much greater control over CPU and IO concurrency and almost eliminate the need for channel busy tests. We assume again that the execution sequence of a main program can be put in the same form as that given at the beginning of Section 6.5.2.1 and employ the same multiple buffer data structure.

The main program procedures *Get_buf* and *Release_buf* then become

```
procedure Get_buf(current);
begin
    while r = n do ; {wait loop; all buffers are empty}
    current := next_get;
    next_get := next_get +ₙ 1
end {Get_buf }
procedure Release_buf;
begin
    r := r + 1;
    if ¬busy[ch] then Read(ch, next(p_rec), buf[next_io])
end {Release_buf }
```

On an IO completion interrupt, the following code (*IR*) is executed:

```
Save Current State;
next_io := next_io +ₙ 1;
r := r - 1;
if r ≠ 0 then Read(ch, next(p_rec), buf[next_io]);
Restore State
```

When an interrupt occurs, the current state of the interrupted program is saved. If there is at least one empty buffer, the channel is restarted and the routine returns to the interrupted program by restoring the original state. Since the *IR* routine is invoked whenever the previous *IO* operation terminates, the channel is kept busy as long as there are empty buffers available. Only when all buffers become full will the channel remain idle. To restart it again, a ¬*busy*[*ch*] test has been incorporated in the *Release_buf* procedure; if the channel is idle at that time, a *Read* operation is issued; *r* is guaranteed to be greater than zero then, since *Release_buf* increments *r* prior to testing the channel.

We initialize the system with

$r := n;$
$next\_io := 0;$
$next\_get := 0;$
$Read(ch, first(p\_rec), buf[next\_io]);$

For reasons of simplicity, we have completely ignored the problem of process synchronization in this solution. In particular, the incrementing of the counter r in *Release_buf* and its decrementing in the interrupt routine constitute critical sections and have to be treated as such. On a single-processor, the simplest and least elegant solution would be to disable interrupts for the duration of the *Release_buf* procedure or at least of the increment statement. Assuming that the interrupt routine cannot itself be interrupted, this would guarantee that the operations on r could not be interleaved and thus yield an inconsistent state similar to that described in Section 2.3.1. More elegant would be the use of semaphore operations or other higher-level primitives to solve this critical section problem.

6.5.3 A Process Model for Interrupt-Driven IO

Having described the various types of interaction between the CPU and the channel, we are now ready to discuss the possible overall organization of the IO subsystem. In older systems, especially those targeted to batch processing, no explicit distinction was usually made between the two levels L2 and L1 discussed in Section 6.1.3. The IO system could be viewed as a monolithic entity, accepting requests to transfer sequences of physical records, creating the necessary channel programs, and initiating their execution. It would then interrogate the channel to detect the completion of any IO operation. Some amount of internal buffering, for example the coroutine scheme discussed earlier, would normally be employed to increase the utilization of devices.

When interrupts are employed, we see a clear separation of the programs involved in the IO processing into two almost independent layers: the "main" program, which executes the *Get_buf* and *Release_buf*, and the IO Driver routine, which services the channel. Save for the last statement of *Release_buf* and the synchronization mechanisms (not shown explicitly in the algorithms) necessary to preserve the integrity of the r counter, there is no explicit connection between the main program and any devices. Rather, the main program's interface to lower levels of the IO subsystem is the circular buffer and the variable r. The tasks of restarting the channel and servicing interrupts is the responsibility of the IR routine, which is invoked automatically whenever the channel terminates.

This principle of separating the routines into those that directly interact with the channel and those that only consume (in the case of input) or produce (in the case of output) the data is commonly applied in modern operating systems. These routines correspond to the two levels of the IO subsystem, L1 and L2, respectively. Typically, L1 and L2 would be separate processes (or sets of processes) communicating with one another by a pool or a queue of buffers as follows. The process at level L2 accepts a request from the next higher level in the form of physical record numbers. It creates an appropriate channel program (or IO request specification) to accomplish the transfer of these records to or from main memory and places that package into a queue, which serves as the interface between the two levels. The package is eventually removed from the queue by an L1 process, which schedules and initiates the processing of the package by the channel. When the operation is completed, an appropriate L1 process is invoked to handle the interrupt, to wake up the corresponding suspended user process, and to make the status of the IO operation available to the reactivated process.

We can express these interactions between the L2 and L1 processes more formally using the resource management primitives *Request* and *Release* introduced in Chapter 3 as follows. We define for each IO device D an IO process p_D that controls the operation of that device. Such processes are usually referred to as *IO drivers* or *device drivers*. Process p_D receives IO requests, typically from a queue, invokes the appropriate allocators or schedulers for channels and controllers, initiates IO operations, handles general transmission errors, processes interrupts, and sends completion messages back to the requesting process.

We assume the lowest-level IO command issued by processes at level L2 consists of a request/reply sequence directed at the selected process p_D; this can take the general form

Release(Dio__queue, ioprog);
Request(Dio__end, Ω, completion__status);

Dio__queue represents the class of IO request packets directed at p_D, while *Dio__end* is associated with replies from p_D. The parameter *ioprog* specifies the details of the request. In general, for each device interface, a different set of conventions is necessary. In the case of DMA, *ioprog* could consist of a physical device address and the number of bytes to be transferred, or it could directly contain channel commands or controller orders to perform some complex IO operation. With programmed IO, *ioprog* would be a simple command, together with the data item to be transferred. The final results of the IO request are returned in *completion__status*, which typically contains the number of units of information actually transmitted and information regarding any errors that might have occurred during the operation.

The main task of the p_D process is to intercept the request, perform the specified operation, and inform the requesting process of the outcome of the operation. The details of the process vary for each device, but a typical organization might be as follows:

p_D: **loop**
　　Request(Dio__queue, Ω, (p, ioprog));
　　Request(Path, D, path);
　　Generate IO instructions from path and ioprog;
　　Initiate IO;
　　Request(IOint, path, message);
　　Decode interrupt; Possible further IO operations;
　　Produce completion status information;

Release(Path, path);
       Release(Dio__end, (p, completion__status));
  end {*loop*}

The first instruction obtains the IO request from the caller, designated as *p*. The second instruction then establishes a physical path between the device *D* and main memory. Depending on the hardware configuration, more than one such path may be possible, as shown in Figure 6-15. In the general case depicted in Figure 6-15c, a channel and controller must be assigned to establish such a path. The resource allocator for *Path* allocates a channel and a controller to p_D, thus defining the physical transmission path for the operation.

IOint designates the class of interrupts associated with IO devices. *Requesting IOint* causes the current process to be suspended until the appropriate interrupt has been caused by a channel. When that occurs, an interrupt handler is automatically invoked by the hardware. In this model, all interrupt handlers are treated uniformly. Their main function is to translate hardware signals into software messages. Abstractly, we view

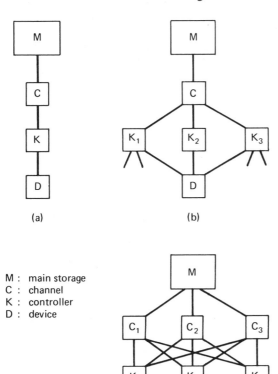

M : main storage
C : channel
K : controller
D : device

Figure 6-15 Paths from memory to an IO device D: (a) Single path (b) Single channel (c) Multiple paths.

each interrupt handler *IH* as a cyclic process that waits for an interrupt, determines the internal process p_D responsible for servicing this interrupt, and *Releases* an appropriate message to p_D. To implement this idea using the structures of Chapter 3, the handler first saves the state of the interrupted process, *, changes *'s status from *running* to *ready__a*, and sets the processor descriptor element *Process*[* ↑ . *Processor*] to *NIL*:

```
IH:    Store__State(* ↑ . Processor, * ↑ . CPU__State);
       * ↑ . Status := 'ready__a';
       Process[* ↑ . Processor] := NIL;
       Determine service process p_D;
       Release(Interrupt__Class, (p_D, interrupt__details));
```

When the *Scheduler* is called within the *Release* in *IH*, it may either reactivate the interrupted process or give the CPU to a process that changed from *blocked__a* to *ready__a* as a result of the *Release*. Interrupts are inhibited during *IH*, since system descriptors are being modified.

Eventually, control is returned to the process p_D, which analyzes (decodes) the details of the interrupt and may take some corrective actions as a result of this analysis. The statement *Possible further IO operations* may be necessary because the original request generates several IO commands (e.g., a disk seek followed by a read) or because of certain IO errors where the system attempts to correctly execute the IO instructions several more times before signaling the machine operator. Finally, p_D generates the completion information, releases the path established previously to the device, and transmits the completion information to the original L2 process by releasing a message to the *Dio__end* resource class.

6.6 COMMAND LANGUAGES AND FILE SYSTEM UTILITIES

At the highest level of interaction, users communicate with the machine through a set of commands provided by the operating system. This interface may be viewed as a program, a *command interpreter*, that accepts and interprets statements issued by the user. So far in this chapter we have dealt with only the commands that permit users to access files (i.e., open, close, read, and write). These commands are only a small subset of a typical operating system interface. Furthermore, they are relatively low level commands, used typically inside of programs rather than being issued directly from a terminal during an interactive session.

To create a more convenient and powerful way of interacting with the operating system, a variety of higher-level commands is provided for different user classes. In a typical multiuser system, commands to perform the following four types of tasks would normally exist:

1. Start and terminate a session (process)
2. Execute programs

3. Obtain information about the system

4. Manipulate files

Let us examine commands in each of the four categories in turn. The first statement of an interactive task or a batch job is a command that identifies the user and establishes a process that will be executing in the system on behalf of that user. This initial statement, usually called the *log-in* command, may require a number of information items to be included as parameters; among these are the user's name, unique identification such as a password, account number, priority, resource limits (e.g., the maximum amount of CPU time or the maximum number of lines to be printed for a batch job), and resource reservations (e.g., memory, IO devices). A *log-out* or *log-off* command is provided to terminate explicitly an interactive session or a batch job. An implicit termination may occur, for example, when a user hangs up the communication line (e.g., telephone) or turns off the terminal, or when the system ends a batch job due to error conditions. To permit a session to be suspended temporarily and later resumed in the same state at which it was suspended, a pair of *detach/attach* commands is often provided. As opposed to the *log-out* statement, a *detach* statement must save the current state of the process and its environment; this information allows correct restoration when the process is reattached at some later time.

The fundamental task performed by the machine as viewed through the top-level operating system interface is the execution of user programs. Thus any command language will contain statements directing the operating system to load and execute user programs, language processors (assemblers, compilers, interpreters), and other utility programs. Typical commands for this program management activity are ones to *link* several modules together, *load* programs, and *execute* programs. Associated with these commands, as parameters or as separate statements, may be resource reservation and limit data, similar to those used for the *log-in* statement. In addition, arguments specific to the particular program invoked, such as the names of files to be used by the program and debugging services requested (e.g., traces or dumps) may also be specified. In interactive systems, commands that aid testing and debugging are also often available. For example, the system could support commands that permit a user to suspend, examine, change, and resume some running process.

The third major set of commands is inquiries about the current state of the system and the state of the user's process(es). Information regarding the system that may be of interest to a particular user includes the current date and time of day, the number of users presently logged in, the system load, memory and device utilization, the configuration of the system, description of individual devices, or availability of resources. Information pertaining to the user's process could include the CPU time used so far, the connect time (i.e., the real time the user has been logged in up to the point the inquiry was made), the number of read and write operations performed, files currently open, devices assigned to the process, and other elements of information useful in determining the next action to be taken.

Finally, the fourth major set of commands relates to file processing. These serve such basic functions as specifying the primary input and output files to be used by programs, requesting allocation of IO devices, and describing the files referenced by user programs. In addition, most operating systems provide a collection of file utilities to perform such functions as *creating*, *deleting*, *copying*, *appending*, *printing*, or *renaming* files and directories or to change their protection status. These commands could form a separate system with its own language, or they could all be contained in the top-level command language of the operating system.

Depending on the level of control exercised by the user, there are a potentially staggering number of detailed parameters corresponding to the file commands. Examples are the following:

1. Disposition of the file (e.g., temporary or permanent)
2. Protection (access control) information
3. Buffering and blocking parameters
4. Space reservations on secondary storage
5. IO devices to be employed
6. File organization (e.g., sequential or direct access)

The collection of all file-manipulation commands and utilities is implemented as a layer of software that utilizes the commands of the abstract program interface presented in Section 6.1.2. For example, to copy a file $F1$ over to a file $F2$, it is necessary to open file $F1$ for reading, open file $F2$ for writing, perform the read/write operations, and close both files. Thus, in many operating systems, the file-manipulation functions are viewed as part of the file system. In the hierarchical model presented in this chapter (Figure 6-1), these could constitute a new level L6.

In addition to the preceding basic commands for program, resource, and file control, several other statements may be provided to increase the user friendliness of the system. These include statements to achieve the following:

1. Declare default parameters for each user.
2. Establish command procedures or macros to permit frequently used sequences of commands to be invoked as a group.
3. Provide user guidance by listing, upon request (e.g., by typing some keyword such as "help" or "?"), the possible commands or parameters expected in a given situation and explaining their effect.

Example

To illustrate some of the concepts outlined, we will briefly discuss the user interface provided by the UNIX operating system. When a user enters the system, a powerful command interpreter, called the *shell*, is started; it expects statements of the form

$$command_1 \ arg_1 \ . \ . \ . \ arg_{kl}; \ . \ . \ . \ ; \ command_n \ arg_1 \ . \ . \ . \ arg_{kn}$$

Proceeding from left to right, the shell interprets each *command$_i$* as a program to be executed. It searches the file system directory and, if a file with the name *command$_i$* is found, it creates a new process using the **fork** primitive. This process then executes the program with the arguments arg_1 through arg_k. When all commands constituting the sequence have been processed, control returns to the shell, which is ready to interpret the next sequence. The following are examples of simple commands:

who	Generates a list of all users currently logged in.
pwd	Prints the name of the current working directory.
cd F	Sets the current working directory to be the file *F*.
ls	Lists in alphabetical order all files recorded in the current directory; several arguments may be specified to modify the basic *ls* command; for example, *ls -t* will list the files according to their last modification date.
du	Returns information about the current disk usage; an argument may be specified to determine the disk usage for only a certain subtree of the current file hierarchy.
*cat F*1 *F*2	Concatenates the two files *F*1 and *F*2 and types them on the user terminal.
lpr F	Sends the file named *F* to the system's line printer.

The shell permits several processes, corresponding to different commands within a given line, to execute concurrently. This is accomplished by including the character ''&'' as the last argument of a command. If this is the case, the shell does not wait for the termination of the corresponding process but immediately proceeds with the next command. For example, the sequence

$$command_1 \ldots \&; command_2 \ldots$$

starts two concurrent processes, executing the files *command*$_1$ and *command*$_2$. When both terminate, the shell returns to the user with a prompt to accept the next line of commands.

In comparison, the sequence

$$command_1 \ldots \&; command_2 \ldots \&$$

also starts two processes concurrently; however, it does not wait for their termination but returns to the user immediately. In this way, background processes may be started and executed while the user is free to continue communicating with the shell.

Each time a shell is started for a user, two files, called *Standard Input* and *Standard Output*, are automatically opened. Any user input statement receives data from the standard input, while any output is sent to the standard output. Normally, the standard IO files are associated with the user terminal, thus permitting the user to communicate directly with the currently running program. The shell, however, permits the standard input and standard output to be reassigned to other files or devices. This is accomplished by specifying one or both of the arguments

$$< in\_file, > out\_file$$

where *in__file* and *out__file* become the input and output files, respectively. The symbols $<$ and $>$ indicate the direction of the data flow (i.e., from *in__file* and to *out__file*). The assignment is valid for the duration of the command.

Frequently, the output of a program is to be used as the input to some other program. This could be accomplished by using a temporary file as follows:

$$command_1 > temp\_file; command_2 < temp\_file$$

where *temp_file* is a temporary file used to hold the data transferred between the two programs.

The shell offers a more elegant solution by permitting the standard output of a program to be directed into the standard input of some other program as follows:

$$command_1 \mid command_2$$

Contrary to the previous solution, both processes are started concurrently. The temporary file used to hold the data between the two programs is now invisible to the user. In UNIX terminology, such an implicit communication file is called a *pipe*. The two processes may be viewed as a producer and a consumer, respectively, with the pipe serving as a virtually unbounded buffer. The necessary synchronization is performed internally by the system.

6.7 RECOVERY FROM SYSTEM FAILURE

Hardware and software errors can be reduced by building reliable and, often, redundant machine components and by the systematic logical design, coding, and debugging of programs. Unfortunately, failures or "crashes" are still very likely to occur in most complex systems. These may be *catastrophic* failures, which essentially destroy vital parts of the system and require extensive reconstruction efforts, or they could be less severe and localized to a small number of tables and/or programs. Modules for analyzing and recovering from such errors should be an integral part of any systems design and not be an ad hoc patch inserted after the rest of the operating system has been implemented.

The basic need is for graceful recovery methods that are transparent to the user, execute rapidly, and require little real-time work by the systems staff at the time of failure; an extreme example of a nongraceful recovery procedure is to simply reload the most current version of the operating system (stored off line on tape or disk usually) and inform users that all current computations have been lost. It is appropriate to examine the recovery problem in this chapter since, from the point of view of systems reconstruction, the file system contains the most vital information—directories of jobs and processes in progress, locations of all programs and data files, allocation details of on- and off-line storage, accounting records, and other critical data.

First, we briefly review some of the causes and effects of systems failures. Hardware errors may result from failures in any of the computer components as well as the communication lines connecting them. An error can produce a complete breakdown of a component, such as a disk drive, or it may be manifested more subtly as a nonreproducible transient, for example a storage parity error caused by a fluctuation in power. Hardware failures are normally detected by the hardware itself and, in many instances, can be localized to a small area; an example is the mechanical breakdown of a peripheral unit such as a line printer. Frequently, however, the situation can be much more serious, causing problems similar to the software errors discussed later; the electronic destruction of information in a memory circuit and the erasure of parts of a disk due to incorrect functioning of the read/write heads or movable arms are in this category.

Systems and user programs are rarely, if ever, error free. Examples of typical coding errors are the transfer of control to an incorrect, perhaps nonexistent, address, mistakes in the operand addressing that result in the retrieval and modification of wrong data items, and infinite looping. Careful systems design and a computer with appropriate hardware protection mechanisms should ensure that user errors are totally isolated from the operating system and from other users; attempts to access data in or to transfer control to memory assigned to the system or to other user processes are normally detected by hardware, while incorrect systems service calls are discovered by systems programs. Thus, software failures can be traced mainly to errors in systems programs rather than to those of users.

The effects of these errors may be as follows:

1. The destruction of critical tables, such as process queues or active directories.
2. Addresses and pointers, for example those in file directories, that do not link to valid list items.
3. Incorrect resource lists, such as the free space tables for main or secondary storage.
4. Writing or reading data from the wrong files.

Discovery of the cause and effects of a system failure is generally a very difficult task, since programs have usually progressed far beyond the actual incorrect code at the time the failure becomes apparent. There are few general rules that one can give, at least for isolating the effects. A common technique is to examine all systems data structures for *consistency*. Examples follow of how consistency may be verified:

1. *Tracing of address entries in tables.* Normally, the set of addresses to which a pointer may link is fixed and relatively small, and each element of a list structure has some identifying header information that can be checked. For example, file directory entries must point to other directories or files, and the pointer structure usually forms a tree with data files at the leaves; the latter can be verified by tracing through the pointers. Another clear example is found in doubly linked lists, where successive forward and backward links must point to the same entry. Secondary storage addresses in tables are also usually valid only within a small range of possible addresses.
2. *Use of redundant information.* It is often convenient for normal processing purposes to maintain several copies of the same information but in different forms. For example, a resource data structure might contain allocation details, such as the name of each process holding some of the resource, while the process descriptors may redundantly contain a list of each resource allocated to the process; the

available and used space lists also duplicate the same information. This redundancy might also be explicitly designed for consistency checking.

3. *Application of checksum methods.* Accountants have long used checksums and hash totals to provide an independent check on the validity of a table of dollar amounts. The idea is to combine *all* the data in a table or file into a single number, for example by summing, exclusive OR-ing, or some other operation; this is done when the table is first created and whenever it is changed. When the table or file is accessed, the checksum is computed again to ensure that all the data are still present and correct.

Numerous other examples exist; many of these fall within normal error-checking responsibilities of programs (e.g., checking that a count of the number of buffers is nonnegative).

Localized hardware breakdowns that do not subsequently result in software damages and that are not critical to the continued operation of the computer are normally handled by removing descriptors of the hardware resources from the data structures and possibly substituting an equivalent resource; a breakdown of a noncritical peripheral unit falls in this class. For more serious hardware problems and for software failures, graceful recovery requires that up-to-date copies of the operating system, the collection of system and user files, and even the contents of main storage be available. This *backup* series of files is the center of all recovery procedures. Failures are then handled by the selective loading of backup files in an attempt to re-create the total system as it appeared immediately before failure. Recovery from catastrophic crashes can be accomplished by a systematic but lengthy reloading procedure, while less severe failures are treated on a more ad hoc basis in the hope of recovering more quickly and more completely.

Backup procedures that *dump* parts of the system must be both convenient and efficient. To dump the entire on-line set of information at selected time intervals is not satisfactory generally because it is both time consuming and cannot be done frequently enough to provide up-to-date copies. The standard approach maintains two types of backup dumps: *selective incremental* dumps obtained at relatively frequent time intervals and more complete *checkpoint* dumps occurring over much longer intervals.

The incremental dumps copy all files that have been either *modified* or *created* since the last such dump; files that have been accessed in a read-only manner are not included. This ensures that the most recent version of any file is available. Dumping can be initiated at a regular, fixed time interval, say every few minutes or hours, when the system has nothing else to do, almost continuously at the end of each process or group of processes, or some combination of these; the second scheme is somewhat dangerous by itself, since no guarantees could be made on the timeliness of the dump. In any case, some record of changed or created files must be maintained.

The purpose of checkpoint dumps is to allow a relatively recent version of the system to be loaded quickly so that processes may be run and further reconstruction can proceed at a more leisurely pace. Typically, this dump copies the *most recently used* parts of the system—both system and user files. A complete checkpoint dump cycle may be accomplished approximately every few days but could be programmed to copy small portions at a smaller time increment. Records of backup files, containing items such as time, type, and location of the dump, may conveniently be included in file directories; that is, the dumps are treated as files. Of course, we run into a familiar problem here: What happens if the directory is destroyed? One clearly needs an off-line record of the backup file directories; but since these directories are changing often, they appear in the incremental dumps, and the record is available.

Given the incremental and checkpoint backup files, recovery from catastrophic failures proceeds in the following manner:

1. Reload the system from the most recent checkpoint dump. The reloaded system is now used to control the remainder of the recovery while other user processes may simultaneously run.

2. Starting from the most recent incremental dump, work backward in time through the incremental dumps, reconstructing system and user files and directories.

It is not possible at this time to outline a systematic procedure for restoring a system after noncatastrophic failures. However, if errors can be isolated to a small set of files or tables, it is often possible to reconstruct these in a consistent manner so as to affect a small, if not empty, set of users and allow almost immediate continued systems operation. For example, if the failure only affects a single process or the currently active set of processes, then one can simply purge the process(es) and rerun it (them); if files are modified during the first failed execution, then either the users will have to be notified about possibly inconsistent files or, more satisfactorily, the most recent file copies can be obtained from one of the backup dumps automatically. Similarly, if only a small set of system files or tables proves erroneous on checking after failure, it may be possible to correct these and continue. One example might be the files and memory-resident tables related to user accounting; if these were partially or fully destroyed as a result of a systems error, they should be easily built from backup files, with the exception of the current process set. Another example is an inconsistency in the available and used space lists in secondary storage; they can be rebuilt by tracing through the directory structure.

Example

> The MULTICS file system described by Bash, Benjafield, and Gandy (1967) includes incremental dumping and both systems and user checkpoint dumping, with copying done in duplicate for even further protection. Systems checkpoints consist of the current accounting, directory, and operating system component files, whereas user checkpoints dump all segments accessed since the last checkpoint. In addition to the reloading process for catastrophic errors, MULTICS has an on-line salvage procedure that attempts to correct less severe failures by ensuring that directories and space tables are consistent.

EXERCISES

6.1. Consider again the directory hierarchy in Figure 6-3.
  (a) What are the shortest path names for each of the nondirectory files starting from the root node?

(b) Repeat part (a) assuming that directory no. 7 is the current working directory.

(c) Assume that all links are eliminated. What are the path names that must be used instead of the two link names (i.e., *F* in directory no. 5 and *L* in directory no. 12)?

6.2. Assume the following form for all directory files:

- Each directory entry contains the symbolic branch name, auxiliary storage address, and length of a child file (directory or data).
- The first two words of the file contain the auxiliary storage address and length, respectively, of the parent directory.

Suppose a working directory *D* resides in main memory at locations $W[i]$, $i = 1, \ldots, w$. Write a Boolean function

$$Search\_directory(Path, n, Addr)$$

that searches the directory tree for a file identified by the path name $Path[i]$, $i = 1, \ldots, n$, relative to *D*. The routine should return *false* if the requested file is not found; otherwise, it returns *true* and the secondary storage address of the file in *Addr*. Each element of *Path* may be an asterick or a symbolic branch name; for example, the path $*.*.B.C$ would be stored as $Path[1] = Path[2] = *$, $Path[3] = B$, and $Path[4] = C$. (Assume that links are not used.) Use the following two given procedures in your program:

$$Read(File\_addr, M, Length)$$

This reads a file of length *Length* located in auxiliary storage at address *File_addr* into main storage words $M[1], M[2], \ldots, M[Length]$.

$$Search(M, Length, Name, Addr, Len); \quad \{Boolean\ function\}$$

This searches a directory file stored in main memory $M[i]$, $i = 1, \ldots, Length$ for the symbolic name *Name*. If unsuccessful, it returns *false*; otherwise, it returns *true*, the auxiliary storage address of *Name* in *Addr*, and its length in *Len*.

6.3. The diagram on page 309 shows a portion of a tree-structured directory hierarchy.

The file system maintains a *referenced file table* (RFT) for each session of each user. This contains the name of every file referenced during that session and its corresponding unique path name. The RFT is cleared when the user logs off. To locate a file, the following search rules are used:

1. Search the RFT; if not found, go to rule 2.

2. Search the caller's parent directory; if not found, go to rule 3.

3. Search the current working directory; if not found, go to rule 4.

4. Search the library directory.

Each time a file is found using rules 2, 3, or 4, the corresponding new entry is made in the RFT.

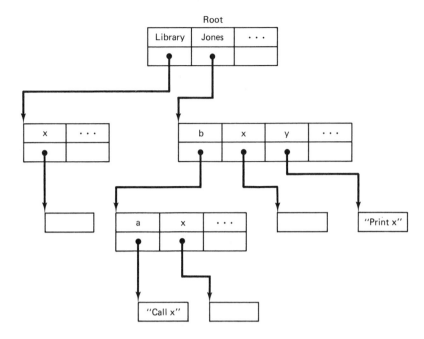

(a) The two files (programs) *Root.Jones.y* and *Root.Jones.b.a* both contain a reference to
x. Which file will x refer to in each of the following situations, assuming the working
directory is *Root.Jones*? (Give the unique path name for x.)

   (i)   RFT is empty; execute *Root.Jones.b.a.*

   (ii) RFT is empty; execute *Root.Jones.y.*

   (iii) RFT is empty; execute *Root.Jones.b.a*; execute *Root.Jones.y.*

(b) Jones wants to execute the program *Root.Jones.b.a* again and to have that program use
Root.Jones.x when referencing the name x. He cannot change the search rules and he
does not want to change any entries in any of the directories. Can he achieve his objective? If so, give a sequence of operations to accomplish that. If not, explain why.

6.4. Consider a logical file of fixed-length records mapped contiguously onto a sequence of
physical records. Develop formulas for calculating the physical record number, given a
logical record number for each of the following cases; ll and pl denote the logical and
physical record lengths, respectively:

(a) $ll = n * pl$, where $n \geq 1$ and n is an integer.

(b) $pl = n * ll$, where $n \geq 1$ and n is an integer.

(c) $ll = k * pl$, where $k \geq 1$, k is a real number, and a logical record never crosses the
boundary between two physical records.

(d) $pl = k * ll$, where $k \geq 1$, k is a real number, and a logical record always begins at a
physical record boundary.

6.5. Consider a disk with c cylinders, t tracks per cylinder, s sectors per track, and a sector
length sl. A logical file L with fixed record length rl is stored contiguously on this disk
starting at location (c_L, t_L, s_L), where c_L, t_L, and s_L are the cylinder, track, and sector
numbers, respectively.

(a) Derive a formula to calculate the disk address (i.e., cylinder, track, sector) of a given logical record n, assuming that (i) $rl \leq sl$; and (ii) $rl > sl$.

(b) How many seek operations are necessary to read an entire file of m logical records?

6.6. Consider a logical file stored index sequentially on a disk. There are two levels of indexing. A master index is kept in main memory; it finds the cylinder on which a record is kept, given the record key. Sector 0 on track 0 in each cylinder then contains a secondary index organized as shown in Figure 6-8; the pointer field contains the track and the sector numbers of the corresponding group of records.

(a) Give an algorithm for translating a given logical record number n into the corresponding disk address, assuming (i) fixed-length, and (ii) variable-length logical records.

(b) How many seek operations are necessary for each direct-access operation to a logical record? How many sectors must be read?

6.7. Consider a single-user system with one input device serviced through programmed IO. For IO completion, a device flag is provided, which is tested explicitly by the programmer. Consider the following simple program, which reads n elements of data, initializes some area in memory, and then processes the input data against the initialized memory area:

```
Input : for i = 1 to n do
            begin
                Read;
                while dev__flag = 1 do ; {wait loop}
                in__area[i] := in;
            end;
 Init : for i = 1 to n do
            initialize(mem[i]);
 Proc : for i = 1 to n do
            process(inarea[i], mem[i]);
```

Assuming that *Init* does not need any data read by the *Input* routine, rewrite the program as coroutines to achieve maximum overlap between the CPU and the input device.

6.8. Extend Exercise 6.7 by assuming the existence of an output device serviced also through programmed IO and an explicitly tested device flag. Implement an additional coroutine that prints a sequence of k characters. Assume that the output routine is independent of the other parts of the program and thus may run concurrently.

6.9. Consider the two coroutines *CP* and *IOP* of Section 6.5.2.1. Assume that each is to be executed as a separate process. Rewrite the programs into a functionally equivalent form that uses semaphore operations instead of the **resume** statements. For each semaphore, specify its initial value.

6.10. Consider the circular buffer example of Section 6.5.2.1 and make the following assumptions about its execution:

- Each *Compute__only* statement takes 4 times units.
- Each *Compute(buf[current])* statement takes 4 time units.
- Each procedure call takes 1 time unit.
- Any executable statement (e.g., **repeat**, **until**, **while** p **do**, **resume**, etc.) takes 1 time unit.

- The *Read* command also takes 1 time unit; when it terminates, the channel begins the IO operation and it remains busy for 5 time units.
- Initially, $r = n = 4$, next__get = next__io = 0, and the channel has just been started.

Using a timing diagram, show the cooperation between the two coroutines. In particular, draw separate timing lines for the main **repeat** loop, the *Get__buf* procedure, the *Release__buf* procedure, and the *IOP* routine, and indicate when each is executing until at least three buffers have been filled.

6.11. Repeat Exercise 6.10 for the procedures and the interrupt routine of Section 6.5.2.2. Make the following additional assumptions:

- Switching to the interrupt routine is instantaneous when the channel terminates.
- Return from interrupt is also instantaneous.

6.12. Show that the *IOP* and *CP* coroutines of the circular buffer example in Section 6.5.2.1 cooperate correctly in achieving the desired buffering system for $n \geq 1$. At the minimum, it must be shown that:
   (a) The system starts correctly, regardless of which coroutine is given initial control.
   (b) It is impossible for either *Get__buf* or *IOP* to loop forever without obtaining a full or empty buffer, respectively.
   (c) The buffers used by *Get__buf* and *IOP* are always the next input-full and next empty ones, respectively.

6.13. Consider the circular buffer example of Section 6.5.2.1. Let each physical record consist of m logical records and the buffers be designated by $Buf[i, j]$, $i = 0, \ldots, n - 1$; $j = 0, \ldots, m - 1$ ($m, n \geq 1$). Assume that the operation $Read(ch, Buf[i, *])$ will read a physical record into $Buf[i, 0], Buf[i, 1], \ldots, Buf[i, m - 1]$. Make the necessary changes to the main and *IOP* coroutines to handle this blocked record situation; that is, *Get__buf* and *Release__buf* are still to return *logical* records.

6.14. In the circular buffer example of Section 6.5.2.1, it was assumed that the compute program CP requests only one buffer at a time. Rewrite the procedures *Get__buf* and *Release__buf* such that CP may request and release k buffers ($1 \leq k \leq n$) at a time, for example, Get__buf(3, *current*). (The variable *current* should point to the first of the k buffers.)

6.15. Repeat Exercise 6.14 for the procedures of Section 6.5.2.2.

6.16. Consider again the circular buffer example of Section 6.5.2.1. Assume that a second circular buffer is used for output.
   (a) Write two procedures *Get__buf__out* and *Release__buf__out* (analogous to *Get__buf* and *Release__buf*) that request and release buffers for output.
   (b) Rewrite the *IOP* routine for the following two cases:
      (i) There are two channels (one for input, one for output).
      (ii) The same channel is used for input and output.

6.17. Modify the circular buffer example of Section 6.5.2.1 as follows:
   (a) Eliminate the counter r; instead, use only a Boolean flag to indicate when all buffers are full.
   (b) Eliminate the counter r; the procedures may use only the pointers *next__get* and *next__io* to determine whether to proceed or to wait. (*Hint*: Enforce that at least one buffer is empty at all times.)

6.18. Write a monitor to implement a FIFO disk scheduler consisting of the following three procedures:

Do__io(operation, cylinder);
Get__Next(operation, cylinder);
Done;

The following diagram illustrates the use of these procedures:

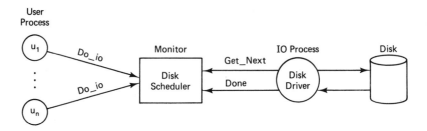

A user process requests a disk operation by calling *Do__io* with the appropriate parameters. The disk driver gets the next request (FIFO) using *Get__Next*. When the operation is completed, it issues the call to *Done*, which wakes up the appropriate user process.

6.19. The UNIX operating system has no general interprocess communication or synchronization scheme. Instead, binary semaphore operations can be simulated by creating and deleting a known file. Show how this idea can be implemented and explain why it works.

7

Protection and Security

7.1 BASIC ISSUES

The increasing dependence on computer systems in industrial corporations, financial institutions, government and administrative offices, and military installations has introduced a new set of problems related to the security of computer systems. These problems result from two basic types of intrusions: *malicious* and *incidental*. In the first case, we are faced with unauthorized attempts to read or destroy sensitive data or to otherwise disrupt the system's operation. In many cases the culprit is a mere "computer hack," who considers the penetration of a computer system a personal challenge; often, however, we are faced with acts of purposeful crime, resulting in great financial losses, injustice, or personal harm. In the second category, we find problems that result from hardware malfunctioning, undetected errors in the operating system and other software components, or from natural disasters such as fires, earthquakes, and power blackouts. The consequences may be as serious as those of intentional crimes.

Due to their intangible nature, the terms protection and security do not have any precise and widely accepted definition within computer science. The main reason is the extremely broad spectrum of frequently contradictory issues comprising this area, which cannot be solved through any single approach. In this book we will adhere to the definitions given in the *Dictionary of the English Language* (Random House), where *protection* is viewed as the *act* or the *state* of defending or guarding from attack, invasion, loss, or annoyance, while *security* is *freedom* from danger, risk, doubt, or apprehension. In that sense, protection may be viewed as the collection of mechanisms and policies necessary (but not sufficient) to achieve security. The latter implies additional attributes such as dependability, firmness, or robustness against failure, which cannot be achieved through protection alone. Hence security is the broader of the two terms; it represents the goal to be achieved through protection mechanisms and other means.

A computer system consists of collections of data, which can be read or modified, and services that may be invoked; both of these will be referred to as *objects*. Active components of the system, capable of performing the read and write operations or able to utilize a service will be called *subjects*. In most conventional systems, processes would correspond to subjects while data files, programs, or even processors would be regarded as objects. Both subjects and objects must coexist in a computer system and share its physical resources such as processors, memories, and IO devices. The sharing of software resources among processes, such as data files and service routines, is also highly desirable, as was discussed in Chapter 5. Unfortunately, the ability to share poses a potential threat to security. Hence one of the major objectives in designing secure computer systems is to provide mechanisms and policies to permit the sharing of data, services, and physical resources but only in a controlled manner according to well-defined policies.

We can divide the issues of protection and security into four basic categories, according to the type of security threat to be prevented.

1. *Information disclosure* is concerned with an unauthorized dissemination of information, either as a result of theft or through illegal actions on the part of a user who has access to that information. Obvious examples of information disclosure are the reading of a forthcoming exam by a student, access to classified or secret military documents, or the theft of research results proprietary to an industrial enterprise. An important part of this problem is the enforcement of the right of *privacy*, a social policy defined as the ability of each individual to control the collection, storing, and dissemination of information about himself or herself. Failing to do so could result in substantial damage or harm to an individual or a social group. For example, monitoring an individual's financial transactions or personal activities could serve as the basis for subsequent blackmail.

2. *Information destruction* is the problem of information loss, which could be the result of an error or an act of sabotage. An obvious example is the loss of an important operating system data structure, such as a process or resource queue. Other examples are the destruction of research or development results of an individual or an institution to eliminate unwanted competition or the deletion of police or court records, which could result in a lack of evidence in a criminal charge. Note that information may be destroyed without being disclosed, and vice versa.

3. *Unauthorized use of services* is concerned with the problem of bypassing the system's accounting policies in order to make unauthorized use of some proprietary services or simply to obtain free computing time. Users of a computing facility often display a different attitude toward data files or programs than they would

toward other resources. For example, a person who has been entrusted an object, for example a car, by the object's owner might hesitate to let a third party use it without the user's consent. On the other hand, letting a third party use an entrusted computer account or a software system may be viewed by the same person as quite acceptable. Especially if the proprietary package were ''only'' a computer game, few would hesitate to make a copy for a friend. In dealing with this problem, one must realize that, while intangible, computer accounts, data files, or programs all represent valuable resources, which might have been created as business assets. Consequently, their unauthorized use must be considered an act of crime.

4. *Denial of service* is the problem of preventing an authorized user from utilizing the system's services in a timely manner. As the dependence of society on computers increases, timely response becomes an important issue. In many situations, any significant delay in service may have severe consequences. Such delays could be caused inadvertently, as a result of system malfunctioning, or deliberately, as an act of sabotage. In both cases, the resulting denial of service could be of *temporary* nature (an unexpected and intolerable delay) or it could result in *permanent* damage or loss of information. For example, a mechanical malfunctioning of a disk's read/write arm may require a service engineer to be called in to perform the necessary repairs. Even if no data are destroyed on the disk when the read/write arm stopped functioning and normal operation is resumed when the problem is eliminated, the unavailability of the system may result in serious damage. For example, the system could be monitoring some real-time events or processes whose uncontrolled behavior might pose a serious threat to human life or property. Substantial financial losses may also result from the unavailability of a computer system in many types of businesses, for example in an airline reservation system. In many instances, hardware or software malfunctioning causes both denial of service and the destruction of information.

From this discussion we see that the issues in protection and security are multifarious, implying that no single scheme is sufficient to provide an adequate computing environment. Rather, a spectrum of various safeguards must be employed to achieve an overall system security. The interplay of these safeguards must be carefully balanced since any chain of policies and mechanisms is only as strong as its weakest link. Two other factors to be considered are (1) the additional dollar cost of providing protection mechanisms, which usually increases with the sophistication of the system, and (2) a possible degradation of performance due to protection.

We can distinguish two types of safeguards to be imposed on a system for the purpose of increasing its security level: *external* and *internal*.

7.1.1 External Safeguards

The main purpose of external safeguards is to control *physical access* to the computing facility. In the case of a single-user system such as a personal computer, external safeguards are limited to deciding who should be allowed to use the system. This is usually decided and enforced by the owner, who also has the freedom to perform any modifications of the system's hardware or software. Shared computer systems, on the other hand, are usually installed in buildings or rooms where entry is restricted to authorized personnel. Such restrictions are subject to *administrative policies* and may be enforced through a variety of *physical safeguards*, such as locks, badges, sign-in procedures, or TV cameras. Inadequate control of physical access to any part of the computing facility could result in any of the four threats to security discussed previously. For example, an intruder may read or modify information, employ some service, or cause a denial of service by using the operator's console or by physically altering some components of the system to bypass the protection mechanisms.

Additional administrative mechanisms are frequently employed as a deterrent to potential violators. These may usefully be combined with appropriate internal safeguards implemented for this purpose. The most common safeguards of this type are surveillance mechanisms that automatically record all activities that may be indicative of potential security violations. Examples of such activities are unsuccessful log-in procedures, attempts to use privileged instructions, or invocation of protected internal system procedures. Chronological sequences of such events, called *audit trails*, may be used in real time to expose a potential intruder; this approach is referred to as *threat monitoring*. Audit trails may also serve as the basis for subsequent external safeguard procedures to analyze or *audit* potential threats.

The security of a system requires not only adequate protection mechanisms to prevent disclosure, destruction, and misuse or information and services, but also some means to guarantee a certain level of reliability and dependability. The backup and recovery procedures discussed in Section 5.7 are an important part of the overall security of a system.

7.1.2 Internal Safeguards

Assuming that sufficient external safeguards are provided to prevent a potential intruder from gaining entry into the system by physically modifying its configuration or through restricted channels such as the operator console, the responsibility for the system's security rests with the operating system. It must contain the necessary internal safeguards to prevent or at least reduce the risk of a possible security violation.

Verification of User Identity.   When an authorized user executes a log-in procedure, a record of her or his presence in the system is created. Normally, this record has the form of a process that will be acting on behalf of the user. When such a process is created, we say that the user has successfully *entered* the system.

An essential task to be performed by any protection system is the verification of the user's identity at the time of entry into the system. This task, referred to as *user authentication*, is usually the first security check performed by the system's internal safeguards. We will survey a number of possible schemes in Section 7.2.1. After successful entry into the system, all actions taken by the user (represented by his or her process) are governed by internal protection mechanisms and policies enforced by the operating system. According to the type of problem to be solved, either of two types of schemes, called *access control* and *information flow control*, may be used.

Access Control.   As the name suggests, we are concerned with controlling the ability of subjects to access objects. The fundamental question to be answered in a particular state of execution is "Can subject *s* perform an operation *f* on an object *o*?" Most existing systems provide this type of control at the file-system level. Subjects are processes confined to their own designated areas within main memory. They may request access to files stored on secondary memory by issuing appropriate commands to the file system. Depending on the sophistication of the file system, various degrees of access control may be provided. In the simplest case, the system does not distinguish between the types of operations a process may perform on a file once access is granted. A more advanced scheme than the all-or-nothing policy would recognize various types of operations, such as read, write, append, or execute, and grant or deny access based on the operation requested. The dissemination of access rights themselves is also controlled by the file system, which enforces the directives specified by the owner of each file.

Information Flow Control.   Access-control mechanisms are not sufficient to solve a number of important protection problems. In particular, they cannot be used to answer the question "Is it possible for subject *s* to acquire the information contained in object *o*?" Note that it may not be necessary for the subject *s* to actually gain *access* to that object; rather, the information could be transferred to it by some other subjects or it could simply be copied into an object accessible by *s*. Since such information transfers cannot, in general, be detected by access-control mechanisms, more sophisticated means to permit the specification and enforcement of policies to control the *flow* of information are necessary.

Cryptography.   From the preceding discussion, it follows that internal safeguards are used primarily to govern the actions of a user who has entered the system legally through the appropriate log-in procedures, while the main purpose of external safegaurds is to prevent individuals from physically circumventing the internal protection schemes. Unfortunately, it is not always possible to guarantee that all parts of the computing facility are physically inaccessible. This is especially true of terminals and other IO devices that may be dispersed throughout buildings or even connected remotely through public telephone lines. Similarly, computer networks make use of communication channels that may not be physically protected. As a result, information may be obtained illegally by tapping into such channels, or it may be distorted by deleting or modifying portions of the data being transmitted.

Additional internal safeguards may be introduced to seal such gaps left open by external safeguards. In the case of communication lines and terminals that cannot be protected physically, the only effective means of protection is the use of *cryptography* to disguise the information being transmitted or to detect possible interference. The study of cryptography is outside the scope of this book. The interested reader is referred to Denning (1982), which provides in-depth treatment of this subject.

7.2 PENETRATION OF A COMPUTER FACILITY

All rights and privileges with respect to a computing facility are initially granted to users by the system's administrator and are recorded in some form inside the system. Due to the nature of electronic systems, the internal record is always some collection of binary information; the user's identity outside the system, on the other hand, may be based on a variety of different schemes. The key issue in security is to verify the correspondence between the external identification and the internal record. To penetrate a computing facility, the intruder must either bypass the verification mechanisms, for example by physically altering the system's hardware, or impersonate a legal user by providing false or stolen identification. Before studying the possible penetration attempts, we must first examine the various user authentication methods employed in existing computer systems.

7.2.1 User Authentication Methods

To make any internal protection mechanisms effective, it is necessary to guarantee that only authorized users be permitted to enter the system. Hence any multiuser computer facility must have some means of verifying the user's identity and establishing the connection to the appropriate internal record describing the user's rights and privileges. This process is referred to as *user authentication* and may be based on one or more of the following:

- Knowledge of some information
- Possession of some artifact
- Physical characteristic of a person

The most common representative of the first category is the knowledge of a *password* to be presented to the system at the time of entry. To decrease the likelihood of password guessing, the scheme can be extended to a short *dialog* during which the user must answer a series of questions before entry is granted. The latter is similar to the security procedures employed by banks and other institutions, in which a client may be asked to give the mother's maiden name, date of birth, or similar types of information before any services are performed.

Another type of knowledge that must be possessed by a potential user may be a secret combination for a lock used to prevent physical access to the terminal room or to an individual terminal. Such physical safeguards are usually employed in addition to logical means of user authentication such as passwords or dialogs.

The most prominent example of user authentication based on the possession of some unforgeable item is the use of cards with machine-readable information. To alleviate the threat of loss or theft, such items are usually employed in combination with a secret code or a password. For example, ready-teller machines permitting 24-hour access to a bank's computer are controlled in this manner. Other common examples of unforgeable items are *badges*, used for visual inspection by a guard, or physical *keys* necessary to enter buildings and terminal rooms or to operate terminals.

User authentication methods in the third category are based on physical characteristics unique to an individual. Perhaps the best known such characteristic, other than a person's appearance, is *fingerprints*. Unfortunately, their examination and comparison by a machine is difficult and costly to implement. A related scheme is based on *hand geometry*, that is, the lengths of individual fingers and their curvature, which yield a unique pattern for each individual. The recognition of *voice patterns*, produced by measuring the frequencies and amplitudes of spoken phrases, offers another possibility to verify the identity of an individual. Finally, the *dynamics of signatures*, that is, the speed of writing and the pressure exercised while producing a signature, have also been used successfully for user authentication.

In addition to being rather costly to implement, the main problem of all the preceding methods that use the physical characteristics of an individual is a certain factor of doubt in the recognition process. This may lead to two types of error: (1) rejection of an authorized user, known as false alarm, or (2) acceptance of an impostor. To understand the relationship between these two cases, assume that a given authentication mechanism, instead of producing a simple yes/no answer, returns a number between zero and one. This number corresponds to the certainty with which the recognition has been performed. The problem is to determine the threshold between *genuine* attempts (i.e., those issued by authorized users) and *false* attempts, originating from impostors.

Assume that all genuine attempts result in a number between n and 1 ($0 \leq n \leq 1$), whereas impostor attempts yield a number between 0 and m ($0 \leq m \leq 1$). If m is smaller than n, as illustrated in Figure 7-1a, the threshold of acceptance could be placed anywhere between m and n. Unfortunately, this is not always the case. Figure 7-1b shows a situation in which a certain number of genuine attempts overlaps with attempts by impostors. The shaded area to the left of the threshold represents rejected genuine attempts, while the area to its right corresponds to accepted impostor attempts. By moving the threshold between the two values n and m, different policies may be implemented. However, the total number of erroneous recognitions cannot be changed.

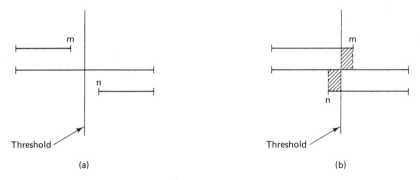

Figure 7-1 Sensitivity of user authentication mechanisms.

7.2.2 Penetration Attempts

Penetration refers to the act of illegal entry into the computer system and may take two basic forms:

1. A user may completely bypass the authentication mechanisms, thus gaining uncontrolled access to information maintained inside the system.
2. A user may obtain information or alter the system such that she or he may be permitted to enter the system legally as an authorized user.

Either form may lead to information theft or destruction, unauthorized use of services, or service denial. The following paragraphs survey a number of potential penetration attempts and suggest some possible safeguards to prevent such actions.

Wire Tapping. Communication lines connecting terminals and other devices to the host computer or lines interconnecting nodes of a computer network cannot always be protected from physical access and thus constitute a vulnerable point for an attack. *Wire tapping*, defined as the act of establishing a physical connection to a communication line, can occur in two forms: *passive* or *active*. In the first case the intruder is merely listening to the communication on the tapped line without altering its contents. It may be used to copy sensitive data, thus bypassing the user authentication mechanisms, or it may be used to obtain information (e.g. a password) that would permit legal entry on subsequent occasions.

A method similar to, and thus used for the same purpose as passive wire tapping is *electromagnetic pickup*, which is the monitoring of electromagnetic signals emanating from the system or its components. This usually does not require any physical modification of the system's hardware and consequently may be accomplished without leaving a trace. Communication lines and cathode ray terminals are the most susceptible to this type of attack.

Active wire tapping occurs when the data being transmitted are modified by the intruder. Two special cases of active tapping are *between lines* transmission and *piggyback* entry. The first refers to insertion of additional messages into the communication while the legitimate user is temporarily inactive, for example between individual lines or characters transmitted by a terminal. The authentic messages themselves are not altered in any way. Piggyback entry, on the other hand, requires that original messages be intercepted and modified or replaced by entirely new messages before reaching their destination. This is usually accomplished by breaking the communication line and letting all messages pass through a third computer, pretending to be the geniune source and destination of messages. A typical application of this technique is to intercept and discard a log-off command transmitted by a legitimate user and, after returning to that user a faked acknowledgment of the session termination, continue the session with the same privileges as the original legitimate user.

In general, the only effective means of preventing tapping is the use of encryption to make the transmitted information illegible to an intruder. Malicious disruption of communication, resulting in information loss or denial of service, cannot, however, be avoided by any means other than preventing physical access to any component of the system.

Trial and Error.   Where user authentication schemes are based on the knowledge of a password or some other information, an intruder may attempt to *guess* the necessary information. Most systems permit a password to be an arbitrary sequence of alphanumeric (or even special) characters; the only possible restriction might be the maximum length of the resulting string. This permits very large numbers of distinct passwords to be created. For example, with an alphabet of 26 letters and 10 digits available on any keyboard and a password length of only 4 characters, more than 1 million distinct passwords may be created. Thus, on the surface, the possibility of guessing a valid password would not seem likely to succeed. Unfortunately, studies of actual systems have shown that most users tend to select passwords based on some personal data, such as the names or birth dates of the person or an immediate relative, which may easily be obtained by a potential intruder.

Penetration by trial and error may meet with success, especially when a second computer is employed to generate large numbers of possible passwords. Furthermore, an intruder may not have to search for the password of a given individual but may be content with guessing *any* password that would permit access to the system. This would be the case, for example, when the intruder wishes to utilize the system services without proper authorization. Since a system may recognize thousands of different passwords as valid at any given time, a trial and error approach performed rapidly by another computer might soon discover one that permits legal entry.

Several measures can be taken to eliminate this danger or at least to reduce the amount of damage that could result should a password be disclosed. To limit the probability of guessing, passwords may be generated by the system as random strings of characters. To alleviate the difficulty of dealing with such random passwords, the system could apply certain rules to make the generated strings pronounceable and thus easier to remember. Another way to reduce the success ratio of trial and error methods is to limit the number of accepted incorrect guesses or to increase the response time with each unsuccessful attempt.

Passwords are frequently limited by an expiration date or a number of uses to reduce the possible damage caused by a successful penetration. When this limit is reached, a new password must be obtained. Such restrictions are useful, for example, in preventing intruders from employing the system's services free of charge over extensive periods of time. Their effectiveness in preventing theft or destruction of information, however, is minimal.

Browsing.   The term *browsing* refers to searching of storage for unauthorized information. When a portion of memory is allocated to a process, few systems will actually erase all data that may have remained there from previous computations. Browsing through this storage may compromise sensitive information belonging to other users or to the operating system itself. Similarly, unused space on disks or tapes, allocated previously to other users or the operating system, is usually easy to get access to and may contain sensitive information.

Trap Doors.   A *trap door* refers to an unspecified and undocumented feature of the system that may be exploited to perform unauthorized actions. A trap door could be the result of a flaw in the system design or it could have been implanted intentionally by a systems programmer for future use. For example, insufficient checking of legal parameters, the use of undefined opcodes, or an unusual and thus untested sequence of operations may result in some obscure system state, making it vulnerable to attack. A trap door may also be implanted into the system by a Trojan Horse, a program offered for public use that, when employed, performs unadvertised actions by misusing the additional privileges possessed by the unsuspecting user.

Searching of Waste.   Finally, and with a surprisingly high success ratio, the examination of old printer ribbons, listings, memory dumps, notes, discarded tapes and disks, or similar such artifacts found conveniently in waste paper baskets may yield important information leading eventually to the penetration of a system.

7.3 ACCESS AND INFORMATION FLOW CONTROL

7.3.1 The Current Execution Environment

In the course of its execution, a process will reside in various parts of the storage hierarchy comprising the underlying computer system. Ordered by speed, these may be registers, various associative memories (e.g., caches or look-aside buffers; see Section 5.4.2.4), primary memory, and secondary memory.

Registers are normally visible to programmers at the assembly level. However, since context switching automatically saves and restores all registers, each process can be viewed as having its own private set. Associative memories are entirely transparent (not accessible) to application programs. Thus, as long as the appropriate system programs operate correctly, no unauthorized information flow through registers or associative memories is possible.

The components of a computing facility that are usually visible to processes are the primary and secondary memories and a number of other hardware devices. Most of these are scarce resources; thus controlling the amount and type of sharing is one of the main tasks of the operating system. At any given time, a process is able to access a certain collection of resources comprising the facility. These could be software components, such as programs, data files, or even other processes, residing on one of the two types of memory; these could also be some of the hardware components such as IO devices or special processors. We will refer to the collection of all objects, hardware or software, accessible to a subject (process) at a given time as the *current execution environment*.

Depending on the sophistication of the system, the current execution environment (sometimes also called the current access environment in the literature) may be *static*, that is, constant for the life span of a process, or it may vary *dynamically*. To keep the extent of damage a process may cause to itself or to other processes as small as possible, some protection policies require that processes operate at all times in the smallest environment necessary to carry out the current tasks. A dynamically changing environment must be supported to satisfy this requirement, patterned after the need-to-know principle enforced by the military.

7.3.2 Protection in Primary Memory

Memory protection facilities are required both to control a process's access to its own instructions and data and to prevent a process from accessing (e.g., reading, writing, or executing) the information associated with other processes; that is, processes must be protected from themselves and from others. An obvious example is the protection of the operating system from overwriting or erroneous execution by user programs. Other examples occur naturally in sharing situations, when one is dealing with proprietary information, and in program debugging.

There are two main problems to be solved. First, processes must be *confined* to areas of main storage that have been assigned to them by the appropriate mechanisms of the operating system (i.e., they may only read from, write into, or execute in these areas). Enforcement of such confinement depends greatly on the type of memory management scheme implemented in a given system, for example physical versus virtual memory. We will explore the various possibilities shortly. The second problem is concerned with the *type* of access by a process to different areas of main memory. Ideally, each process should have its own set of rights with respect to a given memory area S; these rights are typically a Boolean combination of the following values:

1. *Read* (R). S may be read; instructions that load information from S into a register or into some other storage area or that compare elements of S are permitted; storing into S or executing from S, for example by transferring control to some address in S, is illegal if access is R-only.

2. *Write* (W). S may be written into; storing from a register or some other area of memory into S is permitted. A special case of *Write* is *Append*, which permits data to be stored but only at the end of S; that is, no data in S may be overwritten.

3. *Execute* (X). S may be executed as a program; instructions may be fetched from S and executed; internal reads for constants are usually also allowed.

Often the R protection is interpreted to include X as well. In terms of these basic modes, the most common forms of access restriction are the following:

$\neg(R \lor W \lor X)$:	No access is permitted.
$R \land \neg(W \lor X)$:	Read only. A table of constants or part of a data file, for example a historical file on student grades, might be given this designation.

$(R \vee W) \wedge \neg X$:   This protects a read/write data area, for example an array in a scientific computation, from attempts at execution by an incorrect program.

$\neg(R \vee W) \wedge X$:   Execute only. The security of program instructions in systems programs and propriety programs is possible with this combination. S cannot be treated as data.

$R \vee X \wedge \neg W$:   Writing is not permitted.

$R \vee X \vee W$:   Unrestricted access is provided.

Let us now distinguish between systems with and without virtual memory. For each, we examine the two problems of confining processes into specified memory areas and permitting different types of access to an area.

Systems without Virtual Memory. In the absence of relocation registers, paging hardware, or segmentation facilities, programs must address physical memory directly. To guarantee that processes will remain in their own partitions, each physical address must be checked for its validity; it must refer only to the area assigned to the process. This can be enforced through the use of one or a combination of the following: (1) *bounds registers* that specify the upper and lower addresses of a contiguous storage area, (2) *length indicators* containing the size of a storage area, or (3) identification *keys* associated with storage blocks.

The use of bounds registers is illustrated in Figure 7-2. Each time a reference to a physical address *pa* is made, the hardware performs the check

$$LR \leq pa \leq UR$$

where LR and UR point to the first and the last memory cell assigned to the process. Only if the check is successful is the reference carried out; otherwise, an error condition is signaled and the process is aborted. Instead of the upper bound register, a length register, say L, could be used. In this case the check performed by the hardware would be

$$LR \leq pa < LR + L$$

The use of identification keys requires that storage be divided into blocks, usually of equal size. A combination of n bits, referred to as a *lock*, is associated with each block. Each process has a pattern of n bits, called the *key*, as part of its process state.

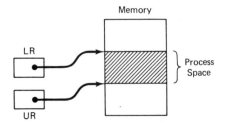

Figure 7-2 Bounds registers for memory protection.

Upon each reference the hardware compares the current key with the lock of the block to be accessed; only if a match is found is the process permitted to proceed with the operation.

The use of bounds or length registers is the simplest form of access control; it permits only an all-or-nothing type of protection to a given area, without being able to distinguish different types of access. The use of memory locks and keys offers potentially greater flexibility in that each lock could incorporate the type of access permitted to the corresponding memory block. Associating protection information directly with physical memory, however, is very restrictive when programs or data regions are to be shared. To permit different processes to have different rights with respect to the same information, the contents of locks would have to be reloaded each time a process switch occurs. A much greater flexibility is possible in systems with virtual memory, where protection is associated with the logical name spaces rather than physical memory.

Systems with Virtual Memory.   In systems that employ simple relocation registers to implement virtual memory, the problem of confining processes to assigned areas is similar to that in systems without any dynamic relocation capabilities. A given virtual address *va* is first transformed into the corresponding physical address by adding to it the content of the relocation register *RR*. The resulting physical address is then compared to the contents of the paper and lower bounds registers. The modified *NL_map* function would have the following form:

```
function NL_map(va): pa;
begin
    pa := va + RR;
    if ¬ (LR ≤ pa ≤ UR) then error
    else NL_map := pa
end
```

This prevents a process from accessing information outside its legal bounds. The problem of allowing different types of access to a given area, however, still persists and additional mechanisms to solve it must be provided. One possibility is to associate the necessary access information with physical blocks of storage (locks and keys) in the same way as under static relocation discussed earlier. A much better approach is to associate the access information with the executing process and extend the *NL_map* procedure to perform the necessary checks as part of the address translation process. This would permit each process to have a potentially different set of access rights with respect to a physical memory area.

The same approach can be taken in paged or segmented memory systems, where it may be exploited to its full extent. A segment or page of a virtual memory system is accessed indirectly by an entry in a page or segment table (or both). Such tables are private to a process; hence, by incorporating protection information into individual table entries, each process can have a different set of rights with respect to any segment or page (private or shared) accessible by that process. The necessary checks are performed at each address translation step by the *NL_map* procedure. We consider the case of segmentation followed by paging, where each table occupies at most one page. Access information is specified on a per-segment basis and hence it is kept in the segment table. The table entries and the associated pointers could be as follows.

The segment table is an array of *ST_entries*, each corresponding to one segment *s*. It is located and delimited by the following two values (registers):

1. *stb* is the pointer to the beginning of the segment table.
2. *stl* is an integer that gives the number of valid entries (segments) in the segment table.

Each entry in a segment table may have the form:

```
ST_entry = record
                pt_base: ptr_to_page_table;
                pt_len: integer;
                pt_resident: Boolean;
                access: access_rights
           end
```

where *pt_base* points to the beginning of the page table for the segment *s*, *pt_len* gives the number of valid entries in the page table (i.e., the number of pages constituting the segment), *pt_resident* indicates whether the page table is currently resident in main memory, and *access* lists the access information (rights) the process has for the segment.

Each page table entry corresponds to one page *p* of the segment *s*; it could have the form

```
PT_entry = record
                pg_base: ptr_to_page;
                pg_resident: Boolean;
           end
```

where *pg_base* is a pointer to the beginning of the page *p*, and *pg_resident* specifies whether the page *p* is currently resident.

Under the preceding assumptions, the *NL_map* function for translating a virtual address (s, p, w) into a physical address, including all protection checks, may be described as follows:[†]

```
function NL_map((s, p, w)): pa;
begin
    if stl < s then error('Invalid Segment Number')
    if stb ↑[s].access ⊉ type of access requested
    then error('Invalid Access Type');
    if stb ↑[s].pt_resident = false
    then page_fault('Page Table for Segment Not Resident');
```

[†]We will ignore the associative registers here.

if *stb* ↑[*s*].*pt_len* < *p* **then error**('Invalid Page Number');
ptb := *stb* ↑[*s*].*pt_base*; { *ptb* points to page table}
if *ptb* ↑[*p*].*pg_resident* = *false* **then page_fault**('Page Not Resident');
NLmap := *ptb* ↑[*p*].pg_base + w
end

7.3.3 Protection in Secondary Storage

In systems with virtual memory, data kept on secondary storage are accessible in two ways: *implicitly* through the virtual memory mechanisms (page and/or segment faults) or *explicitly* through a file system. In the first case, protection is enforced through the address translation mechanisms (*NL_map*) as described previously. In this section, we consider the second type, where the file system is responsible for enforcing the specified protection policies. To accomplish this, the file system must maintain information about each subject's rights to access a given object; this information may be organized in two different forms, as *access* lists or as *capability* lists.

In the access-list approach, a list of subjects is associated with each object (e.g., a file). Each entry of this access list specifies the rights the corresponding subject has with respect to the object. This concept is illustrated in Figure 7-3a, which shows the access list for an object *o*.

Many operating systems simplify this general form of an access list by segregating users into different classes or groups. The access list then specifies the access information for the various user types or classes, rather than for each individual user.

Example

1. The following philosophy has been adopted by the UNIX operating system. A file's access list distinguishes three types of users: (1) the file's owner, (2) members of a specific group, and (3) all other users. The file's owner is that user who originally created the file. The purpose of the group is to permit a selected team of users to access the file with rights different from those granted to the general public (i.e., the third user type). Within each of the three user types, a file may be readable (r), writable (w), or executable (x). For example, a file designated as rwxr-x--x would permit unrestricted access (rwx) by the owner, read and execute access by any member of the group (r-x), and execute-only access by all others (--x).

2. A more elaborate scheme has been implemented in the TOPS-20 operating system executing on Digital Equipment Corporation's PDP-2020. It also segregates users into the

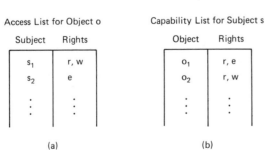

Figure 7-3   Organization of protection information: (a) Access list (b) Capability list.

three classes of owner, group, and others. Within each class, however, access information is encoded as a two-digit number with the following meaning:

77   Unrestricted access

40   Read only

20   Write or delete only

10   Execute only

04   Append only

02   List file specification (i.e., return descriptive attributes of the file)

These rights may be combined arbitrarily by adding the appropriate codes. For example, 44 would give read and append privileges, while 60 would permit reading, writing, and deletion.

3. Different sets of rights are often provided with respect to directory files. In UNIX, a directory may have the rights r, x, and w, with the following interpretation: r permits the directory to be read as if it were an ordinary file; x permits using the directory to locate existing files; w permits new files to be created and existing ones to be deleted.

In the second approach to recording access privileges to objects, the protection information is segregated by subjects. That is, each subject has a list of entries called *capabilities*, each of which consists of a pointer to an object and a set of rights determining the type of access permitted. The basic concept is illustrated in Figure 7-3b, which shows the capability list for a subject (procedure) *s*.

By far the most common approach to organizing protection information is in the form of access lists. However, the concept of capabilities, developed more recently, is gaining popularity. Let us compare the virtues and drawbacks of the two approaches in more detail.

7.3.4 Capabilities versus Access Lists

By analogy, a capability may be viewed as a ticket, for example a theatre ticket, that entitles its holder to exercise certain privileges (e.g., enter a theater). An access list, on the other hand, is comparable to a reservation list, for example in a restaurant; only parties whose names appear on that list are permitted to enter.

On the surface there appears to be little difference between capability lists and access lists since the same amount of information is recorded in both cases. This is true if capabilities are used only to control access to objects residing on secondary storage, while access to objects residing in main memory is governed by other mechanisms. In such a case, the file system is responsible for maintaining all capabilities and for verifying the validity of each request. The concept of a capability, however, viewed as a ticket that authorizes its holder to perform certain operations on a given object can be extended to become the *only* means of referring to objects, regardless of where these currently reside. This extension has a number of important consequences that yield a more powerful protection environment.

Capability-based Addressing.   Let us compare the idea of a capability list with a segment table of a virtual memory. Both of these consist of pointers to objects, each augmented by a set of rights to control the permissible operations. The only real difference is that segment table entries point to objects residing in directly accessible memory (physical or virtual), whereas capabilities, as introduced so far, point to objects guarded by the file system on secondary memories. An important consequence of this distinction is that segment table entries are temporary: they are created during the linking phase and become meaningless when the process terminates.

As an example, consider the dynamic linking mechanism discussed in Section 5.6.4. When a process references a new segment, the file system is invoked to find the requested segment on secondary storage and to verify the process's access rights to that segment by consulting the corresponding access or capability list. If the request is legal, a new entry in the segment table is created. This entry is then used directly by all subsequent references to the same segment. Hence, in a segmented system, there are *two* distinct schemes that determine a process's current environment: for objects residing on secondary storage, the environment is defined by access lists or capability lists, depending on the implementation of the file system; for directly accessible memory, on the other hand, the contents of segment tables define the collection of accessible objects.

The similarity between capability lists, used for secondary storage objects, and segment tables, used for virtual storage objects, suggests that a uniform approach could be taken; instead of having different mechanisms for secondary and virtual memories, capabilities could be used as a *single* means of referring to objects. This approach, termed *capability-based addressing*, associates a unique capability with any object, regardless of its current location in the system. Consequently, the same capability is used by the file system to retrieve the object and by the memory mapping mechanisms when reading, writing, or executing the object in virtual storage.

This uniform approach to addressing thus erases the distinction between pointers to objects residing in virtual memory (the former segment table entries) and those pointing to objects accessed via the file system. That is, a capability is permanent for the lifetime of the object. This can be accomplished by using a *global object table* as shown in Figure 7-4. Each entry in this table points to exactly one object, regardless of where it currently resides. When the object is moved to a different location in the same memory or even between different types of memory, the corresponding entry is updated. A capability is then an index into the global object table, augmented with a set of rights. This permits each subject to have different rights with respect to a given object.

Dynamic Execution Environment.   In a system with a segmented virtual memory, the current execution environment within the directly accessible memory is defined by the contents of the segment table. This table is constructed in most systems when the corresponding process is created and remains constant until its termination. Such a process executes in a static environment. In systems with dynamic linking, such as MULTICS, the individual segment table entries are not filled in until the corresponding segments are actually referenced during execution. The current execution environment of a process is thus changing as new segments are being referenced and entered

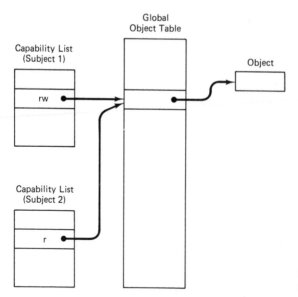

Figure 7-4 Addressing through a global object table.

into the segment table. The change, however, is only in one direction: the current execution environment may grow; however, since segments are never "unlinked," it will never shrink.

To implement a truly dynamic environment in which the number of objects accessible to a process may increase or decrease as execution progresses, additional mechanisms must be provided. In MULTICS, a scheme of concentric protection *rings* has been implemented for this purpose. Each segment is assigned a ring number ranging from 0 to 32. Segments appearing in inner rings are most highly protected, whereas those in outer rings are more accessible in general. Figure 7-5 shows the initial ring assignments in MULTICS; ring assignments are fixed for a given segment and appear as part of the file directory entry for each segment. The operating system occupies the first three rings, with the most critical parts, the nucleus, occupying ring 0; most of the system is in ring 1, and the remainder, the less sensitive segments, reside in ring 2. Rings 3 to 32 may be employed by user processes.

Let E_i be the set of segments residing in ring i at any one time. The basic idea underlying this scheme is that a process executing in any segment S in E_i may access a segment T in E_j in its virtual memory only if $j \geq i$; each access is also subject to the X, R, W protection mode recorded in the access list of T. An attempt to access an inward ring (i.e., $j < i$) results in an interrupt, and control is transferred to a systems routine to verify the validity of the reference. Actually, both inward ($j < i$) and outward ($j > i$) calls generate interrupts. In both cases, if control is successfully transferred out of the current ring, the "executing" ring number must be changed to that of the new ring, and arguments must be checked. For example, a call to a procedure T in an outer ring j might include, as arguments, addresses of variables in ring i (the calling ring); T in E_j will not be able to access these inner ring variables. The solution chosen is to copy the arguments into a data area accessible to T.

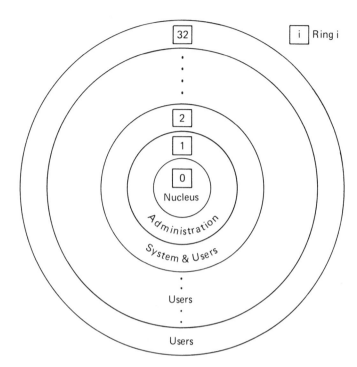

Figure 7-5   Ring protection in MULTICS.

Example

Consider a process p in MULTICS executing two procedures, $P1$ and $P2$, in sequence. The process p has read access to a segment (file) Q, which is recorded in the access list of Q as shown in Figure 7-6a. Assume that we wish to enforce the following constraint: p may access Q only if it is executing in $P1$ but not if it is in $P2$. This can be accomplished by assigning a ring number to Q that is smaller than the ring number of $P2$ but larger or equal to that of $P1$. The assignment shown in the figure satisfies this requirement.

Note that the rings implement a dynamically changing current environment by *restricting* the rights specified by the access lists of different objects. In this example, process p has, in general, read access to Q; the rings, however, restrict this privilege to only a subset of the procedures ($P1$) constituting that process.

The fact that only a very small number of the originally planned 64 rings have been implemented indicates the inadequacy of this scheme. One of the main constraints is the linearity of the ring-based protection mechanisms; objects must be ordered according to the rights they have to one another. Such ordering may not always be possible or convenient since, in general, object references could form an arbitrarily interconnected (e.g., cyclic) graph.

With capability-based systems, implementation of a dynamically changing environment is a natural extension of the basic scheme. Instead of providing a single capability list for the entire process (user), separate capability lists are associated with each

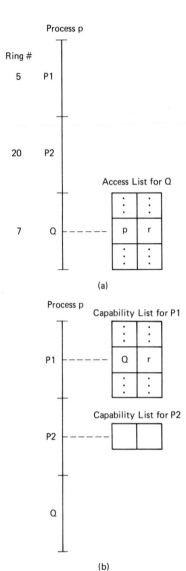

Figure 7-6 Example of protection information: (a) Access lists (b) Capability lists.

object, in particular, a procedure. Thus as a process executes, its current environment is determined by the capability list of the currently executing procedure.

Example

Consider the same process p consisting of the two procedures $P1$ and $P2$, as in the previous example. This time, however, protection information is organized in the form of capability lists. A separate capability list is associated with each of the two procedures $P1$ and $P2$. The requirement that process p may access Q only when executing in $P1$ is then enforced simply by including the capability for Q only in $P1$'s capability list, as shown in Figure 7-6b.

In general, capabilities provide greater flexibility in expressing various protection constraints than the ring-based scheme. For example, we could easily express the constraint that the procedure $P1$ should have only read access to Q, while $P2$ should also have write access to Q. With ring mechanisms, this constraint cannot be expressed, since rights are associated with the object and no discrimination can be made among distinct procedures of the same process. With capabilities, the desired rights are simply included in the appropriate entries of each capability list.

Privileged System States.   Most conventional architectures distinguish between two sets of instructions, privileged and unprivileged. The former are used to access and manipulate various internal registers, control IO devices, or change the current state of the CPU. Consequently, they must be executed only by systems programs. To guarantee that ordinary user programs execute only unprivileged instructions, the CPU may be executing in two distinct states: in the privileged (or system) state, any instruction is valid; in the user state, executing a privileged instruction causes an interrupt that stops the offending process and reports an error. More than two states are distinguished in some systems. For example, VAX-11 distinguishes four processor states, kernel, executive, supervisor, and user, each capable of using a different subset of the existing instructions. This permits a finer subdivision of the operating system into separate levels for further protection.

In capability-based systems, no distinction between different instruction sets and, consequently, between privileged and unprivileged states is necessary. If a purely object-oriented point of view is taken, all operations are viewed as functions applicable to various classes of objects. A given operation can be performed only when it is defined on the desired object type and only when the executing process is in possession of a capability for the object to be manipulated. Hence any process (system or user) is able to perform only those operations reflected by its current environment. For example, scheduling and dispatching of processes is a highly sensitive operation, usually performed by the most privileged parts of the operating system (the kernel). In an object-based system, the tasks of scheduling and dispatching may be viewed as a form of interprocess communication, where processes, seen as objects, are passed among various ports (see Section 3.4.1). There is, however, no need to make such operations privileged in any explicit manner, since only a process with the necessary capabilities for the scheduling and dispatching ports will be able to perform these operations.

The main drawback of capability systems is their relatively high cost and slower speed of execution. These are the main reasons why the majority of computer systems currently on the market are still based on the principles of access lists in file systems and separate protection and addressing mechanisms for main (or virtual) memory.

7.4 PROTECTION PROBLEMS AND SOME PARTIAL SOLUTIONS

Protection systems based on access lists concentrate primarily on the problem of controlling access to objects, without providing any means for specifying and enforcing policies for information flow. Processes are typically seen as the owners of certain objects and have the ability to decide which other processes should be permitted to read, write, or otherwise utilize any of these objects. In systems based on capability addressing, the uniform mechanisms for accessing both primary and secondary memory, together with the ability to vary the current execution environment dynamically, make it possible to solve more sophisticated protection problems. The same is usually true of systems based on non-von Neumann models of computation. For example, Bic has investigated the problems of protection in the context of dataflow systems (Bic, 1982).

The majority of protection problems arise because various subsystems need to cooperate. To illustrate the variety of these problems, let us consider the following general scenario in which two mutually suspicious subsystems wish to exchange different types of information with each other. Assume that a user provides a service subsystem to be employed by other legitimate users of the system. The owner of this service wishes to charge these users for the services rendered. For concreteness, let us assume that the service is a program that calculates the amount of income tax an individual owes to the IRS. To perform this calculation, the service must be supplied the necessary personal data such as income, number of dependents, and deductions. Having completed the appropriate calculations, the service returns the results to its caller. In addition, it should send to its owner sufficient information about the user to be able to generate a bill for the services rendered. This scenario, depicted in Figure 7-7, illustrates a general scheme of mutually suspicious subsystems. Both parties, the owner and the user, involved in the use of the service have different concerns regarding their own security and the security of the service itself. The owner would like to have the following guarantees:

1. No user should be able to steal the service by making a private copy.
2. No user should be able to destroy or otherwise damage the service.
3. No user should be able to employ the service without the owner's permission.
4. The owner should be able to revoke the access of an authorized user to the service.
5. No user (authorized or not) should be able to prevent authorized users from employing the service.

The user's concerns, on the other hand, are the following:

1. The service, when invoked, will not be able to steal, destroy, or otherwise compromise any information or services the user did not explicitly supply to the service.
2. The service should be able to send nonsensitive information to its owner (or some other party) for the purposes of billing or accounting; however, it must not be able to disclose any sensitive information supplied to it by the user.

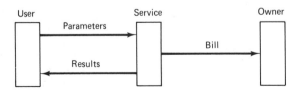

Figure 7-7 General scenario of mutually suspicious subsystems.

Let us consider each of these problems in turn and investigate possible solutions for each.

Access-control Problems.   Problems 1 through 3, expressed by the owner of the service, are typical issues in access control. The first two, theft and destruction of information, are solved through the enforcement of execute-only privileges for an object, some form of which is normally provided in both access-list-oriented as well as capability-based protection schemes. Problem 3, unauthorized use of the service, is more difficult to solve in the case of capabilities since the notion of object ownership has been eliminated. When a process creates a new object, it receives a capability for that object, which may be viewed simply as a pointer with a set of rights. The process may replicate this capability freely, and pass it to any other process it is able to communicate with. When the capability is replicated without restricting any rights, both processes have exactly the same privileges to that object; hence neither (or both) can be considered the object's owner. Even when the rights are reduced before the capability is passed on, the ownership property is not clearly defined. In particular, the original creator process cannot revoke the capability once it has been passed to the other process (see next section). As a consequence, an authorized user of a service could pass the capability for the service to any other user.

To prevent this problem, referred to as *propagation of capabilities*, additional mechanisms must be provided. To illustrate the basic principles, we consider here the HYDRA operating system (Cohen and Jefferson, 1975), that provides extensive access-control mechanisms. A capability for an object o in HYDRA contains a set of generic rights. Here we consider four of these: r, w, s, and l. The first two are the read and write rights (originally called get and put rights in HYDRA). They control the ability of a subject to read/write the contents of the object o. The s and l rights, on the other hand, control the storing and loading of capabilities into/from the object o. That is, s and l control the access to the capability list of o, rather than o's contents. If a subject's capability for o contains the right s, then that subject is permitted to copy any capability from its own list into the capability list of o. Conversely, if x's capability for o contains the right l, then x is permitted to copy any capability from o's capability list into its own list.

To control undesirable propagation of capabilities, HYDRA provides a special right, called *environment right* (e-right, for short). A capability lacking the e-right will be prevented from being copied into any other capability list and thus from propagating through the system. The following example clarifies this concept.

Example

Figure 7-8a shows four objects, A, B, C, and D. A has a capability for object B with the s-right (store), which permits it to copy capabilities from its own capability list to the capability list of B. A's capability for C can be copied into B's list, resulting in the configuration of Figure 7-8b. (We assumed that the e-right was masked out during the transfer.) This transfer is possible for two reasons: A has a capability with an s-right for B *and* the capability being copied has the e-right (i.e., it can be copied). A capability lacking the e-right, such as A's capability for the object D, cannot be copied into another object's

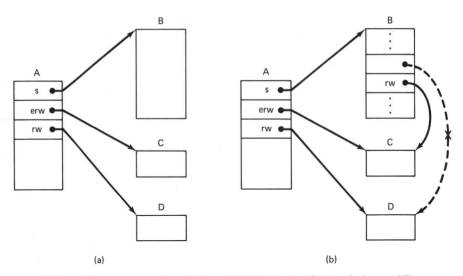

Figure 7-8 Propagation of capabilities: (a) Initial state (b) After transferring capability for C to B.

capability list. Hence, *B* can never gain access to *D* in this constellation. The crossed-out pointer in Figure 7-8b indicates that this connection cannot be established.

Revocation of Privileges.   Closely related to the problems of access control is the fourth concern expressed by the owner, the problem of *revocation* of previously granted privileges. When access lists are used, the owner of the object can simply remove the user's rights from the access list associated with the service. Revocation is much more difficult in capability-based systems, since copies of the same capability may be dispersed throughout the system. To avoid searching for all copies, the idea of indirection may be used. A dummy object, called an *alias*, is created that contains the capability for the service. Individual users are given capabilities for the alias instead of the service itself, as illustrated in Figure 7-9. When revocation of access to the service is desired, the alias is simply destroyed, thus breaking all indirect connections to the service. Using this approach, only *total* revocation may be achieved; that is, *all* users pointing through the same alias have their capabilities removed. It is not possible to remove privileges from users selectively on an individual basis.

Denial of Service.   The last concern expressed by the owner is that of denial of service. In practice, denial of service occurs any time a user is prevented from making sufficient progress. This intuitive measure is, of course, very subjective since insufficient progress may not necessarily be caused by malicious actions on the part of some user or the malfunctioning of hardware or software components. It could be the result of an unexpectedly high demand on some shared resource or a general overloading of the system. Hence, in general, it will not be possible to guarantee that denial of service does not occur. We can, however, provide mechanisms to detect denial of service for some

Capability List

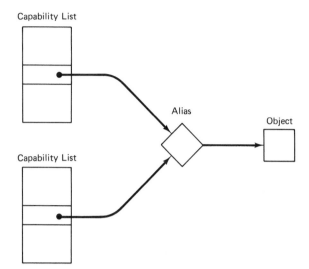

Alias

Object

Capability List

Figure 7-9 Use of aliases for revocation of privileges.

critical resources and inform the user or some higher authority of such situations so that some corrective actions can be initiated. The detection can be accomplished by associating with each service to be monitored a time limit called *maximum service time*. When this time limit is exceeded before the requested service is performed, the process is considered to be making insufficient progress, thus incurring denial of service.

The Trojan Horse Problem.   The first concern expressed by the user of the service is known as the Trojan Horse problem. Analogous to the wooden horse used to sneak enemy soldiers into the city of Troy, who caused its destruction after a 10-year long siege, an unsuspecting user may accept a ''gift'' in the form of a program intended to circumvent the existing protection mechanisms. Because the current execution environment of a process is static in most existing systems, any program, including those borrowed from other users or from the system, will run with the same privileges granted to the currently executing process. Thus a service, such as the tax program discussed previously, might be used as a Trojan Horse to disclose or destroy any information belonging to any user employing that service or to disclose the user's authentication information (e.g., the password) to gain subsequent unauthorized access to the facility.

Systems based on capabilities usually provide a dynamically varying execution environment that enables a user to restrict the privileges of an untrusted service routine. Typically, the procedure calling mechanisms permit the user to explicitly specify as parameters those objects that should be accessible to the procedure after control is transferred. To illustrate this principle, consider the following example, which introduces a simplified version of the procedure call mechanism used in the HYDRA operating system; similar mechanisms exist in the Intel iAPX 432 and other object-oriented systems.

Example

Assume that the current environment of a potential user of the tax service described previously consists of four capabilities as shown in Figure 7-10a: the first points to the code

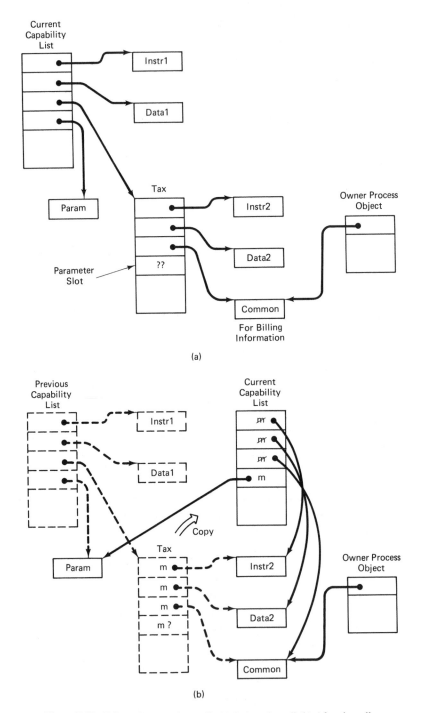

Figure 7-10 Effect of a procedure call: (a) Before the call (b) After the call.

segment *Instr1* of the currently executing procedure (i.e. the procedure that will be issuing the call to the service); the second capability points to a data segment *Data1* used by the current procedure; the third capability points to the procedure Tax to be called; finally, the fourth capability points to a data segment *Param* to be passed to the procedure Tax as a parameter. The latter contains the caller's personal data to be processed by the service.

The procedure Tax itself is represented by a capability list containing capabilities for instructions (*Instr2*) to be executed and data (*Data2*) to be used when Tax is invoked, and a capability for an object labeled *Common*, which it shares with the service's owner. This object is used to transfer the necessary billing information to the owner.

Execution of the procedure call results in the creation of a new current environment for the Tax procedure as shown in Figure 7-10b. (Ignore for a moment the m-rights in the Tax object.) This environment inherits all capabilities contained originally in the procedure's capability list. These are the three capabilities pointing to the instructions, the data, and the common object. The new environment also contains the capabilities for any objects passed to the Tax procedure as parameters; in our case it is the object *Param*. The procedure Tax computes the results based on the information contained in *Data2* and *Param*, writes these into *Param* (or some other object passed to it as a parameter), writes the billing information into *Common*, and executes a return instruction. This automatically restores the current environment to that used before the call, while the environment created for the procedure Tax is destroyed.

This procedure call mechanism satisfies the requirements of a user invoking an untrusted service to restrict the service's current environment to those objects explicitly passed to it as parameters. The Tax procedure, for example, has no way of accessing the segment *Data1* belonging to the caller. As a result, the threat of a Trojan Horse attack is eliminated.

The Selective Confinement Problem.

While the Trojan Horse problem is concerned with protecting information *not* supplied to a service, the second concern expressed by the user is to prevent sensitive information actually entrusted to the service from being compromised. This is usually referred to as the *selective confinement problem*. A special case of selective confinement is *total* confinement, in which *no* information passed to the service by a user may ever be disclosed to any other party, including the service's owner.

The Trojan Horse problem is largely a matter of access control: the service should be prevented from gaining access to objects not supplied to it by the caller. Selective confinement, on the other hand, is a problem of illegal information flow: the service must be prevented from propagating information, entrusted to it legally for processing, to other users.

Due to the difficulty of distinguishing between sensitive information, which must be prevented from escaping, and nonsensitive information, which is needed by the owner for the purposes of billing, few existing systems provide mechanisms that offer a satisfactory solution for the general case of selective confinement. In fact, it has been shown (Fenton, 1974) that, in theory, this problem is unsolvable.

However, total confinement, which prevents any information from leaving the service, can be enforced for most practical purposes. We consider again the capability-based system shown in Figure 7-10a and b. The objective now is to prevent the procedure Tax from writing *any* information into the object *Common*, as well as into any other object potentially shared with other processes. In HYDRA, this has been solved by providing a special right, called *modify* right (m-right for short), that, when removed from a capability, prevents any write access to the corresponding object. The procedure call mechanism described previously is then extended to permit the caller to *mask* out the m-right from all capabilities in the new environment except those passed to it as parameters. This is illustrated in Figure 7-10b, where the only capability that retains its m-right after the procedure has been invoked is the capability for the object *Param*, passed to it as a parameter. Since this is the only object into which any information may be written by the called procedure, total confinement is guaranteed. (Note, however, that total confinement prevents the owner from billing the user in the tax example!)

  Sneaky Signaling. The objective of confinement (both total and selective) is to prevent sensitive information from escaping out of the service procedure. Unfortunately, there are a number of possible implicit covert channels through which information may be conveyed to an observer. The use of such channels for information disclosure is called *sneaky signaling*. In theory, an element with two different states, representing 0 and 1, is sufficient to encode and transmit any amount of information when interrogated repeatedly over time. For example, the disclosure of a single bit may encode the fact that the caller's income is greater than a certain value.

  There are many possible patterns of behavior a service might display to signal binary information to an observer. For example, using different IO devices, opening certain files, or generating error messages depending on the current information content may be used to convey information outside of the system. Similarly, information may be encoded and passed by controlling the patterns of tape movement or of sound waves emanating from a printing device. The use of different time delays caused intentionally as a way to encode sensitive information is particularly difficult to detect and prevent. For example, the execution of a long loop could be initiated or suppressed based on some sensitive data, thus signaling one bit of information. Since such time delays are potentially unbounded, the problem of sneaky signaling and thus the selective confinement problem are quite impractical to solve, even when limiting assumptions about the system and its environment are made. In their full generality, the problems have been proved to be theoretically unsolvable.

7.5 FORMAL MODELS OF PROTECTION

In Section 7.4 we discussed the general issues in access and information control and presented a number of concrete problems and some possible informal solutions. In many situations, however, users will not be satisfied with an intuitive description of the protection system. Rather, a formal model that permits one to specify the exact policies and mechanism required to guarantee system security is needed. Such a model may then be used to formally reason about possible access and information flow policies in the system and prove various properties of the protection scheme.

7.5.1 The Access Matrix Model

Following a number of attempts at modeling protection systems (Dennis and Van Horn, 1966; Graham and Denning, 1972; Jones, 1973; Lampson, 1971), Harrison, Ruzzo, and Ullman (1976) developed a formal model of protection, called the access matrix model, that permits the *proof* of various global properties of protection systems. The major objective of this research was to solve the *safety* problem, defined as the ability to determine in a given situation whether a subject can gain access to a given object.

Definition of the Model.   A protection system is modeled as a set of *subjects* S, a set of *objects* O, where S is a superset of O, and an *access matrix* A. For each subject s and each object o, the access matrix records the *rights* the subject has with respect to the object. Rights are selected from a finite set of *generic* rights defined for a given protection system. Each right may be viewed as representing an operation that can be applied to an object. Typical representatives of generic rights are read, write, and execute rights.

The basic form of the access matrix is depicted in Figure 7-11, where $s_1, \ldots, s_n$ denote subjects and $o_1, \ldots, o_m$ denote objects; the first n objects are assumed to be the subjects $s_1, \ldots, s_n$; that is, $s_i = o_i$ for $1 \le i \le n$. The intersection of the ith row with the jth column in the access matrix contains a possibly empty set of rights that the subject s_i has with respect to the object o_j. Each *row* of the access matrix may be viewed as a *capability* list for the corresponding subject, while each *column* may be viewed as an *access* list associated with an object. Hence the access matrix model presents a unifying view of modeling the two different approaches to protection.

The triple (S, O, A), where S is the set of subjects, O is the set of objects, and A is an access matrix, is referred to as the *state* or *configuration* of the protection system. To change the state of the protection system, the access matrix model provides the fol-

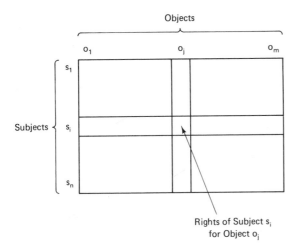

Rights of Subject s_i
for Object o_j

Figure 7-11 Access control matrix.

lowing six *primitive operations*, each of which may be executed only when the corresponding conditions are satisfied:

1. enter r **into** $A(s, o)$
    Actions: Enter the right r into the matrix A at the coordinates (s, o); if r already exists in that cell then there is no change.
    Conditions: s is an existing subject; o is an existing object.

2. delete r **from** $A(s, o)$
    Actions: Remove the right r from the matrix A at the coordinates (s, o); if r is absent from that cell, then there is no change.
    Conditions: s is an existing subject; o is an existing object.

3. create subject s'
    Actions: Create a new row *and* a new column in A labeled s'; all entries in that row and column are empty.
    Conditions: s' is not an already existing object.

4. create object o'
    Actions: Create a new column in A labeled o'; all entries in that column are empty.
    Conditions: o' is not an already existing object.

5. destroy subject s'
    Actions: Remove the column *and* the row labeled s' from A.
    Conditions: s' is an existing subject.

6. destroy object o'
    Actions: Remove the column labeled o' from A.
    Conditions: o' is an existing object but is not a subject.

Each of these primitive operations p changes the state of the protection system; this is denoted as

$$(S, O, A) \vdash_p (S', O', A')$$

For example, the operation **enter** r **into** $A(s, o)$ would create a new state in which $S' = S$, $O' = O$, and $A'(s, o)$ contains the right r.

To model a variety of protection systems, the access matrix model permits primitive operations to be combined into *commands* of the form

$$c(x_1, \ldots, x_n) \equiv \textbf{if } c_1, \ldots, c_m \textbf{ then } p_1; \ldots; p_k$$

where $x_1, \ldots, x_n$ are formal parameters of the command c; each x_i may be a subject or object used as a parameter in the command body
    $c_1, \ldots, c_m$ are conditions of the form $r \in A(s, o)$
    $p_1; \ldots; p_k$ are primitive operations as defined previously
Only if *all* conditions $c_1, \ldots, c_m$ are satisfied, will the sequence of primitive operations $p_1; \ldots; p_k$ be executed; else the entire command will fail.

In the case where $m = 0$ (i.e., there are no conditions), the command degenerates to the form

$$c(x_1, \ldots, x_n) \equiv p_1; \ldots; p_k$$

Each successful command c results in the following sequence of transformations:

$$(S_0, O_0, A_0) \vdash_{p_1} (S_1, O_1, A_1) \ldots \vdash_{p_k} (S_k, O_k, A_k)$$

where $p_1, \ldots, p_k$ are the primitive operations constituting the command c and (S_0, O_0, A_0) is the state of the protection system prior to executing c. We will abbreviate the sequence of transformations as follows:

$$(S_0, O_0, A_0) \vDash_c (S_k, O_k, A_k)$$

Example

> To illustrate how the access matrix model may be used to model an existing protection system, assume we wish to implement the following protection policy: Any subject may create an object for which it will be granted the rights r, w, and *own*. The first two of these are the obvious read and write rights for that object, while the *own* right designates the subject as the sole owner of that object. Rights may propagate through the system according to the following two rules:

> **1.** The owner of an object may confer the read or write rights to any other subject.
> **2.** Any subject with a read right to an object may confer that right on any other subject.

> This policy may be implemented by providing the following commands:

> $create(s, o)$ ≡ **create object** o; **enter** r **into** $A(s, o)$; **enter** w **into** $A(s, o)$;
>   **enter** *own* **into** $A(s, o)$;
> $owner\_confer\_read(s_1, s_2, o)$ ≡ **if** $own \in A(s_1, o)$ **then enter** r **into** $A(s_2, o)$;
> $owner\_confer\_write(s_1, s_2, o)$ ≡ **if** $own \in A(s_1, o)$ **then enter** w **into** $A(s_2, o)$;
> $nonowner\_confer\_read(s_1, s_2, o)$ ≡ **if** $r \in A(s_1, o)$ **then enter** r **into** $A(s_2, o)$;

> The first of these four commands permits the creation of an object o; note that there is no condition associated with this action. The *owner_confer_read* and *owner_confer_write* commands permit the owner s_1 of an object o to confer the respective read and write rights for the object o upon another subject s_2. Finally, the last command permits any subject s_1 that possesses the read right for an object o to confer that right on some other subject s_2.

> ***Deciding System Safety.***   The main objective of the access matrix model was to investigate the problem of safety, that is, the ability to determine in a given situation whether a subject may acquire a particular right to an object. Formally, we can define safety as follows:

> **1.** Given a protection system, we say a command $c(x_1, \ldots, x_n)$ *leaks* a generic right r from a state (S, O, A) if c, when issued in state (S, O, A), can execute a primitive operation that enters the right r into a cell $A(s, o)$ that did not previously contain r.

2. We say a protection system is *safe* in state (S, O, A) for a generic right r if there does *not* exist a state (S', O', A') and a command c such that

   (a) (S', O', A') is derivable from (S, O, A) via a sequence of commands $c_1, \ldots, c_n$; that is,

$$(S, O, A) \vDash_{c_1} \ldots \vDash_{c_n} (S', O', A')$$

   (b) c leaks r from (S', O', A').

Informally, a protection system is safe for a right r in a given state if r is never copied into a cell $A(s, o)$ that does not already contain it, regardless of which commands provided by the protection system are executed. Harrison, Ruzzo, and Ullman (1976) have shown that, for an arbitrary set of commands, *it is undecidable[†] whether a given state of a protection system is safe for a given generic right*. While this result may seem rather disappointing, we are not always faced with the safety question in its most general form; rather, a number of restricted cases may be considered for which safety is decidable. For example, when each command is restricted to perform only *one* primitive operation, there exists an algorithm that decides whether a system is safe in a given state for a given right. Such systems are called *mono-operational*. Another example of a restricted system is the take-grant model presented in the next section. This is also a derivative of the general access matrix model for which safety may be decided. Hence the access matrix model in its most general form serves as the basis for a large variety of more specialized protection models.

7.5.2 The Take-Grant Model

The access matrix in an actual system is normally very sparse. Hence the same information conveyed by the matrix may be represented more efficiently in the form of a graph, where objects and subjects are represented by nodes and rights are represented by directed labeled arcs pointing from subjects to objects or to other subjects. Depending on the possible rights and the rules governing their propagation, there exists a variety of take-grant models. In this section we present the results derived by Jones, Lipton, and Snyder (Jones, Lipton, and Snyder, 1976; Lipton and Snyder, 1977; Snyder, 1977; Snyder, 1981).

Definition of the Model. We will define the take-grant model as consisting of the following components:

1. A set of subjects, represented as solid circles (●).
2. A set of objects, represented as empty circles (○).

Together, subjects and objects constitute the nodes of the take-grant graph. If we do not need to distinguish whether a node is a subject or object, we represent it as a crossed circle (⊗).

[†] Informally, a problem is undecidable if there does not exist an algorithm to solve it. For a formal definition, see for example Hopcroft and Ullman (1969).

3. A set of *generic rights* $r_1, \ldots, r_n, t, g$, where $r_1, \ldots, r_n$ can be any generic right such as read, write, or execute, while t and g are special rights called *take* and *grant*, respectively. Five graph-rewriting rules govern the propagation of rights throughout the system. These rules are defined as follows:

* *create__subject*(s_1, s_2, ρ)
  Action: Subject s_1 creates a new subject s_2 with the set of rights ρ to it. Graphically, this may be depicted as follows:

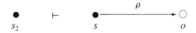

* *create__object*(s, o, ρ)
  Action: Subject s creates a new object o with the set of rights ρ to it. Graphically, this may be depicted as follows:

* *take*(s, x_1, x_2, r)
  Action: Subject s takes from x_1 (which could be an object or a subject) the right r for x_2 (object or subject).
  Conditions: s must have the right t for x_1, and x_1 must have the right r for x_2. Graphically, this may be depicted as follows:

* *grant*(s, x_1, x_2, r)
  Action: Subject s grants to x_1 the right r for x_2.
  Conditions: s must have the right g for x_1 and the right r for x_2. Graphically, this may be depicted as follows:

* *remove*(s, x, r)
  Action: Subject s removes the right r from the set of rights α it has for x (object or subject). (*Note:* When the set of rights becomes empty, the arc from s to x is removed.) Graphically, this may be depicted as follows:

As with the access matrix model, each of the graph-rewriting rules changes the state of the protection system represented by a graph G; this is denoted as

$$G \vdash_p G'$$

where p is the graph-rewriting rule and G' is the new state. The following example illustrates the application of the graph-rewriting rules.

Example

Consider the graph in Figure 7-12a, which shows that x has read and take rights for a subject y and read and grant rights for a subject z. We wish to answer the following question: Is it possible for y to read z? In other words, is there a sequence of transformations $G_0 \vdash_{p_1} G_1 \vdash_{p_2} \ldots \vdash_{p_n} G_n$ such that G_0 is the initial graph (Figure 7-12a) and G_n contains an arc with a read right from y to z? The answer to this question is yes; Figure 7-12b shows one such sequence of transformations that leaves the graph in the desired state.

Deciding System Safety. As was the case with the access matrix model, the main objective of the take-grant model is to determine system safety. Jones, Lipton, and Snyder (1976) have captured the safety question in two predicates, *can__share* and *can__steal*, defined as follows: Assume that G_0 is a protection graph, x_1 and x_2 are vertices in G_0, and ρ is a set of rights. The predicate

$$can\_share\,(\rho, x_1, x_2, G_0)$$

is defined to be true if and only if (1) there are graphs $G_1, \ldots, G_n$ such that $G_0 \vdash_{p_1} G_1 \vdash_{p_2} \ldots \vdash_{p_n} G_n$ and (2) there exists an edge $x_1 \overset{\rho}{\to} x_2$ in G_n. Informally, this may be paraphrased as follows: The predicate *can__share* yields the value true if and only if there exists a sequence of transformations such that x_1 can gain the rights ρ for x_2.

The second predicate,

$$can\_steal\,(\rho, x_1, x_2, G_0)$$

is defined to be true if and only if (1) there are graphs $G_1, \ldots, G_n$ such that $G_0 \vdash_{p_1} G_1 \vdash_{p_2} \ldots \vdash_{p_n} G_n$, (2) there exists an edge $x_1 \overset{\rho}{\to} x_2$ in G_n, and (3) if some subject y_1 has the right ρ for x_2 in G_0, then no graph-rewriting rule p_i in the sequence $G_0 \vdash_{p_1} G_1 \vdash_{p_2} \ldots \vdash_{p_n} G_n$ has the form $grant(\,y_1, y_2, x_2, \rho\,)$ for any y_2.

The first two rules of *can__steal* are the same as those for the *can__share* predicate. The third rule states that no subject y_1, who originally had the right ρ for x_2, will ever grant it to any other subject y_2 during the transformation of G_0 to G_n. This rule implies the following fundamental difference between the two predicates. In the case of *can__share* we were interested in determining whether or not there was *any* way for x_1 to gain the rights ρ for x_2. This assumed that other subjects were willing to *cooperate* in making this transfer possible. In the case of *can__steal*, such cooperation was precluded by rule 3. The *can__steal* predicate becomes true only if x_1 succeeds in gaining the rights *on its own* (i.e., without relying on some other subject to grant the ρ rights to someone else).

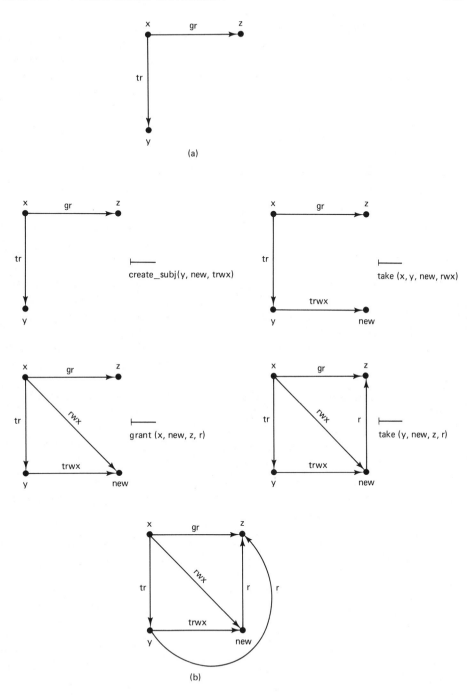

Figure 7-12   Transformation of a Take/Grant graph: (a) Initial graph (b) Sequence of transformations.

Snyder has formulated necessary and sufficient conditions for testing the truth value of the two predicates. By applying these tests, which can be performed in linear time, to a given protection graph, the system's safety can be decided. To illustrate the type of conditions one has to evaluate, we first consider a restricted case of a protection graph, where *all* vertices are subjects. In this case, the following theorem can be proved.

Theorem 1.   The predicate *can__share*(ρ, x_1, x_2, G_0) is true if and only if the following conditions hold simultaneously:

1. There exists at least one vertex y_1 in G_0 such that $y_1 \xrightarrow{\beta} x_2$, where $\rho \subseteq \beta$. Informally, this requires that initially at least one subject must have the ρ right for x_2.

2. x_1 and y_1 are tg-connected, where two vertices are defined as being tg-connected if, ignoring the directionality of the edges, there is a path between them such that each edge on the path is labeled t, g, or both. Informally, this condition requires the existence of a path along which the right can be propagated.

For a given protection graph, condition 1 is easily verified by simply examining all edges incident to x_2. To verify condition 2, a number of well-known connectivity algorithms may be applied. Hence, under the simplifying assumption that all vertices of a protection graph represent subjects, safety can be determined in linear time.

For unrestricted graphs, a simple sufficient (but not necessary) condition to test the *can__share* predicate exists. This is given by the following theorem:

Theorem 2.   The predicate *can__share*(ρ, x_1, x_2, G_0) is true if the following conditions hold simultaneously:

1. There exists at least one subject y_1 in G_0 such that $y_1 \xrightarrow{\beta} x_2$, where $\rho \subseteq \beta$. (This condition is the same as for Theorem 1.)

2. x_1 and y_1 are *directly* tg-connected, where direct tg-connectivity is defined as a special case of general tg-connectivity: two vertices are directly tg-connected if they are connected by an edge labeled t or g; the direction of the edge is irrelevant.

Similar results have been obtained for the *can__steal* predicate in unrestricted protection graphs. The interested reader is referred to Snyder (1981).

7.5.3 The Bell–LaPadula Model

The access matrix model and the take-grant model presented in previous sections have the following two major characteristics in common:

1. They are concerned mainly with the problem of *safety* (i.e., the question whether a subject may gain access to a given object).

2. They model only policies in which each subject is *responsible* for the dissemination of information to which it has access.

These characteristics imply that it is not possible to guarantee unauthorized information flow since sensitive information may be disclosed without explicitly granting access rights to the object containing or able to obtain such information. For example, there is nothing to prevent a process having legal access to secret documents to read or copy their contents and pass the obtained information to some other process with no clearance for secret materials. Consequently, models based on only access control must rely on the proper conduct of the involved subjects; if these choose not to obey the imposed rules, no guarantees regarding information dissemination can be given. Hence access control models are not sufficient in many areas of application.

The security requirements of the Department of Defense motivated much of the research in controlling the flow of information. The military, as well as a number of other institutions, base their information management policies on a hierarchy of *security classes*. Each object is associated with a particular level in that hierarchy and each subject is assigned a certain *clearance*. Permission to access an object is then governed by rules that take into account the type of access requested, the object's classification, and the subject's clearance. Such policies are called *nondiscretionary* since access to objects is granted based on a security class, rather than a subject's identity. Note, however, that the need for *discretionary* security policies, which grant privileges on an individual basis, is not eliminated. The military, for example, enforces the principle of *need-to-know*, according to which each subject should be permitted to access only those objects it needs to perform its duties. Such policies must be based on the subject's identity.

An important requirement imposed on a security system is the ability to formally *verify* its correctness. The complexity of such a task dictates that the programs to be verified are kept as small as possible. This requirement led to the idea of a *security kernel*, a small nucleus of the system containing all mechanisms associated with protection and security. Most existing security kernels today are based on the fundamental principles formulated by Bell and LaPadula at the MITRE Corporation. The resulting model, named after its creators, thus represents one of the first attempts to formalize the problem of information flow control.

Basic Principles of the Model.   The Bell–LaPudula model (Bell and LaPadula, 1973a, b, c; 1984) can be viewed as an extension of the access matrix model in that discretionary policies, enforced individually for each subject, have been augmented by a layer of nondiscretionary policies, based on a classification hierarchy. A protection system is viewed as a finite-state machine, where the current state is represented by a set of subjects, a set of objects, and an access matrix. Each entry of the access matrix may contain a set of generic rights, which represents the discretionary access information. The following four generic rights were defined: read, append, execute, and read/write.

To change the state of the system (i.e., the current contents of the access matrix), the following set of operations, similar to those of the access matrix model, are provided:

1. *get* permits a subject to acquire one or more of the generic rights (read, append, execute, or read/write) to an object.

2. *release* accomplishes the inverse of *get*; it permits a subject to give up one or more of the generic rights it has to an object.

3. *give* permits a subject to confer generic rights for an object upon another subject.

4. *rescind* accomplishes the inverse of *give*; it permits a subject to remove from another subject some generic rights for an object.

5. *create* includes a new object in the access matrix.

6. *delete* removes (deactivates) an object from the access matrix.

7. *change security level* allows a subject to alter its security level.

In addition to the discretionary information recorded in the access matrix, each subject is assigned a clearance and each object is associated with a classification level. It is assumed that these assignments do not change during execution, a property called the *tranquillity principle*.

The heart of the information flow control mechanisms implements the following two properties:

1. The *simple security condition* requires that a subject *s* may not read from an object *o* unless the classification level of *o* is less than or equal to the clearance of *s*. Formally, this can be denoted as $c(o) \leq c(s)$, where $c(o)$ and $c(s)$ are the classification level of *o* and the clearance of *s*, respectively. This establishes a simple hierarchy such that a subject with a certain clearance may read information only at the same or lower classification level. For example, given the four-level military hierarchy of unclassified, confidential, secret, and top secret, a subject cleared for secret documents may also read those classified as confidential or unclassified, but not top secret.

2. The *∗-property*[†] requires that a subject may not have write access to an object *o* unless the classification level of *o* is greater than or equal to the clearance of *s*. Formally, $c(o) \geq c(s)$. Intuitively, the ∗-property prevents any copying of information to lower classification levels than the level of the subject performing the operation. For example, a subject classified for the secret level may create documents with only secret or top-secret status, but not confidential or unclassified.

The consequence of the two properties is that information can flow only in one direction, from lower to higher classification levels in the hierarchy. Figure 7-13 illustrates this graphically for two objects with security clearances *i* and *j*, respectively; the possible flow of information due to reading is shown by dashed lines, while solid lines indicate the information flow due to writing. Note that a subject *s* requiring both read and write privileges to an object *o* must have a clearance *equivalent* to the classification of *o*; formally, $c(o) = c(s)$.

Bell and LaPadula have shown that each of the seven operations provided by the model to change the state of the protection system preserves *both* the simple security

---

[†]Pronounced "star property."

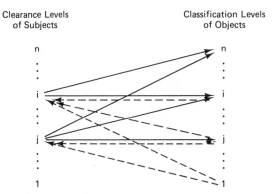

Clearance Levels
of Subjects

Classification Levels
of Objects

Figure 7-13 Possible flow of information
in the Bell-LaPadula model.

condition and the ∗-property. Thus it is guaranteed that no unauthorized flow of information is possible in a system based on this model.

7.5.4 A Lattice Model of Information Flow

The Bell–LaPadula model presented in Section 7.5.3 attempted to constrain the flow of information among objects by providing a classification scheme that, together with a set of legal rules, guarantees that information will flow from one object to another only if the target object has the same or higher classification level than the source. Unfortunately, such a *total ordering* of objects is too restrictive for many applications and, as a consequence, a number of useful policies cannot be expressed. Consider, for example, four objects, x_1, x_2, y_1, and y_2, and the following policy: information may flow from x_1 to y_1 and from x_2 to y_2 but not from x_1 to y_2 or from x_2 to y_1. Using only the simple security condition and the ∗-property of the Bell–LaPadula model, this policy cannot be specified. This is because any linear ordering of the four objects will place either x_1 above y_2 or x_2 above y_1, thus permitting an undesired flow of information.

To permit the specification and enforcement of permissible flow of information among objects in a simpler and more elegant manner, Denning proposed a new model, called the lattice model of secure information flow, which extends the basic flow-control mechanisms of Bell and LaPadula.

Definition of the Model.   The lattice model (Denning, 1976) is defined by the following five components; the first three are the same as those introduced with models presented earlier:

1. A set of *subjects* S; these are the active agents capable of causing information flow.
2. A set of *objects* O capable of storing information. Depending on the desired granularity of the protection system, these could be files, program segments, or even individual variables. Subjects could also be included in the set of objects.
3. A set of *security classes* C corresponding to disjoint levels of protection. Each

object from the set O is assigned a security class; we will consider only the case where the assignments are performed statically (i.e., the security class of an object may not change during execution).

4. A *class-combining operator* $\oplus$; for any operation involving two objects the operator $\oplus$ specifies the security class of the resulting object.

5. A *flow relation* $\rightarrow$; this specifies the legal flow of information between any two security classes.

The set of security classes C, the flow relation $\rightarrow$, and the class-combining operator $\oplus$ is required to form a mathematical structure called a *lattice*. A lattice is defined as a partially ordered set in which each pair of elements has a least upper bound and a greatest lower bound with respect to the class-combining operator. In the case of the tuple $(C, \rightarrow, \oplus)$ a lattice will be formed under the following assumptions:

1. C is finite.

2. C is partially ordered with respect to $\rightarrow$; this will be true when $\rightarrow$ is reflexive, transitive, and antisymmetric.

3. C has a lower bound l such that $l \rightarrow c$ for all $c \in C$.

4. $\oplus$ is a least upper bound operator on C; this can be shown by proving that, for all $a, b, c \in C$:
   (i) $(a \rightarrow a \oplus b) \wedge (b \rightarrow a \oplus b)$
   (ii) $(a \rightarrow c) \wedge (b \rightarrow c) \Rightarrow (a \oplus b \rightarrow c)$

Examples

1. Consider the simple linear classification ordering used by the military consisting of the four levels of unclassified, confidential, secret, and top secret. This ordering forms a lattice, since it can be shown to satisfy the four properties as follows:
   (a) The set $C = \{$ *unclassified, confidential, secret, top-secret* $\}$ is obviously finite.
   (b) C is partially ordered with respect to the flow relation $\rightarrow$:

   $$unclassified \rightarrow confidential \rightarrow secret \rightarrow top \; secret$$

   (c) The lower bound l is the element *unclassified*.
   (d) The class-combining operator $\oplus$ on C is the higher of any two given elements; formally, $C[i] \oplus C[j] = C[\max(i, j)]$, where $C[1] = $ *unclassified*, $C[2] = $ *confidential*, $C[3] = $ *secret*, and $C[4] = $ *top secret*. It is easily shown that $\oplus$ is a least upper bound operator.

2. Consider a system containing three types of records: medical, financial, and criminal. An object can be classified as containing one or more of the three types of information; for instance, an object could contain purely medical information, a combination of medical and criminal, or perhaps all three types. Information of a given type may flow only into objects classified as containing that information type. This can be expressed by the lattice shown in Figure 7-14 where:
   (a) The set of security classes C is the *power set* of the set $\{$ *medical, financial, criminal* $\}$; hence C is finite.

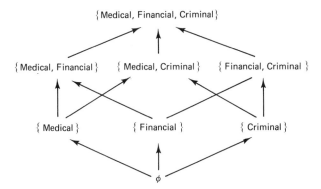

Figure 7-14 Example of an information flow lattice.

(b) The flow relation $\rightarrow$ is the subset operator $\subseteq$; hence C is partially ordered with respect to $\subseteq$.

(c) The lower bound of C is the empty set $\varnothing$.

(d) The class-combining operator $\oplus$ is the set union $\cup$; this is also a least upper bound operator on C.

Enforcement of Secure Information Flow.   The lattice defines the legal flow of information among all objects constituting the system. By definition, a system is considered secure if it does not cause any information flow that violates the given flow relation $\rightarrow$. Hence we must guarantee that no operation performed by a subject can cause information to flow against the arrows of the given lattice. For this purpose, we can distinguish two types of statements, unconditional and conditional, and define a program to be an arbitrarily nested sequence of the two types of statements.

Let the following expression be representative of the class of *unconditional* statements, which includes all arithmetic and logical operations as well as simple assignment statements:

$$o_{result} := f(o_1, \ldots, o_n)$$

This causes explicit information flow from the input objects (variables) $o_1, \ldots, o_n$ into the output object o_{result}. To guarantee that the flow relation is not violated, the security class of the result produced by the function f is determined by applying the operator $\oplus$ to the security classes of the individual objects o_i. Only if the resulting security class is lower than or equal to the security class assigned to o_{result} is the operation permitted; otherwise, a security violation error must be reported. Formally, this test can be expressed as

if $c(o_1) \oplus \ldots \oplus c(o_n) \le c(o_{result})$ **then** proceed **else** error

where $c(o_i)$ denotes the security class assigned to object o_i.

Consider again the lattice of Figure 7-14. Assume that $c(o_1) = medical$ and $c(o_2) = criminal$. Since $c(o_1) \oplus c(o_2) = medical \cup criminal = \{medical, criminal\}$, any function that combines information from o_1 and o_2 into a result object o_{result} will be permitted to proceed only when $c(o_{result}) = \{$ *medical, criminal* $\}$ or $c(o_{result}) = \{$ *medical, financial, criminal* $\}$.

Let the following expression be representative of the second type of statement, which performs an assignment based on a *condition*; examples of such statements are the **if-then-else** or the **while-do** statements.

$$\textbf{condition: } p(o_1, \ldots, o_n)$$
$$\textbf{action: } o_{result} := f(o_{n+1}, \ldots, o_m)$$

where the assignment statement is performed only if the corresponding condition is satisfied. (Note that the sets of objects $o_1, \ldots, o_n$ and $o_{n+1}, \ldots, o_m$ do not have to be disjoint.)

This statement causes *explicit* information flow from the objects $o_{n+1}, \ldots, o_m$ into the object o_{result} if the predicate p yields the value *true*. In addition, and less obviously, information will flow from the objects $o_1, \ldots, o_n$ into o_{result}, regardless of whether the assignment statement is actually executed or not; such information flow is called *implicit*.

To illustrate the implicit type of information flow, consider the following sequence of statements in some programming language:

$$Z := 1;$$
$$Y := 2;$$
$$\textbf{if } X = 0 \textbf{ then } Z := Y$$

After execution of these three statements, we will be able to deduce some information about the value of X by testing the new value of Z: if $Z = 2$ then X must have been equal to zero. Thus, in addition to the explicit information from Y to Z when the conditional assignment statement $Z := Y$ is executed, some amount of information flows implicitly from X to Z, regardless of whether that assignment statement is actually executed.

To prevent any unauthorized flow of information, explicit or implicit, the following test must be performed for each conditional statement:

$$\textbf{if } c(o_1) \oplus \ldots \oplus c(o_n) \oplus c(o_{n+1}) \oplus \ldots \oplus c(o_m) \leq c(o_{result}) \textbf{ then } \text{proceed } \textbf{else } \text{error}$$

where each $c(o_i)$ denotes the security class assigned to object o_i.

The lattice model offers a powerful formalism that permits the specification of a wide variety of flow-control policies. In particular, the lattice model is one of the few existing schemes that offers a solution to the selective confinement problem discussed in Section 7.4. The necessary confinement is accomplished by assigning different security classes to objects containing sensitive and nonsensitive information passed to a service. Computations that use only nonsensitive information will yield results that may be propagated to other subjects, for example for the purposes of billing. The use of sensitive information, on the other hand, raises the security level of the result, thus preventing it from being disclosed.

We have presented two basic types of formal protection models. The first was concerned primarily with access control, that is, the problem of preventing unauthorized access to objects for the purpose of information disclosure, destruction, or unauthorized use of services. The second type addressed the problem of information propagation. This can take place without any violation of access privileges to objects; hence controlling the dissemination of information is, in general, more difficult to specify and enforce than the dissemination of access privileges.

The choice of a model will always depend on the type of system or application in which it is to be implemented, the type of problems to be solved, and the cost of its implementation. The latter may further be subdivided into the actual dollar cost of turning a given model into a working hardware/software subsystem and the indirect cost of possible performance degradation due to the protection mechanisms.

Regardless of the protection model, however, one must always keep in mind that there is no total solution to the global protection problem. Any model will address only some part of the general problem but will leave many gaps in the protective "fire walls" of a system for possible attacks. Some of these, for example the sneaky signaling problems discussed in Section 7.4, cannot theoretically be solved. Others will require combinations of various internal and external safeguards to guarantee a reasonable level of system security. In general, the system designer will have to weigh the cost of providing the various protection mechanisms against the cost of possible damage resulting from security breaches.

EXERCISES

7.1. Passwords may be stolen through wire tapping on the communication line between the system and a terminal. Assume that the system and each terminal are equipped with an encoding/decoding unit. Simply encoding the password in the terminal and decoding it in the system would not solve the problem. (Why?) Using the available decoder/encoder units, devise a scheme to make wire tapping ineffective in this case. (*Hint:* Let the system generate a random number and send it to the terminal when a log in is to be performed.)

7.2. Consider two users *A* and *B* with the following privileges: *A* can read and write a file *F* and read, write, and execute a service program *P*; *B* can only read *F* and execute *P*. An intruder has managed to:
   (a) Guess *A*'s password.
   (b) Guess *B*'s password.
   (c) Place a passive tap on *A*'s terminal line; however, the password transmission is protected through encryption (see Exercise 7.1).
   (d) Place an active tap on *A*'s terminal line (password transmission is protected as in part (c)).
   For each of these cases, describe a simple scenario (if one exists) that would lead to each of the following problems:

   • Information disclosure

- Information destruction
- Unauthorized use of services
- Denial of service

7.3. Consider the *NL_map* procedure used by systems with both segmentation and paging (Section 7.3.2). Simplify that procedure for systems with only segmentation; show the new procedure and the corresponding *ST_entry* record.

7.4. Repeat Exercise 7.3 for systems with only paging; show the new procedure and the corresponding *PT_entry* record.

7.5. Consider again the compiler of Exercise 2.12 and assume a protection system based on access lists.
   (a) For each of the data structures (files) *AL*, *ILC*, and *OM*, show the minimal access lists that still permit the compiler to operate correctly.
   (b) Assume that the process p_1 is divided into two procedures A_{om} and A_{both}. Using the scheme of concentric protection rings, assign ring numbers to the appropriate procedures and data structures such that A_{om} can access only *OM*, while A_{both} can access both *OM* and *AL*.
   (c) Is it possible to assign protection rings such that each procedure can access only one of the data structures but not the other? Explain.
   (d) Assume that process p_2 is divided into three procedures, A_{om}, $A_{om/ilc}$, and A_{all}. Assign ring numbers to the affected procedures and data structures such that A_{om} can access only *OM*, $A_{om/ilc}$ can access *OM* and *ILC*, and A_{all} can access all three data structures.

7.6. Repeat Exercise 7.5 for a capability-based protection system. In particular, show the capability lists associated with the appropriate procedure and data structure objects to satisfy the stated requirements.

7.7. **(a)** Consider five objects *A*, *B*, *D*1, *D*2, and *D*3 in the HYDRA operating system. Show the graphical representation of the objects' capabilities such that the following operations may be performed:

- *A* can call *B*.
- *B* can read and write data from/to *D*1.
- *B* can give its capability for *D*1 to another object, *D*2.
- *A* can read and write the capability list of *D*1.
- *A* can read data from *D*3.
- *B* can read and write data from/to *D*3.

Each object should have only the minimal set of capabilities and rights necessary to accomplish the preceding operations. Assume that the capability for a procedure must contain the right *c* (for call) in order to be called.
   (b) Answer the following questions based on your diagram:

- Can data from *D*3 ever get into *D*1?
- Can data from *D*3 ever get into *D*2?
- Can data from *D*1 ever get into *A*?
- Can data from *D*2 ever get into *A*?

7.8. Consider two processes in the HYDRA operating system. Process p_1 is currently executing in procedure $P1$ and process p_2 is executing in procedure $P2$. Another procedure X and three data objects $D1$, $D2$, and $D3$ exist in the system. The capability lists are as follows:

	Capability for Object	Rights
$P1$	X	cms
	$D2$	emrw
$P2$	$D1$	1
	$D3$	1
X	$D1$	ews
	$D2$	mrws

(a) Show a graphic representation for this configuration.

(b) Assume $P1$ calls X and passes to it the capability for $D2$. Show the current capability list, assuming the m-right was masked out during the call.

(c) Answer the following questions:
- After the call, can X write into any of the objects $D1$, $D2$, $D3$, $P1$, or $P2$?
- Can X store capabilities into the capability lists of any of the objects $D1$, $D2$, $D3$, $P1$, or $P2$?
- Which capabilities can propagate from $P1$ to $P2$?

7.9. Consider the example of Section 7.5.1.

(a) Construct an access matrix with the smallest possible number of entries such that each of the following commands leaks the right r.

$$create(s1, new\_o)$$
$$owner\_confer\_read(s1, s2, o1)$$
$$owner\_confer\_read(s2, s3, o2)$$
$$non\_owner\_confer\_read(s3, s2, o1)$$

(b) Is the protection system state described by the matrix of part (a) safe for the rights w and own? If not, can it be made safe? Explain.

(c) Construct a similar matrix such that none of the commands $owner\_confer\_read$, $owner\_confer\_write$, and $nonowner\_confer\_read$ leak any right, regardless of their parameters.

7.10. Assume that the generic set of rights in the access matrix model contains also the rights t (take) and g (grant), similar to the take-grant model.

(a) Define the corresponding operations $take$ and $grant$ (specified for the take-grant model) as commands in the access matrix model.

(b) How could the $remove$ operation of the take-grant model be expressed as a command in the access matrix model? Sketch the necessary algorithm (assume a loop construct may be used in the command body).

7.11. Construct a take-grant graph G in which a given subject $s1$ can never gain direct access to an object $o1$, that is, the predicate $can\_share(r, s1, o1, G)$ is false for any r, yet it is still possible for information contained in $o1$ to reach $s1$ (i.e., to flow from $o1$ to $s1$).

7.12. **(a)** For each of the following take-grant graphs G, prove that the predicate $can\_share(r, x1, x3, G)$ holds:

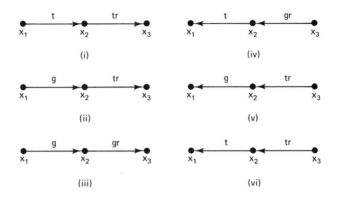

(i)

(b) Show the corresponding sequences of transformations from G to G_n, where G_n is the first state containing the edge $x1 \overset{r}{\to} x3$.

(c) Which of the six transformations are still valid under each of the following assumptions:

    (i) x_3 is an object; x_1 and x_2 are subjects.

    (ii) x_2 is an object; x_1 and x_3 are subjects.

    (iii) x_1 is an object; x_2 and x_3 are subjects.

    (iv) x_2 and x_3 are objects; x_1 is a subject.

7.13. For each of the graphs in Exercise 7.12, try to find transformations to show that the predicate $can\_steal(r, x_1, x_3, G)$ holds.

7.14. Consider a set of subjects $x_1, \ldots, x_n$ in the take-grant model connected into a linear chain as follows:

- Each pair of subjects x_i, x_{i+1} ($1 \le i \le n - 1$) is connected via an arc labeled t or g; the orientation of the arc is arbitrary.
- There is an arc labeled r from x_{n-1} to x_n.

Show that the predicate $can\_share(r, x_1, x_n, G)$ holds for any $n > 1$. (*Hint:* Use the results of Exercise 7.12.)

7.15. Consider a system consisting of two subjects s_1 and s_2 and four objects o_1 through o_4.

    (a) Assign clearances to both subjects and classification levels to all objects according to the Bell–LaPadula model, such that the following conditions hold (use only as many levels as is necessary to achieve your goal):

- s_1 can write only into o_3 and o_4.
- s_2 can write only into o_3.

    (b) Determine which objects can be *read* by which subjects under the assignment of part (a).

    (c) Modify the assignment such that s_1 *cannot* read o_4.

7.16. Consider the set of security classes $C = \{00, 01, 10, 11\}$ in the lattice model of information flow. Define the flow relation $\rightarrow$ and the class-combining operator $\oplus$ such that $(C, \rightarrow, \oplus)$ forms a lattice with the following:

    (a) 00 and 11 as the lower and least upper bounds, respectively.

    (b) 11 and 00 as the lower and least upper bounds, respectively.

7.17. Repeat Exercise 7.16 for the set of security classes $C = \{(XYZ) \mid X, Y, Z \in \{0, 1\}\}$ and the bounds 000 and 111.

References

Aho, A. V., P. J. Denning, and J. D. Ullman. 1971. Principles of optimal page replacement. *J. ACM* **18,** No. 1 (Jan.), 80–93.

Andrews, G. R., and F. B. Schneider. 1983. Concepts and notations for concurrent programming. *ACM Computing Surveys* **15,** No. 1 (Mar.), 3–43.

Baer, J. L., and G. R. Sager. 1972. Measurement and improvement of program behavior under paging systems. In W. Freiberger (ed.), *Statistical Computer Performance Evaluation*, Academic Press, New York, 241–264.

Bash, J. L., E. G. Benjafield, and M. L. Gandy. 1967. The Multics operating system—an overview of Multics as it is being developed. Project MAC, MIT, Cambridge, Mass.

Batson, A., S. Ju, and D. C. Wood. 1970. Measurements of segment size. *Comm. ACM* **13,** No. 3 (Mar.), 155–159.

Belady, L. A. 1966. A study of replacement algorithms for a virtual storage computer. *IBM Syst. J.* **5,** No. 2, 78–101.

Bell, D. E., and L. J. LaPadula. 1973a. *Secure Computer Systems: Mathematical Foundations*, MTR-2547, Vol. 1. MITRE Corp., Bedford, Mass.

——, ——. 1973b. *Secure Computer Systems: A Mathematical Model*, MTR-2547, Vol. 2. MITRE Corp., Bedford, Mass.

——, ——. 1973c. *Secure Computer Systems: A Refinement of the Mathematical Model*, MTR-2547, Vol. 3. MITRE Corp., Bedford, Mass.

——, ——. 1974. *Secure Computer Systems: Mathematical Foundations and Model*, M74-244, Vol. 3. MITRE Corp., Bedford, Mass.

BERNSTEIN, A. J., and J. C. SHARP. 1971. A policy-driven scheduler for a time-sharing system. *Comm. ACM* **14,** No. 2, (Feb.), 74–78.

BIC, L. 1982. A protection model and its implementation in a dataflow system. *Comm. ACM* **25,** No. 9, (Sept.), 650–658.

BRINCH HANSEN, P. 1970. The nucleus of a multiprogramming system. *Comm. ACM* **13,** No. 4 (April), 238–241, 250.

———. 1973a. Concurrent programming concepts. *ACM Computing Surveys* **5,** No. 4 (Dec.), 223–245.

———. 1973b. *Operating System Principles.* Prentice-Hall, Englewood Cliffs, N.J.

Burroughs Corporation. 1964. B5500 Information Processing Systems, Reference Manual. Detroit, Mich.

———. 1967. B6500 Information Processing Systems, Characteristics Manual. Detroit, Mich.

CAMPBELL, R. H., and A. N. HABERMANN. 1974. The specification of process synchronization by path expressions. In *Lecture Notes in Computer Science*, Vol. 16. Springer-Verlag, New York, pp. 89–102.

CAMPBELL, R. H., and R. B. KOLSTAD. 1980. An overview of path Pascal's design. *SIGPLAN Notices* **15,** No. 9 (Sept.), 13–24.

CARR, R. W. 1981. Virtual Memory Management, STAN-CS-81-873. Stanford Linear Accelerator Center, Stanford University, Stanford, Calif.

COFFMAN, E. G., JR., and L. C. VARIAN. 1968. Further experimental data on behavior of programs in a paging environment. *Comm. ACM* **11,** No. 7 (July), 471–474.

COHEN, E., and D. JEFFERSON. 1975. Protection in the HYDRA operating system. *Operating Systems Rev.* **9,** No. 5, 141–160.

COMER, D. 1979. The ubiquitous B-tree. *ACM Surveys* **11,** No. 2 (June), 121–138.

COMFORT, W. T. 1965. A computing system design for user service. *Proc. AFIPS 1965 Fall Joint Computer Conf.* **27.** Spartan Books, New York, pp. 619–628.

CONWAY, M. E. 1963. A multiprocessor system design. *Proc. AFIPS Fall Joint Computer Conf.*, Las Vegas, Nevada, pp. 139–146.

COURTOIS, P. J., F. HEYMANS, and D. L. PARNAS. 1971. *Concurrent Control with "Readers" and "Writers." Comm. ACM* **14,** No. 10 (Oct.), 667–668.

DALEY, R. C., and J. B. DENNIS. 1968. Virtual memory, processes, and sharing in MULTICS. *Comm. ACM* **11,** No. 5 (May), 306–312.

DENNING, D. E. 1976. A lattice model of secure information flow. *Comm. ACM* **19,** No. 5 (May), 236–243.

———. 1982. *Cryptography and Data Security.* Addison-Wesley, Reading, Mass.

DENNING, P. J. 1968. The working set model for program behavior. *Comm. ACM* **11,** No. 5 (May), 323–333.

———. 1970. Virtual memory. *Computing Surveys* **2,** No. 3 (Sept.), 153–189.

———. 1980. Working sets past and present. *IEEE Trans. SE*, Vol. **SE-6,** No. 1 (Jan.), 64–84.

———, et al. 1976. Optimal multiprogramming. *Acta Informatica* **7,** No. 2, 197–216.

DENNIS, J. B. 1965. Segmentation and the design of multiprogrammed operating systems. *J. ACM* **12,** No. 4 (Oct.), 589–602.

———, and E. C. VAN HORN. 1966. Programming semantics for multiprogrammed computations. *Comm. ACM* **9,** No. 3 (Mar.), 143–155.

Digital Equipment Corporation. 1982. *VAX Software Handbook*. Maynard, Mass.

DIJKSTRA, E. W. 1965. Cooperating sequential processes. Mathematics Dept., Technological University, Eindhoven, The Netherlands.

———. 1968a. The structure of the "THE"-multiprogramming system. *Comm. ACM* **11,** No. 5 (May), 341–346.

———. 1968b. Co-operating sequential processes. In F. Genuys (ed.), *Programming Languages*, Academic Press, New York, pp. 43–112.

———. 1975. Guarded commands, nondeterminacy, and formal derivation of programs. *Comm. ACM* **18,** No. 8 (Aug.), 453–457.

VAN EMDEN, M. H., and R. A. KOWALSKI. 1976. The semantics of predicate logic as a programming language. *J. ACM* **23,** No. 4 (Oct.).

FENTON, J. S. 1974. Memoryless subsystems. *Computer J.* **17,** No. 2, 143–147.

FINE, E. G., C. W. JACKSON, and P. V. MCISAAC. 1966. Dynamic program behavior under paging. *Proc. ACM 21st Nat. Conf.* Thompson Book Co., Washington, D.C., pp. 223–228.

FOGEL, M. 1974. The VMOS paging algorithm. *Operating Systems Rev.* **8,** No. 1, 8–16.

FRANKLIN, M. A., G. S. GRAHAM, and R. K. GUPTA. 1978. Anomalies with variable partition paging algorithms. *Comm ACM* **21,** No. 3 (Mar.), 232–236.

FREIBERGS, I. F. 1968. The dynamic behavior of programs. *Proc. AFIPS 1968 Fall Joint Comput. Conf.* **33,** Part 2, 1163–1167.

GELENBE, E., P. TIBERIO, and J. BOECKHORST. Page size in demand paging systems. *Acta Informatica* **3,** No.   , 1–24.

GRAHAM, G. S., and P. J. DENNING. 1972. Protection—Principles and Practice, AFIPS Conf. Proc., 1972 SJCC, Vol. 40. AFIPS Press, Montvale, N.J., pp. 417–429.

GREY, J. N. 1976. *Lecture Notes on Database Systems*, Springer-Verlag, New York.

GUPTA, R. K., and M. A. FRANKLIN. 1978. Working set and page fault frequency replacement algorithm: A performance comparison. *IEEE TC*, **C-27,** (Aug.), 706–712.

HABERMANN, A. N. 1969. Prevention of system deadlocks. *Comm. ACM* **12,** No. 7 (July), 373–377, 385.

———, L. FLON, and L. COOPRIDE. 1976. Modularization and hierarchy in a family of operating systems. *Comm. ACM* **19,** No. 5 (May), 266–272.

HARRISON, M. A., W. L. RUZZO, and J. D. ULLMAN. 1976. Protection in operating systems. *Comm. ACM* **19,** No. 8 (Aug.), 461–471.

HAVENDER, J. W. 1968. Avoiding deadlock in multitasking systems. *IBM Syst. J.* **7,** No. 2, 74–84.

HOARE, C. A. R. 1972. Toward a theory of parallel programming. In C. A. R. Hoare and R. H. Perrott (eds.), Operating Systems Techniques, Academic Press, New York, pp. 61–71.

———. 1974. Monitors: An operating system structuring concept. *Comm. ACM* **17,** No. 10 (Oct.), 549–557.

———. Communicating sequential processes. *Comm. ACM* **21,** No. 8 (Aug.), 666–677.

HOLT, R. C. 1971a. Comments on prevention of system deadlocks. *Comm. ACM* **14,** No. 1 (Jan.), 36–38.

———. 1971b. On deadlock in computer systems. Ph.D. thesis, TR 71-91, Computer Science, Cornell University, Ithaca, N.Y.

———. 1972. Some deadlock properties of computer systems. *ACM Computing Surveys* **4,** No. 3 (Sept.), 179–196.

HOPCROFT, J. E., and J. D. ULLMAN. 1969. *Formal Languages and Their Relation to Automata.* Addison-Wesley, Reading, Mass.

IBM Corp. 1963. IBM 7090 data processing system multiprogramming package. IBM Special Systems Feature Bulletin L22-6641-3. White Plains, N.Y.

———. 1965. IBM system/360 operating system. Concepts and facilities. Form C28-6535. Poughkeepsie, N.Y.

Intel Corp. 1981. iAPX 432 General Data Processor Architecture Reference Manual. Santa Clara, Calif.

JONES, A. K. 1973. Protection in programmed systems. Ph.D. thesis, Department of Computer Science. Carnegie-Mellon University, Pittsburgh, Pa.

JONES, A. K., R. J. LIPTON, and L. SNYDER. 1976. A linear time algorithm for deciding subject-object security. *Proc. 17th Ann. Foundations Computer Sci. Conf.*, Houston, Tex., pp. 33–41.

KEEHN, D., and J. LACY. 1974. VSAM data set design parameters. *IBM Syst. J.* **3,** No. , 186–212.

KILBURN, T., et al. 1962. One-level storage system. *IRE Trans. EC-11,* 2 (April), 223–235.

KNUTH, D. E. 1968. *The Art of Computer Programming, Vol. 1.* Addison-Wesley, Reading, Mass.

LAMPSON, B. W. 1971. Protection. *Proc. Fifth Princeton Symp. Information Sciences and Systems*, Princeton University, March 1971, pp. 437–443. Reprinted in *Operating Systems Rev.* **8,** No. 1 (Jan. 1974), 18–24.

——— and D. D. REDELL. 1980. Experience with processes and monitors in Mesa. *Comm. ACM* **23,** No. 2 (Feb.), 105–117.

LENFANT, J., and P. BURGEVIN. 1975. Empirical data on program behavior. *Proc. ACM Int'l. Symp.*, E. Gelenbe and D. Potier (eds.). North-Holland, Amsterdam, pp. 163–170.

LIPTON, R. J., and L. SNYDER. 1977. A linear time algorithm for deciding subject securing. *J. ACM* **24,** No. 3 (July), 455–464.

MADNICK, S. E. 1968. Design strategies for file systems: a model. Scientific Center Report, 2nd Revision, April 1970. IBM Corp., Cambridge Scientific Center, Cambridge, Mass.

——— and J. W. ALSOP, II. 1969. A modular approach to file system design. *Proc. AFIPS 1969 Spring Joint Comput. Conf.* **34,** AFIPS Press, Montvale, N.J., pp. 1–13.

MATTSON, R. L., et al. 1970. Evaluation techniques for storage hierarchies. *IBM Syst. J.* **9,** No. 2, 78–117.

MORRIS, J. B. 1972. Demand paging through the use of working sets on the MANIAC II. *Comm. ACM* **15** (Oct.), 867–872.

OPDERBECK, H., and W. W. CHU. 1974. Performance of the page fault frequency algorithm in a multiprogramming environment. *Proc. IFIP Congress*, pp. 235–241.

OPPENHEIMER, G., and N. WEIZER. 1968. Resource management for a medium scale time-sharing operating system. *Comm. ACM* **11,** No. 5 (May), 313–322.

PETERSON, G. L. 1981. Myths about the mutual exclusion problem. *Information Processing Letters* **12,** No. 3 (June), pp. 115–116.

PRIEVE, B. G., and R. S. FABRY. 1976. VMIN—An optimal variable space page replacement algorithm. *Comm. ACM* **19,** No. 86 (May), 295–297.

REDELL, D. D., et al. 1980. Pilot: An operating system for a personal computer. *Comm. ACM* **23,** No. 2 (Feb.), 81–92.

REED, P. D., and K. R. KANODIA. 1979. Synchronization with event counts and sequencers. *Comm. ACM* **22,** No. 2 (Feb.), 115–123.

RODRIGUEZ-ROSELL, J. 1973. Empirical working set behavior. *Comm. ACM* **16** (Sept.), 556–560.

RUSCHITZKA, M., and R. S. FABRY. 1977. A unifying approach to scheduling. *Comm. ACM* **20,** No. 7 (July), 469–476.

SADEH, E. 1975. An analysis of the performance of the page fault frequency (PFF) replacement algorithm. *Proc. 5th ACM Symp. Operating Systems Principles*, pp. 6–13.

SHATZ, S. M. 1984. Communication mechanisms for programming distributed systems. *Computer* **17,** No. 6 (June), 21–28.

SHAW, A., et al. 1975. A multiprogramming nucleus with dynamic resource facilities. *Software— Practice and Experience* **5,** 245–267.

SNYDER, L. 1977. On the synthesis and analysis of protection systems. *Proc. 6th Symp. Operating Systems Principles*; ACM SIGOPS *Operating Systems Rev.* **11,** No. 5 (Nov.), 141–150.

———. 1981. Formal models of capability-based protection systems. *IEEE TC*, Vol. **C-30,** No. 3 (March), 172–181.

SPIRN, J. R. 1977. *Program Behavior: Models and Measurement.* Elsevier/North-Holland, New York.

TRELEAVEN, P. C., T. R. BROWNBRIDGE, and R. C. HOPKINS. 1982. Data-driven and demand-driven computer architecture. *ACM Computing Surveys* **14,** No. 1 (March), 93–143.

U.S. Department of Defense. 1981. Programming language Ada: Reference manual. *Lecture Notes in Computer Science*, vol. 106, Springer-Verlag, New York.

WEGNER, P. 1968. *Programming Languages, Information Structures, and Machine Organization.* McGraw-Hill, New York.

WEIDERMAN, N. 1971. Synchronization and simulation in operating system construction. Ph.D. thesis, Tech. Rep. 71-102, Computer Science, Cornell University, Ithaca, N.Y.

WOLMAN, E. 1965. A fixed optimum cell-size for records of various lengths. *J. ACM* **12,** No. 1 (Jan.), 53–70.

Indexes

wait in Monitor, 63
  with priority, 67–68
wait/notify primitives, 66–67
Waiting list, 107–108
Wire tapping, 320
Working file directory, 268
Working set model, 226–228
Write (see Access to files, IO instruction)

AUTHOR INDEX